13.III 7.VIII

MOZART

The Man · The Musician

SCHIRMER BOOKS

A Division of Macmillan Publishing Co., Inc.

New York

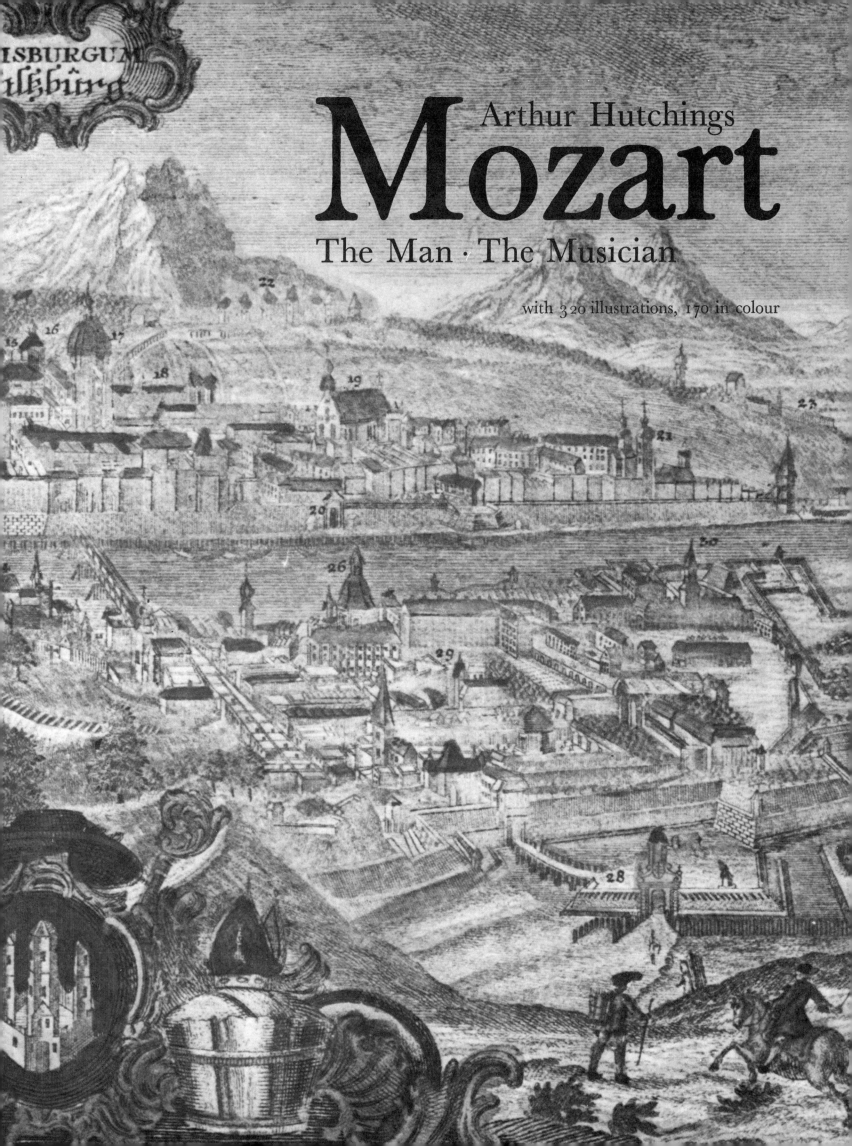

Arthur Hutchings
Mozart
The Man · The Musician

with 320 illustrations, 170 in colour

To ROBERT LEWIS

SCHIRMER BOOKS, A Division of
Macmillan Publishing Co., Inc.
New York

Library of Congress Catalog Card Number: 75-13790
Editorial: A. David Hogarth
Illustrations: Gaston H. Richter

Set in 11/12pt Baskerville by Fletcher & Son Ltd, Norwich

Lithos, printing, and binding by Georg Westermann Verlag,
Druckerei und Kartographische Anstalt, Brunswick, West Germany

Published in the United Kingdom by
Thames and Hudson, 30 Bloomsbury Street, London WC1B 3QP

CONTENTS   *Note: the two parts of this book, Mozart: The Man and Mozart: The Musician, are numbered independently*

CONTENTS

Note: the two parts of this book, Mozart: The Man and Mozart: The Musician, are numbered independently

MOZART: *The Musician*

FOREWORD *by Kingsley Amis*

Discussing musical matters the other evening with a young acquaintance, the son of a distinguished conductor, I said, "Arthur Hutchings is the man who really understands Mozart. Remember that marvellous summary of the A major piano concerto?" – and went on to paraphrase, I hope not too inadequately, what Hutchings wrote. My companion was far from impressed: "I've read something like that in heaven knows how many programme notes." With my wits about me for once, I retorted, "No doubt you have. The word must have got round. Hutchings was writing [his 'Companion to Mozart's Piano Concertos'] in 1948." The lad muttered that he knew little about the programme notes of that period and the subject dropped.

The point I tried to make that evening might well have been valid in itself; it would not do to extend it into a general statement that writing about music has come to take its time from Hutchings. If only it had! With a few intermittently shining exceptions in journalism, we are more and more faced with a choice between technical treatises on the one hand and sleeve notes and leaflets – gossipy, short on musical information, badly written – on the other.

The likes of me (and I suspect there are plenty of us) cannot aspire to be called musicians, but we have a great interest in the subject and bring to it a modest amount of technical knowledge, enough to learn things from a score and recognise a musical example. We want to be helped to comprehend, as far as we are able, how this symphony or that concerto works, how its parts are related, what in it is to be expected and what is not. This is where Hutchings comes in. He is not a populariser; he wants his readers to understand, not just to feel that they understand; he offers no short cuts in the form of easy analogies or appeals to sentimentality. He is the finest sort of teacher: what an experience, to have been one of his pupils at Durham or Exeter!

His distinction is nowhere better shown than in his style – lucid and straightforward, yet varied and graceful; full of happy turns of phrase, yet in firm control of itself; effective without ever striving after effect. I think that somebody who knew and cared nothing about music (if one can imagine such a miserable being) would still be able to recognise, on reading a single randomly-chosen page of Hutchings, that he had achieved a triumphant mastery of his subject and of his task.

I had known for years that he was my best guide to Mozart's music; to write about Mozart's life clearly called for a rather different set of abilities. Hutchings has turned out to possess those too. He shows us what the man was like by showing what he did and said, how he behaved to his family, his friends, employers, patrons, colleagues, and rivals. The story tells itself without manipulation from the historian, and its principal character is, with the inevitability of truth, an amalgam, irreducible to any comprehensive description. We have heard often enough of inspired Mozart, hard-working Mozart, affectionate Mozart, malicious Mozart, intelligent Mozart, commonplace Mozart; Hutchings's Mozart is much more than all these put together. And, thrown in for good measure, there is a fascinating account of what musical life was like in the later eighteenth century: the lodgings and the coach-journeys, the courts and concert-rooms, the jobs, the money, the disappointments, the illnesses, the passing moments of glory. Arthur Hutchings has succeeded in his undertaking, which, in view of the stature of its central figure, is saying a good deal.

Kingsley Amis

MOZART

The Man

I

What was the man like?

"Il était toujours si gai"
"He was fond of reading"
His Appearance

1. Salzburg, looking towards the castle and the Nonnberg. Anonymous lithograph, c. 1840.

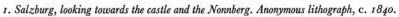

1. Salzburg, looking towards the castle and the Nonnberg. Anonymous lithograph, c. 1840.

During 1829 Vincent Novello, a charming London musician who founded a music-publishing business which still bears his name, took his family through north France and Holland, down the Rhine, and across the south German states to Austria. The journey was a pilgrimage. He and his wife had long prepared for it. They were amongst the first devotees of Mozart who had never actually seen their idol.

Like later pilgrims they saw a striking parallel between the beauty of Salzburg and that of Mozart's music. Art alone could not have produced Salzburg: its enchantment came from its natural setting and the fact that artifice had wedded nature. To an older generation than Novello's, nature in wild scenes was not an object of veneration. "Nature" usually meant human nature, the moods and passions which could be prolonged and heightened by poetry and music; but Novello's generation was Wordsworth's, with its ascendant cult of solitude. Mozart himself was not affected by it. While a shaking coach took him across plains and hills remote from cities he preferred musical composition to the views through a window. A garden summer-house in which to write an opera was a civilised blessing: a cottage on a mountain-side far from urbane society was merely a place of exile.

The Novellos took a sum of money, subscribed by English Mozart-lovers, to the bedridden Maria Anna Sonnenburg (Mozart's sister Nannerl), who assured them that she had not been in great need, but that she took great pleasure in London's appreciation of her brother's music. They learnt later that when the publisher André had suggested a subscription concert for her benefit she had disliked the proposal as she "did not wish to be the object of public observation." They were fortunate in calling upon Constanze Nissen, Mozart's widow, at a time when Mozart's son Karl happened to be visiting his mother. Soon after Mozart's death her financial straits had been relieved, chiefly by André's purchase of Mozart's manuscripts, and she had lived comfortably with her second husband. When the Novellos arrived in Salzburg she had an attractive little house in the street leading to the slopes of the Nonnberg and was very proud of her garden flowers. She was twice widowed, aged 65, but still agile and vivacious. Conversation with her was conducted in French, which she had used in letters to England, and she was pleased to answer Novello's carefully prepared questions about her first husband.

Like Novello, we are curious to know what sort of *man* so great an artist was. The testimony of a wife is held to be at a natural disadvantage in a court of law, and we could suppose that the elderly Constanze "romanticised" the past and was anxious to paint Mozart only in the finest colours. In fact she seems to have made neither of these errors. Mary Novello wrote in her diary: "Madame

2. Vincent Novello. Oil painting by Edward Petre Novello.

Nissen's manner in speaking of her illustrious husband was not quite so enthusiastic as I should have expected in one so near and dear to him." Even so, she admitted that Constanze was tender and affectionate. Moreover nothing said by Constanze disagrees with other evidence, such as Mozart's letters and the recollections of singers and people who knew and worked with him. We shall consider her opinions concerning the best portraits of Mozart, but at the outset of our own pilgrimage, which concerns the child and his upbringing, our chief interest is in the effect upon the grown man of his early treatment and experiences. If the man suffered from no morbid obsessions, was not considered emotionally, nervously, sexually, or socially peculiar, if he was abnormal only as Monteverdi, Handel, Wagner, or any other musical genius was abnormal, then we need care in blaming his father and condemning his upbringing.

Constanze did not expect Novello's first question – "Was his general disposition lively or melancholy?" Her immediate answer has already been quoted in the original French. To that, "He was always so gay," she added the surprising information that Mozart was actually "speaking playfully only a few minutes before his death, which was at last sudden." This is credible, for his childlike playfulness is well documented. On the other hand, no portraits of the adult Mozart show this trait; some suggest a satirical, even a sardonic turn of mind; most of them suggest pride (in the sense of class-consciousness) and the most famous one, the unfinished profile of a head bent as if making music, conveys an expression of tender melancholy. We have to remember, however, that throughout the eighteenth century a dignified stance and manner was usual in a portrait; the painter did not anticipate the photographer with his request for a smile and a relaxed pose. No musician from Vivaldi to Beethoven grins at us from a picture unless it be a satirical cartoon.

If Mozart was *always* gay, by nature playful, then the misery that drove him to begging letters and the depression caused by the onset of the kidney disease (uraemia), which is believed to have killed him, were adventitious; they could have affected a temperament as genial as Haydn's. They did not come from any psychotic condition nor, as far as we know, did they cause one until death was very near. Though not regarded as physically robust, Mozart seems to have had plenty of physical and nervous stamina until his disease depressed his spirits. Today even if uraemia is not completely cured it can be so treated that the patient need fear neither painful symptoms nor a shortened expectation of life. Relief for uraemia was discovered soon after Mozart's death. Without that disease he would almost certainly have done well financially by a projected visit to England, possibly by a state appointment, certainly by the international popularity of "The Magic Flute" which might have been the first of a series of great *Singspiele*.

"He was fond of reading"

Novello proceeded to the question: "Was he in possession of aptitude towards any other art or pursuit than his own science?" and Mary Novello's diary records Constanze's answer. "He was fond of reading and well acquainted with Shakespeare in the translation. One of his favourite authors, which Madame Nissen frequently perused, was in nine volumes; but as it was forbidden fruit in the Austrian states she would not name it. I suspect some of the French revolutionary works." The Novellos were told that Mozart was fond of painting and sculpture and could draw well himself. They were shown one of his albums of drawings and paintings. They already knew that he could converse and read in French and Italian as well as his native tongue and, though entirely educated by his father, understood Latin as well as one who had been sent to a school.

This, too, is important to our consideration of Mozart's childhood. It is sometimes supposed that his total training was musical, and that his knowledge of other languages than German, chiefly Italian, was no more than any other well-equipped musician's. This is not true. His favourite study in childhood was mathematics, and he was so indulged as to be allowed to cover walls and floors with figures. He is not considered an intellectual yet he

3. Mary Sabilla Novello. Oil painting by Edward Petre Novello.

was invited to the houses of intellectuals and numbered such people amongst his friends before the Mozarts became Freemasons. Many were also his father's friends, not only because Leopold Mozart had written a treatise on violin technique which brought him some fame but because, like his son, he was of wider culture and greater general intelligence than most musicians.

Wolfgang was better educated by Leopold than were boys at such a famous school as the imperial one in Vienna – far better educated than boys like the two Haydns and Schubert who went there as choral scholars to be trained in little else than Latin and music, vocal and instrumental. Even religious practice and doctrine must have been instilled by the devout but highly critical Leopold with far more solicitude and intelligence than boys of that time could expect from the school catechist. It should also be remembered that Mozart was never beaten or punished as schoolboys were – indeed as princes were by their tutors and with their royal parents' approbation or total indifference. Our only reason for noticing that Mozart *was* properly educated – that is to say prepared as acceptable company to those who paid for schooling – is to stress the fact that he did not lack avocations from music. He knew the solitude of genius only too well; he knew that his best music was thought too complex by the "wider audience" which one who has cast off patrons hopes to enchant. But Constanze's "He

3

was fond of reading" means to the psychiatrist much the same as "He was fond of dancing" (as he was indeed) or "He was interested in the arts," or "He enjoyed his Masonic lodges," or "The Mozarts were invited to dinner by the Glucks." It proves that, as a man amongst other men, he was no oddity; he may even have seemed extrovert. His feelings towards other musicians must be considered later; for the moment we ask only: "Did his inherited nature or his upbringing make him a withdrawn and lonely figure?" All we know about him suggests an unqualified "No!" The man was ebullient and sociable; only the artist kept himself to himself while imagining or fashioning his work.

During much of this century we have been affected by the work of Freud and his disciples. Their probing of the subconscious mind (as well as our conscious motives and indulgence of imagination) has made us interested in "secret" lives. It has also led biographers – not just those with an itch to "debunk" the great – to treat famous artists as the subjects of psychiatric analysis, often thereby eliciting new understanding and sympathy. Mozart has been the subject of an enormous number of books during the past 50 years, and at first it seems remarkable that none of them has revealed a secretly psychotic Mozart, an artist tortured as was Beethoven, Tchaikovsky, Wolf, or Mahler; but a little reflection tells us that a malicious biographer or pseudo-psychologist could easily be disproved if he attempted a false portrait of Mozart, for more is known about Mozart's private and daily life than about Haydn's. Documentary evidence covers some part of almost every month of his 35 years. Consequently we are even better informed than was Novello, and know that he was wrong when he wrote: "It is quite evident that Mozart killed himself with over-exertion." Mozart was killed by a malady. His exertions, his great pains, were the concomitants of the supreme pleasure of creation. He would not easily "stoop" to the exertion of teaching or "pot-boiling" even when in dire financial distress; nor would he leave his beloved Vienna to accept appointments, e.g. in Prussia, which might not have proved congenial – and might not have enabled him to devote his time to the kind of opera that delighted him.

Since by definition a genius is unbalanced, unfitted to share his work or imagination with any other creature, the most remarkable fact about Mozart is that, during most of his short and restless life, he was happier than more fortunate and more successful musicians have been.

His Appearance

(For illustrations of works described here the reader is referred to the special colour section on Mozart portraits.)

"No earthly remains of Mozart survived save a few wretched portraits, no two of which are alike." That is Alfred Einstein's verdict on the pictures which so many of us cherish, even gaze at for long, hoping that they will convey at least something of the man as he appeared to those fortunate enough to know him. Since there is no more perceptive writing on Mozart than Einstein's "Mozart: His Character, His Work," it is not easy for us to dismiss his opinion. Unless a wonderful child-portrait by Greuze is of Mozart, which the German iconographers have so far denied, then no artist of the first rank ever attempted his likeness. One of the disappointments of eighteenth-century portraiture for those of us who claim

4. Mozart. Boxwood cameo by (or after) Leonhard Posch, 1789.

5. Mozart. Copperplate by Johann Georg Mansfeld, after Posch, 1789.

no great connoisseurship of the graphic arts is that we are often able to admire them as paintings or drawings, but rarely feel them to be what they were so often called – "likenesses."

In 1923 Arthur Schurig, who had already published an essay on pictures of the child Mozart in an account of Leopold's travels, brought out in Leipzig the second edition of his "Wolfgang Amadé Mozart." It contained a commentary upon portraits of the composer from his sixth year to his death and said: "Mozart has been the subject of more portraits quite unrelated to his actual appearance than any other famous man. An adoring posterity has not conceived a more incorrect physical image of any other notability." This declaration led the Viennese musicologist O. E. Deutsch and several art historians to make an examination of all paintings, engravings, sketches, cameos, etc. claiming to represent Mozart, and it is now thought that only eight of them, whether good or bad as likenesses, can have been made with Mozart's knowledge or by artists who at least looked at his face while sketching. Since several Mozart "biographies in pictures" have been beautifully produced, many dubious portraits are still in music-lovers' minds. For instance Robert Bory's "La Vie de W. A. Mozart par l'image," a very attractive publication of 1948, which has been used as a quarry for other books, contains amongst its many pictures no less than 62 supposed portraits of Mozart (including medallions, silhouettes, etc.).

It does not follow that every picture made in the absence of the composer, or after his death, is valueless. It may include details of buildings, instruments, personalities, and possessions which we are glad to have, and for that reason materials are used here in which the actual facial appearance of Mozart may be inaccurate. It therefore seems right to give a list of artists whose names are associated with portraits that have not been authenticated. These, as well as anonymous portraits which do not concern us, are catalogued and discussed by the Munich collector Max Zenger in his contributions ("Falsche Mozartbildnisse") in the issues of the "Neues Mozart-Jahrbuch" for 1941 and 1942. The pictures not authenticated are those attributed to Battoni, Bosio, Breitkopf, Duplessis, Grassi, Greuze, Klass, Langenhöffel, Rigaud, Saint-Aubin, Van Smissen, Thelott, Tischbein, and Zoffany. The inclusion of the Greuze in this list is saddening. It is a masterly and beautiful painting of a child in thought, not in fine surroundings or fine clothes, but as we imagine the child Mozart might have looked when not preened for public performance. It is not really doubted that Greuze painted it but that his subject was Mozart. Nevertheless, our present quest is for the appearance and manner of the man, not the child.

The credibility we attach to this or that "likeness" must be influenced by any comments upon portraits made by those who knew Mozart, especially his sons or his wife, and also by a passage in the "Reminiscences" of Michael Kelly, an Irish actor-singer at the Vienna "Italian" opera (where he was billed as Signor "Oc-

6. Mozart. Lithograph by Edvard Lehmann after the Lange portrait.

chelli"!). He frequently visited the Mozarts and played billiards with the composer, whose musical advice he found "infinitely valuable," but whose friendship he secured more freely than did most of Mozart's musical acquaintances. (Mozart was obviously reserved towards other composers except Michael Haydn.) This passage from Kelly is almost more valuable than a fine painting of Mozart, and it is worth quoting fully:

He favoured the company by performing fantasias and capriccios on the piano-forte. His feeling, the rapidity of his fingers, the great execution and strength of his left hand particularly, and the apparent inspiration of his modulations, astounded me. After this splendid performance we sat down to supper, and I had the pleasure to be placed at table between him and his wife. After supper the young branches of his family had a dance, and Mozart joined them. Madame Mozart told me that, great as his genius was, he was an enthusiast in dancing.

He was a remarkably small man, very thin and pale, with a profusion of fine fair hair, of which he was rather vain. He gave me a cordial invitation to his house, of which I availed myself, and passed a great deal of my time there. He always received me with kindness and hospitality. He was remarkably fond of punch, of which beverage I have seen him

5

take copious draughts. He was also fond of billiards and had an excellent billiard table in his house. Many and many a game have I played with him, but always came off second best. He gave Sunday concerts, at which I was never missing. He was kind-hearted, and always ready to oblige; but so very particular, when he played, that if the slightest noise were made, he instantly left off.

Kelly's words may be compared with Constanze's – "He did not play much in private, but would occasionally extemporise when he was sitting alone with me. Nor did he like playing at all to strangers unless he knew them to be good judges. Then he would exert himself to the utmost for them." Still more reassuring is the correspondence between Kelly's pen-portrait and the sketch in oils made by Joseph Lange during the winter of 1782–83, now in the Mozart Museum at Salzburg. Asked by Novello which she considered to be the "best likeness" of her first husband, Constanze replied: "The painting in oils done by the husband of Madame Lange. It is unfinished but admirably done." Lange was Mozart's brother-in-law, having married Aloysia Weber to whom Mozart paid court before he transferred his love to Constanze. Even without Constanze's opinion and assurances of authenticity we should surely consider this Lange picture convincing. If the face and head, fortunately without wig, are not fully finished to every detail of the "profusion of fine fair hair," then they are as vivid as could be wished; the unfinished part is evidently prepared to show Mozart's hands playing the piano, and his face suggests concentration upon a passage of poignant expression.

Lange also painted Constanze at about the same time and the portrait is generally believed to be the one in the University of Glasgow. Mary Novello's notes concerning Constanze's opinion of the Lange portrait are a little puzzling. "She assured us that it exactly resembled him, and is much more beautiful than the engraving." Plainly this engraving is also genuinely from the life, be it well or badly done; but was it of a preliminary sketch by Lange or the silverpoint by Doris Stock of Dresden, made in 1789 and owned by Peters of Leipzig? Was it one of the "good likenesses done in wax by an artist at Berlin" which Constanze praised? Wax cameo reliefs of Mozart's head and shoulders by Leonhard Posch of Berlin were exhibited both at Salzburg and Vienna before the war, but they have disappeared; an engraving from one of them by Johann Mansfeld can be seen at Salzburg in a wooden frame. Posch made his medallions in 1788, and if Constanze thought them good likenesses of Mozart then we cannot think the same of a silhouette, one of four representing Joseph Haydn, Gluck, Mozart, and Salieri, made by Hieronymus Löschenkohl for the 1786 Austrian National Calendar.

Most pictures of the child and boy Mozart are in wigs and court clothes and one would expect them to flatter; they are interesting for other features than those of the

7. *Mozart. Engraving by G. A. Sasso after G. B. Bosio, c. 1785.*

boy himself. A few years after his death his sister wrote to the publisher Breitkopf: "My brother was a very pretty child. But after he had smallpox he was much disfigured, and still worse when he came back from Italy he got the Italian yellow hue which made him quite unrecognisable." Later, in a letter to Joseph Sonnleithner, she commented on the oldest of the portraits held by her which had been made in 1772–73 during Mozart's stay in Milan. "He was then only 16 years of age; but as he had just recovered from a very bad illness, the picture makes him look sickly and yellow." She thought well of the family group "made when he was 22." She was mistaken about her brother's age in this picture, an oil painting made by Johann della Croce at Salzburg during the winter of 1780–81 when Mozart was 24. This is very much the proud family picture. Nannerl and Wolfgang are duetting at the piano, their prowess implicit in the crossed hands which they need not even watch, for their eyes are towards us; Leopold leans against the piano

8. Mozart. Silverpoint drawing by Doris Stock, 1789.

9. *Haydn, Gluck, Mozart, and Salieri. Silhouettes by Hieronymus Löschenkohl, 1785.*

showing his violin, and the inkstand with pen just behind him are reminders of his famous treatise; from the wall the dead mother's portrait looks down on them – no, at us, like the rest of them, all with the grandest clothes, coiffure or wig.

In 1819 Mozart's stock was fast rising and a fashionable painter, Barbara Krafft, was asked to make a portrait of him for Joseph Sonnleithner's Gallery of Composers, later acquired by the Gesellschaft der Musikfreunde. It was in connexion with this undertaking that the composer's sister was consulted, and we have quoted from one of her letters. Evidently she arranged for the artist to use the Lange portrait and the family picture. Barbara Krafft's work has been commended purely as a good piece of painting, and it was also regarded as a good portrait; but the similarity between Mozart's expression in this posthumous work and that in the family picture is obvious. It does not flatter, but it is true to other evidence concerning Mozart's slight build and pallid complexion. Do we imagine too much in seeing there a man who, however gentle and playful amongst friends and relatives, could be sarcastic and defiant upon occasion, and for all his known ability would not easily commend himself to most aristocratic employers in the era of decaying feudalism?

In the only other portrait to be considered Mozart is made to look both taller and more dignified, and therefore older, than he was. Painted in 1777, it shows him as a Chevalier of the Golden Spur, an honour bestowed on him by the Pope in 1770. The artist is not known. The picture was made for Padre Martini and is still in Bologna. If it were not for the fact that on such occasions most eighteenth-century people would adopt a grave and proud pose, we might say that this portrait revealed a gravity which is belied by people who knew Mozart and a pride which he inherited and was exacerbated by his treatment.

Leonhard Posch, whom Constanze called "the artist from Berlin," not only made the wax medallions which she commended, but also Mozart's death mask. He was employed in Vienna by Count Joseph Deym, owner of the exhibition called the "Panoptikum" for which Mozart composed the pieces to be played by clockwork mechanism. We do not know how long the death mask remained intact, but Constanze admitted responsibility for its accidental breakage. Our loss is not as great as we might suppose, since we know so much more about Mozart's appearance, manners, and speech than about those of other composers of genius. We even know that he had a tenor voice, and that he spoke quietly except in the excitement of rehearsal, when he could let out a penetrating shout.

Pictorial Essay:
Mozart Portraits

"We must be satisfied with a dozen authentic portraits of Mozart and the contemporary variants. Of these, only eight give an approximate representation of his appearance at the various stages of his life." So writes Otto Erich Deutsch in his preface to "Mozart and his World in Contemporary Pictures," published in 1961 as a supplement to the "Neue Mozart-Ausgabe." All 12, except the drawing by Doris Stock and the Löschenkohl silhouette (reproduced on Pages 7 and 8 respectively), are included in this pictorial section *(Nos. 1, 4, 5, 7, 8, 9, 11, 12, 13, and 14)*. This does not mean that all are good likenesses or that other portraits are valueless. The "authentic" portrait *(No. 11)* of Mozart as a Knight of the Golden Spur makes him look older and taller than we know him to have been. Yet the striking portrait by Barbara Krafft *(No. 15)*, painted 28 years after the composer's death and based on the family portrait *(No. 8)*, is probably truer to his actual appearance and character than any other except the unfinished Lange painting *(No. 14)*. It is Professor Hutchings's opinion that Mozart's natural pride, acquired through birth and upbringing, was exaggerated by his familiarity as a child with the great and powerful. In this respect, we might imagine the first portrait here beginning a cycle which ends with Krafft portraying a man in whom the years have tinged that pride with sarcasm.

1. Mozart in gala dress. Oil-painting, 1763, attributed to Pietro Antonio Lorenzoni. The costume, given to Wolfgang by the Empress Maria Theresa for a public banquet during his visit to Vienna in 1762, is said to have been originally for the Archduke Maximilian (born, like Mozart, in 1756).

1

2

2. An unauthenticated portrait purporting to be the eight-year-old Mozart holding a bird's nest containing nightingale eggs. The oil-painting by Johann Zoffany, was made in London in 1764/65.

3 and 4. Leopold Mozart with his children. Both these portraits were formerly believed to have been made during the first visit to Paris in 1763/64 by Louis Carrogis, known as Carmontelle, at the request of Melchior Grimm. Doubts have now been cast on the authenticity of No. 3, a red-chalk drawing strengthened with watercolour and gouache. No. 4, a water-colour which includes Nannerl, exists in three almost identical versions in Chantilly, Paris, and London, and it has not yet been definitely established which the original is. The illustration here is the Chantilly version.

3

4

5

5. Tea at Prince Conti's in the Temple. Oil-painting by Michel Barthélemy Ollivier. Painted during Mozart's second visit to Paris in the summer of 1766, the work depicts a typical "salon" gathering of the time. The distinguished company includes the Counts Egmont and Chabot-Rohan. Mozart, now 10 years old, is seated at the harpsichord apparently about to accompany the singer Pierre Jélyotte, who is tuning a guitar.

6. An unauthenticated portrait attributed to Jean-Baptiste Greuze. Previously in the Belle Skinner Collection, the copy illustrated here is now in Yale University. The original is thought to have been painted in Amsterdam in 1766.

7. Mozart in Verona. Formerly attributed to Felice Cignaroli, this oil-portrait, painted early in January 1770 during the first Italian tour, is now known to have been by Saviero dalla Rosa. Mozart here is only a few weeks from his fourteenth birthday. The painting is detailed enough for Deutsch to suggest that the music on the stand is the fragmentary Allegro in G for clavier, K. 72a.

6

7

8

9

10

11. Mozart as a Chevalier of the Golden Spur. This oil-painting by an unknown artist was executed in Salzburg in 1777 and sent to Padre Martini in Bologna where it still remains. It shows Mozart wearing the Order of the Golden Spur which he received from the Pope in 1770. The gravity of expression and dignity of bearing are rather misleading.

8. The Mozart Family. Painted by Johann Nepomuk della Croce in Salzburg in 1780/81, this oil-portrait shows Nannerl and Wolfgang (now almost 24) at the keyboard. Their mother, who had died in 1778, is represented in the portrait on the wall. Leopold holds his violin to the fore, but Professor Hutchings also sees as symbolic of his gifts the pen and inkstand in the background. While the mother's picture is modelled on a previous portrait *(see No. 17)*, the representation of Mozart here was to be the model for a future portrait by Barbara Krafft *(No. 15)*.

9. This anonymous miniature on ivory is believed to have been the one Wolfgang sent to his playful cousin Maria Anna Thekla Mozart, known as the "Bäsle," in 1777 when he was 21. It was painted that year in either Mannheim or Augsburg.

10. Another work by Della Croce, painter of the family portrait *(No. 8)* – this time an as yet unauthenticated miniature in gouache-tempera on parchment, painted in Salzburg around 1780 and rediscovered by Dr. Erich Fiala of Vienna. It is thought that the head alone was painted by Della Croce, perhaps as a study for a bust portrait to match one of Nannerl. The book bears an ingenious monogram of the letters "W.A.M." This intriguing miniature is discussed fully in a monograph by Dr. Robert Haas, "Ein unbekanntes Mozart-Bildnis" (Vienna, 1955).

11

CAV. AMADEO WOLFGANGO MOZART ACCAD. FILARMON: DI BOLOG E DI VERONA

14

12. A miniature on ivory attributed to Martin Knoller and probably painted in Milan early in 1773. Nannerl is thought to have received this portrait from her brother and to have referred to it after Mozart's death as making him look "sickly and yellow" as a result of illness.

13. Replica of a wax cameo relief by Leonhard Posch. This portrait, praised by Constanze, was made in Vienna in 1788

14. Mozart at the piano (detail). Painted in oils by Mozart's brother-in-law Joseph Lange in Vienna in 1782-83, this unfinished but fine portrait was, according to Constanze, the best likeness of her husband.

15. This posthumous oil-portrait by Barbara Krafft was painted in Salzburg in 1819 for Joseph Sonnleithner's Gallery of Composers. Nannerl was asked to help the artist and is thought to have put at her disposal the Knoller miniature *(No. 12)*, a copy (since lost) of the Lange portrait *(No. 14)*, and the family por- trait *(No. 8)*. Of these it was the last, the Della Croce, which provided the basic model, as can be seen from the dress, coiffure, and general features. It is a tribute to Krafft's artistry that her work still remains one of the most highly valued portraits of her enigmatic subject.

II

The Mozarts and their time

Society and Status
Leopold Mozart and His Wife
Getreidegasse No. 9
The Children at Home

10. Germany and Austria, c. 1710. Map by Jeremias Wölff, Augsburg.

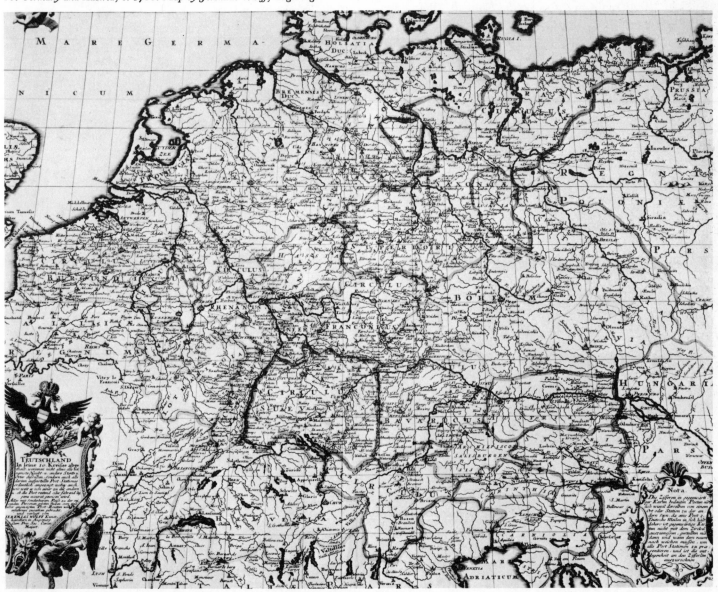

Society and Status

The Mozarts' letters reveal two sentiments which recur enough to seem obsessive – "chips on the shoulder" is the modern phrase. The first is understandable, for it is simply wounded pride; but let us note that the offence was not only the failure of Viennese society to discriminate between Wolfgang's supreme genius and other men's mere talents, but also to accord a musician who was no longer a retained servant less than the social status due to an independent "professional" citizen. The other gnawing sentiment cannot be explained without recourse to the general history of the German states, for it is Mozart's consciousness of being a German and resenting the deference given to writers, architects, painters, and musicians from the Latin countries.

Documentary evidence on the political, economic, and social conditions prevailing in greater Germany between 1750 and 1800 was brilliantly collected by Adrien Fauchier-Magnan for his "Les Petites Cours d'Allemagne au XVIIIème Siècle" published in 1947. In the ensuing paragraphs both the sources and the commentary in this fascinating book will be quoted and paraphrased without further acknowledgment. It should be read by all music-lovers whose gratitude towards music-loving princes of the eighteenth century named in the history of music has not been tempered by knowledge of the human misery they inflicted in pursuit of their admired tastes as well as their disreputable pleasures. It is sometimes forgotten that they were *absolute* sovereigns. To speak of a German confederation is ludicrous, as is also the belief that, except for protective alliance, the petty sovereigns recognised imperial hegemony. Men like Karl Theodor and Karl Eugen, to say nothing of the Salzburg rulers under whom Mozart served, had enough intellect and sensibility to earn our gratitude for their cultural tastes while being just and even beloved administrators of their domains. "The abuse of greatness is when it disjoins remorse from power" or, to paraphrase Shakespeare, the best of men go bad when will and whim may command peremptory execution of orders without check of conscience or thought of responsibility to others. A quick glance at a century of greater Germany's history before Mozart's birth will help to explain the matters which occasionally made a happy man sour.

No earthquake, cyclone, or plague ever afflicted a comparable area as the Thirty Years' War afflicted the states bounded by the Rhine, Danube, Elbe, and North Sea. Between 1618 and 1650 over two-thirds of the people in Dresden perished, while the population of Württemberg fell from 400,000 to 40,000. Some cities, such as Wiesbaden, lost all their houses, and the few survivors lived like hermits with wild animals among ruins already covered by grass and trees. No cattle were left. Trade had ceased. "This tragic period halted the march of German civilisation. Government, religion, fortunes, literature, science, morality – all had to begin afresh after a relapse into barbarism and pillage." It is true that Salzburg escaped, yet like the rest of Germany she looked outside – to France and Italy – for the best artists and thinkers. On the way to Vienna from Italy, indeed at a nodal point for routes in all directions, Salzburg naturally included families of many nationalities. Amongst the Mozarts' predecessors, colleagues, and "superiors" were a great many musicians of Italian or Bohemian provenance as well as some from Austria, Bavaria, and other German states. It was natural for a German prince to think highly of a Frenchman or Italian and to pay him twice as much as a German employee in a similar post, for the demolition of any such concept as "Germany" did not finish at the Peace of Westphalia.

By the terms of that treaty France ensured that there could be no possibility of a unity among German states under Austrian hegemony. She encouraged every petty princedom to regard her as a friend and to imitate her absolutism. French gold was available to hire soldiers or to finance internal aggrandisement. The Peace of Westphalia parcelled Germany into hundreds of independent states, the emperor being required to attend a Diet or parliament at Ratisbon and there settle disputes and hear complaints, e.g. concerning taxation; but France insisted on sending a plenipotentiary, with spies and *agents provocateurs* in his entourage; the policy was to exploit a divided Germany. We are not concerned with political so much as social results – the effect upon the lives and thinking of people like the Mozarts. Social attitudes were directly affected by the ridiculously minute divisions of government. The extent of the division may be imagined from one smallish area at the western side of Bavaria – the district from which Leopold Mozart came. "Swabia comprised 97 sovereigns – 4 ecclesiastical princes, 14 secular princes, 25 lords of the manor, 30 imperial towns (of which Ulm and Augsburg were the most important), and 23 prelates."

Our story of Mozart is not concerned with the power of each petty ruler, who could with impunity shoot a disrespectful huntsman, or order a hundred or a thousand lashes for a soldier or a groom, or hang a starving peasant caught stealing a hare, but with the effect on all society of a ruling class animated (i.e. itself ruled) by pride and protocol, each king, duke, count, landgrave, waldgrave, rhinegrave, margrave, baron, bishop, abbot, or lord of a mere five square miles setting up tolls and customs, thinking only of the possibility of aggrandisement or fearing oppression from others of greater rank. Behind the French-imitated elegance of balls, feasts, and visits were agitations, rivalries, briberies, hatreds, and conspiracies to secure a little more land or climb one more step up the ladder of titles.

"Some took as their model the French king's military pomp, others his mania for building and designing gardens where antiquity and poetic mythology are revealed at each step; nearly all of them aped his Spanish gallantry." That quotation may not well apply to the

Salzburg ruled first by Schrattenbach then by Colloredo, but the social consequences of their predecessors' activities remained. Whatever the "mania" of a small ruler who conceived it his duty to employ a vast number of stewards, bailiffs, financial and administrative officers, down to valets, grooms, gardeners, and others ranking only just beneath musicians, stipends had to be small or the tolls and taxes which provided them would have been unpayable – and the subjects became, like their masters, animated by the hope of rising in social status and the fear of those who had risen, and cursed also by rivalries, briberies, and hatreds. Merely to be directly in the ruler's service was to reflect his pride and require deference. It was a mark of Bach's sturdy independence, and his desire to make the music in the churches of Leipzig outshine that of a court, that he decided to *lose* social status, forgo the exalted title *Kapellmeister* and the duke's grand uniform for that of mere city *Kantor* and its black gown. By the end of the century and with the growth of the Enlightenment into the new thinking of the French Encyclopaedists, the professional man – the lawyer, professor, intellectual, artistic genius – as well as the wealthy merchant not only stood high in a city or bourgeois hierarchy, but had to be respected by any ruler with pretensions to intelligence. These were the people who dominated the revolution in France and have really been the ruling classes ever since, whatever the supposed political ideology of a European state.

Living just before the actual outbreak of revolution Mozart, not Beethoven, was the first supreme genius born into a feudal society who dared to be freelance, seeking a livelihood and even securing friends from both the aristocracy of birth and the professional people and the mercantile citizens of Salzburg and Vienna. He was sufficiently of the old régime himself to think much in English society and manners to be inelegant if not boorish. On the other hand it is worth noting what English people thought of south Germany during his time and even later. Having been impressed with the orchestral playing and opera in Württemberg, Burney was horrified at the beggarly state of the peasantry. The only way to escape near-starvation was to enlist in the army (unless already pressed into that service), which was brutal towards the rest of the population and brutally disciplined itself, reminding Burney of Lamettrie's "Man a Machine"; he finished by execrating Karl Eugen's pride, "for though I love music I love humanity more." Even after Beethoven's death the Novellos thought the "women of Germany [they were writing in Vienna] want air and carriage; the *trottoir* makes them walk as if they had tight shoes and though they stare with the vulgarity of a milkmaid they are shy and at a loss if you address them. As for the peasantry, after 14 they become frightful and are more like men than women in dress and appearance. In Vienna you see them rolling barrows full of stones, conveying up mortar and working amongst men on scaffolding, and some of the loads they bear would astonish an Irish porter. Scarce a shoe is to be seen among them."

The Mozarts were conscious of social status. Leopold remained dignified and reserved amongst the other musicians but was obviously genial and friendly with mercantile and professional people whom he regarded as his equals or, if their status had been achieved by prosperity without his own superior education, his inferiors. No doubt what mattered most in these nice assessments of social rank were people's impressions from a man's appearance, manners, and speech. In command of these Leopold Mozart was fortunate.

Leopold Mozart and His Wife

Wolfgang's father came from a family of Augsburg bookbinders who were able to give him a good education. When Maria Theresa expelled the Jesuits from Austria the cities of Swabia, Franconia, Bavaria, and neighbouring states gained still more good teachers at their excellent Jesuit schools, where the most promising pupils were prepared for the Benedictine university at Salzburg. At the age of eight, boys who passed the entrance test in reading, writing, and general knowledge entered the *Gymnasium*; those good enough might proceed at 16 to the *Lyceum* for two or three years. Leopold was there for only two; it was expected that he would enter the church but

11. Augsburg, c. 1700. Etching published by Pieter van der Aa.

12. Leopold Mozart around 1762. Pencil drawing attributed to Franz Lactanz, Count Firmian, high steward at the palace of the prince-archbishop of Salzburg.

either he or others decided otherwise. (He may have craftily suggested an intention to be a priest.)

It was never the practice of the Jesuits to "overdo" religion in schools. They discouraged any fanaticism or even intense absorption with religious doctrine and observance such as characterised certain Protestant communities. The rational thinking of the Enlightenment affected the Jesuits as, indeed, it did the university at Salzburg, and Leopold Mozart seems to have represented well the strong faith but "good-mannered" religion of his teachers. He was cynical towards superstition and exploitation of "miracles," highly critical of the clergy, yet punctilious in Catholic belief and practice, requiring his family to be so. This behaviour was quite sincere, as was his son's religious adherence. The rebellious, critical, and radical streak in Wolfgang was inherited; yet Leopold, like his son, became a Freemason because the aims of the brotherhood seemed a rational and practical expression of Christianity.

At Augsburg Leopold was taught not only Latin, Greek, French, Italian, history, and mathematics but also subjects amongst the sciences which were thought worth the attention of an enlightened mind though they took little lesson time; they included the elements of geology, chemistry, physics, botany, anatomy, and astronomy. (He owned two microscopes and a telescope, a globe and an atlas.) While at school he sang both at St. Ulrich and Holy Cross, received lessons in organ and violin-playing and, having a good voice and presence, took prominent parts in classical and religious plays. As has already been stressed, he was better equipped than most schoolmasters to be his son's private tutor in general education as well as music. In 1737, aged 18, he went up to Salzburg University and was commended after the first-year examination. He ceased to attend classes regularly in his second year, and when called before the dean offered no explanation of his absences. "He left as if indifferent" to the threat of expulsion and therefore "was

13. The collegiate church of Salzburg University designed by Johann Bernhard Fischer von Erlach and built between 1694 and 1707. Engraving by Karl Remshard after a drawing by Franz Anton Danreiter, c. 1730.

not summoned to further examination." This may mean either that he was not allowed to proceed to the second-year examinations or that he was not again called before the authorities for investigation of his progress or lack of it, having decided to leave. He was shrewd and ambitious, and he may have been earning while enrolled as a student or may have seized an opportunity for employment locally that would not recur when he needed it. It has also been suggested that he left when grants from Augsburg were stopped because he did not intend to be a priest. These are conjectures; we do not know why he left or was expelled, but evidently the decision did not prevent his frequenting the university to take part in its theatrical activities and, within a few years, to supply music for a performance before the court.

He became *Kammerdiener* to a wealthy aristocrat who held one of the Salzburg canonries (he was head of the chapter). The appointment has been mistaken for that of *Leibkammerdiener* or valet, because of the French term *valet de chambre*; the nearest English rendering of his official status is "chamber musician," i.e. member of the orchestra. His employer provided Fauchier-Magnan with some delicious evidence of the foolish envy and rancour that was rife in that society of titles and protocol. Count Johann of Thurn and Taxis belonged to a family which owed its enormous wealth to its monopoly of the imperial postal service. The Counts of Thurn and Taxis had made contracts with the various states to run over 40 coach routes not only carrying mail but offering first and second-class passenger travel. (The vehicles were nicknamed "taxis," and when later on a Magdeburg inventor produced a "taximeter" to measure mileage and therefore amounts to be paid for transport, the description of a hired vehicle with the appliance was shortened from "cabriolet taximeter" to "taxicab.") The Princess Palatine wrote: "The Count of Thurn and Taxis tries to pass for a duke although there are dozens like him." At one of the count's receptions various notables were not assigned to definite places at the dinner table; there and then they began quarrels over precedence which continued in a war of pamphlets. It was brought to the notice of the emperor who satisfied honour by blaming the host for bad organisation!

Leopold Mozart seems to have been treated well, however, and the preface to six trio sonatas which were engraved in 1740 declares that his employer had "in his benevolence . . . rescued the composer from necessity." Yet after three years he left the rescuer for a place amongst the first violins in the court *Kapelle*, which seems to indicate that his compositions were much to the taste of Salzburg. They were numerous in all three of the classifications then recognised – church, chamber, and theatre music ("chamber" including orchestral) – and bear comparison with most works of the pre-Classical era. By 1757 he had secured additional emoluments and a title as "Court Composer," but that year he basked less in his facility as a composer than in the reviews of his *magnum opus* which had been published at Augsburg in

1756 soon after his famous son's birth. It is usually called simply his "Violin School," its full title being "Versuch einer gründlichen Violinschule" (Thorough treatise on violin technique). Even allowing for eighteenth-century piracy he must have taken good royalties from this work over the rest of his life, for it was translated into several European languages and regarded well into the nineteenth century as a standard work. Despite commissions for compositions from places well away from Salzburg, only his book brought him international repute before that reflected from his child prodigies. His pride must have risen particularly at the printed commendations by Marpurg, Zelter, and Schubart which mentioned not only the book's "splendid examples" and "modern outlook" but also its "excellent German"; yet no sequel followed the hint on the last page – "Perhaps I shall dare to add yet another book to the musician's library" – which has been held to prove that he intended to write a comprehensive textbook of music theory and composition. Nor did he produce the biography of his son as promised in the second edition of the "Violin School." That he cherished the idea seems proved by his preserving all Wolfgang's early compositions and writings, including letters, for which purpose his landlord Hagenauer destroyed no letters sent home to Salzburg while the Mozarts were touring.

Leopold served in the Salzburg *Kapelle* for no less than 40 years under five prince-archbishops. The ruler who transferred him to court service was the Baron Leopold Firmian who ordered the erection of Salzburg's much-photographed "horse" fountain and the building of Leopoldskron Castle. He brought many Italians to Salzburg and was so much a man of the Enlightenment that he was suspected of Freemasonry – a charge difficult to reconcile with his cruel expulsion of some 20,000 Protestants. (In Augsburg there was a large Protestant community, led by the Fuggers, and the rise of Freemasonry was only one means towards religious toleration in years when only certain rulers, not the church itself, forbade Catholics to be Masons. Leopold's opinion about the expulsion is not recorded; most Salzburgers were disgusted by it.) Firmian's successor, Count Jakob Ernst of Liechtenstein, incurred adverse comment for very different excesses – he spent much upon carnivals and entertainments and was thought too extravagant for a church dignitary – but he died two years after his enthronement, to be followed by Count Andreas Dietrichstein who, though forced to an initial policy of retrenchment, was himself fond of music and entertainment. He was followed by Count Sigismund Schrattenbach after a much-contested election. It is hard to know why this prince, the first of the two known to Wolfgang, was so much liked in Salzburg whereas his successor, Count Hieronymus Colloredo, was disliked even before he arrived. Appearance, speech, and manner have probably more to do with the popularity of rulers than history conveys; they may help to explain, for instance, the detestation amongst English landed and mercantile classes for Charles I and

14. Leopoldskron Castle. Drawing by Franz Anton Danreiter, 1740.

Laud, both men of high moral standards.

Schrattenbach made it clear that he was not only prince but bishop, and he wished to raise morality in his dominions. He brought "hell-fire" mission preachers to the churches, endowed orphanages and reformatories, yet was thought, in Alfred Einstein's words, "patriarchal and easy-going." He was fortunately fond of music and of the Mozarts, to whom he was obviously indulgent. He was ruler from 1753 to 1771, during which period Leopold was promoted first to court composer then to vice-*Kapellmeister* after the death of Johann Ernst Eberlin, the only German *Kapellmeister* in Leopold's time. He, too, had been educated by the Jesuits at Augsburg and gone to Salzburg University. The depreciations of nearly all Salzburg musicians mentioned in the Mozarts' letters do not include any of Eberlin, whom Leopold evidently admired, for he collaborated with him in certain compositions for local events. What is more, Eberlin seems to have been the better composer. When he died in 1762 Leopold hoped to be made *Kapellmeister*, but Schrattenbach promoted Lolli, the vice-*Kapellmeister*, and Leopold took his place. By an almost openly declared policy ("Never trust another man . ." may be regarded as an *ad hoc* warning to his son) Leopold did not make close friendships with his professional colleagues, but there were exceptions amongst some of those who were Germans – Adlgasser, the court organist, a Bavarian and the composer of operas, oratorios, and many instrumental works, and the violinist Hebelt who deputised for Leopold when he was absent.

If it is true that musical aptitude is much affected by heredity, then Mozart was as much beholden to his mother's family as his father's. Wolfgang Nikolaus Pertl, the maternal grandfather after whom Mozart was given his first name, came from a family of Salzburg cloth-makers. He was musically gifted but read law at Salzburg University and became a civil servant in the revenue division, being still admired as a bass singer and as choirmaster at the school and monastic church of St. Peter. He was promoted to administrative posts in Vienna, Graz, then back in Salzburg, and finally in the St. Gilgen district in the plain near St. Wolfgang Lake to the east of Salzburg. Anna Maria Pertl was born in St. Gilgen in 1720 but was only four when her father died suddenly, leaving debts. He was reckoned a high official, but Salzburg's beggarly stipends were well known in surrounding states as the consequence of using far too many people in the civil service, or rather court service. He was far from extravagant, yet the fact that a good library was sold to meet some of his creditors indicates his cultured tastes. On a very small pension the widow and her small family must have known acute privation; yet it was from them that Anna Maria's future son was to derive his disposition to merriment and teasing, his father's humour being

15

reserved and caustic. Even so, to have "come down in the world" was a harsh fate in that society where one could not accept certain kinds of employment without shame. The widow may have been permitted to go on living in the house or part of the house allotted to her husband, the district superintendent, for she did not move into Salzburg until 1742. She then lived in the Getreidegasse, the very street in which her daughter was to set up home with Leopold Mozart.

Anna Maria was good-looking, for she and Leopold were known as the "handsomest couple in Salzburg." He must have been attracted to her almost as soon as she arrived in the city, for in a letter he wrote home from Milan in 1772 occurs the passage: "It was 25 years ago, I believe, when we had the wise resolve to get married, one we had certainly looked forward to for many years. All good things take time!" She was "uneducated" but intelligent, with an outstandingly affectionate nature. The marriage was one of opposites, and she cannot have

been respected by Wolfgang as his father was, whoever greatly he loved her; yet there is no evidence that during their greatest anxieties Mozart's parents quarrelled or found their love under strain. The fact is remarkable when one considers not only Leopold's absences with his son but also the late hours and long periods he had to spend away from home at his duties with the court.

Getreidegasse No. 9

Visitors to Salzburg should not imagine that in Mozart's time the Mozart *Geburtshaus* merely faced another street running into the Getreidegasse. It was by no means one of the poorer streets of the old city or it would not have been chosen by so status-conscious a husband. That wide and handsome entrance to No. 9 was on the side of an Italianate square, the Löchelplatz,

15. *The Löchelplatz, showing the Mozart Geburtshaus (No. 225), now No. 9. Lithograph by C. Czichna after a drawing by J. A. Wenzl, 1837.*

with a fountain in the middle at which the women drew their daily water. That fountain is still there, now no more than a monument with its plinth against a building instead of charmingly free-standing: for opposite No. 9 Getreidegasse the square was cut by another street very soon after Mozart's death. (Not many Salzburg squares were thus altered during the nineteenth century.) Looking at that wide door we can also see to the right an elegant shop front which belonged to the wholesale grocery business of Johann Hagenauer, the Mozarts' landlord and admiring friend.

The wedding was in the cathedral on November 21, 1747, Leopold being 28 and his bride 27. They lived on the third floor of the Hagenauer house. The best rooms were in the front overlooking the square, but today's thousands of visitors see domesticity in the little rooms at the back – the kitchen as it was in the eighteenth century and the little chamber evidently used for *accouchements* and therefore proudly shown as the place of the great man's birth. It was probably used later as the children's bedroom. Evidently the room for music-making was that which now houses the museum. (More interesting still is the second-floor exhibition of those delightful models showing the stage-settings of various Mozart operas at different periods.) At the end of each of the first three years of marriage Anna Maria bore a child which did not live, and we need no further reason for her increasingly bad health which led to a consultation with Dr. Barisani in the spring of 1750. Silvester Barisani was a near neighbour and good family friend, being also physician to the prince-archbishop. His family had a small estate outside the city and also ran a manufactory of agricultural implements. Anna Maria was advised to visit a fashionable health resort, as was her son's wife in 1789; in neither case could the cost be borne easily, but it is unlikely that the affectionate husband made any demur, and not to have followed the doctor's advice would have been to lose status amongst friends and neighbours. In each case the medicinal waters, or more probably the change from work and worry, sent the wife home strong and well. On July 30 of the following year Maria Anna Walburga, to be known as Nannerl, was born. Two more children died soon after birth and then, on January 27, 1756, Wolfgang Amadeus Mozart was born in that little back room overlooking the courtyard, four and a half years later than Nannerl. Fortunately for Anna Maria, if not for the two children and Leopold, there were no more children to follow.

The more we know about eighteenth-century standards of hygiene the more we may wonder how even two children out of seven survived. It was thought vulgar for the "better classes" to keep infants on their mother's milk, or even on milk at all for very long. They were put out to be wet-nursed and then fed on various physicians' different slops, for instance honey and water, or broth with some patent powder. We may be amused today at different opinions on the nourishment of babies, for medical counsels on the subject differ sufficiently to

16. *Johann Hagenauer. Copy in oils by Sebastian Stief, 1873, of a burial-plate portrait in St. Peter's Cemetery, Salzburg.*

provide a subject for a play by Shaw; but at least most babies survive. When Mozart was born most babies failed to survive their very first year.

The Children at Home

Were the Mozart children "forced" in their general and musical education – taught too rapidly and with inadequate exercise and diversion of body and spirits? Did Leopold exploit their talents for money? Did he culpably risk their health by tiring journeys, long hours of waiting before exhibiting their accomplishments, the exigencies of weather and treatment in lodgings and inns, including a nasty London winter which struck himself severely? Not to say "Yes" to each of these questions merely because there *seem* to be no serious long-term results is surely less than honest; but it would be still less fair to let that "Yes" accompany a conception of Leopold Mozart as a cruel circus-act manager and his children as considering themselves badly used. Nothing they wrote or said either when young or in years of recollection suggests that they thought themselves unfortunate in any way; on the contrary they regarded themselves as divinely favoured by their talents, their parents, their upbringing, which other children might envy; this might be called the result of indoctrination – a point not to be argued here – but certainly the subjects of the process seem never to have resisted its application or to have felt unhappy at its effect.

Both children may have been hypersensitive, but we

know for certain only that the boy was. He showed the abnormality by constantly asking those about him if they loved him, and in weeping if he received a teasing reply. It must not be forgotten that Leopold was the first very musical child in his family and may himself have had to hide hypersensitivity. Wolfgang Mozart had the inestimable advantage of having an artist-father who had the common sense (or artistic perception) to know that his son was a far greater artist. Leopold seems never to have shown angry misunderstanding until his son, on tour while Leopold himself had to remain in Salzburg, seemed to be wasting time instead of seeking "a famous *Kapellmeister*-ship," the only kind of post which would bring the due recognition and reward of genius. It is ridiculous to suppose that Leopold did not recognise the difference between Wolfgang's genius – something which high accomplishment and assiduous training could not produce – and his own talent. When he visited his son in Vienna he marvelled at it, and he recognised it before Haydn assured him of it.

The nearest evidence we have of Leopold's undoubted peremptoriness as a parent (any head of a family who did not expect prompt obedience would have been despised long after the eighteenth century) comes from the Salzburg court trumpeter, Andreas Schachtner, in letters to Nannerl after Mozart's death. He recollects the little boy's asking to participate in the sight-reading of some trios by their colleague Wentzel. According to Schachtner the child had not by that time "received any instruction on the violin," but it is unlikely, in view of his father's chief occupation and the fact that Leopold was regarded as *the* authority on teaching the violin, that Wolfgang had not learnt something about the instrument informally. The trios were about to be rehearsed by Leopold, Wentzel, and Schachtner. "Wolfgangerl asked to be allowed to play second violin . . . Your Papa reproved him and thought he would be unable to make anything of it. Wolfgang said: 'You do not need to have taken lessons to play second violin.' When your Papa insisted that he go away at once and not bother us, he began to cry and went sulkily off with his little fiddle. I asked that he be allowed to play alongside of me. At last your Papa said: 'Play with Herr Schachtner, but so softly that you can't be heard, or you'll have to go' . . . Soon I noticed to my amazement that I was superfluous. Quietly I laid my violin aside and watched your Papa, who had tears of wonder and pleasure running down his cheeks. We played through all six trios. When we were finished, Wolfgangerl was so elated by our applause that he said he could play the first violin part. We let him do it for a joke, and almost died of laughter. His fingering was incorrect and improvised but he never got stuck." Obviously the child was indulged, for his father could not bear to see him distressed.

Apparently there were never tears from the children at the heavy routine of prescribed lessons, musical and otherwise. We misunderstand them if we think of them as we do of normal children of our own time, miserable

17. *Dr. Silvester Barisani. Oil painting by Johann Nepomuk della Croce.*

because they must be at study when they want to be with other youngsters at play. Professor Erich Schenk rightly mentions the effect of Leopold's Jesuit schooling, by which it was a religious duty to "work" faithfully even while to "work" meant to perform school exercises as well as one could. No doubt the Mozart children were taught the same attitude, but it needed no stressing: in modern parlance, they lapped it up.

What outdoor exercise they got, we do not know, but we do know that they played with other children, for instance those of the court chancellor, von Mölk, and the two of the four Gilowsky children nearest to them in age, one of each sex (Gilowsky was the court surgeon). Their closest friends were the children of Maria von Stumb, a widow in comfortable circumstances. Some of these people may have become family friends because they or their children took music lessons from Leopold. Nannerl herself began to teach children while she was in her teens.

Pictorial Essay:
The Family Circle

If the remarkable musical gifts of the Mozart children were inherited then they owed much to both sides of the family. Their mother, who lacked education but not intelligence, was not herself a practising musician, but her father Wolfgang Nikolaus Pertl, was admired as a singer and choirmaster. She met the violinist-composer Leopold Mozart shortly after she moved to Salzburg from St. Gilgen in 1742 and in November 1747 "the handsomest couple in Salzburg" were married. Of the seven children born to them only the two pictured here together survived. It was perhaps a marriage of opposites but it was, in Professor Hutchings's opinion, a happy one, even under the strain of journeys and separations. Affection and respect for one another made the family closely knit and we have this to thank for the fact that Mozart's life is better documented, mainly in the form of family letters, than the lives of many composers who lived much closer to our own time.

16. The Mozart children. An unsigned miniature on ivory purporting to represent Wolfgang and Nannerl. It was painted around 1765 and is attributed to Eusebius Alphen.

17. The mother. Anna Maria Mozart, born Pertl (1720-1778). Unsigned portrait in oils, c. 1775, attributed by Professor Erich Schenk to Pietro Antonio Lorenzoni, though others have suggested Franz Joseph Degle of Augsburg.

18. The father. Johann Georg Leopold Mozart (1719-1787). Anonymous oil portrait, c. 1765, which Schenk attributes, like *No. 17*, to Lorenzoni.

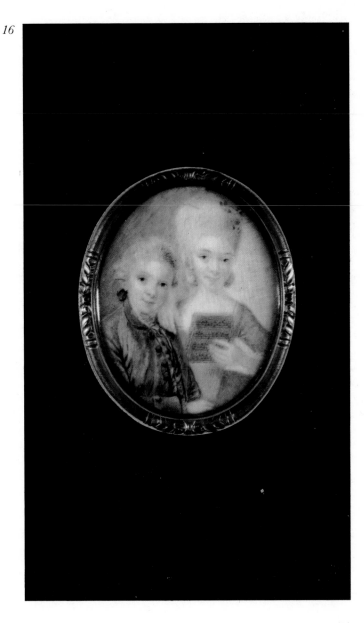

17

(10)

It was inevitable that Nannerl Mozart should to some extent be overshadowed by her brother, even before his true genius as a composer became apparent. When they played together as children before the courts of Europe, Wolfgang, if only because he was four and a half years younger, must have attracted the major share of attention. Yet, like her father, Nannerl seems to have been quick to recognise and accept without question the fact that Wolfgang's gifts were of an order quite different from her own. This seems to have made little difference to the affection they undoubtedly had for each other and the close family bond between them. There is no evidence of any undue bitterness or envy in their relationship either in childhood or in later years. It was to teaching that Nannerl turned after her career as a youthful prodigy. Then, in 1784, at the age of 33, she married Johann Baptist Berchtold zu Sonnenburg, a magistrate of St. Gilgen (as Nannerl's maternal grandfather had been) and settled there in the house where her mother was born. She bore three children, of whom only a son Leopold survived childhood. In 1792 her husband was ennobled and it was as the Baroness von Berchtold zu Sonnenburg that she returned to Salzburg after his death in 1801 and occupied herself with occasional teaching till blindness overcame her in 1820. She lived long enough to meet Vincent and Mary Novello during their visit to Salzburg in 1829 but died the same year at the age of 77.

19. Maria Anna (Nannerl) Mozart (1751-1829). This unsigned oil portrait, attributed to Pietro Antonio Lorenzoni, was painted in Salzburg in 1763 as a companion portrait to that of Wolfgang in gala costume *(No. 1)* and a memento of their appearance together at the court in Vienna in 1762. It was previously supposed that Nannerl's costume here was given to her by the Empress Maria Theresa and originally made for the Archduchess Marie Antoinette. Now it is known that the portrait was "prepared" and only the head is thought to be original.

20. Maria Anna Berchtold zu Sonnenburg. An unsigned oil portrait of Nannerl after her marriage. Dated around 1785, it was probably intended to match one of her husband executed about the same time.

21. Constanze Mozart, born Weber (1763-1842). Oil portrait by Joseph Lange painted (like *No. 14*) about 1782 in Vienna. See also Page 70.

If the marriage of Mozart's parents was one of opposites then his own to the 19-year-old Constanze Weber in 1782 was surely also one. Yet although there was no question of intellectual parity between the pair, they had enough in common for Professor Hutchings to maintain, in spite of many opinions to the contrary, that the two were "suited" psychologically and sexually and that the marriage remained happy even under the clouds of financial insecurity and ill health. It is not perhaps unusual that Mozart should have married Constanze after attraction to and rejection by her older sister Aloysia. (Dvořák's happy marriage to Anna Čermáková nearly 100 years later followed the same pattern.) What is odd is that we owe to the man Aloysia did eventually marry, Joseph Lange, the best portraits we possess of both Mozart *(No. 14)* and his wife *(No. 21)* although he was an actor and not a professional artist.

Eighteen years after Mozart's death Constanze married Georg Nikolaus Nissen, a diplomat and one of Mozart's earliest biographers. (They had, however, set up house together around 1800 – see *No. 77.)* Nissen received a Danish decoration in 1809 but, according to Deutsch, was not ennobled or entitled to the name von Nissen which Constanze used on his book on Mozart, published posthumously by her in 1828.

22. Constanze Mozart. An oil portrait of 1802 by Hans Hansen, probably commissioned by her future second husband, with whom she was then living (see *No. 77)*.

23. Georg Nikolaus Nissen (1761-1826). This oil portrait, by Ferdinand Jagemann, was painted in Vienna in 1809, the year of Nissen's decoration and his marriage to Constanze Mozart.

24. Constanze Nissen. A miniature of Constanze after her second marriage, painted in 1826 by Thomas Spitzer.

Only two of Mozart's children survived him – Karl Thomas (1784-1858) and Franz Xaver (1791-1844). Both seem to have been well provided for by their stepfather Nissen, although he had children of his own. Only the younger, who later took his father's name, became a professional musician and was highly thought of as a pianist, composer, and teacher. Karl, who studied piano and could perhaps have made music his career, eventually settled instead in the government service in Milan. He was able to benefit from royalties for his father's work and died as a result in much happier financial circumstances.

25. Mozart's children, Karl Thomas (right) and Franz Xaver, an oil portrait c. 1798 by Hans Hansen, who also painted their mother *(No. 22)*.

26. Franz Xaver Mozart (also known as Wolfgang Amadeus). Portrait in oils c. 1825 by Karl Schweikart.

III

The exhibition tours

18. The headquarters of the Thurn und Taxis postal service in Brussels. Detail from an eighteenth-century print.

Proving a Miracle

Though Leopold was affectionate towards Nannerl, she became chiefly a willing catalyst in the projection of Wolfgang's talents. Wolfgang's precocity changed Leopold's life and almost turned his head. He became the servant of his son, utterly devoted to him long before the three years of home instruction were finished. "Nowadays when everything called a miracle is ridiculed it has become my duty to prove this miracle to the world." By competing in the flourishing business of travelling virtuosi? Was that the fulfilment of a duty to God or the pursuit of a desire for money? Surely to make money was a strong motive, as it is nearly always in people who have known hardship and won status. The wish to own a carriage and groom, dress well, employ servants, be better housed than other musicians – these were not purely selfish imaginings. Fame and fortune went hand in hand and the two were what he sought in trying to launch his son as the prince of musicians and chief musician of the greatest of princes.

The tours were planned with programmes that included such charlatan tricks as letting the boy play with a cloth covering the keyboard, going into an adjoining room and naming notes played in the audience-chamber, or coming in and playing passages or harmonies he had heard through the door. As the child's skill advanced it became safe to include extemporisations and, as Daines Barrington heard to his wonder in London, the immediate harmonisation of melodies and extemporisation of variations. In some places he was also allowed to show his skill on the organ and the violin. The main plan was to gain a hearing at the most important courts, notably those of the emperor and of the king of France. Whatever the financial reward, success with a sovereign who had a famous musical establishment could be the basis of Wolfgang's later applications for high positions. Already the Mozarts had friends amongst aristocratic families around Salzburg and they were the means of securing entry to still higher echelons of society.

If we regard Mozart as no longer a child after the age of 15, that is to say after 1771, then the children were taken on four exhibition tours, or more accurately on three as a complete family, for Nannerl and her mother stayed at home for the fourth. They were:

1. January, 1762–January, 1763: A trial Austrian tour, going through Bavaria and, while based on Vienna, visiting places in Hungary.
2. June, 1763–November, 1766: The grand tour through Munich, Augsburg, the Rhine, Aix-la-Chapelle (Aachen), and Brussels to Paris and Versailles; thence to London for over a year, back via Holland with a return visit to the French court and, after a visit to Dijon and Lyons, through Switzerland and Bavaria.
3. September, 1767–January, 1769: A second tour of Austria based on Vienna.
4. December, 1769–March, 1771: The Italian tour as far as Naples.

Two further visits to Italy were not planned as exhibition tours, though no opportunity was lost to display Wolfgang's talents, no doubt with the suggestion that he was younger than his actual age – which his small build supported. The visits to Milan in 1771 and 1772–73 were made to supervise performances of works commissioned from Wolfgang as a result of the original Italian tour. Thus, out of the 11 years from 1762 to 1773, Leopold was absent from duty in Salzburg for a total of more than eight, and just because old Archbishop Schrattenbach freely gave him leave (and was probably proud of their success) we should not condemn the less pleasant Archbishop Colloredo for demurring at further requests for absence; but the troubles with him lie ahead of our story. We must first recount just a selection of incidents during the exhibition tours because their circumstances affected Mozart the adult artist.

The First Tour

When they set out the Mozarts had no carriage of their own, and because the whole family travelled we lack the rich abundance of letters that passed between them when some stayed at home. We have only a few sent by Leopold to Hagenauer and other Salzburg friends. We do not know even the mode of transport for every stage of the tour; it was sometimes in conveyances supplied by pleased patrons, sometimes hired carriages, sometimes mail-coach, and sometimes mail-boat. Munich was the obvious destination for a first "trial" excursion, being not only the nearest important capital to Salzburg but also the residence of the Elector Maximilian Joseph III, a minor composer and a good gamba player. The Mozarts were there in midwinter, the early months of 1762, until the carnival season was beginning before Lent. Although we do not have details of their court appearance, it is known that Leopold was pleased with the impact they made and the money they took. So they would surely be as lucky at the episcopal court of Passau, the next nearest to Salzburg after Munich, if one wished to be certain of a munificent and music-loving prince. The Bishop of Passau was Count Joseph Thun-Hohenstein who hoped to be elected to Salzburg. In September the Mozarts set out for Passau, probably by boat down the Salzach to the Danube. They were cordially treated but not highly paid; the chief reward was to have been appreciated by the episcopal member of the highly influential Thun family. They proceeded to Linz where a concert they gave under the patronage of their protector Count Schlick astonished and delighted a young aristocrat who arrived just in time to hear them. He was Count Pálffy, nephew of the Hungarian chancellor, and nobody was of greater service to the children when they arrived in Vienna.

19. View of Passau showing the cathedral (right centre), and the prince-bishop's gardens. Engraving by Jeremias Wölff.

The dean of Passau Cathedral, Count Herberstein, who had accompanied them to Linz, also went ahead of them to Vienna. An audience with the imperial family was almost assured, for Pálffy, Herberstein, and others would surely persuade Count Durazzo, intendant of the emperor's theatres and music and Gluck's ally in presenting "reform" opera, to make the necessary arrangements. They went down river by the mail-boat. Violent storms held them at Ybbs and Stein, and at the former Wolfgang astounded the Franciscans by his trial of their organ. The family arrived in Vienna on October 6, rested at an inn of which Leopold had a poor opinion, and appeared first in Count Collalto's palace. At the first opportunity Leopold went alone to the opera to hear Gluck's "Orfeo ed Euridice," which had had its famous first performance on October 5. We have no record of his opinion but we do know what gave him greater pleasure – hearing the Archduke Leopold talking from his box to someone in the next box about the "wonder boy from Salzburg." Pálffy and others had evidently reported their arrival and they had only a week to await the summons to Schönbrunn on October 13. This choice of date suggests that the Mozarts were regarded as entertainment for the young Archduke Maximilian who had just celebrated his nameday; and Franz I's treatment of the over-serious Wolfgang confirms the suggestion – it was kindly meant, and would have been kindly in effect to most six-year-olds. He called the child "My little wizard" and jestingly said it was no great feat to play looking at the keyboard. He had heard of the trick of playing with the keyboard covered. Having sampled it he said it was not unusual to play using all the fingers, but to make a piece sound well using a single finger for each hand *would* be a remarkable feat. The boy played in that manner to great applause, but said while the emperor was standing by him "Is not Herr Wagenseil here? He understands . . ." a remark which might have been thought offensively ironic from an adult.

Mozart later played a concerto by Wagenseil, the composer turning the pages for him. The imperial family were evidently charmed by the children, for the empress Maria Theresa is said to have gone with some of her own children to show the little visitors the adjoining apartments. Wolfgang slipped on a polished floor, and the Archduchess Marie Antoinette, later queen of France, helped him up and received an immediate offer of marriage in return for her kindness. She was two months older than Wolfgang. Then, according to Leopold, "Wolferl jumped on the empress's lap, threw his arms round her neck and kissed her heartily. We stayed from three until six

20. Georg Christoph Wagenseil (centre). Detail from a painting by Eduard Ender, engraved by Hermann Dröhmer.

21

o'clock and the emperor himself came into the other room to fetch me to hear the archduchess's violin-playing."

It would be tedious to give a list of the Viennese notabilities who sent carriages to bring the children to their palaces, but since we have been at pains not to take sides with those who put Leopold amongst the bad fathers of history we should notice also the kind of treatment from which he should have protected his children on this first tour as on later ones. Immediately after the three hours with the imperial family (preceded by what preparations and waiting?) they were taken to the palace of Prince Joseph of Sachsen-Hildburghausen, formerly the field-marshal blamed for the defeat at Rossbach. He was wealthy, maintained a fine orchestra, took great interest in the arts, and paid handsomely. From him they were dragged off to display before the Countess Kinsky. (Names associated with Beethoven's dedications will often be found in accounts of Mozart's life, for it was thanks to the maintaining of houses in or near the city and the example of the greater rulers in regarding the cultivation of music as an attribute of rank, that Vienna became Europe's musical Mecca during the Classical period. Very often when history speaks of "Italian opera" during that period and for some time before it, we should remember that Italian composers were all over Austria and Germany and staged many of their first performances in Vienna.)

Even though the various patrons usually sent their carriages, the round of three-hour and four-hour engagements must have tired and strained the children to the detriment of their health. This must have specially affected the six-year-old Wolfgang. He was not clear of a cold caught in the bad weather at Linz before there was

21. Dr. Franz (Friedrich) Anton Mesmer. Engraving by Meyer.

a second summons to Schönbrunn on October 21; it had to be declined because he was running a high temperature and had broken out into a rash. The Countess Kinsky's doctor diagnosed scarlet fever – mistakenly, for the rash disappeared after 10 days and the children were taken for walks and to the theatre. (Leopold declared that the boy's illness and convalescence "lost us at least 50 ducats"!) Here we need mention only some of the engagements before and after Wolfgang's illness – those before notabilities who came later to appreciate the adult Mozart in Vienna. They included Count Thun and his Countess, the most liberal and "open-house" of Vienna's patrons of the arts; the diplomat Count Kaunitz, who had heard fine music while in Turin and Paris; the Countess Lodron, for whom Mozart was later to write a concerto; the French ambassador, who wanted them to make a tour to Paris and Versailles; Count Harrach, former governor of Lombardy, who suggested an Italian tour; Dr. Mesmer, the notorious "magnetiser," and Dr. Bernhard, the professor of medicine at the university who had attended Wolfgang in his fever. The performances for the two last mentioned may have done more than others to swell Mozart's later Vienna audiences, for public concerts depended largely upon the intelligent middle classes (among whom there were, incidentally, many Freemasons).

Useful, too, was their invitation to the grand evening concert held on St. Cecilia's Day (November 22) in St. Stephen's, for Reutter, the imperial *Kapellmeister*, showed them such friendship that they not only dined with him but were asked to do so whenever they wished. For a dazzling public banquet the empress sent them gala dresses, which are mentioned here because Wolfgang wore his when he and Nannerl had their portraits painted on their return to Salzburg. (The unknown painter was probably an Italian but Wolfgang's face is lifeless enough in all conscience, and the picture is of value only to show visitors to the Mozarteum the boy's dress, said to have been made originally for the little Archduke Maximilian. The girl's portrait is now disesteemed since the discovery that, as was often the custom, the engaged artist painted only Nannerl's head, the rest having been prepared, probably by a pupil, for portraits of other young girls – indeed, the head seems stuck on and disproportionate.)

Count Pálffy persuaded the Mozarts to make Pressburg their centre for a series of performances before the Hungarian nobility. The journeys were made over bad roads in a particularly unpleasant December. In a letter to Hagenauer there is complaint of the intense cold and of a carious tooth which caused such a swelling of Leopold's face that he was not recognised by an old Salzburg friend in the orchestra at Pressburg. Details like these help us to imagine the unpleasant side of eighteenth-century travelling – was the tooth extracted (without anaesthetics) by the local barber or blacksmith?

But since we are to follow the Mozarts over worse roads and through greater hazards, we should consider other factors contributory to comfort or discomfort away from

22. Wasserburg. Anonymous lithograph.

home. First, it was not only the imperial court that laid down precisely the manner of dress for all who appeared there. Most courts except the Prussian (which affected military plainness, even shabbiness, forbidding the use of foreign materials of dress to encourage local industry), prescribed every detail of apparel from wig to shoes, and without regard to cost; even the tiny Wolfgang had to have his wig. Moreover a luxurious wardrobe was a mark of status. In Mozart's time travel was usually by first or second-class mail-coach or (sailing) boat with extra charge for freight. In all forms of road transport before "macadamising," when the local parish merely filled in a few bad ruts after complaints (or used money from turnpikes to pay labourers), the breaking of axles and wheels was so common that people laid bets as to which way a vehicle would fall next. Postilions had to be humoured or they could be unpleasant. Halts for meals in cold weather could be infuriating, for the wealthier passengers would continue feasting in the warmth of an inn. The changing of horses was often possible only by hiring or buying fresh beasts from local folk and peasants, who would sometimes refuse them. A wise long-distance traveller tried to cross as few frontiers of the many petty states of Germany as he could (provided he could use the better roads and was not dependent upon the mail-coaches) because of halts at customs houses where tolls were required and passports inspected, the process being complicated by changes of currency, often to one deliberately depreciated by the ruler. The value placed on money had to be accepted on the spot.

The discomfort east of Vienna was offset by large financial profit, and the Mozarts were able to buy their own carriage. They were back in Vienna by Christmas Eve and declined Durazzo's suggestion that they should give a public concert; instead they went home to Salzburg and arrived on January 5, 1763 – for which they must have been glad, for poor little Wolfgang immedi-

ately fell ill again, this time with pains in the joints like those of rheumatism. During convalescence and afterwards he did much violin practice and became a very good player. We hear little of Anna Maria, the devoted mother. It is to Leopold's credit that he did not save money by leaving her at home while the children were so young, yet surely such a solidly domestic woman wished that, after making so much money, Leopold would be content without immediately planning a long tour that took the little ones over the sea. Her own health was not as robust as her portrait suggests. We noted her previous illness and shall later note her comparatively early death in Paris, lonely and hardly in full understanding of her son.

The Grand Tour

On June 9, 1763 the Mozarts set out on their grand tour with a servant aged 19, Sebastian Winter. His hands were kept busy attending to the carriage, to packing, unpacking, and other business at inns, and to doing valet's work with the clothes and accoutrements. Just outside Wasserburg on the way to Munich a wheel broke and took more than a day to repair. They had been warned of its weakness. However, the local church had an organ with pedals, the use of which Leopold explained. Wolfgang could not reach them if he sat, so he "pushed away the stool and preambled standing, playing the pedals as if he had practised them for months. All were amazed; this is a new grace of God which most people acquire only by great effort." That is from a letter which Leopold wrote to Hagenauer to pass away the irritating delay. Frankly it seems either exaggerated or naïve, for there are no new principles to explain about a pedalier to a boy skilled on manuals. Boys of far less ability than

Mozart have picked up pedalling without a teacher, but they were rarely boys only just aged seven.

Nannerl kept a travel journal which describes the Nymphenburg Palace near Munich and the four "castles" in the gardens. As usual Leopold made the family advertise their arrival by promenading where somebody influential would see them, if necessary from windows which they were "accidentally" passing. One of the princes they had pleased in Vienna saw them, and their first engagement, leading to a later one at the court, kept the poor mites up till nearly midnight on the day when they arrived travel-worn and tired. Still, they netted a handsome sum and letters of recommendation to the Mannheim court. Leopold's native Augsburg, despite his preparation by a long account in the newspaper of the wonder children by an "eye-witness," "delayed me a long time and profited me little." It was the young performers' first experience of a public as distinct from a court appearance, and to their father's disgust the audiences were nearly all Lutherans, not his Catholic friends. Of course the children were shown the glories of St. Ulrich and Holy Cross, and they had the good luck to meet and hear Nardini on leave from the Württemberg court. Leopold's opinion of his violin-playing was that "for beauty, purity, and evenness of tone . . . nothing better can be heard." They thought Ulm's medieval and Gothic architecture "ugly and dreary," but were fascinated by the great organ in the cathedral, demonstrated by Johann Christoph Walther, son of the first German lexicographer of music. On the way to Stuttgart, the capital of Württemberg, they turned off to Ludwigsburg, hearing that the court had moved to the summer palace there. Despite the letter of recommendation from Munich, Duke Karl Eugen did not wish to hear the travelling wonders and they had to be content to play before Jommelli and members of the orchestra from Stuttgart. Jommelli made the unfortunate observation that such artistry as Wolfgang's was unbelievable "in a German child." Forced to serve under Italians at home, Leopold was angry, being already soured by the magnificence of Jommelli's apartments. He even thought the *Kapellmeister* capable of preventing the duke from receiving the children. Like Burney he was also disgusted at the expensive military display and the poverty of the peasantry and anyone out of uniform. "When you spit, you spit either into an officer's pocket or a soldier's bullet pouch. In the street you hear nothing but 'Halt! March! Wheel!'." The final annoyance was a delay for no better reason than that all horses had been requisitioned by the court and militia.

The Mozarts were glad to leave on July 14 for Schwetzingen, near Heidelberg, the summer residence of Karl Theodor, Elector Palatine. The famous Mannheim orchestra was there and did not disappoint them. Their playing, "the finest in Germany," was noted as coming from "all young people of good habits, not drinkers or gamblers or licentious rogues." Moreover the elector paid well, though he kept the children performing for over four hours. Leopold got on well with Holzbauer and other members of the orchestra who were ready to honour the author of the "Violin School." At Heidelberg Wolfgang's organ-playing so impressed the clerics at the Church of the Holy Spirit that they ordered an inscription recording the occasion to be made on the instrument itself.

They went through Worms to Mainz, which had an archbishop-elector and a court of great distinction, famous for its interest in the arts; but the elector was very ill, so they gave profitable concerts at a place known as the "King of Rome." They took the market ferry to Frankfurt-am-Main where a public concert was so successful that they gave several more. By this time Wolfgang was playing violin as well as clavier concertos. (Goethe in his old age remembered how, as a lad of 14, he saw "the little man with the wig and sword" performing in Frankfurt.) The Mozarts returned to Mainz and used it as a centre for their appearances in Wiesbaden, Biberach, and Kostheim, but they set off north down the Rhine when there was no prospect of the elector's recovery. They went to Coblenz, Bonn, Cologne, and Aix-la-Chapelle (Aachen) where Frederick the Great's sister, Princess Amalia of Prussia, was taking the cure. She made a great fuss of the little boy. Indeed she, and other members of her family, were musical and played various instruments, but Leopold wrote to Hagenauer: "She has no money, and her whole equipage and retinue resemble a physician's as much as one water-drop does another . . . neither innkeeper nor postmaster can be paid by kisses." She hoped he would bring the children to Berlin.

They went on to Brussels, capital of the Austrian Netherlands. The emperor's brother, Prince Charles of Lorraine, was the governor, and kept Leopold waiting nearly a month – "His Highness's amusements just now consist of lacquering, painting, making varnishes, eating, drinking, and laughing so noisily that he can be heard several rooms away . . . ," and "This fine prince does nothing but hunt, eat like a pig and drink, and in the end will have no money." "What with snuff-boxes and leather cases and such-like trumpery we shall soon open a shop"; but he rather liked the "magnifique" swords given by some nobleman to Wolfgang, and the lace for Nannerl. What worried him most was going on paying for lodging and subsistence while the winter was approaching, getting little financial gain from petty aristocracy. He found some sedative for his patience in touring churches and admiring pictures, of which he had a great love. He was rapturous about Rubens's "Christ giving the keys to Peter." His letters contain contemptuous remarks about the interior arrangements of the houses – "a pot on a long chain with meat, turnips, and all manner of things all boiling together . . . The door was left open so that we were honoured by visits from the pigs who grunted all round us. You can best imagine our midday meal from a Dutch painting." But early in November the Mozarts were at last called to the palace to perform before a large audience, and despite the forebodings the prince paid them handsomely.

23. Friedrich Melchior, Baron von Grimm. Wash drawing by Louis Carrogis de Carmontelle, 1758.

24. *The palace and gardens of Versailles. Engraving by Perelle, 1766.*

France

The Mozarts arrived in Paris on November 18, 1763, and it was fortunate that they had Austrian and other German-speaking friends of some standing already there; for it was not only strange to be where there was but one court, entry to which was by a series of elaborate stages, but also to know that high-ranking nobility from Germany were made to feel second-class persons in this proudest of places even after the death of the Sun King. The Mozarts were invited to stay in the residence of the Bavarian diplomat, Count von Eyck, whose wife was daughter of Count Arco, the Salzburg lord chamberlain of whom we shall hear later. The countess treated the children with "incredible affection" and put her two-manual harpsichord in their apartments. Yet Leopold declared that he owed most to Melchior Grimm. "He managed our affairs at court. He arranged our first concert. He himself paid me 80 louis d'or, selling 320 tickets, and even paid for the lighting by more than 60 large candles . . . a hundred tickets are already sold for another concert. So you see what can be done by a man with intelligence and a good heart." The son of a Lutheran pastor in Ratisbon, Grimm became a wit, a social *flâneur*, and something of a philosopher, who first indulged in pamphleteering and criticism of social and artistic events. His championship of Italian opera won him the favour of the Duc d'Orléans who made him his secretary. He knew the Encyclopaedists, but more important for the Mozarts was his editorship of a journal, the "Correspondance littéraire," in which he had published, just before their arrival, a long eulogy of their accomplishments, particularly Wolfgang's. "I fear that this child will turn my head completely if I hear much more from him. I now understand the overwhelming effect of

miracles . . . The emperor and empress have lavished favours on them, and they have enjoyed similar treatment at the courts of Munich and Mannheim. It is a pity that music is so little understood in this country." No doubt Grimm did some paraphrasing from Leopold's own advance notices!

On Christmas Eve they went to Versailles and were invited to stay for a fortnight. They heard a Christmas mass, Leopold approving of the choral portions but finding the solo parts "hollow, chilly, and poor, in other words French." The ceremonial machinery turned to bring them by New Year's Day to a royal banquet. When the royal family enters

> . . . it is not the custom to bow. One stands erect without making the slightest movement . . . You can therefore imagine how these French must have been astounded when the king's daughters, not only in the private rooms but in public, stopped on seeing my children, went up to them, and not only let them kiss their hands, but kissed them and let themselves be kissed innumerable times . . . Not only was room made for us to approach the royal table but also Master Wolfgangus was asked to stand all the time beside the Queen, talk constantly with her and keep her amused . . . and to partake of the dishes which she graciously handed to him from the table. The queen speaks as good German as we do. But as the king knows no German the queen interpreted for him . . .

Let us hope that the Marquise de Pompadour did not understand German, for when she put Wolfgang on a table he bent to kiss her and was repulsed. He said: "Who does she think she is? Why, the empress herself kissed me!"

After the court appearance the nobility vied with invitations. Amongst others the British ambassador, the Duke of Bedford, was delighted with the children. Leopold made plenty of money, but probably of more importance to Wolfgang than the aristocrats were some of the musicians, especially the migrant Germans employed in Paris. At that time the most brilliant keyboard-player was held to be Johann Eckard who, like Leopold Mozart, came from Augsburg. One of the best musical establishments was maintained by the Prince de Conti, for it included Gossec, symphonist and opera composer, Duport, who was one of the first great cello soloists, and Johann Schobert, composer of sonatas and other works for clavier (he had formerly been organist at Versailles and came from Strasbourg though born in Silesia). Leonzi Honauer published much chamber music, including harpsichord sonatas which were popular in London as well as Paris; and Hermann Raupach, whom Grimm reports as duetting with the boy Mozart, was in Paris until 1768 when he took up a court post at St. Petersburg. These Germans in Paris must have had some influence on young Mozart, whether they were already friends of his father or not, for every movement in his first written essays in concerto design has been traced to a sonata by one of the four.

The children's popularity in Paris must have been remarkable, for it was most unusual to obtain any relaxation of the royal order that only the *Concert spirituel* and the *Academie royale de musique* (i.e. the "Opéra") might give public music in Paris. Pressure must have come from the exalted who feared the Mozarts might leave without being able to fulfil enough private engagements. Some of the finest musicians, even the violinist Gaviniès, gave their services at the second public concert on April 9, 1764. The Mozarts left for Calais next day, although when they left Salzburg Leopold had not finally determined to go to London. Before we follow the family to England we may note that Wolfgang sustained another illness in Paris during the February, and it incurred an inflamed throat. (Leopold noted the loss of revenue.) Though strongly urged to have the family vaccinated Leopold objected "on religious grounds."

London

Winter, the manservant, had left for a "superior" appointment with a prince at Donaueschingen and was replaced by an Alsatian, who had the advantage of being bilingual. The Mozarts joined one or two other travellers to hire a private craft from Calais to Dover on April 22, "sacrificed heavily to Neptune," but were the next day at "The White Bear" in Piccadilly. They must have been impressed by the ease of the English as compared with the French court, for they were cordially received by the king and queen within a few days of their arrival. George III was still a comparatively young man. He was very musical, though not as good a player as Queen Charlotte. The king's passion for Handel's music was constant, and though Handel had been dead for five years the boy must

have heard his concertos and choral works at the Academies of Antient Music, as well as some of the dozen or so oratorios given at the Haymarket or the Covent Garden Theatre while he was in London, as were "Acis and Galatea" and "Alexander's Feast." The king asked him to sight-read music by Handel and supply a melody and texture over the bass of a Handel aria. That was at a second concert in Buckingham House on May 19, when the boy accompanied the queen and also a flautist and played organ, harpsichord, and violin. Leopold was particularly charmed when "the king came driving by with the queen and, though we were dressed in different clothes, recognised us and greeted us. The king opened his coach window and smiled, nodding and waving his hands, especially to Master Wolfgang." Yet another royal invitation came for October 25, the anniversary of the king's accession. Between the last two visits to court the family saw London sights, including many which are amusingly misspelt in Nannerl's diary – "St. Paul Kirch, Soudark, enchange, Linconsin fiels, garten Tempel bar, Soumerset haus" – and contributed (Leopold thought it a good advertisement "to earn the love of this very peculiar nation") to a charity concert for the Lying-in Hospital which was given in the Rotunda at Ranelagh.

It was natural for Leopold, as in Paris, to meet German-speaking musicians. This was not difficult since the most popular (in the sense of "fashionable") composer and performer in London was Johann Christian Bach, youngest and most beloved son of the great J. S. Bach. His influence on Mozart need not be examined in this biographical sketch, where it is enough to declare that nobody has yet claimed to be able to tell at a first hearing certain works by young Mozart from some by J. C. Bach. The elder man is known to have been genial and hospitable, but there was more than patronising indulgence in his attitude towards the highly musical boy. Mozart took the opportunity to emulate Bach's style (specially commenting to Nannerl that he must use the horns well) during some six weeks of the summer of 1764 when Leopold himself fell seriously ill and the children could not play instruments, since he had been ordered rest and quiet. "A severe cold" seems an understatement for something which made Leopold write to Hagenauer in alarm as to what might happen to his children.

Some of the most valuable evidence of Wolfgang's abilities in extempore performance is to be found in a paper preserved in the Royal Society's "Philosophical Transactions," Vol. XL, for 1770, and read before the society by the Hon. Daines Barrington, a lawyer, magistrate, and philosopher-naturalist. He so thoroughly scrutinised Leopold's claims as to secure through Count Haslang, the diplomat, a copy of Wolfgang's birth certificate from Salzburg. Leopold having said that Wolfgang might be privately examined by anyone who so wished, Barrington was "alone with him for a considerable time."

I carried to him a manuscript duet which was composed by an English gentleman to some favourite words in Metastasio's opera of Demofoönte. The

25. *The Hon. Daines Barrington. Engraving by Charles Knight, 1795, after a drawing by Joseph Slater, 1770.*

whole score was in five parts, viz. accompaniments for a first and second violin, the two vocal parts and a base . . . the parts for the second voice were written in what the Italians stile the Contralto cleff.

The score was no sooner put upon his desk, than he began to play the symphony in a most masterly manner, as well as the time and stile which corresponded with the intention of the composer . . . His voice in the tone of it was thin and infantine, but nothing could exceed the masterly manner in which he sung. His father, who took the under part in the duet, was once or twice out . . . on which occasions the son looked back with some anger, pointing out to him his mistakes.

Barrington then wished to hear extemporisation, to which Leopold shook his head, but apparently the boy was willing.

Happening to know that little Mozart was much taken notice of by Manzoli, the famous singer, who came over to England in 1764, I said to the boy, that I should be glad to hear an extemporary "Love Song," such as his friend Manzoli might choose in an opera.

The boy on this . . . looked back with much archness, and immediately began five or six lines of a jargon recitative proper to introduce a love song. He then played a symphony which might correspond with an air composed to the single word *Affetto*. It had a first and a second part which, together with the symphonies, was of the length that opera songs generally last . . . it was really above mediocrity, and shewed a most extraordinary readiness of invention.

Finding that he was in humour, and as it were inspired, I then desired him to compose a "Song of Rage," such as might be proper for the opera stage. The boy again looked back with much archness, and began five or six lines of a jargon recitative . . . This lasted also about the same time as the "Song of Love"; and in the middle of it, he had worked himself up to such a pitch, that he beat his harpsichord like a person possessed, sometimes rising in his chair. The word he pitched upon for this second extemporary composition was *Perfido*.

After this he played a difficult lesson, which he had finished a day or two before: his execution was amazing, considering that his little fingers could scarcely reach a fifth on the harpsichord. His astonishing readiness, however, did not arise merely from great practice; he had a thorough knowledge of the fundamental principles of composition, as, upon producing a treble, he immediately wrote a base under it which, when tried, had a very good effect.

He was also a great master of modulation . . . to which I must add, that I have been informed by one or two able musicians, when Bach the celebrated composer had begun a fugue and left off abruptly,

that little Mozart hath immediately taken it up, and worked it after a most masterly manner.

A favourite cat entered the room and Wolfgang left the harpsichord, "nor could we bring him back for a considerable time. He would also sometimes run about the room with a stick between his legs by way of a horse . . . It was in June 1765 that I was witness to what I have above related, when the boy was only eight years and five months old."

The paper was written long after the Mozarts had gone, and Leopold makes no mention of Barrington, whose examination of Wolfgang may have been only one of several. Perhaps he was responsible for their visit to the British Museum, for which Wolfgang wrote the first vocal composition in the record of his works (K. 20, the four-voice motet "God is our Refuge") in what he thought the "antient" or Baroque style of Anglican church music. Leopold published the six sonatas K. 10–15, labelled them "Op. 3," and dedicated them to Queen Charlotte, who sent him no less than 50 guineas for the compliment! England would have paid handsomely if the means of making money could have been fitted into a smaller time, but Leopold thought London had too many rival attractions to make a long stay as profitable as a move into new territory. Moreover, in Salzburg, even the easy-going Archbishop Schrattenbach was getting restive for a return of the family. The grand tour was to be prolonged to three and a half years, yet Leopold wrote petulantly to Hagenauer: "I wish they could let me do what I have set out to do with God's help, and am determined to finish with His help!" He sent money for votive masses at Salzburg and at the nearby pilgrimage church of Maria Plain. He hoped, he wrote, to be rewarded with a calm sea voyage!

J. C. Bach and others in London had convinced him that there were few better musical centres than Milan, where Wolfgang might secure commissions for composition, especially opera. He had therefore thought of returning home through Paris, Milan, and Venice; but the Dutch envoy pressed him "at all costs to go to The Hague for the Princess of Weilburg, sister of the Prince of Orange, is most eager to see this boy of whom she has heard so much." They left London on July 24, 1765, spent a day seeing Canterbury and then accepted Sir Horace Mann's invitation to stay at his country house nearby, described in Nannerl's diary as "very beautiful." They were there a week, and the children enjoyed seeing horse-racing. On August 1, they embarked at Dover.

Holland

At Calais they found their own carriage and travelled through Dunkirk to Lille, where they were held up because first Wolfgang then his father was laid up with a feverish chill. Leopold was so impatient that they went on to Ghent before he had fully recovered. They climbed the belfry to see the chimes and Wolfgang played the big new organ in the Cistercian church; he played again at the cathedral in Antwerp, from which place Leopold's letters are full of admiration for the pictures in the churches, especially "that indescribable Rubens master-piece, 'The Descent from the Cross'." On September 11 they reached The Hague. To modern tourists Amsterdam is surely the most attractive city in the Netherlands, not least because the canals cannot by present regulations be entirely ruined by motor traffic. To the eighteenth century, however, the fine houses of past centuries were merely quaint and old-fashioned, and the mercantile, middle-class society rather staid and dull. Even Burney said ironically that one heard for music only the ringing of chimes and the ringing of ducats. For contemporaries the splendour was round the court and amongst the cosmopolitan society of The Hague.

. They performed before the court and were supported by members of the orchestra, most of whom, to their great pleasure, were Germans. A few days after the arrival at The Hague Nannerl was so ill that Wolfgang alone performed at court. Nannerl was shaking as if with fever or influenza. For nearly a fortnight Leopold's notes show no great alarm; their lists of aristocratic patrons, ambassadors worth contacting and bourgeois intellectuals are not callous, for he expected her to recover soon. Suddenly he can write only of the doctors he has called in, for he sees his daughter "growing daily more emaciated; there is nothing left of her but skin and bones . . . The doctor himself has given her up." She received the last rites and became delirious. (The disease is believed to have been typhus.) Then the princess sent along her own physician, Schwenke, the retired professor of medicine at the university. According to Leopold, "good old Schwenke saved her life." No sooner was she out of bed – time had now dragged on to the middle of November – than the boy succumbed, lay in a coma, and then became delirious. Leopold paid for masses at Salzburg, but the boy was not well until nearly the end of January. He did much composition during his convalescence, the results of which were heard during the rest of his time in Holland. The Mozarts were there for a total of more than seven months, and we know that the financial profit was large. After the serious illnesses should not Leopold have hastened the journey home at least a little? It is difficult not to believe that the success of the tour made him avaricious. The money had to be made while he could still talk of Wolfgang as a "child" rather than a "boy." A tour taken a year or so later would not present *quite* such a pretty little "prodigy of nature" even if it presented a better musician whose compositions were almost unaided!

They gave a concert on January 22 and because Lent came early that year the closing of the opera theatres favoured concerts. In Amsterdam the publisher Hummel acted as their concert manager and engraved Wolfgang's latest works (assisted or wholly original, we are not quite

26. *William V, Prince of Orange. Engraving by Jacques-Firmin Beauvarlet after a drawing by Gerard van Nijmegen, 1765.*

sure) which included six sonatas for harpsichord and violin, K.26–K.31, dedicated to the princess.

They returned to The Hague for the coming-of-age celebrations of the Prince of Orange early in March. A Haarlem printer brought out a Dutch edition of the "Violin School" which Mozart thought "extraordinarily handsome, even more so than my own," and the publisher gave him a copy in the presence of the organist who was in charge of the famous Christiaan Müller instrument in Haarlem's St. Bavokerk, on which of course Wolfgang performed. They went again to Amsterdam for their last concert in Holland and then left via Utrecht, Rotterdam, Mechlin, Brussels, and Cambrai, performing in most of those cities. On May 10, 1766, they were in Paris and were again invited to Versailles. We are told little about this return visit to France. Leopold was flattered by Prince Karl Wilhelm of Brunswick, who played the violin to professional standard (according to Burney) and asked if he had the honour of meeting the author of the "Violin School." Melchior Grimm's faithful eulogies in his "Correspondance littéraire" lay much stress upon the boy's progress as a composer and the girl's as a player. ("Mlle. Mozart, now 13, who has grown very pretty, plays the keyboard in the best and most brilliant way imaginable; her brother alone can reduce her applause.") The end of his article makes a prediction which Leopold wished to come true – to his great irritation and disappointment it did not – "Before long the princes of all Europe will be competing for possession of them."

They left early in July for Dijon, where they played before the Prince de Condé. They stayed a month in Lyons, gave up the idea of going to Italy, but made for Geneva where they spent three weeks despite civil strife

27. *The Grote Markt, Rotterdam, with a statue of Erasmus. Anonymous engraving, second half of the eighteenth century.*

there. Leopold's travel diary seems to have been abandoned after Dijon, but we know from letters by Voltaire that the children performed in Switzerland: "As you know, I live eight miles away from Geneva. I never go out, and I was very ill when this phenomenon shone upon the black horizon of Geneva . . . Madame Denis was ill. For more than six weeks I myself have been in bed. How can you expect me to have seen your young pianist? We are far from giving parties."

Leopold had been advised to give a concert at Ferney. Would he have done so if Voltaire had been well? He taught the children to regard Voltaire as a monster breathing irreverence and agnosticism, and the state of the philosopher's health may have saved Leopold from chicanery. After the three weeks in Geneva, they gave concerts in Lausanne, Berne, and Zürich. They proceeded to Schaffhausen, evidently only for a short rest and to see the falls of the Rhine, and then to Donaueschingen, a little town valued by enterprising music-lovers today for its festivals of modern music. At that time it was the seat of the Prince of Fürstenberg, himself a fine musician and the generous patron of professionals. There they met their old servant, Winter, who had become valet to the prince. They were well treated and well paid. No wonder Leopold wrote: "We all wept on saying farewell."

With another winter approaching Leopold felt the need to hasten home. He wasted little time in Augsburg, and at Munich the children were once again summoned before the elector. "Wolfgang had to compose a piece of which His Highness sang just a few bars of the opening, and after dinner he tried it his princely self in the music-room. You may well guess how amazed everyone was to see and hear it." Then Wolfgang had another of his

rheumatic illnesses and was in great pain. After 10 days he was well enough to appear once more at court – or so his father thought. It is difficult to tell whether the following words in a letter to Hagenauer are those of a sensible or of a cruel parent. They seem cruel, yet let it be repeated that the children seem never to have been punished nor did either of them write or speak a word to suggest that they thought their father at all unkind.

> . . . My children are used to work; if they became used to idleness on the excuse that this or that prevents their getting on with their tasks, the structure I have built would collapse. Habit is an iron shirt . . . But who knows what will happen to us when we get home to Salzburg? Perhaps we shall have such a reception that we shall gladly hoist our luggage on our backs and set off again. However I am bringing my children back to their native land, God willing. If they are not wanted, I am not to blame, but they are not going to be had for nothing.

They were not going to be unpaid court entertainers. They had returned with considerable honour and wealth for mere musicians – servants reckoned at just above the level of good gardeners. But was status won at the expense of the children's health? Many have said that it was – that they were often travel-weary, performed late at night, suffered from being in coach or carriage, inn or lodging, during severe winters. Did not their illnesses show this? No; we cannot be certain that, in eighteenth-century conditions of heating and sanitation, they would not have had the same diseases at home. Children are resilient physically, and Leopold had every reason to watch them carefully if they were cold, tired, or exposed to danger as far as he could tell. Surely if they played late into the night they slept late into the day to compensate, for what impression could tired and fretful children make on a brilliant audience? More than one contemporary witness of their appearances writes of their father as a man to be admired for his *care* of them, not just his training. Undoubtedly they were, as we say today, "conditioned" to musical and other study beyond their years, but we cannot say that Mozart's early death was in any way related to his childhood experiences. He was in some ways tougher than his slight build suggested. Handel and Bach were not the only eighteenth-century musicians to go blind through music-copying by quill and candlelight, yet Mozart was never forced, as were Beethoven and Schubert, to wear glasses. He had strong eyesight. As for Nannerl, though she did go blind in old age, she seems in other ways to have enjoyed good health until she was widowed.

The chief price paid for the enormous success of the tours seems to have been a dangerous alteration in the boy's attitude to the people of Salzburg. It was an inevitable price, and as Leopold himself bore grudges against musicians at Salzburg, to say nothing of their social superiors, he may not have been careful enough to teach Wolfgang his own tactful cunning. There was a great difference in the social proprieties between the times Mozart's full powers became evident and Beethoven's did. The interval saw the progress of the revolution in France; it also brought a respect for the unliveried musician whose eccentricities could be tolerated and even enjoyed if he had real genius. After the grand tour Mozart was nearly 11 – an age when most boys begin to need special discipline unless they are to become self-conceited and rude, aggressive, destructive, and unkind both to the elderly and their juniors. The effects are

28. The Empress Maria Theresa. Engraving by Jacob Schmutzer, 1770, after an oil portrait by Joseph Ducreux.

pretty similar whether the diagnosis be a superiority or an inferiority complex, and it is only fair both to Wolfgang and his father to declare that we have no evidence that Mozart became unpleasant during the years when most boys fight their battles in a senior school, from about the age of 11 to 16; but young Mozart was both self-confident and slightly snobbish, if we may judge by his letters. He had been intimately received by crowned heads, had travelled into capitals and amongst such exalted personages as even the archbishop-elector himself had not known. How then could he be, at least in manner and speech, "your humble servant" to the mere local court officers and citizenry?

The family reached Salzburg on November 30, 1766. Apparently the archbishop was proud of them but he was cunning enough to find out for himself if Master Wolfgang was the composer whom others declared him to be, or if he was helped at home.

The Austrian Tour

Most biographers tell us that during the months at home after the grand tour Leopold required his children to make up for lost time in their general education. He certainly took special care of Wolfgang's musical education, for we have a note-book of this period filled with counterpoint exercises based on Fux's "Gradus ad Parnassum." The exercises were what Mozart needed. Another uprooting he did not need, and little good came of Leopold's decision to leave for Vienna on September 11, 1767, when the family had been at home for only just over nine months. The Archduchess Maria Josepha was to be married to the king of Naples; the children would surely be bright stars at the festivities. Besides they had not yet received a command for performance before the new young emperor, Joseph II. Their stay in Vienna began with disaster. No invitation was forthcoming from the court, and therefore it would have been against convention to give a concert elsewhere; the widowed empress, Maria Theresa, was not yet going to concerts or the theatre. While they waited they became aware that they had arrived during a widespread smallpox epidemic. Suddenly all hopes of a festive celebration were ended by news that the 17-year-old bride had died of the disease. Then the son of the friend with whom they were lodging, a goldsmith, caught it, and the Mozarts fled to Olmütz (Olomouc) via Brünn (Brno) though both children had already become infected.

They put up at an inn which was cold and damp. On October 28, when Wolfgang became delirious, Leopold went to the dean of the cathedral, Count Leopold Podstatzky, who brought the children to his own residence under the care of his own eminent physician. Another princely cleric attached to the cathedral behaved with equal kindness. Nannerl suffered less severely than Wolfgang, whose eyes were covered with pustules and were virtually blind for at least a week; but during convalescence his noble Good Samaritans came daily to play with him, show him card tricks, and teach him fencing. Both declared that they had no fear of smallpox. The family returned to Brünn where Count Franz Schrattenbach, the Salzburg archbishop's brother, gave them rooms in his palace and arranged a concert. He "and all the nobility of Brünn," according to Leopold, showed exemplary kindness. On January 10, 1768 they set off again for Vienna and were soon invited to the court where the "empress talked with my wife about the children's smallpox and our great tour, stroked her cheeks and pressed her hands, while the emperor talked with me and Wolfgang about music and many other things, and often made Nannerl blush."

The Mozarts spent another year in Vienna because of Leopold's wish that his son should shine as an opera composer. The old successes with concerts could hardly be repeated. Some of the nobility, like Kaunitz, were terrified of children who still carried the red scars; others could no longer regard as "wonder children" a girl of nearly 17 and a boy of 12. Like their father they were now rivals to other concert-givers, and Leopold's letters home may not be entirely mistaken in declaring that most professional musicians in Vienna were hostile to him. To what extent they were "schemers" against the children we cannot judge. It was certainly absurd to regard Gluck, aged 54 and at the height of his fame, as the arch-schemer against a boy of 12; more justified were Leopold's diatribes against Affligio, manager of the theatres. This adventurer, at one time an associate of Casanova, ran gaming-tables in Naples until his escape was advisable; by the same means he first came to know influential members of Viennese society when he arrived, self-styled "Count Affligio." He not only became the lessee of several theatres but also ran such disgusting and lucrative spectacles as the baiting of animals. Extravagance and gambling brought him to bankruptcy and he fled in 1770 to run gambling-houses in Milan, then Lyons, and finally Barcelona, where he enriched himself and again managed an opera house. Condemned for forgery, he ended his life as a criminal slaving in the galleys. Had Leopold known this, what a sermon he could have preached on divine justice!

Leopold secured from a librettist recently arrived, Coltellini, the libretto of "La finta semplice" (The Pretended Simpleton) and, with assent from the imperial office, signed a contract for its production. It did not receive a performance during that stay in Vienna, but we must not assume that Affligio intended from the first to prevent it. At the time he was in trouble, having incurred heavy losses from a French troupe engaged for the wedding festivities. No doubt he deceived the Mozarts by delaying tactics and a superficially genial "soon, soon"; and when Leopold was not to be put off he may have made it worthwhile for singers and players originally keen on the work to turn hostile towards it. Leopold was foolish enough to write a long petition to the court, really a long complaint against the manager. It obtained an interview with the emperor and his promise to intervene, but from that time Maria Theresa seems to have lost her affection for the Mozarts, and the whole affair simply added to the distrust felt by other musicians. Whether Leopold judged rightly or wrongly Affligio did not expect "La finta semplice" to be a success. If composers waiting for productions did protest or "intrigue" let us understand them; they lived in Vienna and had to get performances or go poor, whereas the Mozarts were outsiders on a secure pay-roll from their own Salzburg.

The Mozarts had good friends in Vienna. Two of them, Baron van Swieten and Count Sporck, were later to be useful, and Hasse took the trouble to write enthusiastic recommendations to influential people in various Italian cities. The Mozarts were back in Salzburg on January 5, 1769, and remained there for most of the year. Far from reproaching them for their prolonged absence, Schrattenbach wanted to hear "La finta semplice" on his nameday early in May.

The First Italian Tour

Father and son set out happily for Italy early in December. In Hagenauer's words Wolfgang "had received permission to leave for Italy, and notice that he was henceforth to hold the office of *Konzertmeister*, with right to draw the stipend after his return." Recommendations from Salzburg to the Governor of the Tyrol secured a warm reception and a concert as they passed through Innsbruck. Over the Brenner after a short halt at Bolzano they enjoyed another welcome from the nobility to whom they performed in Rovereto. On the second day a path had to be forced through a crowd in the church so that Wolfgang could reach the organ. At Verona, which had its own famous Accademia Filarmonica, their arrival was expected and they were handsomely treated and financially rewarded by both noble and mercantile families. The academy marvelled at his playing on piano and violin, his sight-reading, extemporising, and compositions. A certain Locatelli (not to be confused with the violinist-composer) arranged for the performance of one of his symphonies; poems were dedicated to him and it was insisted that his portrait be painted. Leopold consented though he reflected that money might have been earned during the time required by the painter. This portrait, formerly attributed to Cignaroli but now thought to be by Saviero dalla Rosa, is fascinating despite the wig and fine red jacket and the absence of markings from smallpox, because the facial features of the adult Mozart are so clearly formed. It is easy to see how charming this boy could be, and also how cheeky and sarcastic upon occasion. He was nearly 14, as the portrait well suggests, but Leopold began at this time to declare his age as a year less than it really was.

The separation of the family gives us the benefit of

letters home. Evidently Leopold did not exaggerate the esteem won at Verona, for later in the year the Accademia Filarmonica notified Wolfgang of their honorary conferment upon him of the title *Maestro di cappella*. The travellers met less cordiality at Mantua, and Mozart was worried by a running cold and chilblains. The president of the academy at Mantua was a Colloredo! They were kindly received, however, by Count Arco, cousin of the Salzburg chamberlain, who arranged private concerts. In bitter weather they left for Cremona, where they heard Hasse's "La clemenza di Tito," but were glad to push on to Milan. There Count Firmian, governor of Lombardy and nephew of Leopold's first Salzburg prince-archbishop, had arranged for them to occupy the guest rooms at the S. Marco monastery near his palace, and they were particularly grateful to the monks who warmed their beds ready for their return each night.

Without recounting all engagements or naming all notable persons we should notice just the facts which most affected Mozart's future. The most important was Firmian's not merely paying handsomely for pleasure received but also securing for Wolfgang a contract on excellent terms for the first opera of the following season.

To reach Rome for Holy Week and Easter, which was Leopold's aim, time would have to be restricted in cities that might be eager to hold Wolfgang; yet he must try to shine in Bologna, Italy's Oxford. Nothing could impress society in general and musical society in particular more than commendation from the savants of Bologna, especially if the doyen of Italian musicians and Europe's oracle upon the theory and science of music, Padre Martini, were impressed by Wolfgang. Unfortunately Martini was ageing and had retired to be *parroco* of S. Francesco, rarely leaving his presbytery at night. Even meetings of the Accademia Filarmonica, of which he was still president, were held near his church. Perhaps, however, the Mozarts might call on him and secure a written testimonial. So they left Milan for Bologna on March 15 and made a short stop at Parma, where they were invited to dinner by the great singer Lucrezia Agujari. She so delighted Wolfgang that he included notation of some of her feats in a letter home to Nannerl.

In rain and cold weather the Oxford colleges and university buildings can seem forbidding to people who are not privileged to be inside them. Bologna, too, must have seemed austere and gloomy as the Mozarts entered it in wintry weather. In the eighteenth century it had not spread to brash and lively artisan suburbs; and those arcades along the streets and sides of squares which give cloistered shade from the glare and heat of summer must have added to the gloom. The gaiety of south-German Baroque and Rococo is found only in its smallish city cathedral, not the vast university basilica of S. Petronio; and the brilliant court of the Este family, patrons of the university, was away at Modena. But the necessarily brief stay in Bologna proved one of the happiest periods they had known. They found Count Pallavicini warmhearted and gentle, not at all the dramatic caricature of

29. Bologna. Engraving by Thomas Medland after a drawing by John Smith, 1742.

a field-marshal. They knew they had to contact him but they did not expect him to be their very generous host, nor to be a man of such wide musical and general culture. He assembled a good orchestra for the boy to direct. "One hundred and fifty of the most exalted persons" were present, and they included the cardinal-legate and Padre Martini. This did not prevent the Mozarts from calling at S. Francesco. At each visit Martini gave Wolfgang a subject and bade him write out a complete fugue upon it.

They dared not stay long enough to secure any written testimonial. They called at the country house near Bologna which had been taken by the greatest male soprano of his day, Farinelli, enriched first in England and then as musician and confidential diplomat to Philip V of Spain. They did not intend to stay long in Florence, but their arrival had been announced to the Grand Duke of Tuscany, Prince Leopold, who had heard the Mozart children and played with them when they first visited Vienna. Wolfgang was asked to play at court, and was beguiled into staying over five hours with the violinist Nardini and with the Marquis de Ligniville, whose hobby was devising vocal canons to liturgical texts.

Florence has always been something of an English colony, and there the Mozarts renewed acquaintance with the singer Manzoli, who had captured London audiences along with his friend J. C. Bach and hoped to be in Milan for Wolfgang's opera. The boy's chief delight, however, was the company of an English boy of his own age, already a good violinist, who was studying with Nardini. This was Tom Linley, son of the Thomas Linley who directed music at Bath and whose daughter married Sheridan. The father composed (it is said in collaboration with the son) the music for Sheridan's "The Duenna." Mozart shed tears at having to leave Linley. Poor boy! Away from home, what could the fine gatherings and

30. *The Pantheon in Rome, c. 1745. Detail from a drawing attributed to Antonio Canal.*

adult conversation mean to him by comparison with the uninhibited companionship of another youngster, also a fine musician? After acting as his father's orchestral leader and composing theatre music, Linley was drowned aged only 22, in a boating accident on the Duke of Ancaster's ornamental lake. Mozart often spoke of him and was greatly distressed by his death. As Linley was soon to return to England Mozart could not hope to find him in Rome on his own return visit. This thought, together with the cold, rainy weather and poor inns, made the journey to Rome miserable. The Mozarts arrived on the Wednesday of Holy Week, and their first sight of the papal retinue was not awe-inspiring. Thunder followed by a sudden downpour changed the style of the hierarchs and their attendants from *maestoso* to *affrettando*, but we may presume that ruffled dignity was restored when the procession reformed under cover.

The Mozarts arrived just in time for the ceremony which included the singing of Gregorio Allegri's "Miserere mei Deus," a work in which five-voice and four-voice choirs alternate until a short final section uses all nine voices. The piece, the exclusive property of the Sistine Choir, was regarded as sacrosanct and guarded from copyists. Without actually declaring that Wolfgang wrote it *all* down after once hearing it, Leopold tried to suggest the feat, claiming that Cristofori, one of the singers, had perused the transcription and found it accurate. In fact Mozart was probably already acquainted with the general shape and harmonic tread of the piece, for it had been sung in Vienna and one of the few scores had been made by Padre Martini. Furthermore the work was performed three times in all during their stay in Rome. Even so it is doubtful if anyone except Mozart could have either spaced the chords accurately or remembered their outlay without actually writing them down fully during the performance.

Armed with many letters of introduction, Leopold took the boy to perform in various palaces, including the Barberini and Chigi. Among his auditors was the "Young Pretender," Charles Edward Stuart. After a last concert at the German Jesuit College, father and son went sightseeing and then on to Naples, where they thought the populace "stupid and superstitious and even more impudent than the English." The impudence seems to have been shown chiefly by staring, but when news of their coming had preceded them they were something to stare at; moreover it was Leopold's policy to be seen in extraordinarily fine clothes, which were surely a curiosity when the wearers did not arrive with liveried servants and a carriage bearing a noble crest. The nobility of Naples generously gave them immediate use of such carriages so that they could take part in the torchlight processions along the Strada Nova. Unexpectedly large profits came from a concert in Count Kaunitz-Rietberg's house and it is suggested that the San Carlo theatre wanted to secure an opera from Wolfgang – "If Wolfgang had not already received the contract from Milan he would have been offered one at Bologna, Rome, or Naples." They visited Vesuvius, went over the sea to Baiæ, and toured Pompeii and Herculaneum before they set off in haste for Rome on June 25 – possibly news of a new honour in Rome had reached them. Wolfgang's first letter home from Naples supplies a picture of social conditions – the numbers of brigands and beggars, for instance. "The *lazzaroni* have their own captain or leader who draws 25 silver ducats each month from the king for no other reason than to keep the others in order." On the way to Rome one of the horses fell and Leopold sustained an ugly wound in the right leg which did not heal until he had left Italy.

The honour awaiting Wolfgang in Rome was the conferment upon him by Pope Clement XIV of the Order of the Golden Spur. Like the French Legion of Honour, it has more than one class. The only musician before Mozart to be awarded the first class was the sixteenth-century composer Lassus. Gluck's knighthood was only of the second class, which no doubt Leopold gleefully noted! We have mentioned the painting of Mozart wearing the golden cross on a scarlet ribbon, but he is said to have worn it only once at home, where he declared that it caused mockery and resentment from some of the petty nobility. Yet Gluck wore his, styled himself "Chevalier Gluck" and was so addressed. The contrast may be a reflection of Mozart's touchy pride and his sensitivity to any kind of social criticism; Haydn and Gluck enjoyed their advancement from humble origins, and were not often or obviously dismayed by the arrogance of a bully or the smile of a snob, but Leopold had instilled into Wolfgang that his origins were *not* humble, that the Mozarts were better, *and* better educated, than their supposed "betters." The boy received the papal accolade at the Quirinal Palace on July 8, 1770. A circumstance of the event may later have given him and his father malicious pleasure. The Bishop of Gurk was appointed as his ceremonial sponsor; he was Count Hieronymus Colloredo, the next prince-archbishop of Salzburg.

After less than a fortnight in Rome the Mozarts left for Bologna where Count Pallavicini lent them a carriage to the great relief of Leopold's painful leg. He then brought them to his country house for some lovely summer days in a pleasant suite of rooms. A servant and a courier were provided for them and the count's 15-year-old son ("he is very talented," wrote Leopold) sought Wolfgang's friendship. It seems clear that the presence and manners of the old and the young Mozart could be charming when they so wished. Most of the aristocracy away from home seemed ready to accept them as if the times and conventions did not divide the classes. Not so the jealous small nobility of Salzburg. After Schrattenbach's death, if not before, provincial Salzburg made them feel either unacceptably bold or servile.

Wolfgang was not allowed to spend all his time enjoying the company of his new friend on the estate. There was work to be done on the opera he was to supply for Milan, "Mitridate, rè di Ponto" (Mithridates, King of Pontus). Padre Martini was revisited and Wolfgang eagerly responded to him by attempting motets in the *stile osservato*, at first somewhat stiff and archaic. But his antiphon "Quaerite primum regnum Dei" (Seek ye first the kingdom of God), K.86, was thought good enough to qualify him as a candidate for membership of the Accademia Filarmonica although he had not reached the prescribed age of 20. The rule was waived and he appeared before the examiners in the hall of the academy. He was given a text and a *cantus firmus*, told to set it in *stile osservato* employing the theme and a four-voice texture. He was locked in an adjoining room and, according to Leopold, emerged with the work after half an hour (though Wolfgang's letters later tell us that he took an hour). Then he was sent back to await the verdict. He returned to be greeted by applause and was later given the testamur of membership. He sent news to young Linley, and added his regret that his father's bad leg had to be rested and therefore they would go straight on to Milan instead of taking the projected detour through Florence, Pisa, and Genoa. They had reason to find the enforced stay at Bologna a blessing in disguise, for they enjoyed a few more weeks on Pallavicini's estate, and no doubt Wolfgang began work on his opera.

They left for Milan on October 13. Apartments were provided near the theatre, and it is to Leopold's credit that, finding the boy working till his fingers ached, he tried to make him compose only before noon, and to take exercise and relaxation afterwards; he also asked the people at home to send amusing letters that would keep up Wolfgang's spirits. Despite expected hitches and intrigues "Mitridate" had an enormous success at its first performance on Boxing Day, 1770. Items were encored; more than 20 performances ensued, Wolfgang directing the first three and then preferring to enjoy his triumph from the auditorium. He was asked to compose another

31. Pope Clement XIV. Engraving by Domenico Cunego after J.D. Porta, 1770.

opera for 1773. The copyist was enriched by many demands for complete scores as well as single arias. Invitations to dinner were accepted from Count Firmian and others and, after a brief visit to Turin, the travellers resumed the homeward journey early in February.

They went home through Venice, and enjoyed the end of the carnival season. Gondolas instead of carriages were at their disposal. They went to operas and masked balls, and Wolfgang gave "a fine concert," but we shall not bother to notice any further triumphs of this journey. He may himself have tired of them, and certainly even Leopold seems to have thought that relaxation and sightseeing should be their reward for a little while. They made brief excursions to Padua (where Wolfgang was commissioned to write an oratorio), Vicenza, and Verona with Hagenauer's friend who was their excellent host in Venice; two daughters of the house loved to please the Mozarts and cooked them their favourite Austrian dishes. The weather turned cold, and they returned through Innsbruck in snow, reaching home just before Easter 1771 after an absence of 15 months.

Pictorial Essay:
Travel and Fashion

27. "Une route." Oil painting by Jean Louis de Marne.

Travelling and keeping up appearances were two important aspects of Mozart's life seen from a social rather than artistic standpoint. To some extent one succeeded the other, for when the extensive travelling of the Salzburg period ended and Mozart settled in Vienna, keeping up with changing fashion and dressing in the latest style remained a preoccupation, even when borrowing became necessary to do it.

In fashion and in travel there were important developments in the second half of the eighteenth century which corresponded with the changing social and intellectual climate. In both, France

31

and Britain were the leaders. During Mozart's lifetime the founders of modern road-building appeared – Trésaguet in France and McAdam (born like Mozart in 1756) and Telford in Scotland. Until their arrival road-building had not progressed much since the Romans and the poor condition of roads in the seventeenth century positively hindered the development of transport systems. In England, for instance, stagecoaches were banned for a time after the introduction of iron wheel rims because of damage to already bad roads. In France, however, roads had been improved enough by 1664 to allow a stagecoach service using the kind of cumbersome vehicle, with six passengers inside and others on top, depicted in de Marne's painting *(No. 27)*, which also shows the stone blocks *(pavés du roi)* used to strengthen country roads at that time. Private carriages became lighter and faster as the century progressed *(Nos. 34, 38, and 46)*. But broken wheels on bad roads remained only one hazard among many (see *Nos. 37, 40, and 46*).

As with road development France and Britain led the way for the fashion-conscious traveller, as the colour plates here testify. All are taken from the eighteenth-century publication "Journal der Moden" which contained surprisingly detailed reports of what the best-dressed people were wearing in Paris and London.

28, 29, and 30. These French fashions illustrate some of the general trends in women's dress in Mozart's time – the use of lighter, plainer materials instead of heavy brocades (see also *No. 44*) and a steady decrease in the width of the *paniers* or supports under dresses (see *No. 69*). These eventually disappeared in favour of a pad at the back of the dress *(No. 44)* which gave rise to the bustle. The 1788 summer outfit shown in *No. 28* is a "Robe à Gorge anglaise" in linen with a gauze "Chapeau anonyme." The watches at the waist were fashionable with both men and women at the time (see *Nos. 32 and 45*). *No. 29*, a "Robe à feston" made in Lyons for the autumn of 1788, is in heavy silk and is topped by a taffeta hat "à la Turque." The court influence which dominated eighteenth-century fashion in general and which is apparent here, particularly in the long shoulder sash, was soon to be ousted by simpler country and folk styles as a result of the French Revolution (see *No. 32*). Also described as "à la Turque" is the earlier dress of *No. 30*, in heavy silk and taffeta, also with festoons, from the spring of 1786. The English-style plumed bonnet was to become very popular around the turn of the century. The ubiquitous fan in this case has lorgnettes attached.

31. Children's clothes for spring 1787. When Mozart was born children were dressed as miniature adults (see *Nos. 1 and 19*)

sometimes down to wig and sword. But Jean-Jacques Rousseau's theories of education soon led to a revolution in upper-class children's dress and by the 1770's boys were wearing soft shirts and hats and loose trousers, anticipating a similar development in adult clothing after the French Revolution. A reminder of the past remains in the little girl's corselet; it is, however, made of black taffeta and very light. The undressed hair of both children falls naturally and is gathered in the girl's case by a simple ribbon.

32. A plate comparing the German (left) and French fashions in riding costumes for gentlemen in 1786. The progressive French costume anticipates a trend of men's dress generally in the 1790's away from courtly military style to country style, with long plain square-tailed coats and round-brimmed hats instead of the tricorne. Boots were to become fashionable in everyday dress and swords were no longer carried.

33. The entrance to Schönbrunn (see also *No. 69*), detail from an engraving by Carl Schütz, 1783, showing in the foreground an open four-wheeled carriage with four horses driven by a postilion. In the background are some examples of the Berlin coaches popular at the time.

34. The Viennese suburb called "Wieden und Wien," detail from an engraving by Johann Ziegler, 1780, showing a light two-person private carriage of the type then known as the *désobligeant.*

35. A Viennese postman of the late eighteenth century. Engraving by H. Benedicti.

36. A postilion in the service of the Archbishop of Salzburg. Anonymous watercolour, 1760.

The delivery postman *(No. 35)* and the postilion should not be confused although their names have similar origins and the kind of horn the postilion carries here still remains a symbol of postal service. Postilions, in fact, were mounted drivers who usually rode the near leader in a team or the near horse in a pair when no driver was on the box (see also *No. 33).*

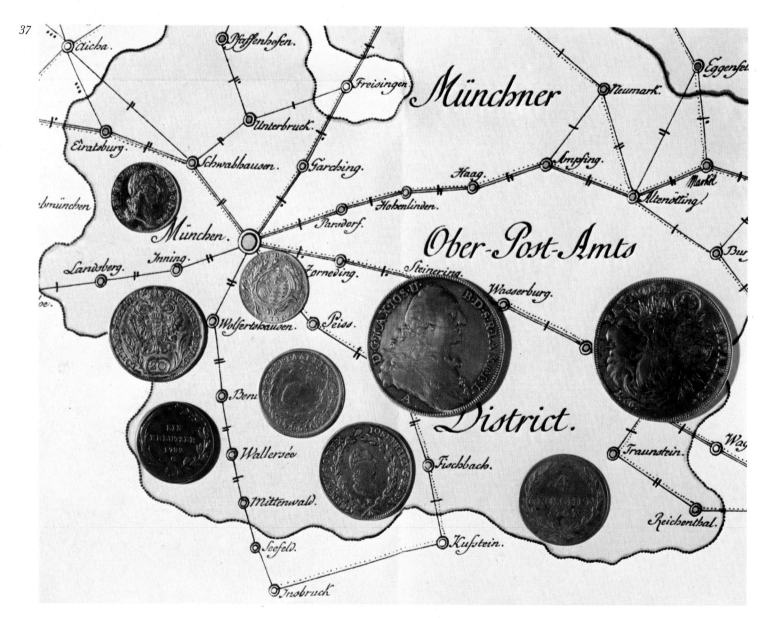

37. Not all the highway "robbers" of Mozart's day operated outside the law. Travelling was made financially hazardous by changes of currency at state customs houses, often to one deliberately depreciated. In *No. 37* some of the many coins which circulated in Mozart's day are illustrated against a map of the Munich area from the Hendschel Atlas of 1793 in the Thurn und Taxis collection.

On the extreme left are three coins from the reign of the Emperor Joseph II – (top to bottom) 1 ducat, 20 kreutzer (1787), and 1 kreutzer (1782). The other small coins are (top to bottom) a Bavarian ducat (1787), 4 Bavarian groschen (1767), with the

head of Maximilian Joseph III; the obverse of the Joseph II 20 kreutzer and the reverse of the Bavarian 4 groschen. The large coins are the obverse (Maximilian Joseph III) and reverse of a Bavarian reichsthaler (1766).

The gold ducat (4 1/2 gulden) was worth 72 groschen or 270 kreutzer. There were three reichsthalers to the ducat.

38. "The Travellers' Halt." An eighteenth-century engraving by the Augsburg artist Martin Engelbrecht depicting a typical scene during the change of horses. The hooded carriage is probably a fast two-wheeled phaeton.

39 and 40. Two engravings originally published with accompanying poems in Augsburg in the 1740's. *No. 39* extols the virtues of a country at peace where one can travel in safety on foot or by carriage. *No. 40* illustrates the dangers of travel in a country at war, where want drives the populace to plunder and violence.

41. A Paris outfit for gentlemen of breeding for spring 1786. Mozart himself seems to have favoured this rather conservative style of dress with starched ruffle, lace cuffs, and finely worked shoe-buckles – in this case eight-sided buckles of English silver. But though conservative in these respects and in retention of embroidery, the sword, and the tricorne (carried in its last days so as not to disturb the hair), the illustration has progressive features in the cut of the coat and the absence of the wig. As the century progressed gentlemen turned again to their own hair, powdering it at first – a distinguishing mark of the upper classes which faded in the 1790's. From Kelly's "Reminiscences" and the Lange portrait *(No. 14)* we know that Mozart dressed his own hair in this manner and was rather proud of it.

44. A German example of the revolutionary change in women's fashion after 1789. The plain, light dress from Westphalia, designed for summer 1790, is of white muslin. Supports under the dress have disappeared except for a pad at the back.

45. An artist's impression of the main features of men's fashion to be seen in Paris in 1788. Particular emphasis is laid on buttons which were minor works of art at the time, sometimes costing more than the clothes they adorned. They came in all kinds of materials from cut-glass to jade and some featured miniature paintings on porcelain or ivory.

41

42. "The Old Augarten Bridge." Anonymous oil painting, Vienna, c. 1782. This bridge over the Danube canal leading to the Augarten (see *No. 74)*, was a natural stopping-point for travellers by road or water at that time.

42

43. A view of Vienna's Leopoldstadt, showing barges on the Danube canal. Engraving by Johann Ziegler, 1780.

44

45

46. "The attack on a diligence." Oil painting by Goya, 1787. The term "diligence" was applied to different types of coaches and carriages in different countries. Early in the century it referred to any large public vehicle (and was used in German in this sense by Mozart when he complained of the coach which crawled "at a snail's pace" on his return from Paris in 1778). After 1783 in England it was limited to a mail-coach of the Berlin type. In France it came to be applied to a fast two-wheeled post-chaise, pulled, like this four-wheeled Spanish example, by three horses abreast. These were driven by a postilion and the absence of a driver on the box (used instead for mail or luggage) allowed windows in the carriage front.

IV
A child no longer

32. Salzburg Cathedral. Engraving by Karl Remshard after a drawing by Franz Anton Danreiter.

Except in mental and musical perception Wolfgang's growth seems to have been normal. Sexually he was slightly in advance of most boys. He was aged 15 years and three months when he returned to Salzburg in 1771, and he began to take a new interest in the girls. If he had not been at home we should have had more letters like those written during his next absence, in the course of which Nannerl was asked to convey his regards to "certain persons." One letter was written in Italian. As that language would be understood by likely interceptors, though not Mama, it was used for enjoyment of the idea of secrecy. At first the object of this conspiratorial tenderness was one of Dr. Barisani's daughters; she seems to have been supplanted by one Barbara von Mölk – he favoured brunettes!

Even if his parents had allowed or encouraged the gallivantings of calf-love he would have had little time for them. Almost immediately he arrived home he heard that he would be asked to supply a *serenata* for the wedding of the Archduke Ferdinand to Princess Beatrice of Modena. The festivities were to be at Milan during October, and leave from Salzburg would be readily granted for an imperial occasion. He also had to compose the oratorio for Padua, "La Betulia liberata." Furthermore, since he now held office at Salzburg, he had to justify his stipend and produce church music.

Father and son went off to Milan on August 13 and were received by the bride. The wedding was to be in the cathedral on October 15, and there would be a concert in the evening. On the next evening the *festa teatrale* would be Hasse's "Ruggiero." On the third evening the court would attend Mozart's *azione teatrale*, a two-act pastoral *serenata* entitled "Ascanio in Alba." Mozart worked happily and speedily, despite his report to Nannerl concerning his former lodgings by the theatre. "Above us is a violinist, below us another, next to us a singing-master who gives lessons, and in the end room opposite ours an oboist. Splendid conditions for composing! They give one plenty of ideas!" The Mozarts called on Hasse who treated them most cordially. (He seems always to have been charming; even Handel thought so.) "Ascanio" eclipsed "Ruggiero" with tumultuous acclaim and calls for encores, and it was more frequently repeated on subsequent nights. Hasse generously said: "This boy will consign us all to oblivion." Maria Theresa topped Mozart's fee by presenting him with a gold watch studded with jewels and containing her portrait in enamels. She may have done this only at the prompting of the newly married couple, for she soon struck a blow to the Mozart pride. Leopold lingered in Milan until the archduke returned from his honeymoon; since Wolfgang had already conceived a dislike for the limitations of Salzburg, his father hoped to secure another appointment for him. He was thwarted by the old

33. Maria Barbara von Mölk. Anonymous silhouette.

empress, who wrote to her son telling him not to engage "a composer or other useless people who run about the world like beggars." Three years previously Leopold had surely made a tactical error when he lingered in Vienna and sent the emperor his petition against Affligio concerning the non-production of Wolfgang's opera there.

The celebrations included horse-and-carriage racing and a public largesse of viands and wine. If the Mozarts had not arrived late for these they might never again have seen their family, for the scaffolding from which they intended to view the proceedings, and for which they had tickets, suddenly collapsed and killed more than 50 people. Providence enabled them to be reunited with the rest of the family in Salzburg before Christmas. On December 16 Archbishop Schrattenbach died after a long illness. Rome, the emperor's advisers, the political ambitions of feudal families – these were some of the factors which made the election of his successor take some time. By March it was known that Hieronymus Joseph Franz de Paula, Count of Colloredo, the Hapsburg nominee, was to be the next (and last) prince-archbishop of Salzburg.

The fact that several officials in Salzburg were dismayed at Colloredo's election, and expected him to be a difficult man to please, suggests that the pride and covert insolence of the Mozarts should not be blamed entirely for the troubles that lay ahead with their sovereign. Of course the Mozart biographers are prejudiced towards their hero, even if they concede that it takes a highly intelligent employer to be indulgent towards a spirited servant of genius. Yet there is no doubt that, by any standards but those of a tenacious feudal despot, Wolfgang was not well treated by Colloredo. All the more necessary does it seem, therefore, to find all the good we can in Colloredo before we reach the account of his causing Mozart to be kicked out of his service.

Colloredo could have been regarded as highly intelligent if we did not consider lively exercise of imagination and sympathy to be a concomitant of high intelligence. He was neither voluptuary nor obscurantist, but very much the product of the Enlightenment, determined to govern punctiliously and exact punctilious service, for he thought it his duty to educate. He reformed the administration and curriculum of the schools and promoted reading of philosophic and scientific papers and meetings of cultural societies. One of his chief interests was in the theatre, for both tragedy and comedy were liberally educative; but he was dissatisfied with provincial productions and wanted good visiting players. This seemed offensive, as did even the cutting down of ceremonial which, to simple folk, is an unacknowledged and colourful entertainment. The citizens and peasantry hated him for reducing the number of locally observed saints' days and days of obligation, for these had been holidays in the secular meaning of the word. His musicians took as an affront the directive that liturgical settings had to be so short that, even on a high day, mass did not exceed three-quarters of an hour. Mozart himself was scandalised at the portrait of Voltaire that hung in the archbishop's audience room. Moreover there had to be economy and exactitude in financial management, and nothing spent on unnecessary junketings like fairs, race-meetings, and firework displays.

The would-be intellectual or even the morally admirable ruler who lacks charm, or is not *simpatico*, can be more detested than the lazy voluptuary. In an earlier chapter it was suggested that something in voice and manner turned people against Charles I, a good husband and father, and Laud, whose clergy included some of the most dedicated to pastoral duty of any England has known. This can be imagined even while looking at their portraits, and that is why we show two portraits of Colloredo. Surely this is the unsmiling face of one too proud to explain his purposes, of a bureaucrat to whom people are things rather than persons because they are known by documents and statistics. They are "personnel," "staff," "clerks," "officers." Only a noble title made one an individual man or woman distinct from a component in the moribund machine of feudal society.

It may never have occurred to Colloredo that he was ungracious or in any way a bad example of the exalted ecclesiastic. Like most Austrian aristocrats he had received training in music, and he was a good enough violinist to play, when he deigned to do so, before distinguished visitors. He had given concerts at a country house which he owned near Salzburg before becoming ruler of the principality, for he was given a canonry at Salzburg back in 1747 before attaining a bishopric. His attitude to Wolfgang cannot therefore have come from ignorance of his outstanding talent, even if he did not (from what he heard while the young man was in his service) regard him as a genius to be ranked with Joseph

Haydn, whose brother Michael was on the Salzburg establishment. Musicians were as much servants as were bailiffs and gardeners, and the Mozarts seemed to give themselves airs above their place. The father, having received a good education and made his name as the author of the "Violin School," did not regard himself as a liveried servant like others and, instead of putting the boy under the discipline he himself had known, toured him as a prodigy, absenting himself from duty to be with him, and encouraging advance in conceit and superciliousness. It was not good for the young, other than princes and the sons of high diplomats, to have the entrée to palaces all over Europe and be intimately treated by the great. Obviously the Mozarts were unusually good musicians and no doubt the boy was exceptional; but musicians they were and as such must expect to be treated. What else should they expect?

Regarding Wolfgang simply as a musician and servant, Colloredo was fair in acknowledging the number of church pieces, symphonies, and divertimenti he had produced during his short time in Salzburg, and it was ensured that he received his salary promptly – not a large one but, by the standards of the day, not a poor one for a youth of 16. Moreover Colloredo commissioned an *azione teatrale* to mark his accession (the libretto, Metastasio's "Il sogno di Scipione," which had served similar occasions before, was taken from the shelves). The work was given on April 29, and soon after it the composer produced a number of symphonies, dances, and a "Regina coeli." All this represented proper application to work, which according to Colloredo should be recognised if not specially rewarded. At this stage, whatever his forebodings or natural antipathy to the young man, he was honourable enough to show no enmity, but rather to let his approval of Mozart's industry be known, no doubt haughtily, for *hauteur* was normal in Colloredo.

Possibly Wolfgang's exemplary industry was planned to obviate trouble in getting leave for the production of his Milan opera, "Lucio Silla," K. 135. He left with his father on October 24, 1772, and was away longer than he should have been. Leopold lingered there in the hope that his son would be engaged by the Grand Duke of Tuscany in Florence. He sent excuses to Salzburg – that rheumatic attacks made the journey over the Alps unthinkable, that he was buying Italian music for Salzburg – but when he heard from Florence that no appointment was open (he knew nothing of Maria Theresa's letter) he came to the conclusion that Italy offered no prospects. In March he took Wolfgang back to Salzburg where he was to remain for more years than he expected. The average musician of his time would have thought his position enviable; Mozart thought it parochial, a hateful servitude. To the end of his life Italy, the nursery of opera, of renascent architecture and the other arts, remained more El Dorado for Mozart than for German artists before and after him. There he was not addressed as "My man," "Fellow," and so on. Translation cannot convey Colloredo's attitude to his social inferiors. To judge by

34. Hieronymus, Count Colloredo, last prince-archbishop of Salzburg. Oil portrait by Franz Xaver König painted in 1772, the year of his election to the archbishopric in succession to Archbishop Schrattenbach. Another portrait appears in the colour pictorial section "Rulers and Residences" (No. 54).

Mozart's accounts of verbal skirmishes with him, the feudal master thought it demeaning to suggest that he remembered even a servant's proper name. To savour the atmosphere we must see some pre-1900 social comedy in which a titled or wealthy harridan calls to a maid-servant, "Creature, pick that up," or "I sent for you, girl." There are still parvenus who affect the "My good man" and "My good woman" style, but they must pay for their whims (in the armed forces the taxpayer pays for them) whereas Colloredo was amongst the last feudal rulers outside a few countries (e.g. Russia) who could with impunity treat a servant as a thing instead of a man or woman. We still do so when we compile statistics or regard the non-officers of institutions as "cases" or "personnel," but in democratic countries we can usually secure the reprimand of an efficiently inhuman bureaucrat who fails to address us by name. We still meet him, and Colloredo was one of his forbears. We have tried to do justice to Colloredo because he would have acted as a cold, efficient bureaucrat if he had been a minor servant of the court and not its sovereign. There is evidence that the emperor regretted his choice for Salzburg, but no evidence that Colloredo was, by his own standards, unjust, neglectful of duty, or given to habits unbecoming to an ecclesiastic. He was the child of his day, and that day was fast declining.

The Restless Years

However dull the first two years in Salzburg may have seemed to Mozart when he indulged in memories of his triumph or longed for Italy, it has actually been said that those or later years in Salzburg may have been the happiest in his life. Men are not always most miserable where and when they most grumble. Whatever his own opinion, the Salzburg output of music proved that his time there was more conducive to his artistic advance than would have been the continued excitements and depressions of the touring life which, for all its quality, came near to "show business," for it involved speculation about the tastes of different audiences of different nations and regions and classes, together with the discomforts and worries of travel and the likely emotional tensions with a father whom he loved but wished to cease dominating him both as man and artist.

As far as Mozart's art was concerned Colloredo was no villain. Mozart regarded himself as the local composer, not just the court musician, and we have no evidence that his employer ever objected to his composing for friends amongst the citizens, for musicians outside Salzburg, or for performances by the family that were not within the court and its institutions. Colloredo did not prevent his musicians from taking fees for teaching. The only music he actually commanded from Mozart was for the entertainment of important visitors or for special occasions; he had no need to command music for the

cathedral, which was what he chiefly expected from Mozart, because plenty was forthcoming. As for theatre and chamber (i.e. orchestral) music, "dinner music," and music for the keyboard, Colloredo was like many other German snobs in supposing that the best, most tasteful, could come only from Italians, and he infuriated the Mozarts by saying that Wolfgang ought to go and study in Naples. If he ever presumed to speak adversely of Wolfgang's music we have certainly not heard of it, and surely we should have done so from one of the family letters. All we do know is that when he was complimented by his grand visitors, or by his own superiors in Munich and Vienna, on possessing such a genius, he made no further comment than a shake of the head with a shrug of the shoulders.

Leopold was probably more restless than Wolfgang because of his impatience to see his son launched on a safe and prosperous voyage through life. To him that meant securing a post as *Kapellmeister* to a court of some standing, which could come about only by unusual good fortune. There was no precedent for the offer of such an appointment to a youth not yet 20. (N.B. it had to be "a court of some standing," not one of the small north-German courts with which J. S. Bach was content while still young.) There might, however, be the chance of a post carrying the title *Konzertmeister*, like that at Berlin formerly occupied by C. P. E. Bach who was really the harpsichordist and composer there. With that title, or one carrying similar status, Wolfgang might be composer and organist, or musical director of a court theatre (which Wolfgang himself hoped most to be) for his present *Konzertmeister*-ship was unpropitious as a launching-pad for the ultimate fame of a directorship at Vienna or Munich.

Why not try first at Vienna itself where the old triumphs had been? Maria Theresa was well aware of the Milan triumph, and Leopold knew nothing of her letter to her son there. Leave was granted to go to the capital in July 1773 simply because Colloredo himself was going to be absent from Salzburg. Indeed the leave was extended when Colloredo deferred his own return. The emperor was away in Poland. The empress, though she received the Mozarts graciously, made it clear that there was no vacancy for Wolfgang to fill. When the emperor returned he gave the Mozarts no audience and they were back in Salzburg in October, having renewed friendship with Dr. Mesmer and others, but the richer only by the D major serenade, K.185, and the six quartets, K.168–173, composed during the Vienna holiday.

At home in Salzburg during 1774 and what remained of 1773 Mozart composed his first string quintet, K.174, his first original piano concerto, K.175, a bassoon concerto, divertimenti, and several new symphonies, including "the earlier G minor," K.183. Then came something to eclipse interest even in symphonies, a commission from the very court to be cultivated if Vienna could not offer employment. The Elector of Bavaria asked for a comic opera, "La finta giardiniera" for the carnival of 1775, and he wished Mozart to be in Munich to rehearse and direct the performance. Colloredo could hardly refuse leave, for his own presence would be expected. Father and son set off on December 6, and had a miserably cold journey despite the bundles of hay spread on the floor of the carriage. Wolfgang's face was swollen with a bad tooth, and on arrival in Munich he stayed indoors for a week. During this period he often had toothache and evidently did not submit to the terrors of eighteenth-century dentistry without anaesthesia! Yet he wrote home in high spirits, with plenty of the word-play and coarse humour which in later days distressed a father who wanted evidence of seriousness and attention to the worldly wisdom which might lead to a lucrative appointment. Between comments on their ancient landlady's "bewitching lingerie" Nannerl is told that she is to be allowed to join them in Munich, and must bring this and that music which Wolfgang forgot.

"La finta giardiniera" was a huge success, and most arias had to be repeated. According to Leopold the Munich performances "killed" a rival opera by one Antonio Tozzi, who had to leave hurriedly because of his seduction of a noble lady which caused a scandal. The delighted Leopold observed that "people were beginning to notice that Italians were rogues everywhere." He was even more delighted to see "how embarrassed" Colloredo was, arriving too late for the opera, when its praises were sung by the elector and all the nobility. Presumably he was further embarrassed during a concert given to honour his visit. The Mozarts stayed till March and Wolfgang competed with Ignaz von Beecke in one of those silly piano-playing contests. Leopold failed to mention that many were more pleased with Beecke's prepared pieces than Mozart's, conceding Mozart to be the more brilliant sight-reader and improviser. Baron Dürnitz commissioned six piano sonatas after hearing Mozart play. As for the elector himself, he was so impressed by some church music given in Munich that he asked Mozart for the offertorium "Misericordias Domini," K.222, but gave no indication that he coveted the composer's services. We do not know if Colloredo disparaged Mozart to him during conversation, but he did not even ask for another opera, and Leopold was too shrewd to seek an interview which might only make his son's service at Salzburg less comfortable. However, it became known that there would be an early opportunity to impress (and perhaps speak to) the Archduke Maximilian, for he would be in Salzburg during April on his way back from a visit to his sister, Marie Antoinette, in France.

At home again the Mozarts were soon made aware that the tastes of Maximilian were to be indulged during his visit. Wolfgang was ordered to compose a *festa teatrale* to Metastasio's "Il rè pastore." The suggestion that Mozart was deliberately insulted when "Il rè pastore" was mounted on April 23, the second night of the royal visit, is hardly acceptable. An opera by Fischietti was given on the previous night and Mozart being much the

35. *The Archduke Maximilian. Engraving after a bust by M. Anna Meruielle born Torricella.*

younger man, took second turn but not second-class treatment. Colloredo did not spare expense on scenery and costumes. Probably at Mozart's request a fine castrato and a solo flautist were borrowed from the Munich *Kapelle*. They may have been sent specially, or at least in time for rehearsals, for it is possible that Maximilian took good musicians with him to France and that they were therefore available at Salzburg. Even so, Mozart was also brought before the archduke as a virtuoso pianist in concertos and solo pieces. We do not need the dubious evidence of radiance and ebullience in his music at this period to suppose that, when not recalling brilliant occasions on his travels or being badgered by his father to imagine them in the future at some grand capital, he was happy at Salzburg until at least the beginning of 1777. Colloredo's active dislike for him does not seem to have been openly manifest until the Mozarts once more wanted leave of absence with the obvious intention of seeking employment elsewhere.

That Wolfgang was well enough appreciated in Salzburg is made plain by several works of 1775–76, such as the "Serenata notturna," K.239, the three-piano concerto for the Countess Lodron and her daughters, K.242, and the piano concerto for Colloredo's niece, Countess Lützow, K.246. Add to these the church music, the lovely violin concertos and divertimenti which delighted Mozart's fellow musicians at court, above all his first really great piano concerto, the E flat "Jeunehomme" of January, 1777, and we have the fruits of activity which seems to have precluded any notable unhappiness.

Signs of discontent there are, however, as early as September, 1776, when a now famous letter was sent to Padre Martini. Colloredo had just closed the theatre in

36. The gardens of the Mirabell Palace, summer residence of the archbishops of Salzburg. Engraving by J. A. Corvinus after a drawing by Franz Anton Danreiter.

the winter palace, where Mozart's operas had been given, and ordered the reconstruction of the city assembly rooms near the Mozart house where the Landestheater now stands. This new theatre was to be well enough appointed for travelling companies but would not be used by the court artists and musicians. Therein lay insult. The letter to Martini, no doubt supervised by Leopold, begins with the submission of motets for the "most esteemed father and maestro" to judge, but passes in the second paragraph to:

> Oh, however often do I wish I were nearer to you, so that I could discuss things and converse with you! I live in a country where fortune does not favour music . . . We are badly served at the theatre for lack of singers. We have no castrati and are unlikely to get them, for they want paying well and liberality is not one of our faults.

There follows the information that his father has served the Salzburg court for 36 years "and is aware that the archbishop does not like to be surrounded by elderly persons." Then after a complaint about new official requirements in the composition of masses, the letter finishes with greetings to the Accademia Filarmonica and a repetition of the sentiment that it gives the writer "endless sorrow" to be separated from Martini, the one person in the world he most loves and esteems.

If the Mozarts thought Martini could secure the sort of appointment they wanted for Wolfgang they were surely mistaken. Martini was not to be drawn into discussion of anything but the enclosed compositions, and his return letter says no more than that they gave him great pleasure. He heard no more from either Wolfgang or Leopold until, a year later, they wrote to him about

the "Bolognese" painting of Wolfgang wearing the insignia of a Chevalier of the Golden Spur.

In March, 1777, father and son applied for leave of absence to undertake a concert tour. It was refused, for Colloredo expected the emperor to visit Salzburg that summer. In August Wolfgang, under Leopold's supervision, wrote a long petition for his discharge. "I owe it to God to be grateful to my father . . . to lighten his burden so far as I am able, and to provide for myself, and later for my sister . . . Three years ago, when I asked permission to travel to Vienna, Your Grace himself graciously declared that I had nothing to expect here and would do better to seek my fortune elsewhere." His dismissal was granted. Leopold was distressed when the time came (in September) for the parting, for he knew he must stay in Salzburg; but Wolfgang was not to have his freedom even at 21. His mother would travel with him.

Munich

The details of Mozart's last real tour (for his visits to produce operas in Prague and his later travels in Germany are hardly tours in the proper sense) have been fully documented in standard works. Here they must be summarised, since our main concern is with the tour's worrying concomitants. In any case it cannot be said that what was actually produced in musical notation was at all proportionate to the composer's high expectations. The main product was a rich harvest of letters to and from Salzburg, now available to English readers through the devoted translations made by Emily

Anderson. For some years they had some adventitious interest because to readers of the early twentieth century it seemed incredible that the composer of such pure music, or a man with such pretensions to civilised refinement, could include such coarse scatalogical expressions in letters to his father and sister – include them deliberately for the delight of writing them and giving pleasure to his readers. It is greatly to Emily Anderson's credit that she did not hesitate to translate by words used amongst Englishmen when in adult male and intimate company the equivalents of the forceful German slang which in Salzburg might be used in female or mixed intimate company. Thus Wolfgang tells of the surprise of Munich aristocrats at hearing the "shit story" of his break with Colloredo, who is called an "old prick." Indeed Mozart's mother rivals her son in coarseness sometimes, and supplies the added documentary delight of much misspelling and mispunctuation.

While mother and son were in Munich, Leopold's letters were full of fussy advice – after a pathetic first letter about his, Nannerl's, and the dog's misery at the parting. Wolfgang should see the cellist Woschitka who will best know the elector's tastes; Wolfgang must bear in mind that the elector plays the gamba; he must remember to mention his honours from the Verona and Bologna academies; he is glad Count Seeau greeted him so pleasantly for he is in charge of the court music, but Count Zeill has charge of theatres and is himself a fairly good musician; Wolfgang might mention his ability to supply ballets, *Singspiele*, and various kinds of opera. When these nobles had already told Mozart that they saw little prospect of an appointment for him, it does not seem to have occurred to him that, however kindly disposed they felt towards him, the feudal code of behaviour made them unwilling to appear as critics of Colloredo's behaviour, for Colloredo was their neighbouring sovereign and visitor, or that by the same code of the *ancien régime*, Mozart was not unlike a runaway servant or deserter. They did not secure him any formal interview with the elector, but Woschitka posted him in a narrow room through which the elector passed on the way to mass. Even as reported in Mozart's letter home the elector's words seem to bear out what has just been suggested:

I said: "Allow me, Your Highness, to throw myself humbly at your feet and offer my services." "So you have left Salzburg for good? You've actually left?" "Yes, Your Highness." "Why? Have you had a quarrel?" "Oh, no indeed, Your Highness; I merely asked leave of absence for a tour; he refused, and therefore I was forced to take this step. Yet I had for some time thought of leaving, for Salzburg is no place for me, I assure you." "Good God how young you are! But I take it that your father is still in Salzburg." "Yes, Your Highness. He sends you his humble respects . . . I have already been to Italy three times, written three operas, am a member of the Bologna Academy and had to pass a test which I

finished in an hour though many musicians laboured and sweated over it four or five hours. That may serve as proof that I am capable of serving in any court, but my sole wish is to serve Your Highness…" "Yes, my dear child, but there is no vacancy. If only there were a vacancy."

The "Good God how young you are!" faithfully reported by Wolfgang, might have been calculated to rouse Leopold's fears concerning his son's lack of worldly wisdom and his (understandable) care-free happiness off both employer's and father's leash. His music-loving inn-keeper gave Saturday-evening concerts, no doubt with refreshments, and when Mozart played the violin so well in quintets and divertimenti by Haydn, and then the piano in some of his own concertos, it was hoped that he could be persuaded to remain in Munich at least for the winter. A scheme was proposed by which 10 music-lovers guaranteed a monthly subscription, Mozart being free to take fees for other engagements and for teaching until Munich provided a salaried post. Leopold's reaction, after slight hesitation, was: "You must not make yourself cheap. Do not throw yourself away." He quite understood his son's wish to live in Munich, but "how the archbishop would sneer" if he heard that young Mozart was not serving a court but earning his living amongst tradesfolk by an arrangement he could have found in any city, not just Munich or Vienna. Leopold reacted very differently to another piece of news from Munich. Wolfgang had visited the Bohemian composer Mysliveček in hospital, where he was suffering from advanced syphilis. His nose had been cauterised and his appearance was both pathetic and horrible. Both musicians were deeply affected at their meeting, and the older man begged Wolfgang to go to Italy, where they had first met in 1772 at Bologna, and showed him several letters to prove that his name was often mentioned in that country. Knowing his own inability to undertake the composition and direction of operas for Naples, Mysliveček had proposed to the opera directors there that they ask Mozart to sign a contract. Leopold immediately wrote several letters both to Naples and to Venice on his son's behalf but received no reply. Italy remained a mirage. Wolfgang was ordered to move on to Mannheim, passing through his father's native Augsburg where old friends would welcome him and his mother.

They stayed at an inn, but were almost daily in the family home of Wolfgang's uncle, Franz Mozart, where the chief attraction for young Mozart was his gay, tomboyish cousin, Maria Anna Thekla. "Our cousin is beautiful, intelligent, clever, and merry because she has seen something of the world. In fact we suit each other well because she is also a bit naughty. We play jokes on people together and have much sport." This girl, nicknamed "The Bäsle," was the recipient of the coarsest of all Mozart's high-spirited letters and returned the same sort of smut amongst her own news. Yet Mozart could not easily disguise his distaste for Augsburg's stolid, mercantile bigwigs. He had been ordered by his father to

37. Mozart's cousin, Maria Anna Thekla Mozart, known as "The Bäsle." Pencil drawing, 1777–78.

wear his papal decoration, and was asked at dinner by the son of the organiser of the city music club how much one paid for the Order of the Golden Spur. According to himself he retorted, "You need no spur. You already have one in your head," and left the table and house. In fact he played for the club and received an apology from the offender. He was led in by a baron and seems to have behaved with a good deal of haughtiness which may have prompted the dinner insult. The supporting orchestra was "enough to give you the St. Vitus's dance" and he would be "right glad to reach a place with a court." Not wishing to disparage relatives and friends Leopold wrote to say that at home they had laughed a great deal about the discomfiture of "Herr Longotabarro" (his real name was Langemantl), whose father failed to get his law degree and had risen to become a magistrate in Augsburg only after serving in the lowest offices. Leopold then rubbed in the lesson of wasting talent on mere burghers.

Wolfgang was held in Augsburg chiefly by his admiration of Andreas Stein's pianos. Stein was a great enthusiast both as a maker and player of instruments and loved to have Mozart playing in his workshops and at home with his family. Mozart played, sight-read, and improvised to the astonishment of his old friends, the monks at Holy Cross. He gave a much publicised and admired concert in the Fugger Hall but was dissatisfied with the payment. To our benefit he exchanged portraits with his cousin, the spritely "Bäsle," promised to write to her wherever he was, and set off with his mother for Mannheim towards the end of October.

Mannheim

The tourist coming from other historic places on or near the Rhine finds Mannheim a typically cosy German city that has expanded from a feudal capital to an industrial centre. Admittedly it is a little more pleasant than some of its neighbours in that industrial belt, but it is not easily imagined as "The Palatine Athens" or the nearest rival to Versailles for the size and magnificence of its palace and ancillary buildings. Its splendour during the second half of the eighteenth century must be guessed from studying old prints. It was the Elector Karl Theodor's intention to emulate the court of Versailles from chapel to mistresses, but he was fortunate in having a greater love of the arts than of military glory, thus differing from the nearby ruler of Württemberg who also boasted musical connoisseurship.

Perhaps he was fortunate in not being dragged into war but indirectly benefiting from it, particularly the war between Austria and Prussia right in the middle of the century, for it brought to Mannheim the fine Austrian and Bohemian musicians who had no need to escape farther in order to enjoy their art where it was appreciated. Holzbauer and Filtz were from Vienna, Johann Stamitz and Cannabich from Prague. The fine players

38. *Karl Theodor, Elector Palatine. Oil portrait by Anton Hickel, 1780.*

and composers whom Mozart met there were of the second generation, including the younger Cannabich, the younger Stamitz, Toeschi, Filtz, Fränzl, and Beck. The orchestra was the most famous contributor to the fame of the Mannheim court, but Karl Theodor should also have credit for his art gallery, museum of antiquities, museum of natural history, academy of painting and sculpture, and academies of sciences and languages. He took his court to Munich in 1778. Before that time Mannheim rather than Munich was Germany's most enviable artistic Mecca.

Mozart's important contacts there during 1777 were not with aristocrats but with musicians and with the Weber family to which his future wife belonged. When he was eventually able to speak with Karl Theodor he rose to the remark: "I hear you wrote an opera for Munich." He eagerly expressed the wish to compose one for Mannheim, adding: "May I ask Your Highness not to forget me. I also know German." This reply was pointed towards the elector's creditable attempt to promote opera in the vernacular. While in Mannheim Mozart heard some examples. He thought poorly of Anton Schweitzer's music to an "Alceste" by Christoph Martin Wieland. He actually directed the music of Schweitzer's "Rosemunde" during its composer's illness, and was happy to be thus occupied while impatiently awaiting further audience with the elector. Wieland himself arrived to hear the setting of his text. He greatly admired Mozart, but Wolfgang's opinion of the poet's personality was not flattering:

39. Christoph Martin Wieland. Engraving by Nicolas Schenker after a portrait by Gerhard von Kügelgen.

He has a rather childish voice, a continuous goggling stare through his glasses, a kind of aggressive erudition, yet sometimes a silly condescension. I am not surprised, however, that he should behave like this here (even if he does not do so at Weimar) for people regard him as if he had come down from heaven. They are embarrassed in his presence and stand silent, waiting upon every word he says – a pity they often have to wait a long time, for he has a speech impediment that makes him unable to say more than six words without hesitating. Despite this, however, we all know that he has a brilliant mind. The face is ugly, covered with pock marks, and with a rather long nose; I should say he was a little taller than Papa.

Mozart could not have been active in the theatre unless welcomed there by the leading musicians. Their family friends and the Webers were more important than the elector for Mozart's future, though he did not know it; a series of letters showed that his father feared this "demeaning" of his son with people who, once out of their court uniforms, were "loose-living rogues" – according to him irreligious or at best bohemian. This sweeping classification came from Leopold's impatience at his son's prolonged stay when neither an appointment nor adequate money was immediately forthcoming.

It is difficult to tell how far Leopold's opinions of other musicians were justified. Evidently the fine oboist Ramm was indeed a bohemian type and so was the flute-player Wendling, for one of his daughters was a discarded mistress of the elector; yet their artistry elicited from Mozart music that is still treasured and regularly performed, and certainly the Wendling family, all of them competent musicians, were kind to Mozart and his mother, as were the Cannabichs. Through these friendly people the travellers were saved the expense of board and lodging at an inn, and no doubt it was they and their colleagues who secured for Wolfgang the means (chiefly by giving lessons) of earning enough to prevent the Mannheim stay from being financially disastrous. But were all the Mannheim musicians sincerely friendly? Some of them could fear for their own promotion if Mozart were favoured by Karl Theodor; others, especially the composers and keyboard players, had cause for jealousy. Open dislike for Mozart seems to have been shown only by Peter von Winter, in charge of the theatre orchestra. He must have stood well with the elector because, when Karl Theodor succeeded to the throne of Bavaria, Winter was made *Kapellmeister* in Munich. But when Mozart was in Mannheim the musician most greatly favoured was probably the Abbé Vogler. He had come from Würzburg and been sent at Karl Theodor's expense to Italy where Martini declared that he had ability but lacked patience and perseverance.

We know of no coolness between Vogler and Mozart, who wrote to his father in somewhat depreciatory terms about Vogler's playing and extemporising because Leopold had told his son to cultivate the Abbé as a "strong contrapuntist in charge of a music academy for young people . . . a very clever man he must be for he stands so high in the elector's favour." (Young Mozart did not like to be kept standing while Vogler took most of the time playing an organ which he, Mozart, was supposed to be trying. Vogler must have seen Mozart's very great ability.) If, however, the elector was not influenced by the musicians he so greatly valued, why did he continue to show a gracious manner without offering an appointment to Mozart? The elector had a great affection for his children by the actress Josepha Seyffert, whom he had made Countess Haydeck. Their music teacher was not jealous but flattered when Mozart managed to play to them and compose variations for them to learn, and since the elector seemed pleased at discovering him with his darlings and sat quietly and approvingly while Mozart played his pieces for them, there seemed hope that he might become their tutor as a step to some higher appointment. On one of these occasions Karl Theodor said: "So you will be staying the winter here?" to which Mozart answered: "Whatever Your Highness commands." Why should the elector have said this unless Cannabich or other musicians had put the thought in his head? And from what musician would he be more likely to take advice than Vogler, who was also his court chaplain?

Another priest-musician had followed Vogler from Würzburg. He was Johann Sterkel, and since his piano compositions were to be greatly admired by Beethoven, can they or Sterkel's playing have been as bad as Mozart's letters home suggested? Was Vogler "a wretched musical clown, an extremely conceited creature of small talent"? May not young Mozart have appeared conceited and given to clowning? Was he too young to disguise his enmity towards people like Sterkel and Vogler? These questions are asked but not answered. Mozart may have been a far more attractive young man than are most artists aware of their outstanding ability. He was an affectionate son, husband, and father, and when he set up his own home he was evidently a gay and frank host; but we do not know exactly how he appeared to those who did not become intimate with him or with whom he was unable or unwilling to become intimate. He may have revealed some of the contempt that constantly appears in his letters. His father knew how easily Wolfgang could show indiscreet frankness on one occasion, or to one person whom he liked, and an indiscreet coolness, perhaps arrogance, on another occasion or to other persons. Leopold had cultivated an equable manner that revealed neither forwardness nor coolness during early acquaintances. His son lacked the politician's ability to develop what is now called an "image." The stay in Mannheim, so much shorter and less eventful than the subsequent stay in Paris, is given this lengthy consideration here because it may have affected his public as well as his domestic future. It may have ensured that he would never secure a directorship of royal music at Munich, nor rise to high appointment at Vienna; and the delay in his official promotion by the monarchs may not have originated with Colloredo but with other musicians whose opinions reached princely ears.

In his constant letters to Mannheim (and Paris) Leopold Mozart is shown as a man greatly to be pitied. At the age of 58 he was now too old to be accused of seeking his own reputation or enrichment by his son's talents, and he was a fine enough musician to know that Wolfgang had such genius as his own talent could no longer advise in purely musical matters. The world in which he had grown up could not envisage any future but beggary or disreputable bohemianism for the artist, however great, whose gifts were not recognised by a high official post. Lonely and miserable, unable to "manage" the tour, Leopold dreaded his son's obvious satisfaction with freedom, or freelancing, as he understood it. To admonitions on what to say, what to show ("your Italian diplomas," etc.), how to behave or dress he received playful replies and comic descriptions of people which would have delighted him in earlier days but now worried him. The most pathetic feature of the correspondence is the father's recoiling when the son protested that he could endure fussy solicitations but would not tolerate his father's doubts on such matters as his religious observance, including confession. Leopold must have been wounded by the words, "I ask you one thing: do not think so badly of me," and "I ask you in the coming year to love me with the same fatherly warmth you have always shown me." He sent tender replies, but was forced to add the wish that Wolfgang would "do all he could to win fame, honour, and money to help us and save your father from the scorn and ridicule of certain persons whose names I may not mention. Your fortune and fame will be our sweet revenge, which we are already enjoying a little."

48

The Weber Family

Leopold's greatest alarms began when he received the following news in a letter dated January 17, 1778:

Next Wednesday I am going to Kirchheimboland to spend a few days with the Princess of Orange [Caroline of Nassau-Weilburg] . . . A Dutch officer was strongly reproved by her for failing to bring me with him when he went there to give her New Year greetings. I shall receive eight louis d'or at the least. She is so very fond of singing that I have had four arias copied for her, and I shall also take her a symphony. She owns a good little orchestra and has a daily concert. The copying of the arias will not cost me much because it is done by a certain Herr Weber who is going with me. He has a daughter who sings splendidly and has a pure, lovely voice, but she is only 16. She lacks only acting ability; if she had that she could be *prima donna* anywhere. Her father is a thoroughly honest German who is bringing his children up decently, and because of that the girl is much sought after here. He has six children, five daughters and one son. For 14 years he had to support wife and children on a salary of 200 gulden, and since he always discharged his duties well and provided the elector with a fine singer he is now granted the munificent sum of 400 gulden.

In this and further letters came enthusiastic tributes to Aloysia Weber's virtues and accomplishments, including her singing and her sight-reading of Wolfgang's piano sonatas. There was no mention of the younger sister, Constanze, for Aloysia was assessed through the mind of a youth head over heels in his first great love affair. She certainly did become an opera singer in Munich when the Mannheim musical establishment moved there (and the musical glory of Mannheim faded) but she was no singer-actress of international fame.

Despite letters from his wife as well as Wolfgang, Leopold may not have guessed the whole truth immediately. But its possibility can never have been far from his mind. In itself it was not his chief dread; it was, however, one of the chief obstacles, maybe with such a headstrong young man the very chief obstacle, to a glorious future as conceived by Leopold. The fear must have been in the father's mind when he parted sadly from Wolfgang and, from the gay and silly letters, knew him to be unfeignedly happy at the prospect of his "golden liberty" from imposed and regular duties. Leopold may have been relieved that the spirited Augsburg cousin provided only flirtatious merriment; if the friendship developed into anything more serious *that* was preferable to marriage into some impoverished and loose-living family of musical lackeys, which is no more than most orchestral players were. He was to learn that the Webers were theatrical and musical bohemians not above breeding a monarch's courtesan. His own marriage to a woman of no fortune

40. Aloysia Lange, born Weber, as Zémire in Grétry's opera "Zémire and Azor." Engraving by Johannes Esaias Nilson, 1784.

had been a love-match with solid prudence on both sides. If his son's could not be socially more brilliant, it must at least be as sensible. Against the opinion of some biographers it must be asserted here that Mozart's marriage into the Weber family actually *was* fortunate in the most important ways that concern a gifted musician and artist, but that is a matter to examine later; for the moment we must, as it were, share Leopold's fears.

The Webers had come down in the world from ancestors who had attained to university education and some literary pretensions, especially in the theatre; they had held posts as tutors, secretaries, and bailiffs. The father of the family known to Wolfgang, Fridolin Weber, like his own father, had been shabbily treated by a Baron Schönau who had dismissed him as a scapegoat for malpractices he himself had initiated. Father and grandfather had secured legal redress from successive barons but only after expenditure that left little profit, and Fridolin moved to Mannheim to earn a precarious livelihood as prompter and copyist as well as chorus and minor-part bass singer in the court theatre. His brother was the father of the composer Carl Maria von Weber. Undoubtedly the Webers were intelligent and gifted, with what may be called either broad-minded attitudes or lax standards, according to our leanings towards Leopold's concept of virtue or theirs. There is surely no doubt that a Weber could be a more congenial and understanding life-companion than a bride chosen by Leopold for his son, destined to live in a metropolis and in a fast-changing society. How well today, unlike Mozart's father, we can understand a young man in love who sublimates his love energies in social and political idealism! Welcomed in a home where "Schönau" was a symbol of feudal oppression as "Colloredo" was in Salzburg, young Mozart had the generosity (and the self-conceit) to imagine himself as their protector and with God's help their ultimate rescuer from poverty and persecution. His was too frank a nature not to declare these feelings in letters – except the private feeling he entertained for Aloysia, which Leopold was experienced enough to read into the other expressions of magnanimity.

Leopold had little to do at home but to worry about his wife and son and to read their letters again and again. He may therefore have been alarmed even at Wolfgang's comments upon the news of a wedding in Salzburg. He wrote that, if he had known in time, he might have composed some minuets, but added:

This is simply marriage for money. I do not want to marry for that. I want to make my wife happy and secure, not to get my fortune from her. I shall therefore let events take their course and enjoy my golden liberty till I have enough to support wife and children. It was necessary for Schiedenhofen to pick a wealthy wife, for a titled man has to do that. The aristocracy can never marry for love but only for convenience and all kinds of secondary considerations to their desires. Nor would it suit the high-born gentleman to go on loving his wife once she had done

her duty and brought a healthy male heir into the world; but we poor commoners . . . our riches die with us for we carry them in our brains, and nobody can take away our treasure except by chopping our heads off.

Greater distress must have been caused by a sarcastic account of the trip and short stay to perform before Princess Caroline of Nassau-Weilburg. In the evenings "we could have dined at the officers' table," but preferred not to do so because "we were never merrier than when we were alone." The remuneration was rather less than expected, and it was plain that the Webers enjoyed a pleasant little holiday largely at Wolfgang's expense. Then followed the final blows. After a general indictment of the Mannheimers, e.g. "We do not like the Wendling way of life. Wendling is honest and kind but quite without religion . . . his daughter has been a mistress. Ramm is a kind man but a libertine," Wolfgang wrote:

I am so fond of this oppressed family that I wish nothing more than to make them happy; and maybe I can do that. My advice is that they should go to Italy. Will you write to our good friend Lugiati as soon as possible and inquire how much is paid to a *prima donna* in Verona . . . I would stake my life that she will do me honour by her singing. Even in this short time she has made great headway under my instruction . . . If this comes about, Herr Weber, his two daughters, and I will have the honour of visiting my dear Papa and my dear sister for a fortnight while passing through Salzburg. My sister will find Mademoiselle Weber a kind friend and companion, for her reputation for good conduct here is like my sister's at Salzburg; her father is like mine, and the whole family like the Mozarts . . . I expect we shall go to Switzerland, and then perhaps to Holland.

Before the letter was despatched, Wolfgang's mother added hers:

From this letter you will see that when Wolfgang makes new friends he wants to sacrifice everything for them. It is true that she sings splendidly, but we must never forget our own interests. I never felt happy about his association with Wendling and Ramm, but he would not listen to me . . . he prefers being with other people to being with me. I object to various things he does and he does not like it . . . I do not think the journey to Paris with Wendling at all advisable; I would rather go with him myself later on. It will not be very expensive by mail-coach. Perhaps you will receive a letter from Herr Grimm. Meanwhile we are losing nothing here. I am writing this in the greatest secrecy; he is out at dinner and I do not want him to discover me writing.

At risk of boring the reader with sentiments that have only too often filled pages written by parents to children, we must quote extensively from Leopold's letters to Mannheim – less to know more of Leopold's suffering than to know how strongly affection could have pulled his son away from his determination. Quite definitely

Leopold played upon Wolfgang's feelings; but with supreme genius is often given an ability to guard it, and we do not need to cite the lonely Beethoven or the monstrously egocentric Wagner to prove that most great artists have defences against the opinions of others, even those whom they love. To imagine what *might* have happened if history had not been exactly what it is, to imagine how Handel might have fared if he had lived elsewhere than in England or what music might have come from Schubert if he had lived only 10 more years – this is merely to enjoy a game; yet it is surely safe to say that if Mozart had succeeded as his father understood success, even if he had become *Kapellmeister* to the emperor in Vienna, either he would not, by the age when death took him, have made the artistic adventures for which he is honoured by posterity or he would have been unhappy in the royal service. His was *not* the age of Beethoven; and the most important fact about his real success is that, in his own way, he produced what pleased his own artistic conscience just as Beethoven did. However foolish he may have been, he was aware of his artistic purpose, and we quote at length from his father's letter to show how hard, how reliable his artistic conscience must have been not to capitulate.

My dear son, I read your letter of the 4th with surprise and horror. I am answering it today, the 11th, because I have been unable to sleep and am so tired out that I have to write slowly, word by word . . . if I am to finish by tomorrow . . . I should not recognise my son in that letter but for his familiar fault; he takes everybody at his word, opens his soft heart to flattery and fine speeches, lets everyone influence him in all directions, and is so led away by sudden ideas and illusory visions that he is ready to fling his own reputation and profit to the winds, and even the interests of his old and honourable parents and his duty to them . . .

Gone are those happy hours . . . when you would not go to sleep without first standing on a chair and singing "Oragna fagata" to me, then kissing the end of my nose and saying that when I grew old you would put me in a glass case with a lid to protect me from the wind, and would always have me with you and honour me! Listen, therefore, patiently to me. You know our woes in Salzburg. You know my wretched salary, and you know why I kept my promise to let you go on your travels. You are aware of all my miseries.

There were two basic purposes for your journey: either to seek a permanent and good appointment or, if that failed, to move forward to some place where there were prospects of big earnings . . . It depends on you alone to raise yourself to a greater eminence than any musician has ever attained. You owe that to the extraordinary talents you have received from a most merciful God, and it depends only upon your own wisdom and behaviour whether you want to die as a mere musician forgotten by everyone, or as a famous *Kapellmeister* of whom posterity will read; whether, lulled to inertia by some woman, you die on a straw pallet in a room full of starving children or, after a Christian life of happiness, honour, and fame you pass away with your family well provided for and everybody respecting you.

How much money had he wasted in Munich for nothing? Had he not "had his little dance" in Augsburg "with my brother's daughter"? How much time had he spent with Cannabich who was seeking his own advantage in two ways? What *prima donna* ever took the stage in Italy before frequent appearances in Germany, and with the most powerful patrons behind her? What manager would not laugh at the recommendation of a girl of 16 or 17? The idea of travelling around with Weber and two daughters "almost deprived me of my reason . . . Your letter reads like a novel." What great composer would descend to Switzerland? Then came the climax:

Off to Paris with you! And at once! Take your place among important people – *aut Caesar aut nihil* . . . From Paris the name and fame of a talented man marches over the world. There the nobility treat men of genius with the greatest respect and courtesy. There you will see a degree of refinement which compares amazingly with the coarseness of our German nobles and their ladies.

Leopold told his son that Nannerl had wept for two days on hearing the last letter from Mannheim, that "both of you" lacked the honesty to send a true account of what happened either at Munich or Mannheim, but the whole story had to be told in the end! Wolfgang must immediately say how much money he has in hand. Leopold then mentions friends with whom he must get in touch. Let him make his name and fortune in Paris so as to secure commissions for operas in Italy, and *then* propose the engagement of Mlle. Weber for their performance.

If we read between their lines, Leopold's letters to Mannheim and then to Paris are pathetic documents. We go from outbursts of anger to pleadings for patience with an ageing father, from reproaches to appeasements, and then back to curt commands.

At last it appears that you could have had pupils but, because once or twice you did not find them at home, you gave them up. You would rather give lessons as a favour. Oh yes, no doubt you would! It is far more proper for your poor father to run about at the age of 58 working for a wretched pittance to support himself and his daughter by toil and sweat . . . I look like poor Lazarus. My dressing-gown is so frayed that if someone calls in the morning I run and hide. While you have been away I have had no shoes made and I no longer have any black hose; on Sundays I wear my old white hose. To crown all this I have neither wife nor son, and God knows when we shall meet again. My supreme joy is gone – hearing you play and listening to your compositions. Your sister is now my only care, and I try to banish my tormenting thoughts by playing the violin to her accompaniment each night from six to eight – arias, symphonies, masses, vespers, and so on. To my astonishment she has made such fine progress that she can now sight-read anything I bring home from the cathedral, no matter how elaborately fugal. And do you know what has given her this new determination and diligence in practising? My death! She recognises and foresees the misery into which she would be thrown if I were now to leave this world. What do you think would become of your Mama and sister then? She did not weep for nothing when she wept over your letter.

By the next post the mood is more hopeful, and includes a "Hurrah!" because Leopold has managed to contact Grimm in Paris.

More to be pitied than Leopold was Anna Maria. She had too much native stamina and common sense to be hurt by recognition of her lack of general education or musical ability. In Mannheim German was spoken by her associates. In Paris she had greater loneliness because of her inadequate command of French. She knew that young people had not lost their filial love merely because, with the callousness of youth, they spent their active hours away from their parents. She knew that Wolfgang needed her humanly if not artistically until he married, however much he was infatuated by Aloysia Weber. Whatever she wrote to her husband, she must have been grateful for the gossip and companionship of the mothers and wives of other musicians. Yet she longed to be at home, where the round of domestic work was in her own hands and appreciated; away from that she was entrusted with a task which she knew she could not fulfil at all well, and surely her husband knew it. She was often tired, sick, and weak, though she cannot have known that death was so near. Wolfgang's plan to take the Webers with him to Italy via Salzburg gave her a ray of hope. Was it disloyal secretly to encourage him in a scheme that would take them home where, perhaps, she could demand to be left? Poor woman! The letters from Salzburg sternly dissuaded her from pleading. After delays to give concerts Wolfgang and she went off to Paris on March 14, 1778, and her excuse for the delay was the time to find a person who would buy their carriage after he had driven them to France.

Tragedy in Paris

The period of Mozart's stay in Paris, from March to September, 1778, was the most frustrating and the least productive in his life. He was to know greater pain, anger, strain, and stress, but never quite the bleakness of the months during which he faced his inability to impose his genius on Paris society. He was not yet old enough to take defeat with a shrug of the shoulders, to see life's ups and downs as chance turnings of the wheel of fate, for his father had not taught him to meet misfortune with cynical courage, but to regard *himself* as responsible for worldly success or failure. Today it is not easy for us to believe that a young man of his intelligence could suppose adversity to be a judgment of God, or to feel guilt at a lack of acclaim which was only to be expected from a nature designed for production, not advertisement, of treasure.

Nor did his father, who could not have steered his son's second appearance in Paris to resounding success, accept the fact that the immediate popularity or failure of music is not related directly to its worth. He had to seek explanation of failure. Since Wolfgang was obviously not enjoying the pleasures of Paris, and therefore could not be losing his chances by his own folly, he must be the victim of intrigue. Mozart wrote a sinfonia concertante for flute, oboe, horn, and bassoon for the Mannheim players in Paris – Wendling, Ramm, Punto, and Ritter. When the day of performance arrived the score was "mislaid" by the conductor. The players were furious; Mozart was merely amused. Like his father he had learnt to expect intrigue; unlike his father he did not put Gluck, then triumphing in Paris, amongst his enemies. Why should Gluck wish to intrigue against a kind of music in which he was no competitor? Why should a man of 64, secure in public esteem, intrigue against a man of 22 whom Paris remembered only as a boy prodigy? Later in Vienna Mozart and his wife dined with the Glucks, and the older musician seems always to have admired the younger. Gluck was a splendid schemer for his own advancement, but he never schemed *against* other composers. He simply possessed the worldly wisdom which Mozart lacked – knew how to secure useful allies and how to avoid offending likely enemies.

Some of Anna Maria's last letters betray the misery of their stay. Without the kindness of German friends Paris would have been intolerable for her. They found their first abode, after a wretched, cold journey, in a room with two beds. It was above the premises of a German dealer in scrap iron. The March wind and rain sank their spirits. Anna Maria was now 57, ailing, homesick, weakened by the cold and the travelling.

I sit alone all day as if I were in prison. The room is dark and looks out on a closed, small yard. I can neither see the sun nor tell what the weather is. By great effort I can knit by the poor light. And for this we have to pay 30 livres a month! The door and stairs are so narrow that it would be impossible to get a piano up here. Wolfgang has to go out to M. Le Gros's house where there is a piano, and so I do not see him all day. I shall soon forget how to talk. Fasting days are unendurable.

These could be the words of a miserable, poor sempstress in a novel by Dickens or Daudet. To understand how they could come from a member of the well-dressed Mozart family is more important than to trace Mozart's steps in Paris. By eighteenth-century standards the

Mozarts were by no means poor musicians of the servant class. Leopold would have arranged with agents to supply any extra money required, and nobody would have been more angry if he had thought that his wife and son gave the impression of poverty. Why, then, did they not lodge at a good inn? Why did Anna Maria go without meals which her ailing body needed while her son dined with Le Gros, Gossec, Noverre, or Grimm?

When Leopold himself undertook an independent enterprise, as when he toured his children, and when his son was not to be restrained from adventure, the precarious nature of independent action in a closely ordered society was not forgotten. One should spend only what one earned away from one's fixed employment. In Mannheim Mozart had not fully paid his way; his mother would therefore economise in Paris until he was earning. Old friends and Grimm were ready with introductions to important people.

Unfortunately the money which might justify better lodging and the use of carriages (Mozart complained of the distances he walked through filthy streets) was not forthcoming from composition but from giving lessons. Since Leopold was not asked to send money Mozart must have done more playing and teaching than we know. Grimm sent him to the Duchesse de Chabot first. Her behaviour was "of the utmost politeness," but she had neither piano nor harpsichord in good tune and order; she kept Mozart waiting in a very cold room while her company arrived, and then let them indulge in drawing while he played. He wrote home of the manners of French nobility: "They say 'O c'est un prodige, c'est inconcevable, c'est étonnant.' Then it is goodbye. At first I spent a good deal of time and money running round to them, often to find nobody at home." He was introduced to the Duc de Guines, whom his father particularly hoped he would cultivate – "I often read of him in the papers. He must have great influence at court." This gentleman played the flute. His daughter played the harp "magnifique" and had a huge repertory by heart, but her father was anxious to boast that she was also a composer. If Mozart could only get her to write an original minuet! The "stupid and lazy" girl "had not an idea in her head" and it is interesting to hear of the modern methods – now used in English state schools – by which Mozart tried to elicit music from her. For instance he began such short pieces as marches and dances and asked her to add the completing phrases, or to repeat a passage he supplied but to introduce some kind of variation. He explained these methods to his father, who approved, but begged him not to be impatient. Fortunately the girl's marriage brought the futile lessons to an end. Mozart was kept waiting for inadequate fees both for them and for the Concerto for Flute and Harp, K. 299, which he wrote for father and daughter to play together.

In April 1778 mother and son moved to better quarters in central Paris. Grimm seems to have called and been surprised at their miserable living conditions, for the new lodgings were found by his friend Mme.

41. Anton Raaff. Engraving by G. F. Touchemolin.

d'Épinay. It was a big room with a piano; according to Anna Maria

> . . . in this Rue Clery it is the first street on the left, going in from the Rue Montmarter [sic], a handsome street and mostly peopled by gentlefolk, very clean, not too far from the *pulvar* [Anna Maria's phonetic "boulevard"] with healthy air. The people in this house are good and honest, not mercenary, which is rare in Paris.

Unfortunately the healthy air did not prevent her suddenly becoming the victim of headache, toothache, a sore throat, and other pains. She wrote to her husband for a supply of the family's standby nostrums – "Black Powder and Markgraf Powder." In a month she seemed to recover, and it is pleasant to know that she was happy, for the first time since she reached Paris, during the month or so before her final illness. The singer Anton Raaff, then an old man, talked to her almost daily and delighted her by singing to her son's or his own accompaniment. One François Heina, a horn-player who knew Leopold and with whom they had made friends almost as soon as they arrived, introduced her to his wife and invited her to dinner. He also took her to the Luxembourg Gardens and to picture galleries. It is unlikely that she fully recovered from an illness that had been recurrent since she left home. Her husband repeatedly begged her to be bled. (Bleeding was still regarded as a panacea and protection which even healthy people were advised to seek in the spring!) At last she consented. A few days later she had a feverish chill from which she declined into delirium and coma. She died on July 3 and was buried in the graveyard of Saint-Eustache in which church a memorial tablet to her can still be seen, though none was put there at the time.

Several biographies of Mozart comment upon Mozart's composure, or apparent composure, as suggesting callousness towards his mother. We live in an age of verbosity when politicians and eminent persons vie in expressions of sanctimonious horror after a disaster or the death, natural or contrived, of a public figure. They might lose popularity and office if, to a reporter's ridiculous question "What did you feel?" they gave Cordelia's answer, "I cannot heave my heart into my mouth." Do we love the dead any the less because we take the meal or the sleep we need? Is it better to go about one's business after bereavement or to be an idle figure of pity? Religious or rationalist, many a man or woman would not attend their most beloved creature's funeral, nor spend more than the minimum on customs or memorials of death, except to avoid hurting the feelings of others; for what can fine words and a fine coffin do to express love or sorrow, or how avail the dead? When the deceased is a beloved parent, many of us find our most obsessive thought to be of self-accusation, justified or not; even if we have not pursued our own way with culpable selfishness, the age gap may have led us to give the parent less of our conversation, company, attention, and understanding than, we tell ourselves, we would give if time could be rolled back. Surely such thoughts afflicted the hypersensitive and affectionate young Mozart, whose age and absorption with matters which he could not share with his mother may have made him less considerate towards her than he might have been. That possibility is not denied; what cannot be accepted is that his unwillingness to write and moralise about his mother's sufferings and death should be regarded as callous. Rather his epistolary behaviour suggests delicate consideration for those at home.

He had begun a letter describing the success of his "Paris" Symphony before his mother died; after the shock he calmly finished it, saying no more about his mother than that she was not well. He then sent a long letter to the Abbé Bullinger, a friend of the family, revealing the anxiety with which his mother's state had oppressed him since, a fortnight previously, he had been convinced that her death "was inevitable." He had prayed that her end would not be painful for her and that he himself should have strength to endure. "God in his goodness" had "granted these two blessings to the fullest measure." He then asked Bullinger to go to his father and sister and "prepare them for the truth" without telling them that Anna Maria was dead. He then contradicted this by writing, "Do as you think best, but use every means in your power" to spare their feelings. Leopold had the grace not to fill his next few letters to his son with reproaches, not even the usual ones saying he could not understand his dislike of Paris nor his failure to be highly successful there. Even so, it is to be hoped that any self-accusations in Wolfgang's heart were unaffected by his father's inability to avoid the word *Opfer* (sacrifice) in and out of season. "Remember the sacrifices we made for you . . ." or "Your mother had to sacrifice herself to help

her son." Leopold could not help believing that deferment of blood-letting had contributed to his wife's death, nor could he help bothering about the return of his wife's clothes and other belongings!

Before we discuss the interval between the mother's death and Wolfgang's return to Salzburg we should consider a matter on which we may easily be misguided by the selection of documents we are likely to know, especially Mozart's own letters. He objected to being ordered to Paris and constantly wrote home in disparagement of Paris, suggesting that he was unable to be in any way successful there except by odd performances which brought in little money. Financially he may not, in the few months of his stay, have reaped any considerable reward, but he may have gained far more admiration than his own letters suggest. He was offered the post of organist at Versailles at a reasonable salary. His father advised him to accept, but he declined, his letters suggesting that he did so on good advice. One of Anna Maria's letters told her husband that his son was "once again so famous and popular here" that she could scarcely believe his success in a place so full of intrigue. Leopold had another confidential agent as well as his wife – Grimm. A letter from Grimm written about a month after Anna Maria's death said:

Wolfgang is too generous, not pushful, too easily deceived, too little occupied with the means that lead to his fortune. To make headway in this place needs craft, enterprise, and boldness. For his own sake I wish he had half the talent and twice the social dexterity (*Gewandheit*) . . . There are only two means of gaining a good standing here. The first is to give lessons on the piano. Apart from the fact that one cannot secure pupils unless one actively tries, even by being a bit of a showman, I doubt if his health would stand the rigours of such an occupation, for it is extremely tiring to run to the four corners of Paris . . . Besides . . . it would keep him from composition which is what he has most at heart. He therefore ought to have the means to devote himself to it exclusively . . ."

After his mother's death Mozart accepted the offer of board and lodging with Grimm and Mme. d'Épinay. He liked the lady sincerely but at times could not easily remain cordial towards Grimm who, he complained, was in the habit of reminding him, directly or indirectly, of his favours. Nothing could make Mozart more touchy than any matter which hurt his pride, and unfortunately he had to borrow money from Grimm which his father arranged to return. For his part Grimm wished that Wolfgang would not stay in Paris now that his father was no longer counselling patience but imploring him to return. By declining the post at Versailles Mozart had shown that he could not envisage his happiness in France, even if he rose to favour with a royal family of which the queen was Austrian and his admirer already. (It is foolish but tempting to imagine the future course of European music if Mozart had prospered as the chief

54

musician of France during the whole revolutionary period.) Why did he now linger in Paris while Grimm tried to speed him on his way?

First there were hopes of work for the stage, and they were increased when his old friend J. C. Bach crossed the Channel with the castrato Tenducci in August in order to produce a French opera. With the visitors from England Mozart was invited to Saint-Germain by Marshal de Noailles, sumptuously entertained, blessed with fine summer weather, and enabled to enjoy some of his last days in France. Back with Grimm, who may have been anxious to prevent his incurring more debts, he stayed in hope of seeing proofs of six of his violin sonatas from Sieber, the publisher. There were "harsh words" from Grimm and irritating evidence that Leopold was more inclined to believe Grimm than his son. The final insult was to be put on a diligence "which crawls at a snail's pace and without change of horses . . . Twice I have had to rise at one in the morning because the coach was to leave at two." The journey, which began on September 26, 1778 was eased by a passing friendship with a German merchant travelling home with whom Mozart took meals apart from a despised company, one of whom had advanced syphilis. Since the coach took eight days to reach Nancy, which Mozart thought charming and elegant, the two decided to proceed in a private carriage. One can imagine Leopold's reaction to the expense, and to his son's trusting a flatterer who spoke German and might be a thief! The wonder is that Mozart ever reached Salzburg. He even wrote in his letter to Bullinger of August 7:

> You, dearest friend, know quite well how I detest Salzburg, and not only because of the injustices which my dear father and I have endured there, which would be enough to make us want to forget the place and put it out of our thoughts for ever! But, overcoming that wish, if only we could manage our affairs to live there respectably! To live respectably and to live happily are very different matters and to do the latter [in Salzburg] I should need recourse to witchcraft . . . I have far more hope of living happily in any other place. Perhaps you will mistake me as supposing that Salzburg is too small for me? If so, you are quite wrong.

The letter complains of the attitude to musicians in Salzburg, the lack of good singers and of a proper opera theatre. Even the orchestra was not what it should have been for lack of a good *Kapellmeister*. "Tomorrow I intend to hire a carriage and drive round to all the hospitals and infirmaries to find a *Kapellmeister* for them. Why . . . did they let Mysliveček slip, and he so near? . . . He would have been the man to terrify the orchestra." There was plenty of money. Why wasn't it used? They were longing for a good musical director as eagerly as the Jews awaited their Messiah. The only female singer of any accomplishment was Mme. Haydn (Michael Haydn's wife) who was in poor health. "I am surprised that she has not lost her voice long ago by her perpetual scourgings, fastings, hair-shirt wearing, and night praying." (Later Mozart calls her "our weeping Magdalene.") Until there is a change, the letter finishes, Mozart will not go to Salzburg. When it has been made, despite his hatred of the place, he is "willing to come and turn over the page whenever I see V.S." (*Volti subito*, turn quickly; the letters are used chiefly on orchestral parts.)

The Traveller Returns

Leopold enticed his son home by assuring him that Salzburg *could* offer him a reconstituted musical establishment with better prospects than he had had when he left. Soon after the organist Adlgasser had died of a stroke while actually playing in the cathedral, Lolli, the *Kapellmeister*, also died. Leopold Mozart deserved to succeed to the office, was expected to apply for it, and did. Before his high hopes were disappointed yet again he used the utmost diplomacy to ensure that his son could return on favourable terms to the court *Kapelle*. To enquiries about Wolfgang he blandly replied that he was doing splendidly in Paris, and how his father, now a lonely widower, wished he had both his company and his talent to enjoy! When Adlgasser died several of the Salzburg nobility, especially Count Arco, who had always befriended Leopold, began to ask if it were likely that Wolfgang would be induced to return. The situation was manipulated adroitly through the agency of a widow, the Countess Wallis, who was Colloredo's sister and lived in the archiepiscopal residence. Before the end of August she let it be known that His Grace was minded to offer Adlgasser's place to Wolfgang. Leopold himself was now in debt, though not dangerously so. With himself *Kapellmeister* while his son, appointed to compose, play the organ and piano, and direct music from the keyboard, took the office and stipend of *Konzertmeister*, the family fortunes and honour would soon be restored.

If the present situation could be used well and speedily, the conditions of appointment would make Wolfgang's return far from humiliating. Leopold had to impress the fact upon him:

> My dearest son, You may be sure that without you I shall die the sooner, but with the joy of having you with me I should last many years longer . . . This matter must be dealt with properly, both with due deference [to Colloredo] but with care for our own reputation. I told him [Baron Grimm] that we should be glad to have you here once more because if the result is not satisfactory you can leave Salzburg again without damaging your prospects . . . I had no doubt that you would accept the offer for my sake if it were made, adding that the archbishop would surely permit you to go to Italy every alternate year, since it was his belief that a musician should hear fresh works from time to time, and that he would furnish you with letters of recommendation.

Before Wolfgang left Paris his father was able to tell him that the archbishop had agreed to these conditions. He had even said that he would grant leave to fulfil an opera commission anywhere, and deigned an explanation of his former objection to another tour by father and son – "he could not bear our running around the world like beggars." (Colloredo was no doubt sincere when he used this expression with which the empress had also expressed contempt. Mozart was no longer a child and even if he had been, Colloredo probably thought performing tours resembled the ways of circus troupes.) It must have been difficult for Leopold to write the following passage:

> Demoiselle Weber has got under the skin of the prince and everyone else too; they are all mad to hear her. When she comes she can stay with us.

Yet Wolfgang kept his father waiting for his definite acceptance. He gave a private concert in Strasbourg though his father had arranged for him to draw what money he needed from a merchant there. The good takings induced Mozart to hire the theatre for a public concert, which was badly attended. "Nothing is sadder," he wrote, "than to see a great T-shaped table spread for 80 when only three persons are eating at it." Then he was detained by floods and gave a third concert which brought a small profit, and he played on the town's fine Silbermann organs. He reached Mannheim on November 6. Since the court had gone to Munich and so had the Webers, Leopold regarded this detour as indicating that Wolfgang was determined not to return to the hated Salzburg. Then a letter suggested that he was fool enough to delay deliberately:

> Please, dearest father, make use of this news in Salzburg. Talk about it so often and so emphatically that the archbishop may suppose I shall not return; he may then decide to offer a better stipend.

"This news" was a request to compose for the Mannheim theatre, now taken over by a well-known troupe which achieved popular success with a form of lyric play then called "duodrama," but later "melodrama." Like *Singspiel* it was in German and used spoken dialogue, but like opera it took its stories from classical mythology and ancient history. Mozart admired two examples, a "Medea" and an "Ariadne auf Naxos" by the Bohemian composer resident in Berlin, Georg Benda, and began to set a "Semiramis" which was shown to him by Baron Dalberg, who became manager of the theatre. Dalberg asked him also to consider a libretto written by himself. Living with the Cannabichs and enjoying the admiration and kindness of other old Mannheim friends, Mozart would have stayed if he could have made Dalberg produce a contract which clearly stated the fee to be paid and the time of its payment.

Early in December his father wrote peremptorily demanding his return. He moved on to Munich in the splendid entourage of the Abbot of Kaisersheim who had become one of his admirers. Mozart found his expansive and genial company pleasant enough, as well as the com-fort and good food the cleric provided, but he wrote sarcastically of the military pomp and ceremony that surrounded an abbot! They arrived in Munich on Christmas Day, and Mozart at once sought out the Webers. Leopold had heard of their prosperity now that Aloysia took thrice her father's salary at the opera and so greatly attracted Karl Theodor:

> Like many such folk, Herr Weber turns poverty to advantage and then forgets he was ever poor . . . He flattered you when he needed you; maybe now he will not admit that you taught her.

Aloysia Weber was not in the least coy or delicate in letting Mozart know that she was now bent on her career and foresaw attachments more profitable than one to a musician husband. It is said that Mozart was broken-hearted; if so the heart soon mended. It is also said that, immediately after his passionate declaration was scorned, he sat down at the piano and strummed the opening of a popular song which went to the words "I'm glad to leave the girl who doesn't want me." The blow was hard enough for him to write to his father: "I am keeping all [news] until I have the happiness of being able to speak again to you, for today I can only weep. I am too soft-hearted." Since his father was not told the "news" he did not know what the weeping was for. He merely insisted on a speedy homecoming: Did Wolfgang not know that people in Salzburg, who had been told he had left Paris in September, thought he was deliberately trying to exacerbate the archbishop's impatience? Good heavens, it was now January! And by the way there were good things to see nowadays at the Salzburg theatre. A most convenient new wardrobe had been made for Wolfgang's clothes, etc., etc.

Mozart had told the merry Bäsle, his cousin from Augsburg, to join him in Munich, and she had arrived. He had hoped that she would hear Aloysia at the opera and be present at his formal engagement to her. After the distressing meeting with Aloysia, the cousin, who had no matrimonial designs on Wolfgang, no doubt helped to comfort him, especially on the journey to Salzburg. Leopold had written to assure his niece that a warm room would be ready for her. The two therefore set off home as soon as Mozart had seen Gluck's "Alceste" and gone with Cannabich to the electress to present the violin sonatas he had brought from Paris and which he had dedicated to her. The reunited Mozarts feasted in Salzburg on January 17, 1779, and Mozart was destined to stay with his father and sister there for nearly two years. In that time he produced the first examples of his really great and original works – works with a peculiar atmosphere of ardent youthfulness. Amongst them was an opera he was invited to compose for the Munich carnival. Colloredo would not offend Karl Theodor by refusing leave of absence but, to be fair to him, we should not suppose that he might otherwise have broken his promise to grant leave for worthy purposes.

V
From servitude to freedom

42. *The Mehlgrube, Vienna, where many of Mozart's public concerts were held. Engraving by Johann Adam Delsenbach after Johann Bernhard Fischer von Erlach.*

There is no evidence that when Mozart left Salzburg for Munich on November 5, 1780 to finish and supervise his opera "Idomeneo," he had determined never to return. (He did return once, but only to present his bride to his father, sister, and friends.) The person commissioned to write the libretto of the carnival opera was Giambattista Varesco, who was the Salzburg court chaplain – a fact which may have eased not only Mozart's negotiations but his securing of leave.

The Archduke Maximilian of the Austrian royal house arrived in Munich a day after Wolfgang. There were illuminations and gala nights – theatre, concerts, ballet – which Mozart enjoyed, especially as he was so happy in the company of his friends from the former Mannheim *Kapelle*. He neglected his opera for a fortnight and had to work hard to finish it in time. It was done, including "the damned dances" for the ballet, by January 18. Before then Mozart had held several rehearsals with the orchestra alone. Just before Christmas Karl Theodor listened to one of them "incognito from an adjoining room" and called out "Bravo!" at the end of the first act. "Since we did not know whether he would stay much longer, we had to play the concertante aria and the thunderstorm . . ." The elector again praised the work and added: "Who would imagine that anything so great could be hidden in so small a head?" Apparently this was not sarcasm, for his good opinions of the work and his encouragements of the composer were retailed not only among the aristocratic music-lovers who invited Wolfgang to meals but also in Salzburg. Leopold wrote:

> The whole town is talking about the excellence of your opera. Baron Lerbach began the rumours; the chancellor's wife told me that he told her it was receiving unusual commendation from all sorts of people. The second excitement came with Herr Becke's letter to Fiala [oboist at Salzburg] which Fiala gave everybody to read . . .

It must be remembered that both father and son were anxious for a great success because of the possibility of getting honourable employment and leaving Salzburg. Earlier Leopold had begged Wolfgang to remember that the "battalion of musicians" Karl Theodor employed in Munich might find themselves destitute when that music-loving elector died. Now, however, his letters were full of advice directed to impressing Karl Theodor.

> See that you keep the whole orchestra in good spirits by flattering them . . . your style needs the utmost concentration incessantly from all players, and it is no easy thing to keep them all intense and hard at work for at least three hours . . . Even the poorest viola player is heartily moved by direct personal commendation and will then work more keenly and attentively. A gesture of that kind costs you no more than a few words.

The two of them hoped that during rehearsal days no trouble would arise from the fact that the agreed six weeks' leave had passed.

> I am resolved to keep quiet, but if I hear any talk I shall say that we understood that you were given leave to stay six weeks in Munich after finishing the composition of the opera, in order to supervise rehearsals and production.

They both knew quite well that what Colloredo granted was a plain six weeks' furlough. Fortunately His Grace himself left Salzburg for Vienna, on January 13, to the relief of Leopold, who was on edge because Colloredo's departure had been postponed several times – the first when Maria Theresa died. (She might have played Mozart her last disservice by deferring her demise until 1781, and then the period of public mourning would have caused the postponement of the carnival opera!)

Leopold and Nannerl arrived in time for the dress rehearsal on Wolfgang's birthday, January 27, and were at the first performance two days later. Otherwise we should have letters to them giving details of the performance, about which we sadly lack details. The Munich paper reported that "Libretto, music, and translation were all of Salzburg origin. The scenery, with the very realistic prospect of the seaport and of Neptune's temple, was by our famous theatrical designer, Court Councillor Lorenz Quaglio, and was admired by all." Local pride? Not entirely. Composers and music still had rare mention in the local press. The opera is known to have been a resounding success.

After it, Nannerl and Wolfgang, possibly Leopold as well, thoroughly enjoyed the Munich carnival. It should not be forgotten that, despite the heavy preparatory work for "Idomeneo," Mozart found time to compose in Munich a wind serenade, a quartet, and a Kyrie, as well as several concert arias. This fact is mentioned because otherwise it is not easy to understand why, in letters to his father written later in the year from Vienna, Wolfgang excuses himself for abandoning himself to pleasure after the opera was over. "In Munich . . . I amused myself too much, it is true. Yet I can swear on my honour that until the première of the opera I did not go to the theatre or anywhere except the Cannabichs'. Afterwards I went gay; that was youthful folly for I thought 'Where will you be after this? Back in Salzburg! Enjoy yourself while you can.' . . . Do not worry about the salvation of my soul, best of fathers . . . It is not true that I boasted of eating meat on fast days; what I said was that it did not matter to me, that I thought it no sin because to me fasting means abstinence . . . I attend mass on all Sundays and holy days, and on other days if I have time . . ."

Colloredo's leave of six weeks had become four months when Mozart was summoned to his employer in Vienna, there to be with the other Salzburg musicians and perform to the archbishop's credit. We have tried almost too hard to see Colloredo's point of view in dealing with a servant who drew salary for absence, and we can understand his instructions that Mozart should be quartered in his residence while Brunetti and Ceccarelli could live in Vienna with a lodging allowance. (In any case Mozart thought that the room allotted to him, over-looking St. Stephen's Cathedral, was "charming.") We are now fast approaching the climax of Mozart's relationship with Colloredo – his famous "kicking out." Since other people in Salzburg, not only musicians, detested an ungracious sovereign, we do not take the archbishop's part unduly by commenting that we have *only* Mozart's account of the events before his dismissal, and it is quite possible that they incurred no special harshness towards him that would not have been shown towards another rebellious servant. After all, it was not Colloredo himself who gave the kick, but Count Arco – son of the Count Arco previously mentioned as belonging to a family which had always befriended and admired the Mozarts.

Mozart's first complaints in letters from Vienna can easily make us angry, for we know the great Mozart, not just the Mozart who was still Colloredo's property according to the generally accepted beliefs of the time. He complained that he was fed with the other servants, and that the food was poor, which seems unlikely, for at the same table sat the cooks. He complained that the valets were at the head of the table, and that Brunetti, Ceccarelli, and he had only the cooks between them and the lowermost end. "Stupid, coarse jokes are made, but not with me, for if I have to speak at all I do so with the utmost gravity, and leave as soon as I have finished. At night we do not feed together, but each man receives three ducats, which is a relief." Evidently Mozart's attitude to the "lower" servants was similar to Colloredo's attitude to musicians. He would have known the same conditions at meal times when in Salzburg if his own home had not been there; but it is quite possible that Colloredo's orders for him to be "kept in his place" were deliberate. In fact Mozart did not often take his midday meal as he described. He admits that he was on such good terms with several of the Viennese nobility, especially the Countess Thun, that he was frequently invited to dine in their houses.

Another humiliation to Mozart, but common usage long after his time, was what may be called "ante-chambering." I personally have sometimes thought it worth the fee offered to wait beyond the time of a summons with others to perform – until a servant bade us enter the grand hall or music-room. If we knew that we were kept waiting while vulgarians finished their eating, drinking, or conversing, we could always leave the place and payment. No doubt in later society if one had complained there would have been genuine apologies and the assurance that no humiliation was intended. In feudal society Mozart must certainly have expected "ante-chambering," waiting for the footman or valet to usher him into, say, the emperor's or another prince's presence; but he was also likely to be rewarded for the experience. Why then did he complain? Because he

43. Maria Wilhelmine, Countess Thun. Anonymous oil portrait.

knew himself to be famous. On his tours he had been received as a visiting notability, usually at a concert during which he was treated differently from the locally employed orchestral players. In Vienna, having to go with the archbishop to some grandee's house, he was ranked merely with Brunetti and Ceccarelli, with whom he waited until a lackey bade them enter. His piano-playing, like their singing or violin-playing, redounded only to their master's honour. On at least one occasion, at Prince Galitzin's, he boldly strode straight in and talked with his friend, the prince – "I had forgotten about that pair Ceccarelli and Brunetti . . . hiding behind the orchestra." Colloredo could take no immediate action, but his mean mind could discipline the young upstart by ordering him to attend and perform in his presence on evenings when Mozart had invitations elsewhere, probably well paid.

The archbishop enjoys a reputation for goodness and the honour his servants win for him, and then robs them of their earnings while paying them nothing himself . . . I shall wait and see if I get no money, and if I am not paid I shall go to the archbishop and tell him plainly that he must pay me if I may not earn outside.

The Last Straw

Rightly or wrongly Wolfgang believed that if he had been free to give public and private concerts in Vienna he could have earned during two months the equivalent of his annual salary at Salzburg. It was at this time, early in April 1781, that he first seems carefully to have calculated the financial effect of his desired independence in Vienna. Naturally he hoped to reach the emperor – "I should enjoy going through my opera for him, and then being a good boy and playing fugues, which he so much likes." But his chance to capture the concert-goers of Vienna came when Starzer, president of the Vienna Society of Musicians, asked him to participate in a concert in aid of widows and orphans to which no less than 180 orchestral players were giving their services. The Countess Thun would lend her Stein piano. Colloredo forbade his participation, and though he yielded when pressed by others, knowing how he would be despised if he did not, Mozart was wounded into desperate rebellion. The concert, on April 3, was an enormous personal success for him – his first appearance before the Viennese public and his first at the Kärntnerthor Theatre, which was to be the scene of later triumphs. The programme included the C major symphony, K. 338, played by that magnificent orchestra, as well as Mozart's piano-playing which was such that he "had to start all over again because the applause would not stop." A few days afterwards at the archbishop's residence the works he had composed for Ceccarelli and Brunetti received nothing like the applause accorded to his piano-playing. Colloredo had not paid him any extra fees, and Mozart heard that the emperor had been present at the Thun residence on a night when the performers, whom Mozart had not been allowed to join (because of a concert at the archbishop's residence), received huge fees. He wrote home of his intention to stay in Vienna, for Brunetti had been told by the younger Count Arco, that the servants would "soon be receiving money for the diligence" to Salzburg.

Leopold was afraid, not only for Wolfgang's future but his own, and it is at least to Colloredo's credit that the father seems never to have been reproached for the son's behaviour nor to have been given cause for uneasiness about his own status and emoluments. Mozart was ready to return with the others when Colloredo chose to humiliate him further. Even allowing for the fact that we depend upon the victim's story, there can be little doubt of at least that intention. He knew Mozart to be abnormally gifted but did not know the size of his genius, and even if he had, he found him difficult to deal with, requiring different treatment and assuming a different status from other musicians of the court. How could the *Kapelle* be kept in good spirit and service if one of their number assumed special privileges? The humiliations were intended to lower his self-conceit and ensure that he did not take the very step which he did take. They consisted of forbidding him to give a public concert in Vienna organised by himself and ordering him to take back "an important parcel" with him to Salzburg. Since the rest were going home this last order was not planned with reference to the importance of the parcel but of the proposed carrier.

Was the first order defied? Not directly; but the last concert at the archbishop's residence was on April 27

and Mozart wrote to say that he had much "worry over the arrangements," particularly in "securing a better orchestra than Brunetti." Does this mean that he arrogated to himself Brunetti's task of making "the arrangements" and securing players, presumably to be paid? After the concert he played variations on the piano, the archbishop proposing the theme. He said he "played with fire and inspiration as though nothing were wrong . . . the ladies kept me at the piano a full hour"; and of course there was much applause. "I should still be playing there if I had not stolen away, for I thought I had already done enough for no payment." As for the second order, concerning the parcel, Mozart told the valet that he could not oblige, as he wished to stay a few days in Vienna "to collect money owing to me . . . I have left the residence and am living at my own expense." Nor would he take the valet's advice to say that the mail-coach was already full. He was summoned to his master's presence. All we know of the interview is Mozart's account in a letter of May 9, 1781, which also told his father where he was lodging:

My patience has been so long tried that at last it is exhausted. I am no longer so unfortunate as to be under Salzburg servitude . . . Twice the – I do not know what to call him – has hurled at me the greatest *sottises* and insults . . . I remained silent; you wished it so. A week ago the footman-courier came unexpectedly to my room and said I was to move out without delay. All the others had been given a day's notice, but I was not. So I hastily packed all I had into my bag and old Madame Weber was kind enough to offer to take me in. There I have a pleasant room, and live with kind people who bring me all the things I suddenly need but cannot always have at hand if I live alone.

Then follows the account of the valet's message that Mozart was to take a package with him back to Salzburg for the archbishop, and of the refusal:

Then it all came out in one breath; that I was the most disorderly fellow he knew, that nobody else served him so badly, and that if I did not leave today he would write home to get my stipend stopped. I had no chance to get a word in for he raged on like a fire . . . He lied to my face, saying that my salary was 500 gulden, called me rogue, villain, and conceited fool. Indeed I should not like to put it all down in writing. Finally my blood rose to boiling and I said: "Isn't Your Grace satisfied with me?" "What, do you dare to threaten, you fool? Oh you conceited fool! There's the door; I'll have no more to do with such a wretched scoundrel." Finally I said: "Nor will I have anything more to do with you . . . You will have it in writing tomorrow." . . . As long as the archbishop remains in town I shall not give a concert. You are quite wrong if you fancy that the nobility and the emperor will think the less of me for this. The archbishop is hated here, most of all by the emperor. That is the real reason for his temper – the emperor did not invite him to Laxenburg. I shall send you a little money by the next mail to show that I shall not starve here.

Wolfgang was not too selfish to imagine his father's plight:

> Now my good fortune is beginning, and I hope that it will also be yours. Write to me in code and tell me that you are pleased, for indeed so you ought to be. But condemn me in public so that nobody will think that you are responsible. If the archbishop shows you the slightest insult, bring my sister and join me immediately in Vienna. I can assure you on my honour that all three of us can make a living here. Yet the wisest course would be to endure another year. Do not send any more letters or parcels to the Deutsches Haus [i.e. the palace of the Teutonic knights where Colloredo resided when in Vienna].

Post was to go to "God's Eye" ("Zum Auge Gottes"), No. 11 Petersplatz, and the request deeply offended Leopold. He did not like the Webers . . . theatrical and musical riff-raff, the very sort of people from which he, an educated man, author of a famous book, wished his son to distinguish himself. Aloysia's leading parts and large salary at Munich lasted only one year, for like previous actresses she had outlived Karl Theodor's "interest." She was engaged in Vienna at the theatre which gave German operas and *Singspiele*. As in Munich she secured box-office employment for her father, but he died before Mozart again joined the family. Madame Weber therefore took lodgers. One of them, the actor Joseph Lange, who was a 29-year-old widower, married Aloysia after agreeing to the stipulation that he pay her mother an annual allowance. This arrangement was concealed from Mozart who was naturally not disposed at first to like Aloysia's husband – "Luckily for me he is a jealous fool and will not let her go anywhere, so that I seldom get a sight of her."

Father and son kept up an acrimonious correspondence. In spite of requests not to interfere Leopold sought Count Arco's help towards a return to Salzburg. When on May 10 Wolfgang tried to hand Arco his resignation and the money for his journey to Salzburg, Arco would accept neither, saying that Mozart had a duty to his father, who should be consulted. "I assured him at once that I knew my duty to my father as well as he did, perhaps better."

Mozart worried himself into a feverish state, imagining what might be sent home to his father by Arco, who asked him to call a week or so later. He told the messenger he would not attend without guarantee that the interview would be a calm and friendly one. Arco

44. St. Peter's Church, Vienna, with (second left) the house called "God's Eye" where Mozart lodged with the Webers. Drawn and engraved by Carl Schütz.

45. *Joseph Lange, actor and gifted amateur artist whose portrait of Mozart is among the finest, together with his wife, Aloysia (see also No. 40), Mozart's sister-in-law. Engraving by Daniel Berger, 1785, after a drawing by Lange himself. For Lange's portrait of Mozart see the colour pictorial section "Mozart Portraits" (No. 14).*

received him "with the best manners, and I answered his plausible speeches with the unvarnished truth." Again, however, Arco would not accept the money or the dismissal petition. His wise counsel is faithfully reported by Mozart:

> He said: "Believe me, you are letting yourself be dazzled here. A man's fame does not last long in Vienna. At first you may hear nothing but praise, and earn a good deal of money, but for how long? After a few months the Viennese want novelty." [I said] "It is the archbishop's fault, not mine, that this has happened in Vienna. If he knew how to treat men of talent it would not have happened. Count Arco, I am the most amiable person in the world, provided that people are the same with me." "Well," he said, "the archbishop thinks you insufferably insolent." . . . "Certainly I am towards him, for I do to others as they do to me. When I perceive that someone insults and belittles me I can be as proud as a peacock." Amongst other things he asked if I did not suppose that he also had frequently to swallow harsh words. I shrugged my shoulders and answered: "You must have your reasons for tolerating them; I have mine for not doing so."

By Mozart's own witness Arco was thus very heavily provoked. Negotiating the affairs of Leopold, the archbishop, and Wolfgang was a thankless task. On June 8, 1781 six days after that reported interview, he lost his temper and pushed Mozart out of his presence with a now notorious kick.

> So this is the way to win people over, to soften them up! By refusing from innate stupidity to accept petitions, by not daring to say anything to one's master from cowardice and sycophancy, to keep one on tenterhooks for a month and finally when one is forced to present the petition . . . throwing one out of the door with a kick on the behind. That's the style!

Aged 61, Leopold felt deeply the certain loss of his son, and was terrified at the thought that he might have lost his own security, for Wolfgang wrote threatening reprisals upon Arco:

> I shall soon write to the count telling him what he can expect from me as soon as I am lucky enough to meet him again – never mind where, provided that it is no place where I must show him respect . . . Keep my stick and carry it all the time. Who knows whether in your hands it might not avenge its former owner upon Arco? . . . The heart ennobles a man. Although I am not a count, I have more honour in my heart than has many a count. Lackey or count, whoever insults me is treated by me as a rascal.

Leopold's terrors were groundless. His son might vent his spleen and boost his besetting pride in a letter or two, but he was no longer an intrepid youth. Within a few years he was to know the truth of Arco's comment upon the fickleness of the wider Viennese musical public, but the immediate future saw him happily married and rising to such popular favour in Vienna as few musicians had managed to maintain for a few years, and none for the whole of his active life in that one city, either as performer or composer.

Bachelor Gay

Two superstitions obscure people's conceptions of great artists. One is the belief that they must be admirable and intelligent in all walks of life. The other, its converse or corollary, is the belief that, though they must behave unconventionally and hold revolutionary opinions, they must also be excused such habits as Wagner's helping himself to other people's money and wives. Neither error allows the hero to be abnormal *only* in the powers that made him famous. How can a genius be happy among undistinguished people? How can he be content with a wife and children who do not share his talents? How can he accept the injustices of society without public protest? In short, how in all matters except his art, can he be so much like thousands of other men, common men, of his time and place? If there is any trait in Mozart which shows him to have been made of our common clay, except as an artist, it is the very fear, the distaste shared by a million suburban citizens, of being thought common and not a "cut above" the nearest shopkeeper, clerk, or orchestral player.

These reflections are particularly advisable as we now deal with a Mozart who, at least to the biographer, presents a different figure from that of the dissatisfied youth protected by his father and employed by the Salzburg ruler. The young man who (violently, his family thought) had taken a step towards artistic independence more daring than any taken by Beethoven has, of course, been the victim of the superstitions just mentioned; but he is as poor a captive for superstitious and romantic people, as he is for envious and unpleasant people who would like to prove him a young libertine. Intelligent, but not a great intellectual, we know that he was a sharp private critic not only of arrogance, injustice, and corruption, but also of immorality. Possibly reports of his sharp tongue discredited him, especially since he rarely spoke generously of other musicians; but he is falsified by those who suggest that he anticipated Beethoven's political and social ideals. He was of his own century, within which Pope had written "Whatever is, is right"; the same sentiment was affirmed by the disrespectful Voltaire despite his mockery of it in Candide's refrain "So all must be for the best in the best of all possible worlds." It was Voltaire who declared: "I would rather be governed by one lion of good breeding than by five hundred rats of my own species" – so much for parliamentary government! With neither the mind nor the time for prolonged speculation, Mozart accepted "Establishment" as his father's child, defying it only

63

when it was personally unjust to him; similarly he practised religion, but like his father could speak and write with contempt of its officers when they seemed to him bad ones. It is foolish to deny his ingrained sense of social respectability and superiority, and we can well understand it by comparing his nurture with that of any of the other three classical giants of music associated with Vienna.

Haydn's father was headman of his village, but classifiable as a peasant. He was a flourishing wheelwright for whom prosperity meant income just above a general level of poverty. The Haydns, including the great Haydn, felt no shame in touching the cap to wealthier people as well as to the feudally privileged. No magistrate would call Beethoven's a good home. Schubert's was respectable enough, but maintained by an ill-paid parish schoolmaster who, like Haydn's father, deferred to local clergy and bigwigs and had relatives in domestic service. Mozart's father was educated and class-proud, and his son was just as thin-skinned if his respectability was questioned. His religious punctilio was not the less sincere for being bound up with respectability.

The point is important, for if Mozart had not been restrained by sincere beliefs (whether of religion or family pride or both), what else need have withheld him from casual licentiousness now that he was an "independent" bachelor of some fame in a city well provided for dalliance? During the period of the congresses after Napoleon's downfall Vienna had a bad reputation for venereal disease, but she was then comparable with large seaports, for she catered for international pleasure-seekers and was filled with the lackeys, soldiery, and dependants of a vast number of diplomats, officers, and sight-seers. The belief that in the eighteenth century Vienna was more depraved than other capitals may be based on a false impression of Viennese *Gemütlichkeit* – the natural gaiety and fondness for amusement which was a facet of Mozart's character although he was not born in Vienna. Northern nations, among whose people Bible-reading Protestantism inculcated decorum of speech, could be deceived by the frank coarseness and cynicism of Bavarians and Austrians in otherwise polite conversation, and forget that it was not only confession-going that made most of them shun actions which justified more than teasing accusations of sin. They showed tolerant amusement towards the amours of the feudally privileged, whose marriages were not of their own choice; but most of them regarded overt fornication among their neighbours as matter for contempt or reproach.

A conceited bachelor of distinction was fair game for observation, and Mozart not only knew it but also knew how easily scandal could reach his father. Leopold was less deceived by the reported "kindness" of Madame Weber than was Wolfgang. She had moved to the larger house in a good district especially to take male lodgers to whom she might marry her daughters. Common musicians and theatrical folk came very low in Leopold's

assessment of honesty and respectability. He had once been anxious about his son's games with the "Bäsle" (who later had a bastard child) and wrote with ill-concealed malice that she "had been made happy by a gentleman of the cathedral." Einstein illuminates this phrase by quoting from a travel diary of 1781 – "The freedom of Augsburg citizens is as cheap as the virginity of their daughters, who are bought every year in dozens by the gentlemen of the cathedral." Leopold rubbed in the sting, telling his son that the most admired of his cousin's wedding presents were "from her uncle in Salzburg. What an honour for me!" He did not at heart distrust his son's morality. Jesuit-trained himself, he had the Jesuit assurance of the training and example he gave, and he was probably more pleased than annoyed when Wolfgang angrily answered any serious suggestion that his devotions or morality had become lax; what Leopold feared was his son's innocence and kindness of heart when a woman mothered him and flattered him by suggesting that she needed gallant protection. That, indeed, was Madame Weber's game with her eligible bachelor lodgers. Why did not Wolfgang take the room offered at Dr. Mesmer's house? We shall see that, at the time, Wolfgang needed no welcome to wealthy houses and homes. He visited Mesmer and maintained his friendship, but would not live where one whom he regarded (in true Mozart tradition!) as a musical rival also had a room. This was the Bolognese singer and composer Righini, on one of whose arias Mozart wrote a pleasant set of piano variations.

> I have for some time thought of taking other lodgings, but only because people are gossiping . . . I wonder what pleasure it gives people to chatter without the slightest factual basis. Just because I am living with them I am going to marry the daughter! If ever there was a time of life when I had no intention of marrying it is now . . . God has not given me a talent so that I might hitch it to a wife and drift through young manhood idly . . . I have nothing against matrimony, but just now it would be a misery.

Madame Weber was deliberately stirring up the gossip and had an agent in one Thorwart, an astute lackey who had worked himself up to the post of adviser to the aristocratic intendant of the National Theatre. When Weber died he had become guardian to the widow and her daughters. Did Mozart know that he had better not offend Thorwart if he wanted production in that theatre? He certainly did not know (at the time) of his future mother-in-law's duplicity. He blamed neither her nor Thorwart for the gossip but, being a Mozart, blamed another musician, the opera composer Peter von Winter whom he had marked out as a rival and enemy at Mannheim.

> Certain scandalmongers and swaggerers like Herr Winter must have shouted into his [Thorwart's] ears all sorts of lies about me, though he does not know me – that he should beware of me, that I have

no fixed income, that I am far too intimate with her [Constanze Weber], that I am likely to jilt her and then she will be ruined . . . The mother, who knows I am honourable, lets things take their course. He came to the house and told her to forbid me to associate with her daughter until I made a written contract with *him*.

For a moment we must leave the story of Mozart's growing love for Constanze Weber and the weak answers he sent in reply to fulminations from Salzburg. Leopold was all the more enraged by the dreary course of his son's dealings with the Webers because his prospects in Vienna were so bright as actually to make his determination to break with Salzburg seem wiser than expected. Mozart lodged with the Webers from the beginning of May to the beginning of September, 1781, and then moved to less convenient quarters in the Graben, making daily visits to the Webers when he was not staying with wealthy friends and patrons. During the summer the privileged were away at their country properties, and Mozart's chief concern was to have music ready for the coming season. He finished the Munich serenade, K.361, and had an immediate success with Artaria's publication of six sonatas for clavier and violin. Later in the year Artaria published two sonatas for piano duet, K.381 and K.358, soon to be eclipsed by the sonata for two pianos, K.448.

He rose early to compose, and disliked the interruption on those mornings when he went to a pupil. He frequently went to the theatre at night and wrote home enthusiastically about the high standards of production and acting in Vienna. He explained that he had to take pupils "to make ends meet" until he achieved security, but would accept only one or two and those at high fees.

> It is a basic rule here that you must not be cheap. The boldest are the most respected . . . With only two pupils I am better off than at Salzburg. My fee for 12 lessons is six ducats, and I explain that I teach only as a very special favour.

His first two pupils were the Countess Rumbeck and Josephine Aurnhammer. The latter was already a good player, and her further progress under Mozart made compensation for her pitifully gross appearance. Unfortunately she adored her new teacher and could not resist expression of her passion.

> She took liberties, and tenderly reproached me when I came a little later than usual or could not stay long. I was forced to tell her that I did not want to make a fool of her, but she became even more demonstrative. When she began her nonsense I had to be harsh, but she took my hand and said: "Please do not be angry, dear Mozart. Whatever you say I shall still love you."

This information about Josephine was answer enough to Leopold's wondering why his son did not live with the Aurnhammers, whom the Mozarts evidently already knew, or came to know, during their previous visit to Vienna; for when Leopold reminded Wolfgang to call

upon them he replied that he "did so almost daily." Her mother sent ribbons to Nannerl and asked if she could "be of service" to her. As a performer Josephine must have brought honour to Mozart as well as herself, for her public career lasted at least until 1813, when she was the soloist in Beethoven's third piano concerto. (It is pleasant to record that she made a "good" marriage with a court councillor and that it proved happy.) Her important public début with Mozart was at a concert given in the Aurnhammers' big house in November. An audience which included the Thuns, Count Firmian, and Baron van Swieten heard the first performance of the new sonata in D for two pianos and also the two-piano concerto in E flat, which was given again in May, 1782, in the Augarten, a public park with a concert pavilion (now the national porcelain factory) and the Viennese counterpart to London's Vauxhall Gardens.

During the summer and autumn of 1781 Mozart's mind was most occupied with a German opera, "Die Entführung aus dem Serail," which he hoped to have ready by the end of the year. We have already pointed out that German operettas and more ambitious, opera-like *Singspiele* were encouraged by the emperor, and Mozart must have imagined the pleasure of securing an imperial appointment by the very sort of work he most wanted to compose; but he had little chance of high appointment while the Italian composer Antonio Salieri, made imperial *Kapellmeister* in 1788, remained in favour, and that excellent courtier outlived Mozart. Needless to say the story that Salieri poisoned Mozart, used as the plot of an opera by Rimsky-Korsakov, is without foundation. It is more important to stress the fact that Gluck seems to have shown Mozart admiration and friendship, for undoubtedly it was his recommendation which ultimately brought "Die Entführung" to production in 1782. The work (commonly called "The Seraglio" in English but more properly translated as "The Elopement from the Harem") was to a libretto by Gottlieb Stephanie, an actor and official at the Burgtheater, and it proved an enormous popular success.

After swiftly finishing the first act Mozart took an unusually long time with the rest, for 1781 was full of distractions other than his courtship of Constanze. During the summer he enjoyed the welcome to a country villa outside Vienna extended to him by Count Cobenzl, diplomat, intellectual, scientist, and music-lover who had first known Mozart as a boy prodigy. Wolfgang was so delighted with the grounds which Cobenzl had laid out "in English style," and was so charmed with a "natural grotto," that he continued his first visit for a week. November and December brought news from the court itself. Two notable visitors were expected with their families and retinue, the Duke of Württemberg and a Russian grand duke. Princess Elisabeth of Württemberg was being brought to Vienna to finish her education as bride-elect of the Archduke Franz who became emperor but at the time was aged only 13 and in Italy with his tutors. Mozart's friends arranged a concert which might recommend him as piano teacher to the princess. The emperor probably considered nobody else for the appointment than Salieri, but he had to entertain his guests, and he invited Mozart to court on Christmas Eve for a piano-playing contest with Muzio Clementi, who was four years older than Mozart and probably the more virtuosic technician as distinct from the greater musician. He had not previously been in Vienna, and was at the height of his powers when the two were matched. His pupil Ludwig Berger received his reports of Mozart.

> Entering the music-room I found there a man whose elegant attire made me think that he was one of the imperial chamberlains; but we had no sooner begun conversing than he turned to musical topics, and we soon recognised each other, with the utmost cordiality, as colleagues . . . I have never before heard anyone play with such intelligence and grace. I was particularly overwhelmed by an *adagio* and by several of his extempore variations for which the emperor had chosen the theme, and which we were to devise alternately.

Clementi was generous concerning Mozart. The generosity was not mutual, even allowing for the fact that we are quoting from words written to Salzburg.

> He is a fine pianist but that is all. He has great control of the right hand. His strongest point is playing passages in thirds. Beyond this he has not the least feeling; he is a mere *mecanicus*.

The thought of Clementi's virtuosity rankled. After perusing Clementi's sonatas Mozart wrote to Leopold:

> All who hear or play them must feel that they are worthless. They have no original or noteworthy passages except the sixths and octaves . . . and I beg my sister not to practise them too much and spoil her quiet, even touch, so that her hand loses its natural lightness, flexibility, and smooth velocity.

46. The "Reisenberg" (later called "Cobenzl"), estate of Count Cobenzl, in the Vienna Woods. Mozart stayed there in 1781. Lithograph by Johann Josef Schindler after a drawing by Christiane Luise Hummel.

For what is to be gained? Suppose you manage sixths and octaves with the utmost speed (which nobody, not even Clementi, manages to do), you merely produce a nasty chopping effect and nothing at all else. Like all Italians, Clementi is a charlatan. He writes *Presto* or even *Prestissimo* with *Alla breve* over a sonata, and then plays it himself *Allegro* and 4/4. I know this because I have heard him do it. What he does really well are passages in thirds, but he sweated over them day and night in London. Apart from that he can do nothing, absolutely nothing, for he has not the slightest taste or expression, let alone feeling.

Mozart stretching the truth to calm his father, even Mozart indulging in a little boasting – these are more pardonable than the petty spite which, in that letter to Leopold, shows how fear can make a great artist into a small critic, unable to recognise truth or unwilling to acknowledge it. According to Mozart's friend Giuseppe Bridi, the emperor laid a wager with the grand duchess that Mozart would be accorded the greater honour, and won his wager; but the composer Dittersdorf, who witnessed the contest, does not mention this, nor does he suggest that either player was named victor but that the competition was enjoyed for its own sake.

Mozart did not think much of the palace instruments, and therefore borrowed the Countess Thun's Stein! On this he played his own solo pieces, but the emperor told him to use one of the others for two-piano playing and the "variations" competition, saying "That doesn't matter" to Mozart's complaint that it was not in tune and that dampers might stick. (Surely we can see from this why Mozart was not, though admired, suddenly given an appointment to deal with other musicians.)

Mozart declared that the contest with Clementi brought him "more than half my Salzburg annual salary" and, although public concerts he gave in March and May 1782 were not very profitable, his financial prospects remained good. Artaria paid him better than most publishers of the day, and he took on a few more pupils. They included the Countesses Pálffy and Zichy and, rather more interesting, Frau Maria von Trattner. One of the sights of Vienna was Trattner's paper mill and book-producing factory, the whole called "Trattner's Typographical Palace." Still more astounding, however, was the "Trattnerhof," the bookseller's huge residence with its marble corridors and palatial music-room. The Trattners proved to be generous supporters of Mozart's concerts, but at first Mozart wrote slightingly of the lady, still very young, whom the widower Trattner married when he was nearly 60.

> At 10 I give Frau von Trattner her lesson; at 11 Countess Rumbeck . . . I go to them every day unless they send word for me not to come, which is not very convenient for me. I have arranged with the countess that she need not send word; if I find she is not at home I get paid for the lesson in any case, but the Trattnerin is much too mean for that.

In the same letter Mozart actually speaks of dining with noble patrons and participating in concerts as though he resented the inroads made on the time he had for composition. Early in 1782 he increased his teaching fees:

> I no longer count [fees] for 12 lessons, but [charge] for a month, having learnt to my cost that the ladies often miss their lessons for weeks at a time. Now they will have to pay six ducats whether they use me or not. [The former charge was six ducats for 12 lessons.]

Mozart Married

It is often supposed that all great artists' nerves are sensitive to stress in matters which do not directly concern their main ambition, and that their lives are easily wrecked by mental distress. Mozart produced the crowning glories of his instrumental music against a background of mortal physical illness and financial calamity, still worse against the knowledge that he had not yet secured for most of his music the public response that greeted "The Magic Flute." The circumstances of his marriage also provide an example of his tough nervous constitution and his ability to concentrate under what are now called pressures. The most distracting weeks that troubled his courtship of Constanze Weber came during the final preparations for the production of "The Seraglio," and the wedding took place just after its triumph in July. Though not a grand affair, the marriage was solemnised in St. Stephen's Cathedral on August 4, 1782, and followed by a "supper given by Baroness Waldstädten which was more princely than baronial."

The baroness, a fine pianist and great music-lover, played a part in the sordid manœuvres that preceded the wedding. Thorwart, as we have recorded, forbade Mozart to visit Constanze unless he signed an agreement with him.

> I therefore put my name to a document binding me to marry Mademoiselle Constanze Weber within three years; and if the impossible occurred and I changed my mind she would have the right to receive 300 gulden from me every year.

Thus Madame Weber thought she would benefit financially from Mozart by one means or another, but her trap merely wounded her prey. First Constanze tore up the document in Mozart's presence soon after Thorwart had secured the signature. Then, as Mozart wrote in a letter of January 30, having already become "aware of the mother's designs," the couple would not be lured into sharing the comforts of her home with its two claviers and spacious rooms.

> Madame Weber will find herself sadly mistaken, for she expected us to live with her. [On April 10:] She is more fond of the bottle than a woman should be . . . I intend to extricate Constanze from such a life.

She needed no extricating, for after Mozart left the Weber house so did she. In November–December 1781 she stayed for a month with Baroness Waldstädten. In April she moved in with the baroness, and thereby increased the Weber–Thorwart pressure on Mozart. As far as he dared, Thorwart suggested that the baroness would lead Constanze into evil ways, and Mozart's credulity could be played upon because of an incident during a game of forfeits that caused a short quarrel between the lovers.

> You were so shameless and bold as to tell your sisters in front of me that you let a young gallant measure the calves of your legs. No woman who cares for her honour does a thing like that . . . If the baroness allowed it to be done to her, that is quite another matter, for she is an old woman who can no longer entice men. Besides she is all too fond of you-know-what, and I should hope, my darling, that you would not want to pursue a life like hers even if you decided not to be my wife. If you could not resist the temptation to join in what the others were doing . . . you could have taken the tape and measured your own calves, as decent women have done in similar circumstances when I have been present.

The baroness was the subject of scandal because she was separated from her husband, though whether he or she was originally the aggrieved partner is not known. In the middle of the performances of "The Seraglio" Mozart wrote a letter to the baroness, telling her that Madame Weber's maid had brought alarming news from Sophie Weber, who had said: "Tell Mozart to send Constanze home at once, for my mother is determined to have her fetched by the police." He asked if the police were allowed to walk into houses in Vienna, or if this were a trick to make the girl return.

> If the threat were acted upon I could have no better way of foiling it than by marrying Constanze to-morrow morning – today if possible. For I should not wish to leave my beloved exposed to disgrace, and no such harm could reach her if she were my wife . . . The Webers have sent for Thorwart. I beg your ladyship to advise and help us poor creatures . . . I kiss your hands a thousand times and remain ever your most grateful servant . . . Constanze does not know about this yet. Has Thorwart called on your ladyship? Ought the two of us to go and see him after dinner?

Mozart's father caused extra anxiety; in fact, his blessing did not arrive until the marriage had been celebrated, though in desperation Mozart would have proceeded even if he had thought it would not be forthcoming. We have made little reference to the many pages of moralising and oblique recrimination that came from Salzburg during 1781–82, or to the excuses, protests, and endearments sent in return from Vienna. From early in 1782 Leopold could not disregard reports from his many musical acquaintances in the capital about his

47. *Maria Cäcilia Weber, Mozart's mother-in-law. Anonymous silhouette.*

son's growing repute with the "right people"; and some letters suggest that he was prepared to bow to the inevitable marriage with a Weber. But his pride was like his son's, and he worried Wolfgang by evading any direct mention of Constanze by name or the engagement; instead he taunted his son about his way of life in general, and roused him to anger by mentioning the state of his "immortal soul."

An extract from one of Mozart's replies is worth comment. As much as other epochs the eighteenth century idealised romantic love, but it knew how much common sense and animal spirits were powerful in *eros pandemos*; only the healthy fruit produced the romantic bloom. The prudery which became fashionable in the following century was as effective as coarseness in preventing love's young dream from being real and lasting. In Mozart's day, and particularly in the south-German states, the parents and friends of young people recognised two conditions of happy marriage – that the partners were mutually lustful, and that they were "suited," i.e. able to tolerate each other's company even if they lacked room and opportunity for separate pursuits. (Since many civilised people find irritating the continual presence of another person in the same room, probably the second condition is the more dangerous to disregard.) Prudishness does not originate in choice of words but in the suppression of ideas behind words, a wilful blindness to fact. In the eighteenth century, and in coarse Austria, choice of words was a mark of refinement as it has been at most times and in most places. It enabled Leopold to despise the Webers even on reading Constanze's letters with their vulgar expressions and misspellings. Asked to take more food, the man of "taste" did not say: "No; I'm full," but his eating and drinking of his fill were not impolite, as in Victorian times when (of all stupidities!) it was polite to leave so-much soup or other food uneaten. Today's foolish habit is to relish an accepted number of formerly banned words with the immaturity of school-children while retaining much prudery of thought; whereas Mozart could write thus to his father:

> Nature speaks as loudly in me as in any man, per-haps more forcefully than in many a big, strong oaf. Yet I find myself unable to go on as most young men do nowadays. First I have religious scruples and too much respect for my neighbour, too strong a code of honour to seduce a girl; then I am too horrified, disgusted, and afraid of diseases, and too concerned for my health to run after whores. Therefore I can swear that I have never taken a woman in that way.

Much in the same letter seems cynically practical to us after a century and a half during which writers of poems, plays, novels, and operas have inclined us to equate the love that makes "happy ever after" with an irresistible "love at first sight," which makes lovers incapable either of the circumspection of good sense or of physical passion, except in a kind of ecstasy during which Heaven makes them incorporeal!

> I, who from infancy have never been accustomed to look after my linen, clothes, and other possessions, can think of nothing more needed than a wife . . . Constanze, the middle one, is the martyr among them [the Weber girls] and perhaps for that very reason the gentlest, cleverest, and best of them. She takes care of everything in the house, yet they blame her for whatever goes wrong . . . She is not ugly, but by no means a beauty. Her beauty consists in two small black eyes and a pretty figure. She is not witty, but has enough sheer intelligence to fulfil well her duties as a wife and mother. She is not given to extravagance – that accusation is a lie. On the contrary she is accustomed to going plainly dressed, for whatever the mother has managed to do for her children has been spent on the other two rather than Constanze. It is true that she would like to be neat and well dressed, though not according to the latest fashion. Most of the clothes a woman needs she can make for herself. She does her own hair every day, is a good housekeeper, and has the kindest heart.

This does not seem like a character sketch written only to make his father think well of his future wife, but like a frank (to us ungallantly frank) picture of Constanze as she might seem to anyone *not* in love with her. He was 26; she was 19. They were to know only nine years of life together, half of them clouded by increasing anxiety and ill health; yet there is no reason to suppose that Mozart's would not have remained a happy marriage if he had lived for another 26 years or more. The lives of modern artists and intellectuals prove fallacious the belief that such people cannot live happily together unless one partner approaches the other in artistic or intellectual stature; and they also prove fallacious any guarantee of happiness when both partners are distinguished painters, writers, musicians, and so on. Parity of intellect or com-mon artistic interest *may* be an important factor in some happy partnerships; but most of them still depend upon the common-sense criteria of the eighteenth century. Mozart and Constanze evidently fulfilled each other's natural passions, enjoyed the giving and taking of love, and were "suited" – could enjoy, not merely endure, their own company in small houses and lodgings, even with the encumbrance of children. Not one woman in a million could have measured Mozart's full capacity, even for love, but Mozart and Constanze had rather more in common than most partners.

Not only did Mozart find women attractive; many women found him so. Indefinable vitality or artistic gifts have enabled seemingly dull and ugly men to fasci-nate women, and Mozart was neither ugly nor taciturn except when defiant. He was small and lithe, capable of showing sudden animation even when his appearance showed the effects of increasing bad health. His engage-ments and pleasures kept him up to all hours and his feeding was irregular – a period of frugality followed by a day or so of extravagant celebration or an invitation to fine company. He had asked his father to comfort a girl in Salzburg who pursued him. She would hardly have done so if, without telling his father, he had not en-couraged her, either for the pleasure of being admired or because playing with fire was attractive. Among the young ladies to whom he gave lessons only Josephine Aurnhammer is mentioned as one whose advances he firmly rejected.

Just after Mozart's death the "Hofdemel affair" pro-vided a feast for Vienna scandalmongers. Mozart was piano teacher to the wife of a brother Freemason, a court official called Hofdemel, who attacked and wounded her with a razor and then killed himself. It was presumed that the crime was prompted by insane jealousy, but no lover was mentioned. When, however, she had returned to her father's home with a pension from the emperor, she gave birth to a son whose first name was Johann, as also was Mozart's. We do not know to what extent among people of good sense any suspicion fell upon Mozart, but over a year after his death one of the obituaries, by a schoolmaster of Gotha, Friedrich Schlichtegroll, con-tained the following:

> In Vienna he married Constanze Weber and found her a good mother for the two children she bore him (others died in infancy) and an excellent wife who sought to restrain him from his many follies and dissipations.

Now the German words *Torheiten* and *Ausschweifungen* no

48. Constanze Mozart, born Weber. From a lithograph (after an anonymous oil portrait, 1783) published in 1828 in the Mozart biography written by her second husband George Nikolaus Nissen. (See also the colour pictorial section "The Family Circle" Nos. 21–24.)

more definitely convey a meaning of *sexual* indulgence than do the English "follies" and "dissipations"; like the English words they may euphemistically indicate debauchery or take their literal meaning of scattering and wastefulness. (After all Mozart had not concentrated upon the one most esteemed goal – a notable public office.) Many biographers have therefore supposed that there were in Mozart's life liaisons of which we know nothing but, in view of that sentence from Schlichtegroll's necrology, Constanze knew at least something.

Here that suggestion is repudiated, although we have judged Mozart censoriously enough to offend his thurifers. Then why should we take the trouble to declare a belief that he did not overstep a proverbial line which has tantalised most artists? Especially now, when many people do not regard chastity as admirable, why should we vindicate the "fidelity" (in the mere legal and technical sense) of a husband who must frequently have declared before his confessor an indulgence which stopped only short of seduction? Not presenting him as a "better" man than he was according to certain canons of conduct, nor supposing that a musical perfectionist (which he was in all conscience!) necessarily applies his high artistic standards to other activities, we must assert that Mozart was more of an idealist than most nineteenth-century artists who professed and talked about idealism in a way which he would have satirised. We are concerned with the *fact* of idealism, not our approval or disapproval of its motives, which may have been fear, pride, or superstition. Neither his Catholicism nor his Freemasonry were merely fashionable: he took them very seriously and intensely, as he did his right to social respect. He was fastidious in matters of dress and toilet, and spoke scornfully of some musicians with whom he gave a concert and who asked for a certain fee with a "suit of clothes." It was "a beggarly request." In the last days of actual poverty the externals of decency – idealism in symbol – were maintained, down to the laundering and starching of cuffs and cravats. Most certainly Mozart upheld an ideal of marital fidelity and checked philandering, though he may have indulged in the game beyond limits approved by his father.

He was anxious about Constanze's possible flirtations during his lengthy absences when operas were in production away from Vienna. In a letter from Dresden of April 16, 1789, he begs his "dear little wife" to take care of her health. He particularly advises her

> not to go out walking alone, preferably not to go out walking at all, and to feel absolutely certain of my love; for I have never yet sent you a single letter without putting your beloved portrait in front of me. I do beg you in all your deportment to watch your honour and mine, and to have proper regard for appearances. Do not be angry at me for saying this. You should love me all the more for so treasuring our reputation.

In the year of his death when the doctor had ordered Constanze to take the cure at Baden-bei-Wien Mozart begged her to avoid the casino.

> *Primo* the company there is – well, you know – and *secondo* you can't dance in your present condition. As for just looking on . . .? You can do that better when your little husband is with you.

No doubt they were mutually indulgent and gay creatures, and naturally could not help wondering how the one would avoid sources of gaiety when the other was absent. We lack letters from Constanze like those we have mentioned from her husband. If she were seriously anxious about her husband's gallantry she must have been suspicious about his relationship with Nancy Storace, the first Susanna in "The Marriage of Figaro," who was a beautiful and vivacious young woman as well as a magnificent singer. Her brother Stephen was one of Mozart's composition pupils, and later made a fortune in London with stage works, chiefly for Drury Lane. During 1784, while she was in Vienna, Nancy Storace married an Oxford doctor of music called Fisher – a fact which tends to discredit the story that Mozart and she were lovers during the preceding period. (Fisher treated her so badly that she left him within a year of marrying him, and the affair was not generally known in England because Fisher was banished by the emperor.) The sole basis of suspicion that Mozart and she were lovers seems to be the fact that he composed for her a splendid scena and aria, "Ch'io mi scordi di te," which is not simply for voice and orchestra but has a piano part which makes dialogue with the voice. Moreover in Mozart's manuscript catalogue this work is entered as "For Signora Storace and me." He did not compose such a work for Constanze, nor did he seek concert engagements for her, for she was not a great singer nor ever claimed to be. If Mozart envisaged an alliance with Nancy Storace as a wonderful thing beyond fruition he is hardly to be blamed; but we have no right to suppose that he sampled it temporarily and furtively.

Constanze's words to Vincent Novello ring true. She and her first husband understood one another at the level required for other matters than his art, of which she knew only enough to encourage his interest in fugues, which happened to tickle her ears. It is rather silly to complain that she was no Egeria, no ideal confidante of his artistic ideals. What bores, what jealous nuisances have been women who pretended fully to understand great artists! She must have been relieved and happy in her marriage. The child-bearing, the ups and downs of income, the miserable time just before and during Mozart's last illness – all these must be weighed against her enjoyment of genuine and permanent affection, her consciousness of social status, and her knowledge that her husband was a great man, even if not by 35 a wholly successful one. She came from a musical and theatrical family and knew enough about music and musicians to know what a rare talent Mozart's was. To know that it was not necessary to understand all his music. The marriage was a happy one, despite its limitations.

The married Mozarts changed their houses as often as the unmarried Beethoven. In general, but not always, they moved to grander or humbler apartments according to the state of their finances; but their occupying a flat or a separate house was not directly related to their fortunes. Part of one floor in a fashionable part of Vienna would cost more than a whole house on the outskirts. In Mozart's Vienna, as in Bath, and as in parts of London in the eighteenth century, some of the best houses were occupied by more than one family. Normally the finest rooms were not at ground level but on the first floor, and they were often occupied by members of the nobility who had estates outside Vienna, while their attachés and chief servants had rooms below or above them. The humblest, and in winter the coldest rooms were the attics; the rooms just below the attics were often let to commercial and middle-class professional people.

These customs were useful to ambitious young men who needed favour from their social superiors and could approach employees if not their masters or mistresses. It will be remembered that Haydn's fortunes began to rise as soon as the cruelly impoverished young man took an attic in the old Michaelerhaus in Vienna. Among the lodgers below him there was on the third floor no less famous a person than the Abbate Metastasio, imperial poet laureate, while occupying the whole of the first floor was an even more useful person to Haydn, the Dowager Princess Esterházy, whose sons Haydn served for most of his brilliant career.

The newlyweds took second-floor apartments in the Wipplingerstrasse. The Mozart family had stayed in that part of the city, and it gave Wolfgang great pleasure to go with Constanze to the church of the Theatines "... I have never prayed so fervently nor confessed and communicated so devoutly as with her."

The second of two duty visits to the Webers ended in quarrels and tears – we may suppose because the Mozarts refused to become lodgers. Only on such an occasion as her birthday was Mme. Weber to see them again. By the end of 1782 they had already moved farther down the Wipplingerstrasse to a third-floor flat owned by Baron Wetzlar, who was also a music-lover. Mozart wrote to his father of "fine big rooms" with two big empty ones next to theirs. When we consider both Mozart's actual earnings during the first six months of his marriage, which were considerably more than six months' salary at Salzburg, and also his bright prospects, we cannot fail to deplore his optimistic improvidence. He was already borrowing money early in 1783. To judge by the Novellos' impression of Constanze when she had been twice widowed we must imagine her to have possessed some of the qualities of a good housewife which Wolfgang had claimed for her in letters to his father; perhaps she learnt them in the school of misfortune while

49. *Ann (Nancy) Storace. Drawing and engraving by Pietro Bettelini, 1788.*

married to Mozart, for she sold his manuscripts after his death with Beethovenian shrewdness; or perhaps she was acting under very good advice then, and did not run her house well until finances were under Nissen's steady control. Certainly the Mozarts seem to have lived in a hand-to-mouth way. We can reach no other conclusion as we compare Haydn's or Beethoven's early days in Vienna with Mozart's. He was already a "name" and knew plenty of the "right" people, including the emperor himself. We may be certain that his pride kept any borrowing strictly private and that many would have relieved his ultimate straits if they had known of them. Haydn wept at hearing of them.

It is not suggested that he or his wife was wickedly extravagant but that he himself would not or could not adopt a standard of life or appearances lower than his father's. It cannot be stressed too often that in practice Mozart was the social revolutionary of the great Viennese "four." Not for him the domestic or public style of the orchestral player or servant musician! By today's arrangements for composers and performers his assets would have risen consistently during his first three years in Vienna, reaching nothing short of affluence after the production of "Figaro"; and he would have received large fees from the many south and north-German theatres which mounted "The Seraglio." Had he been more like Beethoven he would have declined participation in concerts unless promised payment related to profits. Since he gained most by concerts promoted by himself, we must wonder why he was so willing to play (or let his works be played) for small payments or none. It may be that he could not resist public admiration or the sheer pleasure of spending his evenings making music; but a mystery remains – that he found time for the composition of the great works of 1784 onwards. He may actually have enjoyed taking composition pupils like Storace and Attwood, who lodged in his home; but he disliked wasting a morning walking to the houses of aristocratic young ladies to give them piano lessons – yet he was forced to go on with this teaching and even expand it during his years of triumph.

Just after the wedding Leopold wrote to Baroness Waldstädten thanking her for providing the feast. He said he was "the victim" of his son's conduct, which left him "no choice" but to send his paternal blessing and hope it would "operate to his benefit." He would "implore God not to deny the grace so conveyed." What effect the letter had, or was intended to have upon the baroness we do not know. It is mentioned because it includes a description of Wolfgang's character which might well apply to most of us, but may be more shrewd than we suppose.

> He is too patient and inert, too easy-going, or too haughty. In him is a divergence of tendencies that makes a man idle and indecisive, while on the other hand he can be rash and impatient, unable to wait. He is dominated by extremes – either too much or too little.

Leopold and Nannerl had reason to regard as inconsiderate the long delay of the promised visit of the young couple to Salzburg. The first excuse was a revival of "The Seraglio" in October for the entertainment of royal visitors, then the return of wealthy pupils from their country estates, then miserable weather, and finally Constanze's pregnancy. Yet the Mozarts found time and money to keep carnival (and write home to Salzburg for costumes!) and to give a ball in their own house, using the two big empty rooms for dancing. (Yes, they were extravagant!) Before the first child was born in June they had again twice moved lodgings, first into "wretched" rooms in the Kohlmarkt, though Wetzlar paid the rent and the moving expenses, and then to the Judenplatz. (Obviously Wetzlar was under an obligation to them for letting him accommodate some wealthy or important people in their former quarters.) Mozart had already told his father that the child would be called Leopold or Leopoldine according to its sex, but when the baby turned out to be a boy "Baron Wetzlar offered to be its godfather . . . and said 'Ah, now you have a Raimund!' so what could I have done?" It was baptised Raimund Leopold.

However disorderly Mozart's diary of meals and engagements during his wife's pregnancy and concern with the new-born child, independence and freedom had the effect he predicted upon his composition. By the end of 1782 he had written the first of the great six quartets dedicated to Haydn. The detachment from circumstances that was possible during his concentration on composition has unwarrantably been called callous, because it is known that the second of the "Haydn" quartets (which many regard as the finest) was engaging

him during Constanze's labour and that he finished the minuet during the actual moments of his son's birth.

Mozart admitted that these quartets incurred enormous work. They were certainly not written to please immediate listeners or to make money as were the three piano concertos and a horn concerto finished before the winter was out. Hence the gap between December 1782 and June 17, 1783, separating the completion of the first two quartets of the famous set. The piano concertos, K.413–415, were for his own "academies" (for some years a pretentious name for "concerts," for it was not applied merely to historical or serious concerts). In the spring of 1783 Mozart arranged with Artaria for their publication by subscription at a price which Leopold thought too high. Leopold was right, for Mozart had to borrow money to pay Artaria for the printing, and when subscriptions were not forthcoming fast enough he had to implore Baroness Waldstädten to help "so that I do not lose my honour and good name." Then, however, Artaria brought out the edition and made a profit!

Mozart initiated his greatest triumphs in the concert room from the beginning of 1783. Three notable concerts swept him to popularity during March, the last two of which were attended by the court. The first, on March 11, was sponsored by Aloysia Lange in "the theatre," probably the Kärntnerthor. Mozart directed his "Paris" Symphony and played his Salzburg D major piano concerto, K.175, with its Vienna finale, the Rondo, K.382.

> The theatre was very full . . . I had already left the stage but the applause would not stop, and I had to repeat the rondo. There was a veritable storm of clapping . . . Gluck occupied the box next to the Langes, in which my wife also sat. He could not find enough praise for the symphony and aria, and invited all four of us [the Langes and the Mozarts] to dinner with him next Sunday.

The aria, sung by Aloysia, was "Non so d'onde viene," K.294. On the 23rd came Mozart's own concert at which Vienna first heard two of the new concertos.

> The theatre could not possibly have been more full, and all the boxes were taken. What pleased me most was that His Majesty was there, and how pleased he was, and how he applauded me! His habit is to send the money to the office before he comes to the theatre, otherwise I could have expected much more, for he was extremely delighted. He sent 25 ducats. [Mozart was mistaken. The emperor was quite parsimonious!]

On March 30 Mozart played "at Therese Teyber's concert" and the concerto K.415 was given again. Mozart was expected to repeat the rondo after the shouts of "encore," but

> I had the desk removed so that I could play solo. You should have heard how this surprise delighted the audience . . . The emperor listened until I had finished and then left his box; so he must have stayed only to hear me.

50. View of "The Pulpit," on the estate of Mozart's patron Prince Galitzin. Drawing by Johann Ziegler.

Among patrons who sought Mozart's services for "academies" were Baron van Swieten and Prince Galitzin. Galitzin engaged Mozart to play at all his concerts in the forthcoming season. He was "always fetched and returned in his carriage and most generously treated"; but does that mean well paid? Even by London standards of the period the few fees Mozart mentions for playing at concerts not run by himself lead us to suppose that some of the Viennese noble music-lovers gave Mozart the pleasure his pride most coveted – accepted his fastidious dress and manner as that of a "superior person" (as he would have been called in a Victorian novel) and therefore one who gave music for love of it and for its occasions in fine houses. This does not mean that he received no financial reward, but that he received too little and not promptly, not on a business basis of so-much money for so-much time or so-much music. If Mozart ever had the good sense to come to business terms his letters do not mention the fact. Instead they merely complain that, for instance, Van Swieten is stingy. Handel lost no dignity in "talking business" and Beethoven had little to lose; obviously Mozart could not or would not do so.

It was at Galitzin's, however, that the theatre intendant Count Rosenberg set up in his mind the train of thought that ultimately led to the composition of "Figaro." Rosenberg asked him why he did not attempt an Italian *opera buffa*. An excellent company had temporarily drawn attention away from German opera. It counted among its members two future friends of Mozart to whom we have already been introduced – the *prima donna* Nancy Storace, of Italian parentage though born in London, and the Irish tenor Michael Kelly, whose "Reminiscences" have already been quoted. The company arrived during 1783 and was largely responsible for the success of *opera buffa* in Vienna and for Mozart's anxiety to take Rosenberg's advice. He wrote to Italy for libretti but found none that appealed to him. He then thought of Varesco, and so had an extra inducement to make finally the visit to Salzburg that Leopold still irritably awaited.

Visit to Salzburg

The young people arrived in Salzburg on July 30, 1783, and stayed three months. Mozart saw Varesco but the dealings with him are best discussed later. Leopold was at least convinced that his son's prospects in Vienna were as bright as he had hoped, but he still thought Wolfgang would have the sense to watch his chances of an official appointment. (He did; but at the time he boasted that if someone else offered more than the emperor himself he would not take the emperor's offer.) The train of Leopold's thought was evident soon after Wolfgang's marriage. While the nobility were away in the country and the dazzling engagements were few, Mozart had considered the prospect of trying his fortune in Paris or London, and Leopold wrote at once to Baroness Waldstädten begging her to restrain him. Both Gluck and Giuseppe Bonno, the imperial *Kapellmeister*, were old men; no doubt Salieri would replace one or both; then who would replace Salieri? After all the emperor had often enough called "Bravo!" for Mozart's playing and music. Thus by the summer of 1783 father and son were less likely to bicker than they would have been if the visit to Salzburg had been earlier. The old man was anxious to show off his son, for his fame was known in Salzburg. Mozart had never received written notice of his dismissal by Colloredo and imagined, even in the year of his visit, that the lack of an official discharge was a deliberate means of "catching" him (the word is used in a letter of May 21) if he came within the territory ruled by the archbishop. Leopold could reassure him on the matter. Colloredo did not stoop so low either to favour or to victimise a servant. His pride forbade.

Yet because he still lacked imagination in the treatment of his musicians, we have two superb pieces from Mozart. They had been commissioned from Michael Haydn at a time when he was unwell – two duets for violin and viola without accompaniment. When Haydn asked for an extension of time he was told to obey orders exactly or "take the consequences." Mozart went to Haydn's house below the castle and wrote them for him, a kindness pleasant to record and never forgotten by Haydn, who would not part with the manuscripts. These two works by Mozart outshine anything of their class and it is a pity that they are not as well known as they deserve to be.

Nor, indeed, is Mozart's grandest and most exacting piece of choral composition, the C minor Mass. It was never quite finished, and it is hard to guess why. In a letter dated January 4, 1783 he reiterated his intention to have a new mass composed for performance in Salzburg when he brought Constanze there, and he mentioned "the score of half of it" as being at hand to show that his promise was serious. When he arrived he had finished only a few items of the long Credo, and no clear proof has yet been forthcoming to support the accusation that he finished it from movements in earlier works. It was his original intention that Constanze should sing the soprano solos, and tradition has it that, in fact, she did so. The work was not given in the cathedral, which of course was the archbishop's church, but in the equally large and fine St. Peter's on August 25.

While in Salzburg Mozart also met Maria Theresa Paradis, a pianist, singer, and composer who was on a concert tour with her mother, for she was blind from birth. She was the daughter of a Viennese court councillor and took her Christian names from the empress who was her godmother and gave her an annual allow-ance. As her father was Paradies we are not sure why she spelt her name "Paradis" – possibly because she was so highly applauded in Paris. It is believed that she asked Mozart to compose a piano concerto for her, and that he complied, the one being K.456 in B flat; but there is no evidence that he ever heard her play it or that she did so.

The young Mozarts left Salzburg on October 27. At Lambach, where the abbot wanted Wolfgang to play the organ, he was waylaid by one of old Count Thun's sons who had been sent to await him and bring him to the palace at Linz. The count hoped that he would participate in a concert on November 4 and that he would have a symphony with him. He had not, but while enjoying the count's hospitality he was able to compose a new one in a few days. It shows no sign of haste. He could have omitted a minuet or a slow introduction, as in his previous symphony, but the "Linz," in C major, K.425, has both and is of excellent quality throughout.

Arriving home in Vienna the Mozarts were shocked to hear that their baby, originally described as "a plump healthy boy," had been dead for nearly three months. The diagnosis of dysentery covers the real cause, which we have already touched upon – the crass stupidity of the age towards babies and its appalling standards of hygiene. The rocketing increase in population which now alarms us came only in the second half of the nineteenth century. The century that so exalted Nature lacked the intelligence to connect the hardy survival of farm animals with natural feeding. At least Mozart put the baby out to be wet-nursed instead of bringing it up on honeyed water at home or, while they were in Salzburg, entrusting it to Mme. Weber; but the conditions in which it was kept with other little brats in some filthy Vienna suburb we can but guess. Royal babies were treated no more sensibly.

The Concert Round

Immediately after his return from Salzburg Mozart was absorbed with the Vienna concerts which led to the two peak years of his incredible public activity and understandable popularity. Van Swieten had been impatient for his return; so had Counts Pálffy and Esterházy and Prince Galitzin. Early in 1784 Leopold forwarded to Vienna the score of "Idomeneo," which would be needed during Lent when his son intended to give six subscription concerts "as well as my concert in the theatre." On January 23 the Mozarts moved house again, this time to apartments in the magnificent Trattner palace on the Graben. "Now I must go down to the first floor for Frau Trattner's concert; she is leaving all the arrangements to me" (letter of May 8). The Trattnerhof first floor contained a casino, and a concert hall which Trattner let to Mozart and a piano teacher called Richter on very easy terms. During the first months of the year Mozart played for an agreed sum at Saturday concerts run by Richter; then during March he launched his own subscription concerts on Wednesday evenings. "The hall was crammed full" and, apart from takings at the door, no less than 174 subscribers paid six gulden apiece ("three concerts for two guineas" would be a modern equivalent arrangement).

The heavy round of concerts continued into the early summer until nearly all patrons had left Vienna. Since Mozart was earning so much we must wonder why he complained that "the whole morning" was spent giving lessons at various houses "leaving only the evenings for composition, the work most precious to me," on nights when there was no concert. However at least one of his pupils proved as great a credit to him as Josephine Aurnhammer had been. This was Babette Ployer, daughter of the Salzburg agent at the imperial court, for whom he wrote two concertos, in E flat, K.449, and in G, K.453. The latter may have been played earlier than in June, but Mozart told his father of a concert in June "at Döbling in the country, the home of Herr Ployer, the agent, where Fraülein Babette is playing her new concerto in G."

At this time Leopold, who seemed to have lost his distrust of Gluck, had news that Wolfgang was on cordial terms with two composers who enjoyed enviable success with their comic operas, for they came to Mozart's concerts and one of them was at the Döbling concert:

> I am fetching Paisiello in my carriage so that he can hear my works and my pupil. If Sarti were not leaving today he would also be coming out to Döbling with me.

Many of Mozart's letters written between 1782 and 1785 have been lost, but his crowded activities prevented his writing as frequently as he did formerly. Many of his letters to Salzburg are brief or interrupted. For other reasons he could not attend Nannerl's wedding at St. Gilgen. He had so favoured her former Salzburg suitor, a military officer called Yppold, as to ask him to settle in Vienna with Nannerl, but that engagement was broken off. Aged 33, Nannerl married Johann Berchtold zu Sonnenburg, a magistrate of St. Gilgen who was a widower aged 48. Because of a letter from Leopold to St. Gilgen we know that Mozart was gravely ill at the time of the wedding:

> My son in Vienna has been seriously ill. At Paisiello's new opera he sweated so heavily that his clothes were soaked. Then outside in the cold air he had to find the servant who had his coat, for a regulation forbade servants to enter the theatre by the main doors. Consequently not only he but also several other people caught severe chills which turned to rheumatic fever because no immediate steps were taken. Wolfgang has written: "I have had dreadful cramps at the same time each day for the past four days, and each time they have brought violent vomiting . . . My doctor is Herr Sigmund Barisani, who in any case has been visiting me almost every day since he came to Vienna."

The doctor, son of the Barisani who was physician to Colloredo and an old friend of the Mozart family in the Salzburg days, recognised amongst the symptoms those of the kidney disease from which Mozart died seven years later. This fact is very important towards an accurate understanding of Mozart, because people still blame only the fickleness of Vienna for his later decline in fortune, just as they blame the rigours of his childhood tours (and therefore his father) for his declining health. Since he was physically tough and resilient at Salzburg, in Munich, and then in Vienna, the illnesses of childhood and the strain of touring cannot have affected his health permanently to such a degree as to kill him by the age of 35.

From 1785 onwards disease sapped his strength. We must marvel that he undertook such strenuous work as the supervision of his operas in Prague. He often seemed "listless" – the word used by Attwood, his pupil, later organist of St. Paul's. Leopold had described him to Baroness Waldstädten as sometimes "lethargic, too patient." Without that disease he might have had the energy to pursue the advantages he gained with the public and the aristocracy up to 1786; even with it, if he had lived only two more years, he would have regained financial security, especially if he had managed to follow Haydn's advice and visit London.

Haydn's Accolade

The Mozarts were living above the Trattners for less than a year before they themselves became "first floor" people in the Schulerstrasse, at a rent nearly four times that asked by Trattner. There was certainly no quarrel with the Trattners, nor is it thought that they were asked to make room for others or that their rooms at the Trattnerhof were originally taken as a temporary arrangement. Perhaps they were unable to resist apartments which included a palatially decorated salon where they could hold their own select concerts though, as Stanley Sadie points out, the rent was slightly larger than Mozart's yearly salary in Salzburg. The sun of success continued to shine in 1785 and the time had come to make Leopold an eye-witness. He had already been thrilled by Salzburg performances of the "Linz" Symphony and "The Seraglio." Of the opera he wrote:

> The whole town is pleased with it. Even the archbishop had the tremendous graciousness to say that it was not at all bad.

Leopold halted for a few days in Munich, for at his age he found it hard to endure the unusually severe winter of January and February 1785. He pushed forward so as not to miss the opening of his son's Lent concerts in the Mehlgrube which took place on February 11, the day of his arrival in a bitter snowstorm. He wrote to Nannerl at St. Gilgen:

> It is snowing miserably, with an incredible wind

51. Joseph Haydn. Engraving by Luigi Schiavonetti after an oil portrait by Ludwig Guttenbrunn, c. 1791.

raging which has completely chilled these poorly heated rooms . . . I did not dare to leave the house except to hear mass at St. Stephen's which is close by.

Yet the rigours of the climate were forgotten at Wolfgang's concert:

> There was a huge concourse of distinguished people . . . The concert was incomparable and the orchestra splendid. As well as the symphonies there were two arias by a singer from the Italian opera. Then came a splendid piano concerto by Wolfgang [K.466 in D minor] at which the copyist was still engaged when we arrived, so your brother had no time to rehearse the rondo . . .

A greater thrill was in store on the following day when Leopold met Haydn, with whom his son must have been acquainted personally for some time, though unfortunately we lack letters which might mention the occasions of their meeting. Haydn was in Vienna to be received into a Masonic lodge (making him a brother in the craft to Mozart who had become a Freemason the previous December). The last three of the "Haydn" quartets were played in that grand drawing-room, and after hearing them Haydn used words which have become famous. They were:

> I tell you before God as an honest man that your son is the greatest composer I know in person or by name. He has taste and, apart from that, the most thorough knowledge of composition.

Without vocal theophany Leopold could have wished for no more authoritative testimony that his belief in his son's genius and his nurture of his talents were justified. Throughout Europe Haydn was regarded as the supreme musician. To have met him and to have heard those words from him was the most satisfying experience of Leopold's life, yet Haydn was 13 years Leopold's junior. He was often in Vienna about this time and came to play quartets at Mozart's house in the Schulerstrasse or the lodgings of Stephen and Nancy Storace. Michael Kelly recalls Haydn taking first violin, Dittersdorf second violin, Mozart the viola, and the Bohemian composer Johann Vanhall the cello. Haydn would have been free from duty at the town residence of Prince Nikolaus Esterházy. (He retired to Vienna from Esterház when his prince died, a year before Mozart's death.)

There is no need to give every account that is known about the concerts of 1785, nor even of all those heard by Leopold during his visit; but one or two are worth mention. The B flat concerto, K.456, previously mentioned in connexion with Maria Theresa Paradis, was played in the Burgtheater and greatly impressed the old man:

> I was only two boxes away from the very beautiful Princess of Württemberg, from which place the interplay of the instruments came over so clearly that my eyes filled with tears from sheer joy. When your brother left the piano the emperor flourished his hat and called out "Bravo Mozart!" . . . when

he came out to play again there was tremendous applause.

Within a few days Leopold must have been convinced that he need no longer have fears for his son, however mistaken time proved his conviction to be. Wolfgang seemed to have society and the intelligent middle class at his feet, to be welcome and feasted at a score of grand tables, to be making money, and to be assured of affluence without holding a court appointment – but how could he escape the offer of such an honour?

At first his letters to St. Gilgen were full of approving wonder at the brilliance of the concerts, the invitations to dinner several times a week (with detailed accounts of the food and wines), and his pleasure in meeting old friends like Bonno the *Kapellmeister* and Ployer. Yet the hectic round of events and engagements became something of a burden to the old man. He confided to Nannerl:

> We never get to bed before one o'clock, never rise before nine or eat lunch till about half past two. The weather is filthy. There are concerts every day somewhere, incessant giving of lessons, composing, and so on. Where can I go to be out of the way? If only the concert season were over! It is impossible to describe the muddle and disturbance. While I have been here your brother's piano has been shifted from the house to a theatre or somewhere else at least a dozen times. He has had a large pedal made, about three spans long, which goes under the piano and is very heavy.

On April 19 he enjoyed going out to dine with Baroness Waldstädten, his frequent correspondent whom he was anxious to see. He left Vienna a week later. The last of his son's music that he heard during the visit was on the night before his departure – the cantata for tenor, men's voices, and orchestra, "Die Maurerfreude," K.471, in honour of Ignaz von Born. It was given at the Masonic lodge called "Gekrönte Hoffnung" (Crowned Hope). Earlier in the month Leopold had been made a member of the order and quickly promoted to the rank of master; Mozart's own devotion to Freemasonry deserves more lengthy discussion later on.

Pictorial Essay:
Rulers and Residences

47

48

49

50

51

52

53

54

55

56

57

58

These are the rulers Mozart knew together with their residences where these still exist today and retain something of the atmosphere they must have had in the eighteenth century. For this reason Windsor Castle, for instance, has been illustrated rather than Buckingham House although it was only in the latter that Mozart actually played.

47. Count Sigismund von Schrattenbach (1698-1771), prince-archbishop of Salzburg from 1753 and Mozart's first employer. Oil portrait, 1755. His residence, like that of his successor Archbishop Colloredo *(No. 54)* was the Salzburg Residenz *(No. 57* opposite).

48. The Emperor Franz I (1708-1765), the Empress Maria Theresa (see also *No. 56),* and 11 of their 16 children, pictured on the terrace at Schönbrunn (see also *No. 58* above and *No. 69).* Oil portrait, c. 1750, by Martin van Meytens.

49. Karl Theodor (1724-1799), Elector Palatine and Elector of Bavaria from 1778. Informal oil portrait by J. G. Ziesenis, 1757. For his residence at Mannheim see *No. 61.*

50. Louis XV of France (1710-1774). Pastel drawing, 1748, by Maurice Quentin de Latour. For his residence at Fontainebleau see *No. 65.*

51. Marie Antoinette (1755-1793), wife of Louis XVI of France, and her children. Oil portrait, 1787, by Mme. Vigée-Lebrun. For her apartments at Fontainebleau see *No. 65*. As daughter of Maria Theresa she also had connexions with Schönbrunn *(Nos. 48, 58, and 69)* and it was there that Mozart first met her as a child.

52. Queen Charlotte of Great Britain (1744-1818), wife of George III *(No. 62)*. Oil portrait, c. 1762, by Allan Ramsay. For Windsor Castle see *No. 63*.

53. Frederick William II of Prussia (1744-1797). Anonymous oil portrait. It was for him that Mozart wrote his "King of Prussia" quartets, commissioned during the visit to Potsdam in 1789.

54. Count Hieronymus von Colloredo (1732-1812), prince-archbishop of Salz-

burg from 1772 and successor of Archbishop Schrattenbach *(No. 47)*. Oil portrait by Johann Michael Greiter. For his residence see *No. 57*. Another portrait appears on Page 40.

55. The Empress Maria Theresa (1717-1780). Detail from an oil portrait, 1744, by Martin van Meytens (see also *No. 48*). Much building and reconstruction at Schönbrunn *(Nos. 58 and 69)* was carried out during her reign and her personal tastes (for instance, "Maria Theresa" yellow) are often reflected in their interior decoration.

56. The Emperor Joseph II (1741-1790), eldest son of Franz I and Maria Theresa (see also *No. 48*), who appointed Mozart his court composer in 1787. Oil portrait, 1771, by Joseph Hickel. Schönbrunn *(Nos. 58 and 69)* was both his childhood home and the centre of his empire.

59

60

61

57. The present conference hall, previously the council chamber, of the Salzburg Residenz where Mozart served under the Archbishops Schrattenbach *(No. 47)* and Colloredo *(No. 54)*.

58. The exotic "Vieux-Laque-Zimmer" at Schönbrunn (see also *Nos. 48 and 69)*, decorated in Chinese lacquer, a particular passion of Maria Theresa *(No. 55)*. The portrait on the wall (by Anton von Maron) is of Maria Theresa's daughter-in-law, the empress Maria Louise (1745-1792), wife of Leopold II. It was she who called "La clemenza di Tito" a "Porcheria tedesca."

59. Maximilian Joseph III (1727-1777), Elector of Bavaria. Detail from an oil painting, "Chamber Music at the Elector's Court at Munich," 1758, by Johann Nikolaus de Grooth. His residence was the Nymphenburg *(No. 60)* and it was there in 1762 that Mozart made his first important appearance outside Salzburg.

60. The "Steinerne Saal," the tiled main hall of the central pavilion at Munich's Nymphenburg, palace of the electors of Bavaria. In 1756, under Maximilian Joseph III *(No. 59)*, the hall was redesigned by François Cuvilliés the Elder with ceiling frescoes by Johann Baptist Zimmermann.

61. The "Rittersaal" of the Elector Palatine's palace at Mannheim. Here many important works by composers of the

(29)

62

Mannheim school were performed for the first time and here Mozart played before the Elector Karl Theodor *(No. 49)*. The palace, begun in 1720 and finished about 10 years later, is one of the largest in Germany. Covering 15 acres, it has 1500 windows and a façade 580 yards long.

62. George III of Great Britain (1738-1820). Oil portrait, c. 1770, by Johann Zoffany.

63. The royal bedroom at Windsor Castle, country residence of George III *(No. 62)* and Queen Charlotte *(No. 52)*. Begun in 1068, Windsor Castle is not only the oldest of the royal residences illustrated here but also the only one still in use as such. George named it affectionately his "Sweet retreat."

63

64

64. Louis XVI of France (1754-1793), a portrait painted in 1777, the year before Mozart's last visit to Paris, by Joseph-Siffrein Duplessis. Before the restrictions placed on their freedom after the Revolution of 1789, the ill-fated Louis and his wife Marie Antoinette *(No. 51)* usually spent their autumns at Fontainebleau *(No. 65* below).

65. The games room in the suite of Marie Antoinette *(No. 51)* at Fontainebleau, country residence of Louis XVI *(No. 64)*, Louis XV *(No. 50)*, and a long line of French monarchs stretching back to Francis I, for whom the chateau was built in the sixteenth century. The last major structural improvements were by Jacques-Ange Gabriel in the reign of Louis XV, whose mistress, the Marquise de Pompadour, had this particular room decorated in the style which later bore her name.

65

66

66. Pope Clement XIV (1705-1774). Anonymous oil portrait. It was he who bestowed on Mozart the Order of the Golden Spur during the composer's visit to Rome in 1770 (see portrait *No. 11*). The investiture took place in the Quirinal (*No. 67* below).

67. The gallery at the Quirinal, begun in 1574 as a summer residence for Pope Gregory XIII. It was here in 1770 that Mozart received the Order of the Golden Spur (see *No. 11*) from Pope Clement XIV (*No. 66*). The original architects of the Quirinal were Flaminio Ponzio and Ottaviano Mascherino. Their work was carried further by Domenico Fontana after 1585 and by his nephew Carlo Maderno between 1606 and 1615. Under Pope Clement XII further building was done by Ferdinando Fuga between 1730 and 1740 before the palace reached its final form.

67

VI

Fame and loneliness

The Hidden Mozart
At Work on "Figaro"
Intrigue and Triumph
Prague
Leopold's Death

52. *The assembly hall in the Hofburg, Vienna, where Mozart's music for festivities such as this masked ball was often heard after he became court composer in 1787. Anonymous engraving, c. 1746.*

The Hidden Mozart

We left Mozart in that condition which every normal artist desires – able to please himself in the certainty of thereby pleasing a wide public. Until the end of 1786 he remained the cynosure of Vienna's concert-goers, not seriously harmed by the rivalry of Dittersdorf in that year, for Dittersdorf sincerely sang Mozart's praises. Since therefore Vienna accepted his originality, why does not the phrase "the idol of Viennese society" (Otto Jahn's description of Mozart in 1785) seem apt if applied to him during his last five years? Why could he not maintain without anxiety the appearance and social status without which life for him would have been intolerable? When the regular succession of great piano concertos ceased (the last two were for special occasions near the end of his life) did Vienna neglect him? Was he no longer the city's pride after 1786?

If the general belief is true, then the leading patrons of music in the most musical of European capitals suddenly lost their senses, then recovered them a few years later in order to cherish a challenging genius who did not even trouble to show them courtesy. How absurd to suppose that the aristocrats who ensured that Beethoven should not be in distress had no ears for the supreme works of Mozart's last years! Error comes by equating artistic with financial success. Nowadays a parallel success to that of "Figaro" would enable its composer to live in comfort for the rest of his life. He would receive his performing rights every time the work was given in theatre or concert hall in any country; he would have broadcasting and recording fees for the whole or extracts, and copyright fees or royalties for the score, parts, and any arrangement of the music that was printed or photographed. In Mozart's time the composer could take more money at a season of Lent concerts. The opera composer had no financial claim beyond a fee for delivering the music in time. Enriched by an outstanding success, the theatre manager might allow a benefit performance, by which the composer took the profits only after expenses had been met. Opera composers who fared well were in salaried posts like Salieri's. They sought leave to travel with their carefully guarded vocal and orchestral parts in order to take fees for productions away from home; but as Mozart's fame spread abroad his fortunes declined.

We have no proof at all that Vienna's music-lovers turned against his music, though it is indeed to their discredit that they lacked the imagination to recognise his straits. To whom except Michael Puchberg, a fellow-Mason, did he disclose them? An incident during his visit to north Germany in 1789 proves that others were ignorant of his anxiety. He scraped and borrowed to undertake the tour because he was invited to accompany Prince Lichnowsky, his admirer and later Beethoven's. Just before returning from Berlin the prince found himself short of ready cash and blandly asked Mozart to lend

him a hundred gulden. Demur was unthinkable even if the loan emptied Mozart's purse. We do not know if he was repaid but we may be certain that his pride forbade his asking for repayment. When pride licks the dust and Mozart seems metaphorically to collapse, his letters to Puchberg asking for another, another, and yet another "temporary relief" are harrowing to read. There is no doubt of Puchberg's response to a Masonic brother, for he cannot have expected return of his loans for at least several years. Even if his action showed belief in Mozart's ultimate worldly success, his sincerity is proved by his asking nothing back from Constanze after the advantageous disposal of her husband's music and effects, and her being granted a pension from the emperor.

After Mozart was admitted to a Masonic lodge on Christmas Eve, 1784, his music for Masonic ceremonies and occasions must have made him one of the most valued members. The speed with which he was promoted through the minor orders was reserved for esteemed candidates. During the 1780's the brotherhood was so fashionable in Vienna that it enrolled the cream of the intelligentsia and artistic nobility, many of whom were among Mozart's patrons and special friends. If he had disclosed his trouble to them, would not their doyen, Ignaz von Born (to be symbolised as Sarastro the wise and virtuous) himself have proposed the kind of financial

53. Franz Joseph Anton, Count Thun, surrounded by Masonic symbols. Engraving by J. G. Klinger after a painting by A. Rähmel, 1787.

arrangement which some of the nobility made for Beethoven, according him honour instead of wounding his pride? Haydn, Trattner, Count Thun, Van Swieten, Galitzin, and the rest were as ignorant of Mozart's plight as was Lichnowsky. When the emperor came to the widow's relief he was surely surprised and ashamed, for Mozart's poverty was exposed only by his death. The fault was his.

But why talk of fault? Mozart's biographers are at fault only if they try to apportion blame, collectively or upon individuals. We should be at fault if we forbore to blame Vienna only to blame Mozart. People who saw the man, the writer of those pathetic begging letters, were struck by his elegant appearance. More than one of them mention the rich material and the fine embroidery of his clothes. To the end he had a servant and Constanze a maid; the fine cuffs, cravats, and shirts were laundered; the *friseur* and barber called; such items as the billiard table were not sold; balls, receptions, and Masonic meetings were attended until Mozart was too weak to leave his room. Dr. Closset, who attended the most fashionable patients, prescribed for Constanze a cure at Baden so Mozart had to borrow money to take her. Otherwise he would have lost status. He had been conditioned to maintain status and had taught his wife to do so. It is useless to argue the ethics of the matter. We merely recognise the fact, which many of us remember from our elders, that maintaining status was a part of religion – a duty to God, neighbour, and family.

Other facts need emphasis. The period of constant distress was of three years only. However weak his management of money, Mozart might have been spared the need of borrowing in that time if he could have commanded the nervous and physical energy of 1784–85. His unhealthy complexion and protruding eyes are mentioned by other writers than Kelly, and they are evident in Doris Stock's drawing of 1789. He mustered enough spirit to be "on fire" at rehearsals of his operas, but during his last years he could not have endured the strain of production, and he was exhausted by travelling. Vienna did not suddenly turn against him: it was he who withdrew.

But these reflections have taken us forward in a story which we left after Leopold's return to Salzburg in 1785. Happily we resume the tale with more triumphs. Mozart's first short withdrawal, for the composition of "Figaro," was only *pour mieux sauter*.

At Work on "Figaro"

Mozart told his father that he had read "hundreds of plays" before approaching Varesco during the visit to Salzburg in 1783. At first Mozart seemed satisfied with what he received. Then came letters making objections to this and that which Leopold was to pass on to Varesco. In February 1784 Mozart wrote saying that he must lay the opera aside and "compose things which will bring in money immediately." After that we hear no more of Varesco, who was presumably paid off. Strangely it was to Lorenzo da Ponte and his adaptation of Beaumarchais's banned play "Le Mariage de Figaro" that Mozart finally turned after having previously abandoned the same librettist's "Lo sposo deluso" (The Deceived Husband). Mozart was not averse to handling a banned play and to judge from his own and his father's sarcastic comments on feudal grandees he enjoyed seeing Count Almaviva outwitted by servants.

The flamboyant Da Ponte was ambitious and saw in Mozart a collaborator with whom, indeed *by* whom, he might reach his goal of securing the title *poeta cesareo*

54. Four of the cast in the first performance of "The Marriage of Figaro." Left to right: Dorotea Bussani (Cherubino); Paolo Stefano Mandini (Count Almaviva); Francesco Benucci (Figaro); and Maria Mandini (Marcellina). Silhouettes by Löschenkohl, 1786.

55. Lorenzo da Ponte. Engraving by Michele Pekenino after a painting by Nathaniel Rogers.

either to the emperor or to some other great ruler, for the post carried a very good stipend. He was shrewd enough to know he was not the literary equal of his two bitterest enemies whom he wished to forestall in this – Bertati, the most prolific and admired writer of libretti after Metastasio, and Casti, who became poet laureate in 1790 after Metastasio's death. He lacked their ability in original verse, but he was a master of racy adaptation and free translation from plays. Above all he was ready to hear the requirements of the man whose genius he recognised and to discuss every turn of the opera with him.

No work by Mozart sounds more spontaneous than "Figaro," yet two sources tell us that it took enormous concentration. The first is Leopold Mozart, who complained to Nannerl in November 1785 that her brother had not sent a single line to Salzburg for more than a month, and that when one arrived it was followed by only 11 more! A more oblique testimony is the composer's own catalogue notebook in which entries are spare until the end of the year when Mozart, aware that he could not afford to remain withdrawn from the concert world, prepared for the Lent season with the piano concertos K.482 and K.467, and, early in 1786, K.488 and K.491.

There was a further interruption before the first performance of "Figaro," a commission for another work for the stage, albeit a small one and in German. Early in February 1786 the imperial court received visits from the governor of the Austrian Netherlands and his wife, and a relative of the king of Poland. The emperor entertained them along with 40 courtiers to a banquet in the orangery at Schönbrunn. The building was then much longer than it is now, and it was fitted with a stage at each end. After dinner the guests were to sample each of the rival types of opera in miniature. First the servants arranged the chairs in front of one stage for a German *Singspiel*, then in front of the other for an Italian *opera buffa*. Mozart was asked to provide the music for the former, Stephanie's "Der Schauspieldirektor," usually called in English "The Impresario." The opposition was Salieri with his "Prima la musica e poi le parole" (First the Music and Then the Words) to a text by Casti. Before a note was heard the scales were tipped heavily in favour of the Italian art form and the Italian composer. Moreover Salieri received twice Mozart's fee because his was called a "full opera." Yet "The Impresario" did Mozart no harm. The knowledge that the emperor had commissioned him impressed Vienna and provided advance publicity for "Figaro" which, however, had the best of all publicity – the knowledge that the play from which its story was taken had caused a scandal in France and Austria.

Just after the Schönbrunn festivity Mozart attracted attention at a carnival ball in the Hofburg. He impersonated a Hindu *guru* and distributed leaflets containing epigrams supposed to have come from Zoroaster. They were highly approved by his father; whether the Free-

56. *Nikolaus Joseph, Baron von Jacquin. Lithograph by Joseph Lanzadelly after a drawing by Vincenz Georg Kinninger.*

masons liked them or not, Mozart became a more frequent visitor at the house of a Masonic family, the Jacquins, who would have helped him if his needs had been known, for its members were among his most loyal friends during his last years. Nikolaus von Jacquin was a famous botanist from Leyden who became professor of chemistry at Vienna University. He was also curator of the botanical gardens in the Rennweg which he designed. His elder son succeeded him in both offices, but Mozart was particularly fond of the younger son, Gottfried, and the daughter, Franziska, one of his best piano pupils. All the Jacquins were musical. Mozart composed several works for them, including the trios, K.441 and K.498, and the serenades with basset horns and clarinets, K. App. 229.

That spring of 1786, however, brought to Mozart's house a pupil destined to become famous as a pianist and composer. Aged eight, Johann Nepomuk Hummel arrived with his father, a Prussian military bandmaster who had been enticed to Vienna by Mozart's Masonic friend Emanuel Schikaneder, who later commissioned "The Magic Flute." Mozart was impressed by the boy's playing of some little pieces by J. S. Bach and his sight-reading of a sonata. He took him into his home and treated him as a son. The boy accompanied Mozart to concerts and tasted Vienna's applause when he played duets and works for two pianos with his master. Hummel fortunately did not stay long enough to see Mozart's sad end. His father emulated Mozart's father and toured the boy as a prodigy. While Mozart lay dying in Vienna little Hummel was being commended by Haydn in London.

Intrigue and Triumph

The Duscheks, friends of the Mozarts who lived in Prague, visited Salzburg in 1786 to settle some business connected with a family legacy. According to a letter from Mozart's father to Nannerl, the Duscheks feared that there were powerful "intrigues" afoot to ruin "Figaro," and that "Salieri and his retinue will try to move heaven and earth" to stop it. There were certainly obstacles of malicious origin, probably more from Casti's than Salieri's machinations, for Casti was almost a match for the wily Da Ponte. The emperor himself was our hero's best ally against petty obstructions. First Da Ponte was able to assure him that nothing that would offend him had been taken over from the original play by Beaumarchais. Then fortunately the emperor attended the dress rehearsal. The royal party, including Casti and half the aristocracy of Vienna, saw the first act rehearsed amid general applause.

There is no credibility to be attached to the story that members of the cast were suborned to ruin the first per-

57. The "Karlsbrücke," Prague. Detail from an engraving by Johann Balzer after J. A. Scotti di Cassano, 1781.

84

formance, although nearly all were Italians. So many items had to be repeated on that first night of May 1, 1786, that the opera, which is rather longer than most, took nearly twice the expected time, and for the next few performances the audience was informed that there would be no repeats. This did not prevent them from creeping back before the end of the year. There were in all nine performances, the last in December. After that there were none for more than two years. Once more we must insist that nobody should be blamed for this fact. Other composers had their claims, and one of them, the Spaniard Martin y Soler, achieved a popular success with his "Una cosa rara" in November that rivalled the triumph of "Figaro." Moreover Mozart could have made no more money by extra performances at the same theatre unless a benefit had been arranged.

Naturally his thoughts turned towards travel. He wrote to Le Gros in Paris, and asked his father for addresses in Italy. His English pupil, Thomas Attwood, almost persuaded him to set off for England, but his father made it clear that he would not have children dumped on him in Salzburg at his age. He also thought all the proposals reckless. (In fact, they probably were not.) A third child, named Leopold after its grandfather, was born on October 18 but did not live long. While undecided about travelling Mozart composed many fine chamber works towards the end of 1786, as well as the last and the most majestic of his piano concertos in the unbroken series, K.503 in C, first played at an Advent concert in the Casino. He also composed the Symphony in D, K.504, affectionately known as the "Prague," though it may have been acclaimed vociferously first in Vienna.

Prague

An invitation from Count Thun clinched Mozart's decision to go to Prague instead of London, for he could now take his wife. Staying in Thun's palace they risked no heavy expenses, and Mozart could hope for profit from a public concert and perhaps even from a commission for another opera. Ever since a production of "The Seraglio" at the so-called National Theatre, music-lovers in the Bohemian capital had sought out Mozart's publications for piano, his chamber music, and his symphonies, no doubt influenced by Thun and the Freemasons. Immediately after the run of "Figaro" in Vienna rehearsals began in Prague. A "national" theatre was intended for plays and *Singspiele* in German, but in Prague the manager, Bondini, appointed by Thun, mounted Italian and German works impartially.

The Mozarts arrived on January 11, 1787. A long letter written on the 15th to young Gottfried von Jacquin gives some account of their entertainment, which could hardly have been more lavish if they had been heads of state. Obviously it overtaxed Mozart's strength, though he could only just admit the fact during the enjoyment of the few weeks there. First they went to a ball attended by "the cream of Prague's beauty" which would have set young Jacquin "not running but limping" after the lovely girls, "but I neither danced nor flirted for I was too tired." Mozart was charmed to hear items from "Figaro" arranged "for contredanses and *Teutsche*," for "the folk here talk nothing but 'Figaro'; scrape, blow, sing, and whistle nothing but 'Figaro'." Almost daily there were afternoon concerts at Thun's, invitations to lunch or dinner at the houses of other notables, and days of sight-seeing at libraries and museums till "we had almost stared our eyes out." At their first visit to the theatre they saw Paisiello's "Le gare generose" (The Friendly Rivals), but Mozart could give Jacquin no opinion on its music "because I was talking all the time it was in progress. Maybe the work caused my chattering so much, contrary to my custom." (Paisiello and Mozart were supposedly on friendly terms. Let Mozart's idolaters again consider that Joseph II could have regarded Mozart as a much finer musician than others yet have justifiably hesitated to offer him a *Kapellmeister*-ship.)

On the 17th he attended a performance of "Figaro." Knowledge of the composer's presence had been spread, and the ecstatic applause began immediately the overture was finished. At the next performance Mozart directed from the keyboard, having on the previous day in the same theatre shown himself to Prague as a concert pianist. "Never before had the theatre been so crowded." At the end of the concert he "improvised for a full half-hour," and was rewarded by such a storm of applause that he had to play again, with the same result. Sitting down for the third time and gaining the expectant silence, he was startled by a loud voice calling "From 'Figaro'!" whereupon he produced a series of variations on the favourite tune, "Non più andrai." A pity he did not commit the result to paper!

Naturally the Mozarts saw much of their friends, the Duscheks, through whose influence it is supposed that Mozart obtained his desired commission for another opera before he returned in February. It was to be delivered for production in the autumn, and therefore had to be undertaken immediately. As soon as he reached home Mozart went to Da Ponte, who had to produce libretti for two other composers. It seems safe to accept from his memoirs the assertion that the idea of using the Don Juan story was originally his. Under pressure of time he had the audacity to use an existing Italian libretto by his rival Bertati, "Il convitato di pietra" (The Stone Guest), written for that very year's Venice carnival and set to music by Giuseppe Gazzaniga. Being a Venetian with friends in Venice, Da Ponte could secure copies of any dramatic success there. His adaptation was brilliant, yet he needed a source even for his improvements, and that source was Carlo Goldoni's "Don Giovanni Tenorio" of 1736.

Leopold's Death

Since the opera was wanted in the autumn of 1787 it is remarkable that Mozart had time for other compositions. They are not many in number but of magnificent quality. They include "Eine kleine Nachtmusik," the C major and G minor string quintets, and the biggest of the violin sonatas, that in A major. In February English friends and pupils left – Kelly, Attwood, the Storaces – which must have saddened Mozart while giving him more time to compose his new opera. They went home via Salzburg and were shown the sights there by old Leopold, who heard that his son had made good money in Prague but that the infant named after him had died. Soon after this he wrote: "My health is not as I could wish." He went to Munich in February to spend time with his orchestral friends there. He enjoyed the operas but did not go out to late entertainments because "the beginning of my sixty-eighth year has made a great change in the condition of my old body." In March Nannerl went to stay with him and wrote to Wolfgang that he had dropsy; but as she went home to St. Gilgen in May, saying that her father was no worse, Mozart did not leave Vienna. His father's sudden death on May 28, was therefore a blow to Wolfgang, who was seriously ill himself. He found medical attention an unwelcome cost. At the end of April the Mozarts had given up their fine apartments and moved to the country, first to the Landstrasse, then later to the Währingerstrasse. He could give face-saving reasons for moving – "I now have a pleasant garden" and "I can work in peace." One of the last callers at 8 Schulerstrasse was the dour young Beethoven, aged 17 and sent by the Elector of Cologne. No accounts of what happened or was said at the interview is authenticated or even credible. The two never met again, for Beethoven's sponsored visit to Vienna was cut short by the news of his mother's illness.

One of the last letters written by Mozart to his father (April 4) has some reflections on death which sound entirely sincere, and not merely a dutiful echo of church or Masonic teaching on the subject:

I need hardly tell you how much I hope for comforting news about you, and I feel sure it will come although I have accustomed myself to expecting the worst in everything. Since death, when we think of it properly, is the true goal of our lives, I have for many years made myself so familiar with this best friend of men that his image not only holds no terrors for me but also brings me comfort and fortitude. I thank God that He has given me the benefit and opportunity (you know what I mean) to regard this as the clue to our happiness. I never go to sleep without remembering that, young as I am, I may never see the following day. Yet nobody who knows me can call me melancholy or dejected in society.

Putting little Karl in charge of a nurse, Mozart and his wife went to Prague at the beginning of October, first lodging at the "Three Golden Lions," but then with the Duscheks at the pretty villa with the garden pavilion called "Bertramka's Vineyard" and still shown to visitors. Even now it seems to be in the country, although the city has spread along the river beyond it. There is no reason to doubt the story that Josephine Duschek locked Mozart into the little pavilion with writing materials until he composed an aria for her. He took playful revenge by threatening to destroy the brilliant "Bella mia fiamma" (K. 528) unless she could sing it at sight. Other stories connected with this second visit to Prague are only partially credible. The most familiar is that the overture to "Don Giovanni" was composed at a table in the theatre during the dress rehearsal, the parts being handed out with wet ink although no score existed. Constanze told her second husband the more likely story that, *two nights* before the first performance, she plied Mozart with punch and gossip to keep him awake while he "wrote out the overture," which surely means the score. Another story, once doubted, was proved true in the 1920's – that Casanova was interested in the production of "Don Giovanni." It is now fairly certain that he was at the first performance, for we have discovered his presumptuous revision of the sextet in the second act. He was an old friend of Bondini's for his father had been an impresario, and when Da Ponte left Prague Bondini himself may have asked Casanova to employ his talents on revisions. He had almost exhausted his amorous and commercial adventures and was indulging in (literary) memories at the castle of Dux, near Teplitz, some 50 miles north of Prague, which he visited to see his publisher. An acquaintance of his younger days gave him shelter at Dux as librarian.

Mozart suffered bouts of anxiety concerning Prague's likely reaction to "Don Giovanni," and even asked different friends if they expected a failure. Rehearsals were difficult, not because he was opposed, for many of the cast had sung in "Figaro" and the orchestra loved him, but because "Don Giovanni" notoriously needs patient stage management. Let Mozart's letter to Jacquin written on November 4, 1787 show that his fears were groundless:

> My opera "Don Giovanni" had its first performance on October 29, and was received with immense applause. Yesterday it was given for the fourth time, a performance for my benefit . . . They are trying hard to persuade me to stay a couple more months and write another opera.

Confirming this is the manager's letter to Da Ponte:

> Long live Da Ponte! Long live Mozart! All impresarios and singers should bless their names, for as long as they live we shall not know the meaning of poverty in the theatre!

But Constanze was expecting another baby and news had reached Prague that Gluck was likely to die soon. He was aged 73 and had been ailing for some time.

Mozart's hopes were not disappointed. It is believed that Gluck's condition was among the reasons for Da Ponte's hurrying back to Vienna, and the emperor could hardly overlook Mozart entirely after the reports from Prague. The Mozarts arrived home on November 12. Gluck died three days later, and the emperor, without consulting Rosenberg, appointed Mozart "Imperial and Royal Court Composer" at an initial salary of 800 gulden. It is often suggested that this was a mere trifle. It was eight times what he could expect for delivering the music of an opera, and the duties seem to have been light – chiefly the provision of dances for court balls. If the Mozarts had been careful managers, even allowing for Mozart's declining health, they need not have run into very serious debt. For "Don Giovanni," including the benefit performance, Mozart received the unusually large sum of 225 gulden. Why, then, unless the Mozarts were extravagant, should the first begging letter to Puchberg have been written only six months after the return to Vienna?

In April 1788 "Don Giovanni" was put into rehearsal in Vienna with so brilliant a cast that they demanded extra arias and alterations of the work. The first performance on May 7, 1788 was tepidly received. Haydn declared the music too good for the Viennese; asked for one of his operas, he said: "My works are for the Esterház orchestra . . . even if I should have the good luck to receive a libretto for the Prague theatre, I should think it a dangerous venture for anyone to stand beside the great Mozart. If every music-lover, especially among the nobility, could respond to Mozart's inimitable works with the depth of emotion and understanding which they arouse in me, the nations would compete to have such a jewel within their frontiers." Not knowing of Mozart's court appointment he hoped that Prague would "hold tight to this valuable man, but also reward him as he deserved."

Vienna "came round" to "Don Giovanni" sufficiently to give it 15 performances, the last being on December 15. One of these was attended by the emperor who had been with the army against the Turks. Da Ponte tells us that the emperor said: "The music is divine; I should say even more beautiful than 'Figaro.' But such music is not for the teeth of my Viennese." Da Ponte reported the comment to Mozart, who said: "Give them time to chew on it!" Da Ponte adds that he "strove to procure frequent repetitions of the opera; at each performance the applause increased." What he says may be true, but the work was not given again until its composer was dead.

Pictorial Essay:
Mozart's Vienna

Vienna, seat of the Holy Roman Empire from 1558 until 15 years after Mozart's death, has many claims to fame. Not least among them is the fact that here Mozart's genius came to fullest flower. It is the city that Mozart knew and which witnessed his greatest musical triumphs that is pictured here. Most of the major build-ings associated with him can still be seen today, some of them reconstructed with care after the Second World War, for Vienna can also take pride in remaining one of the least spoiled of the great capitals of Western Europe.

68. Eighteenth-century Vienna looking towards the Danube from the Church of St. Charles *(No. 70)*, an engraving by Piringer after a drawing by Lorenz Janscha. Since 1433 the city's skyline had been dominated – as indeed it still is – by the towering Gothic spire of St. Stephen's Cathedral *(No. 71)*.

69. The emperor's palace at Schönbrunn (see also *Nos. 48 and 58*). Coloured etching by Carl Schütz, 1782. The cost of the original palace, designed by Fischer von Erlach the Elder to rival the splendour of Versailles, proved prohibitive and only the entrance façade of the main building, completed in 1696, is according to his plans. It has been suggested that the figures in the foreground of this etching represent the introduction of the young Mozart at Schönbrunn, but there is no positive evidence of this.

70. View towards the Church of St. Charles (right), the palace of Schwarzenberg (left), and (centre) the Belvedere (see also *Nos. 72 and 76*). The huge Church of St. Charles, designed like the Schwarzenberg palace, by Fischer von Erlach the Elder, was built just outside the city walls between 1716 and 1737. The Roman spiral columns are decorated with scenes from the life of St. Charles Borromeo, to whom the church was dedicated in thanksgiving for the end of a plague which swept the city in 1713.

71. St. Stephen's Cathedral (see also *No. 68*). Engraving by Carl Schütz, 1788. Mozart was first there as a child of six for a St. Cecilia's Day concert in 1762. He was married there on August 4, 1782, and in 1791, while on his deathbed, he was appointed the cathedral's musical director (a post filled instead by Albrechtsberger). Work began on the cathedral in 1147, 10 years after Vienna received its charter as a city. It was destroyed by fire and rebuilt early in the fourteenth century, only the Romanesque west front and two towers of the original being preserved. The Gothic spire, 460 feet high, was completed in 1433. During the Second World War the cathedral was again severely damaged and again rebuilt.

70

72

72. The Upper Belvedere, seen from the ornamental pond (see also *Nos. 70 and 76*). View drawn and engraved by Carl Schütz, 1788.

73. The Pfarrkirche (parish church) in the Landstrasse district of Vienna. Drawing and engraving by J. Ziegler. It was to a small house (no longer existing) in this suburb, just outside the city walls, that Mozart and his wife moved in April 1787 and there they stayed until December that year. The reason Professor Hutchings suggests was that living in town in fine apartments was proving too expensive. It was in the Landstrasse district too that Mozart was buried in 1791 – in the cemetery of St. Marx.

74. The entrance to the Augarten. Drawing and engraving by J. Ziegler. The park known as the Augarten formed previously part of the gardens of the emperor's summer residence at Leopoldstadt, on the other side of the Danube canal. They were opened to the public by Joseph II and soon became a counterpart of the famous Vauxhall Gardens in London which impressed Leopold Mozart greatly during the visit to England in 1764-65. The hall in which Mozart played one of his most important concerts on May 26, 1782, can be seen under the trees in the centre background.

75. The square before the old university building and the university church (right). Drawing and engraving by Carl Schütz, 1785. Vienna University, founded in 1365, is the second oldest German-language university. The original buildings, however, have disappeared. This building, designed by the French architect Jean-Nicolas Jadot de Ville-Issey, dates from 1755. The university church was built in 1628 at the command of the Emperor Ferdinand II and put at the disposal of the Jesuits; it is as the "Jesuitenkirche" that it is known today.

73

74

75

(37)

76. The Upper Belvedere (see also *Nos. 70 and 72)*, seen from the gardens. Drawing and engraving by Carl Schütz, 1785. The Belvedere, built by Johann Lukas von Hildebrandt, for Prince Eugene of Savoy, consists of two separate palaces (the Upper and the Lower) separated by the terraced garden seen here. The Lower Belvedere, designed as a summer garden palace, was erected between 1714 and 1716. The Upper, which is now the Austrian gallery of modern art, was built in 1721-23 and preferred for large-scale entertainment and official receptions.

77. The Michaelerplatz, with St. Michael's Church on the left and the Burgtheater (extreme right). Drawing and engraving by Carl Schütz, 1789. The church, whose tower dates from 1340, was "improved" by Baroque architects in 1781 – one of the last examples of the passion for Baroque restyling which bedevilled Vienna's architecture in the eighteenth century. The domed building is the Riding School (1729-1735), designed by Joseph Emanuel Fischer von Erlach. It was in the building on the left of the church that Constanze Mozart set up house with Georg Nikolaus Nissen *(Nos. 22 and 23)* after her husband's death.

78. The headquarters of the Imperial Hungarian Guard and the gardens of Prince Auersperg. Drawing and engraving by J. Ziegler, 1780. After the unsuccessful siege of Vienna by the Turks in 1683, it was forbidden to build in the area adjacent to the city walls, which became known as the "Glacis," a popular spot for strolling couples. Prince Auersperg was a keen admirer of Mozart's music and it was under his auspices that "Idomeneo" received its first Vienna performance in 1786 in his own private theatre by a company of noble amateur singers.

VII
Illness and anxiety
The Cloud
Journey to Berlin
Desperation
A New Régime

58. Baden, the fashionable spa near Vienna. Engraving by Johann Ziegler after a drawing by Lorenz Janscha.

The Cloud

A cloud descended over Mozart's life soon after his return from Prague and his witnessing of Vienna's limited response to "Don Giovanni." The cloud is widely attributed to constant financial embarrassment but, as has already been suggested, there is reason to believe Mozart's precarious income to be at least partly an effect rather than a cause. He who had formerly been so lively a creature, and had managed to earn more money than most musicians of his time up to the age of 32, could surely have kept solvent for three more years if he had not been overtaken by new advances in his physical malady. He may not have known that his loss of physical energy or his moods of listlessness came from his particular disease, but he must have been aware of declining health, for he complained from time to time of headaches, neuralgia, and "rheumatic pains." He seems to have felt, though still young, the same sort of decline that old men and women expect and accept even when great effort is not expected from them.

Whether one has exaggerated the onset of physical disease or not, for Mozart the worst aspect of the cloud was its menace of disgrace. He dreaded poverty not

59. *Gottfried, Baron van Swieten. Engraving by Johann Ernst Mansfeld after a sketch by J. C. de Lakner.*

because he was self-indulgent in the usual meaning of the word but because life would be intolerable if he could not live it at the standard to which he was accustomed from childhood. Frugality at home and in private was endurable. He probably spent most of the money he borrowed on maintaining entertainment of others and keeping up appearances when he went out. Most of us have at some time enjoyed life with an income lower in the statistics of our own society than Mozart's was in his, but ours was a different society. Few people today are more harshly unimaginative than those who, no doubt by commendable effort, reach affluence yet have neither pity for nor sympathy with those who have fallen from it. Let social pride be satirised; yet let there be pity for the pathos of wounded pride.

To us the worst aspect of the cloud is that it hides Mozart. Can the man we have followed so far have lost all his resilience and become, when alone and not fascinated by composition, as miserable as we might suppose from his letters to Puchberg? Much of what is said in the next few pages is not offered as history but as an exercise of imagination that tries not to falsify the little that is known of Mozart's private history between the last months of 1788 and those of 1791, which he did not quite see to its end. To the question: "Is there any need to probe the likely prevailing moods of Mozart's private hours?" one must answer firmly "Yes." To collect paintings, sketches, and stories, some valueless as a clue to the man and artist, and then add a list of his known movements, is not to study Mozart. We know and love what he *did*; our fascination is to discover at least a glance of what he *was*, and thereby to discover what we are.

We are helped by knowing what he was not. Nothing known about his last years suggests any parallel to Beethoven's fighting of troubles and defying of fate. Mozart had no mood comparable with Beethoven's grim anger and disregard of people round him. Mozart was socially conscious and showed anger only when "worked up" by a supposed insult, or when excited by bad performers or official obstructions. He did not defy misfortune but accepted it, as taught by his father's and his own religion and by their Masonic tenets. Yet it seems to have numbed him as it might a brave but bewildered child. He had lost his English friends and his father, and was soon to lose the emperor Joseph, who was at least musical enough to recognise his genius. He seems to have undertaken no venture, no travelling from home, with the old high hopes, but rather with the thought that he must act or succumb to disgrace. In July Puchberg was asked to raise money on two pawn tickets. Then for at least nine months he was not asked for new loans, nor does he seem to have been made any repayment, but we now know that Mozart borrowed from another Masonic brother.

Mozart's dependable sources of income were the fees for his services at Van Swieten's private concerts and his stipend as court composer. Fortunately Van Swieten conceived the idea of letting a wider musical public hear some of the choral-orchestral masterpieces of "old" composers. In 1787 he inaugurated public concerts in various places, though the favourite one for works requiring large forces was the splendid hall of the National Library. The performers were stiffened by members of the court orchestra and the imperial choir from St. Stephen's, and the director engaged was Joseph Starzer; but Starzer died after conducting the first two concerts and Mozart was asked to take over in 1788. In February and March he directed two concerts at the Esterházy residence, each including C. P. E. Bach's "Resurrection of Christ." For subsequent concerts in the series Mozart made his famous (to purists notorious) "arrangements" of Handel's "Acis and Galatea," "Messiah," "Alexander's Feast," and "Ode for St. Cecilia's Day."

Mozart found it inconvenient and possibly expensive to travel into Vienna from the edge of the country for the rehearsals at Van Swieten's and then the public concerts. He moved back into the city and took a house near the one he had occupied just after his marriage. His new address was 4 Judenplatz. His earnings evidently did not meet expenses incurred before and after the move, for in March 1789 he was lent a hundred gulden by another Freemason, the lawyer and magistrate Hofdemel, whose eventual suicide has already been mentioned. One of the great wonders of Mozart's enigmatic personality is his ability to write down the full scores of the three symphonies which crown his work in their genre during that anxious summer of 1788. Our greatest wonder is not at Mozart's powers of detachment from gnawing worries, for other great composers have produced masterworks when in distress, or indeed when in mortal illness; the greater marvel is that such complex and beautiful organisms, each equally splendid yet utterly unlike the other two, were apparently carried in his head – for months, for years, or perhaps only for weeks. Nothing on any scrap of paper exists to suggest that any passage, even the quintuple counterpoint of the last finale, required a preliminary sketch. Moreover all three symphonies are entered in Mozart's catalogue as "composed" (i.e. written down) between June 26 and August 10, a period of six weeks!

Journey to Berlin

While crown prince, Frederick the Great's nephew, Frederick William II of Prussia, had maintained his own orchestra and played the cello in quartets. His tastes were less rigidly conservative than those of his stern uncle, who to the end kept up the military regularity of performing Quantz's flute concertos, and whose service C. P. E. Bach found irksome. Frederick William admired Haydn and paid him handsomely for the six quartets Haydn sent him soon after his accession in 1786. His interest in the cello and in string chamber music led him

to discover the fact that Boccherini had fallen into dire need and was living in the slums of Madrid. He was rescued from distress and given a good annuity. The latest French and Italian comic operas were brought to Berlin, and the king encouraged *Singspiele*. He was delighted with "The Seraglio," having already come to know Mozart's music through his quartets.

Prince Lichnowsky, a member of the Masonic lodge into which Mozart had been received, and for some time Mozart's piano pupil, held lands in Silesia, annexed by Prussia. He was related by marriage to Mozart's good friend, Count Thun. In April 1789 Lichnowsky had to go to Berlin on business and asked Mozart to go with him. To Mozart the request seemed a godsend, for he could probably give concerts in passing through Prague and Dresden. He was soon to be reassured by news from his friend Ramm who had been in Berlin that the king of Prussia had frequently asked whether he was sure that Mozart would reach Berlin.

Prague was reached in three days, on April 10, and Mozart paid a call on Duschek. He also made tentative arrangements for another opera to be mounted in Prague, but the impresario there soon moved to Warsaw and Mozart heard no more of the affair. The trouble was that Lichnowsky did not want to stop more than the one night in Prague. Before arriving Mozart wrote in haste to Constanze:

> Every moment I look at your portrait and weep, half in joy and half in sorrow . . . Have no anxiety on my account for on this journey I am meeting no discomfort or worry. Nothing saddens me but your absence . . .

At Dresden Mozart made music in several houses, but first in the hotel where the travellers were staying, for there they found Anton Kraft who was on tour. (Music-lovers will remember Kraft from Haydn's cello concerto for him; he was an outstanding member of the Esterházy orchestra.) Josephine Duschek was also on tour in Dresden, and Mozart made straight for the house where she lodged, for he brought a letter from her husband in Prague. Her host, Johann Neumann, was also very musical; he was a Saxon court official and a successful amateur librettist. Probably through him Mozart was asked to the court, though Frederick Augustus III rarely welcomed travelling musicians. Mozart played the D major piano concerto, K.537. Lichnowsky took him to dine with the Russian ambassador, a man of wide literary and musical tastes whom Mozart greatly liked for his kindly manner. This prince and Lichnowsky were anxious for Mozart to meet J. W. Hässler, Dresden's leading keyboard player, and proposed that the party should drive to the church for Mozart to sample the organ. Hässler and Mozart played the organ, and then the piano at the ambassador's house. As usual, Mozart has no good word to say for the other musician:

> Hässler's strength at the organ is in his footwork, but as the pedals are arranged step-wise here that is no great accomplishment . . . He can't play a fugue

60. Prince Karl Lichnowsky. Portrait in oils attributed to F. Gödel.

well. He has learnt by heart the harmony and modulations of old Sebastian Bach ... In my opinion Mlle. Aurnhammer is as good on the piano as he is, so you can imagine that his reputation was somewhat lost on me.

He also had a poor opinion of the Dresden opera. We have no letters from Leipzig on his outward journey, but we know that on April 22 he played without payment on Bach's organ in the St. Thomas Church for about an hour to a large congregation. One who was present, Friedrich Rochlitz, noted particularly his "elegant dress."

After three days the travellers continued to Potsdam where Lichnowsky's business was soon done and he wished to return to Vienna. We have no letter telling us what Mozart did when he first arrived; but we know that Frederick William was anxious to see him at once, and probably made arrangements for his formal appearance before the court and music-lovers. He therefore returned as far as Leipzig with Lichnowsky, for Mme. Duschek and Neumann had come on there from Dresden; he also found there letters from Vienna. (Later Mozart told his wife that Lichnowsky had "abandoned him in expensive Potsdam.") He was pressed to give a concert at the Gewandhaus and "played compositions which at that time existed only in manuscript." He played two concertos, one of which we know to have been the magnificent C major, K.503, and Mme. Duschek sang some of his arias. Rochlitz describes Mozart's trouble with some of the older members of the orchestra at the rehearsal of a symphony. One of the famous last three? We do not know. The players dragged and "he stamped the beat so forcefully that one of his finely worked shoe buckles snapped in pieces ... He laughed and let the pieces lie, shouted 'Ancora!' and made them begin again for the third time." Rochlitz was delighted at the end of the concert when "this obliging man," after two hours' hard work, consented to give piano solos, a brilliant improvisation, and the variations on "Je suis Lindor," K.354. Mozart found the applause unexpectedly great, but the audience smaller than he had hoped, for Leipzig was not accustomed to the high price charged for admission.

The concert was on May 12. Arriving in Berlin on the 19th, he discovered that "The Seraglio" was in progress at the National Theatre. In his honour it had been substituted for the work previously billed. The stories of the way he was recognised in the theatre and brought on to the stage vary so widely that none is worth repeating. The Prussian monarch did not approve of his guest giving a public concert, but Mozart heard one given by his pupil Hummel before he himself played before the king and queen. The king rewarded him more generously than he had expected. The hundred Friedrichsdor were worth more in Vienna than Berlin, and corresponded with 700 Austrian florins. He was asked for six quartets, and when he sent only the first of them to Potsdam he received another hundred Friedrichsdor. The prominent

but not very difficult cello parts in this K.575 in D and in subsequent "Prussian" quartets honour the royal performer, who also hoped for six easy piano sonatas for his young daughter.

No evidence supports two stories about Mozart's visit to Prussia. One is that Mozart declined the offer of a *Kapellmeister*-ship, the other that he rutted with Henriette Baranius who played Blondchen in that Berlin performance of "The Seraglio." (Mozart was the last person to take a romp with someone he knew to be the king's mistress!) A far more interesting story is notably missing, for it might explain why Mozart thought it wise to write to Constanze (who had heard how well he was doing financially): "My dearest little wife, when I get home you must rejoice more at having me again than at having any money I bring." Allowing for the "loan" to Lichnowsky and the possibility that the prince did not leave him a carriage for the return journey, he must have spent money lavishly. The observation will not please idolaters who accept silly stories about philanderings and social butterflies but suppose that other people are always to be blamed if a great artist lacks money. A pity Constanze lacked the strong wife's ability to control the family purse! She seems to have been as spendthrift as her husband.

Yet at this point one is forced to comment, in contradiction of others, upon the basic happiness of the Mozarts' marriage. Their letters during his absence in Germany and then during hers in Baden contain mutual equivalents of "Mind you behave yourself" along with much childish name-calling and punning which baffles translation and makes utter nonsense – or rather seemed to do so for those of our forbears who failed to recognise symbolic references to the intimacies of the marriage bed.

> If I were to tell you all the things I do with your portrait you would certainly laugh. When I take it out of its case, I say: "Hello Stanzerl, little rascal ... kiss and hug." When I put it in again, I let it slide in slowly and keep saying "Ah-ah-ah-ah!" in the special way that meaning demands. Then at last a quick "Good night, little mouse. Sleep tight!"

(The words omitted are not coarse but nonsensical – a series of names like the English "Tinker-puss," "Pip-squeak," etc.) Three days after this letter of April 13 from Dresden, he wrote again in less playful vein; we have already seen part of that letter of the 16th in the pages dealing with Mozart's marriage and the lovers' tiff about the game of forfeits, but let one passage be repeated:

> I do beg you ... to watch your honour and mine, and to have proper regard for appearances. Do not be angry at me for saying this. You should love me all the more for so treasuring our reputation.

We hardly need intimate letters to tell us that the most urbane and civilised of great musicians was also as "elemental" as his Papageno, nor do we need the evidence of "Stanzerl's" regular confinements to prove that the couple were sexually suited. What needs defending is a refutation of the charge that these letters show the "superficiality" of the relationship between a great artist and the wife with whom he had to be content – as though a series of mistresses could have done as much for him. Today, when women increasingly receive the same general or artistic education as men, and when there has come what is called a "sexual revolution," we have been made aware that neither mutual physical pleasure nor intellectual parity can guarantee marital happiness. They are keys to it, as ability to read is a key to literary experience; but one can misuse or waste what is unlocked. It has already been pointed out that Constanze was no Egeria, but she knew enough about artists at least to know the sort of man her husband was and not to wish for a different sort or try to bend him to her own ideal. Moreover Mozart was the dominant partner. Though we are on the debatable ground of opinion based on experience and observation, for we cannot know all the facts of Mozart's private life, most of us can suppose him to have been more happy with Constanze as a wife than he would have been with the Egerias of musical history. What musician would wish to be yoked with poor Liszt's countesses or Cosima Wagner?

Desperation

Mozart arrived home on June 4, 1789 and finished only the first of the "Prussian" quartets and the first of the commissioned sonatas (K.576) before circumstances made composition impossible and he found himself worried and depressed. Constanze was again pregnant; she was also very ill, and the money sent by the king of Prussia was finally eroded on fees for various medical treatments and prescriptions. Within almost a month, on July 12, Mozart renewed his appeals to Puchberg:

> God! I am in a state in which I would not wish to put my worst enemy. If you, my best of friends and brothers, now desert me, wretched man that I am, I shall be lost through no fault of mine, and with me my poor, sick wife and child. The other day I wanted to pour out my heart when I was with you, but I could not find the courage. I could not find it now if I faced you; I can muster it only in writing, and then trembling. I should not dare even in writing if I were not certain that you know me, were aware of my circumstances and completely certain that I am brought *guiltlessly* to this utterly wretched situation. Oh God! Instead of coming to you with thanks I am making new requests; instead of settling I am asking for more . . . Alas, luck is against me, though only in Vienna, where I cannot earn any money no matter how hard I try. For the past two weeks I have sent out a proposal for subscription concerts, and the only name subscribed is Van Swieten . . . Now I am dependent solely upon you, my only friend, and ask if you will or can lend

me another 500 gulden. Until I am solvent I offer to return 10 gulden each month. After that – and this must be in a few months at the longest – I shall pay back the entire sum to you, with whatever interest you ask, and I shall continue to acknowledge myself your debtor for the rest of my life. That I shall be for ever, for I shall never be able to repay you properly for your friendship and kindness. Thank God it is now said. You know all; do not be angry at my admission, but remember that without your help the honour, peace, maybe the very life of your friend and brother will be shattered.

There being no immediate reply, Mozart wrote again in a few days:

> If you cannot possibly help me with the sum I mentioned, I beg you to advance whatever you can spare at this moment, for I really am in desperate need.

Knowing what we do of Mozart's upbringing and character we may be certain that never before, not even in illness or bereavement, had he been so miserable; yet in this very letter he mentions the engagement of Nikolaus Closset, then the most fashionable of Vienna's medical practitioners. (His friend Dr. Barisani was now dead.) Constanze was sent to Baden-bei-Wien, and Mozart's misery prevented his "going out." He did, however, make several journeys to see her. Much has been made of such passages in his letters to her as the following:

> As far as your foot is concerned you have only to be patient, for it will soon be well again. I am delighted to hear that you are enjoying your time; do not doubt that; but I do sometimes wish that you would not make yourself cheap.

How could a woman advanced in pregnancy have played the whore with any gallants taking the fashionable cure? We have to remember that Vienna from Mozart's time to Schubert's was fonder of scandal and tittle-tattle than even Paris was. Leaflets and magazines supposedly devoted to news, theatre criticism, music, dress and fashion, court engagements, which would interest "people of fashion," invented suggestions of the kind Mr. Puff so well describes in Sheridan's "The Critic." When truth was not forthcoming in sufficiently scandalous quantity, tales of actors and actresses, and of carefully unmentioned titled folk who were enamoured of them, and then tales of prominent musicians and their relatives – these could always be invented as credible, and a fashionable spa like Baden was a haunt of literary gossips. Unfortunately Mozart was easily hurt by anything touching his "honour," but it is ridiculous to suppose that he believed Constanze unfaithful to him.

Mozart's despair may have been somewhat alleviated, even though no immediate money was forthcoming, when he heard in July that "Figaro" was to be revived in the following month, and when the emperor commissioned a new opera from the Abbate Lorenzo da Ponte and *Hofkomponist* W. A. Mozart. After this revival,

61. Anton Stadler, the fellow-Mason for whom Mozart wrote his Clarinet Concerto. Anonymous silhouette.

which was most enthusiastically received, "Figaro" stayed in repertory; and though, as we have seen, the composer did not benefit financially, these performances were good publicity for the new opera, "Così fan tutte, ossia La scuola degli amanti" (This Do They All, or The School for Lovers).

The work was a great success, but it was not in rehearsal until the end of the year and not produced until January 1790, so that Mozart had again to ask Puchberg for money. He confessed that he had dismissed a Dr. Hunczowsky "for certain reasons in a somewhat unpleasant interview" – the certain reasons presumably being that he could not afford him. We know that Puchberg was still Mozart's musical admirer, for he was due to come to Mozart's house for chamber music on the last day of the year, but he was invited instead to a brief rehearsal of items from the new opera. "Only you and Haydn are invited. I shall tell you about Salieri's intrigues, though already they have all failed."

As during the composition of "Figaro," the sparse entries in Mozart's notebook catalogue indicate his preoccupation with "Così fan tutte." There is only one significant entry for the second half of 1789, that of September 29 – the marvellous quintet for clarinet and strings, K. 581, for the clarinettist Anton Stadler, a fellow-Mason. Presumably it brought immediate pay-

ment. (The clarinet concerto, completed only two months before Mozart died, was also for Stadler.)

With "Così fan tutte" the Mozart–Da Ponte collaboration finished, for just after its production Joseph II died. He might have done more than he did for Mozart, and probably he would have done much for him if the two of them had lived longer. Certainly Joseph had been a protector of both Mozart and Da Ponte against accusations true and false. So many of those against Da Ponte were true that (so he declared in one of his poems dedicated to Byron) he thought himself lucky to escape from Vienna with his life. He fled to Trieste and married an English girl whom he took with him first to London, then America. He concealed his priesthood and seems to have had a happy married life. She died in 1832 when he was 83. In New York she had occasion to be proud of him when, in 1825, Manuel Garcia arrived with an Italian company and gave "Don Giovanni" among its performances, with huge success. After his wife's death he negotiated with the patriarch of Venice to reconcile himself with the church. He made his confession and received the last rites before he died in 1838 aged 89!

A New Régime

For the rest of 1790 Mozart was in bad health and composed little. Constanze was again ordered to Baden. The new emperor was not particularly interested in music. His wife, Maria Louise, formerly Spanish infanta, who was later to call Mozart's "La clemenza di Tito" a *porcheria tedesca* (a German hoggery), went dutifully to theatrical and musical affairs and maintained an attitude of haughty disdain. But one feature of the new régime was of interest to Mozart and other hopeful artists and officials. The new ruler wished to show who was master. He would choose everybody in imperial employment for himself, and make others notice the fact by dismissing plenty of those entrenched by his predecessor's favour. With glee many musicians passed about the rumour that Leopold had spoken of Salieri (not without reason) as a scheming egoist. Salieri wisely resigned to avoid dismissal, and Joseph Weigl took his place. Fortunately Mozart did not lose his minor title and stipend, and therefore applied for the post of "second *Kapellmeister*," "especially as *Kapellmeister* Salieri . . . did not devote himself to the style of church music with which I have been familiar since youth." Anxious to pick up any royal appointment, he mentioned in the same application his repute as a pianist, which emboldened him "to seek the privilege of undertaking the musical instruction of the royal family."

No immediate reply was forthcoming. But Puchberg seems to have believed in Mozart's "hope of an excellent appointment" because at least the application had not been returned as was usual when requests were declined.

62. Joseph Weigl. Anonymous oil portrait.

No less than seven begging letters were written to Puchberg between April and August, and we can but guess at Mozart's feelings ("Has he told anybody else?") when Puchberg and others came to hear the clarinet quintet or the next two quartets for the king of Prussia (K.589 and K.590) which proved to be the last he wrote. He regretted having to "dispose of them and all their labour for so little, merely to get some money to keep going," but he sent them to the printer. Probably because Puchberg insisted, he was forced to the work he hated most. He again took pupils, hoping that they could come to his house, so that he need not spend time and strength trailing round Vienna, and need not leave Constanze in her bad condition. No doubt Puchberg found some of the pupils, though they probably did not include so lowly a person as the one best known to us – Franz Xaver Süssmayr, to whom was entrusted the finishing of the score of Mozart's Requiem.

During the summer Mozart said he suffered from "colds, sleeplessness, and toothache." Early in June he went with Constanze to Baden "in order to save money." Though he, she, and eighteenth-century doctors were unaware of the fact, there must have been a strong connexion between Constanze's unbroken child-bearing and the bad state of her health; for there were no children by her second marriage and, as the Novellos saw, she then enjoyed excellent health. Except that he might have

received ready money, it was merciful that Mozart was not asked to write an opera for the royal double wedding in September of the daughters of the king of Naples to the Archdukes Franz and Ferdinand. Da Ponte's last libretto in Vienna went instead to the new imperial *Kapellmeister* Weigl. According to Da Ponte's memoirs it had to be written in three days, and possibly that was why he did not suggest Mozart for the music, though no doubt Weigl was expected to show justification for his recent appointment.

At the end of September the Mozarts moved again, to a house near St. Stephen's, 8 Rauhensteingasse. On September 24 the court left for the coronation of Leopold II at Frankfurt-am-Main, scheduled for October 9. Mozart's official post did not bring any summons to the festivities, but in his desperation he conceived the idea of making capital for himself in the crowded coronation city. He pawned his silver to hire a carriage and set off with his brother-in-law, Franz Hofer, the violinist with whom he would play. Quite remarkable was his sudden revival of high spirits as they set out on this venture, evidently without caring how fast they spent their resources. At Ratisbon (Regensburg) they "lunched with divine table music, angelic service, and glorious Moselle wine." They breakfasted in Nuremberg which, true to his century, Mozart thought an ugly "Gothick" town, but Würzburg, episcopal capital of Franconia, was "beautiful and magnificent," words which can still be endorsed despite the attention of a bomb-happy vandal in 1945 after peace had been declared. At Aschaffenburg they were "wretchedly swindled by the innkeeper." Having found lodgings in Frankfurt, Mozart seems to have lost his high spirits while he waited:

> [September 30] I pine like a child to return to you. I should be ashamed if people could read my mind. Everything is cold to me, cold as ice. If you were with me I could enjoy the kindness people show me, but everything is empty.
> [October 3] I have so far lived in retirement here. I do not go out in the morning but stay in my poky little room and compose. My only diversion is the theatre, where I meet many acquaintances from Vienna, Munich, Mannheim, and even Salzburg . . . My peace is coming to an end. People are inviting me everywhere, and though I do not like being quizzed I know that is necessary, and in God's name I must endure it.

He could not hire the theatre until after the coronation when the visitors were leaving and his concert drew a small audience who were "so pleased that they begged me to give another." The programme included the D major piano concerto, K.537, now to be called the "Coronation," but Mozart also played another concerto, which may have been his last, K.595 in B flat, one of the most beautiful and enigmatic.

He decided to go to Mainz where his old patron the archbishop-elector von Erthal might give him an appointment. He was made no offer but received, according to the account books, a good fee (165 gulden) for a concert. In a letter home he said he received "a mere 15 carolins" (30 gulden less). Had he so little control of money that he could not admit the amount he spent to Constanze? He went with friends to see the gardens at Schwetzingen, found Mannheim no longer in its musical glory but attended a performance of "Figaro" there. In the orchestra was Johann André, later to be Mozart's publisher. His description of Mozart's "pallid skin and bulging eyes" tallies with the Stock drawing of about this period and testifies to the advance of kidney disease. Mozart returned through Munich in order to meet his old Mannheim friends, and there played before the king of Naples who was visiting the Bavarian court. This was something of a triumph since he had not been asked to play before him in Vienna. The concert may have been financially rewarding, for Mozart seems to have enjoyed his stay in Munich and he planned to take his wife there.

He reached home in November. Despite begging

letters, we can approach the last year of his life certain that, until his illness struck him its death blow, he was less often thoroughly dejected than in 1790. The chief reason for this assertion is that important commissions had to be fulfilled. He must have been cheered by his travel and meeting of friends, however little his finances had improved since he left home; and he felt the pleasure of returning, especially as he found waiting there the following letter of October 26, from Robert O'Reilly, manager of the "Italian Opera" in London:

Through a person attached to His Royal Highness the Prince of Wales I have learned of your intention to visit England. Because I am appointed to meet men of talent personally, and am at present in a position to be of advantage to them, I offer you, sir, the place of composer in England. If you are able to come here at the end of this coming December 1790, and remain until the end of June 1791, and during this time compose at least two serious

63. The coronation of Leopold II as Holy Roman Emperor in Frankfurt-am-Main, 1790. Engraving initialled "F.L.N."

95

64. *Johann André. Engraving by Daniel Berger after a drawing by Johann Christoph Frisch, 1780.*

65. *Johann Peter Salomon. Engraving by Georg Sigismund Facius after an oil portrait by Thomas Hardy, 1792.*

or comic operas, as the management should decide, I am prepared to offer you 300 pounds sterling. You will also be free to write compositions for any other concert hall, other theatres being excepted. If this appeals to you and you are in a position to accept, please do me the honour of replying by return post, and this letter will then serve as a contract.

During Mozart's absence in Frankfurt, J. P. Salomon, the London violinist and concert promoter, was visiting his native Bonn and heard of Prince Nikolaus Esterházy's death. He had previously tried unsuccessfully to induce Haydn to come to London, but now he sped to Vienna to try his luck by personal contact. As we know he was successful, though Haydn was only two years short of 60. At the farewell dinner to Haydn the impresario from England offered Mozart the honour of a similar visit to London, an opportunity Mozart had long hoped for. It is one of the mysteries of musical history that Mozart did not gleefully accept at once. O'Reilly's and Salomon's commissions could have been fulfilled concurrently. He spoke to Haydn of the danger of travelling, and said: "You are not suited, Papa, for the great world, and you command so few languages." Haydn replied that he had health and vigour and that the language he spoke was understood everywhere. There is a ring of truth about this, for Mozart could not bear the loss of friends. He is said to have broken down as he saw Haydn off in the carriage and said: "I fear we shall never see each other again."

He settled, if that is the word, to solitude and composition – working on Count Deym's mechanical organ pieces, then the two wonderful string quintets in D and E flat, K.593 and K.614 (the latter described in

Artaria's edition as "composed for a Hungarian amateur") and dances for the court. In January he "finished" the last piano concerto, the one in B flat which he may have tried out at Frankfurt. But most important of all, before long, Schikaneder and Mozart were sending back and forth parts of the work now known as "The Magic Flute," thanks to which Mozart's really private life, his hours of composition, were passed in the happiest world he knew. He was delighted with the work, both in its comic and its serious aspects, as he had never been delighted with any other.

Pictorial Essay:
Masonic Symbols
and Ceremonies

The importance of Freemasonry to Mozart extended far beyond the music he provided for its ceremonies and less formal occasions. It coloured almost every aspect of his later life and enriched it socially, artistically, and one might almost say financially, for the generous loans he received from his fellow-Mason Michael Puchberg enabled him to maintain his social standing in Vienna and were never fully repaid.

Freemasonry's particular attractions for him are fully discussed by Professor Hutchings on Pages 98 and 99 and it remains here only to supplement his remarks with a closer look at the movement as it functioned in Mozart's time.

The more immediate origins of Freemasonry lay in the stonemasons' guilds of the medieval cathedral-builders, though Masons themselves attach great symbolic if not historical significance to the temple of Solomon, begun around 950 B.C. It would be an oversimplification to say that when cathedral-building declined guilds admitted outsiders to maintain their existence. Much more was involved: the widening of building activities to ever-more elaborate palaces and other secular projects, for instance, and the rise of architecture as an intellectual and theoretical art rather than a practical craft. In the seventeenth century rituals and symbolism of ancient religions and chivalric orders began to be added to those traditionally connected with the guilds, and the foundation of a Grand Lodge in Britain in 1717 was the last major step in the change-over from operative to speculative Freemasonry.

79

80

With the establishment of the office of Grand Master came the concept of sovereignty within the movement, with attendant oaths of allegiance, charters, and insignia (see *No. 84*). This naturally led to political suspicions and sometimes active persecution. Opposition from the church, culminating in the papal bull of 1738, was also natural. Freemasonry is not religious in any sectarian sense and has been able to flourish under both Catholic and Protestant régimes, but it is based on the fundamentals of any religion – belief in a Supreme Being and in an existence after death. Its principles of brotherhood, charity, faith, and obedience were coincidentally Christian ideals, which led to the mistaken idea that it was a Christian institution challenging the authority of the church.

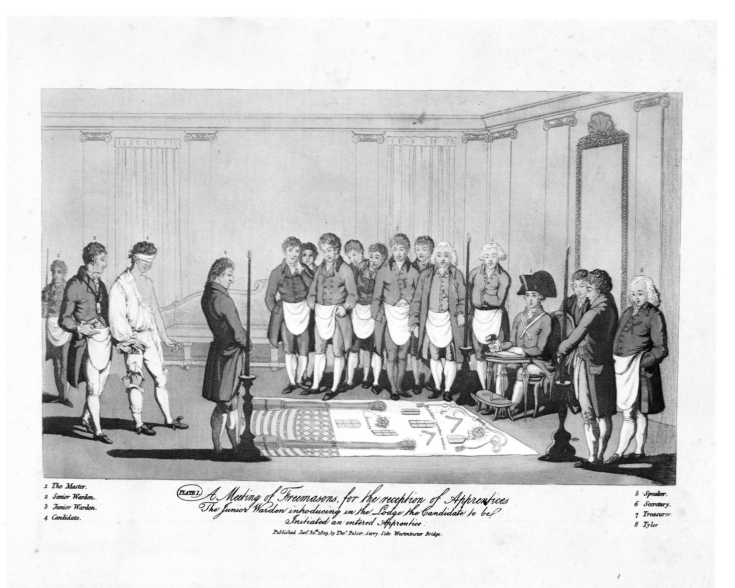

81

1 The Master.
2 Senior Warden.
3 Junior Warden.
4 Candidate.

A Meeting of Freemasons, for the reception of Apprentices
The Junior Warden introducing in the Lodge the Candidate to be
Initiated an entered Apprentice.
Published Jan.ʸ 30ᵗʰ 1809, by Thoˢ Palser, Surry Side Westminster Bridge.

5 Speaker.
6 Secretary.
7 Treasurer.
8 Tyler.

That the pressures on Freemasonry should have been eased in Austria just when Mozart was active in Vienna was a happy accident. It meant he could enjoy to the full the social contact, moral support, and artistic stimulus his sensitive nature required and Freemasonry was able to supply.

79. A Masonic apron of French origin, c. 1800, of hand-painted velvet with a silk border and strings. Its symbolism is centred on the sun, insignia of the Master of a lodge (see *No. 84*), and motifs associated with Egyptian sun worship, notably the phoenix.

80. Two Dutch leatherbound Masonic songbooks, c. 1775, from (left) the Leyden lodge "La vertu" and (right) the Amsterdam lodge "Concordia vincit animos."

In Continental lodges in the eighteenth century ceremonies and official gatherings were usually followed by a meal called the "banquet," not necessarily as sumptuous as that word suggests. Music, including communal singing, was a regular feature of these less formal gatherings (canons were particularly popular) and Mozart's vocal works include a number of pieces, apart from cantatas for formal occasions, which may have been intended for such "banquets." One brother, the "Frère à talent" (nowadays simply designated as the Organist) had the task of organising the musical activity. Few lodges possessed musicians of Mozart's stature, if any at all, and this usually meant hiring non-Mason professional performers, who were admitted only to banquets after taking a simple oath of secrecy. (See also *Nos. 84* *and 88.*)

81. The introduction of a candidate to be initiated as an apprentice, the lowest rank of the order. Symbolically he is presented "neither clothed, neither naked." Although the engraving was published in London in 1809 by Thomas Palser, it represents a much earlier ceremony, being based on an illustration from a French publication of c. 1744 (see also the illustration on page 98) called "Les Coutumes des Francs-Maçons" (The customs of the Freemasons). The clothing of the Masons has been updated but the symbols and ceremony not. After the turn of the century the scene would have been in a proper Masonic temple; there would have been a more imposing altar or throne and the brothers would not have been standing round the tableau. A further clue to the earlier date is the placing of the three symbolic lights.

82. A songbook c. 1800 from the Dutch lodge "The Rising Star" in Goes. (See also *No. 80.*)

83. The initiation of an entered apprentice (blindfolded) at a lodge in Vienna, c. 1780. This clearly aristocratic gathering was probably at either "Zur wahren Eintracht" (True Brotherhood) or "Zur gekrönten Hoffnung" (Crowned Hope).

84. In Freemasonry there are in general three main degrees: the entered apprentice, the fellow of the craft, and the master mason. But in different countries and in individual lodges many additional grades – sometimes hundreds – were superimposed on these major divisions. Professor Hutchings points out that Mozart, who was promoted rapidly through the minor orders, must have been highly valued as a member of the organisation. Naturally, in a movement in which status was important, in spite of the principles of equality and brotherhood, each grade and each official function had its special insignia, although these could vary in form from lodge to lodge. On this page is a selection of insignia from Mozart's time, all in finely worked silver. The offices to which they belong are (left to right): top row – Master of the Lodge (a collection of symbols of other offices crowned by the Master's personal symbol, the sun), Steward, and Senior Warden; middle row – Preparator, Master of the Lodge, and Almoner; bottom row – Frère à talent (see *No. 80*), Deputy Master, and Tiler (doorkeeper).

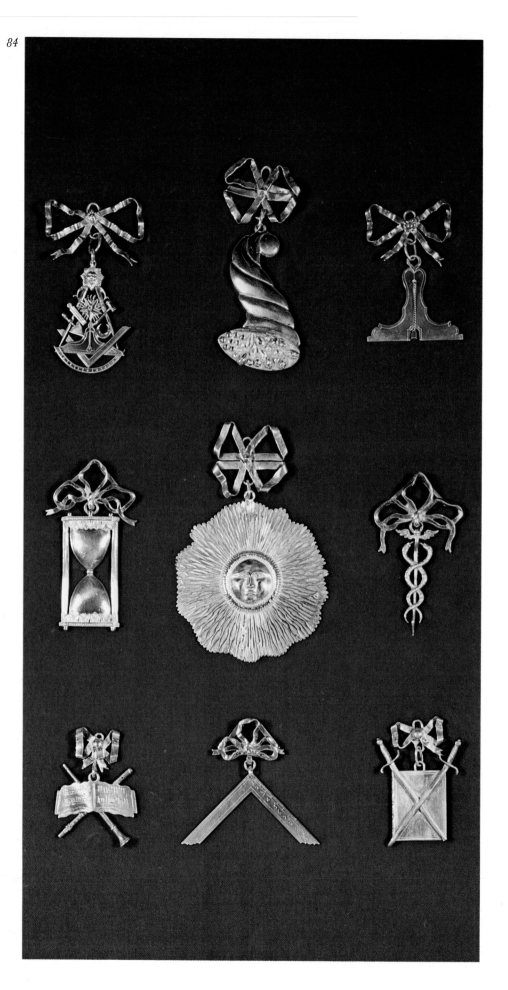

Everything connected with the practice of Freemasonry in the eighteenth century bore in some form or another the symbolism of the order, and as Masonic activities were wide-ranging even within the confines of the lodges it was natural that a great variety of objects should be specially made for ceremonies, social functions, and even for personal use or decoration. If Freemasonry found a place in music through Mozart, it also had a say in the decorative arts of the time, for the manufacture of Masonic articles often brought out the best in craftsmen such as the silversmiths who fashioned the insignia already illustrated *(No. 84)* and resulted in minor works of art like the porcelain figures on this page *(Nos. 86 and 87)*.

85. A Japanese lacquered box with a Masonic tableau motif inlaid in mother-of-pearl, c. 1800.

The Oriental objects, first from China and later from Japan, which began to be imported by Western Europe in the seventeeth century had an important influence in interior design and the decorative arts generally in the Rococo period and beyond. (See also *No. 58*).

86 and 87. That Masonic emblems should be found in eighteenth-century porcelain ware is hardly surprising. After European potters discovered the secret of making true porcelain to match the quality of highly valued Chinese imports and the first European factory had been established at Meissen in Saxony under the patronage of Frederick Augustus, porcelain attained such popularity that it might be regarded as the art most typical of the Rococo period. Both *Nos.* 86 and 87 were made at Meissen and designed by Johann Joachim Kändler, who brought the art to its highest point after 1731 when he was appointed by the elector to reorganise the Meissen modelling department. The designs are thought by some to date from the early 1730's but the modelling of *No. 87*, which exists in several versions, was probably after 1745 for the symbolic hand gestures featured were introduced

88

generally only in that year. Further, both pieces feature the pug dog (known in German as "Mops"). This suggests a connection with the Mops Order, a German sister organisation of the mid-eighteenth century to which women were admitted. *No. 86* depicts simply the Master of a lodge but *No. 87* poses a number of problems of interpretation which still have not been settled among Masonic historians themselves. One English theory is that the piece represents a lodge Master (seated) with either Adolf Fredrik of Sweden, a master mason, or Frederick Augustus of Saxony who happened to be Grand Master of the Mops Order. German historians, however, point to the fact that the apron of the standing figure is not folded down – a mark of apprenticeship. A further confusing detail is that the seated figure wears the insignia of Deputy Master (see *No. 84*). Whatever the truth, the globe clearly symbolises the spread of Freemasonry internationally at that time.

88. An eighteenth-century Masonic glass with engraved symbols in gold. Glasses like this were specially designed for use at Masonic banquets (see also *No. 80*) where there was an elaborate drinking ritual which involved at some points thumping the glasses on the table (the so-called "cannonades") – hence the sturdy design and the thick, heavy base. The form was unique when first introduced but soon became widely popular for both its capacity and its stability. In general manufacture the type became known as a "Mason" (not to be confused with the nineteenth-century English pottery called Mason ware or the glass preserving jars of the American John. L. Mason).

89. A porcelain snuffbox from the middle of the eighteenth century, an example of the many articles, such as plates, clocks, and even pipes, made with Masonic motifs for personal use. This box, mounted with bronze, depicts under the lid the Master of a lodge receiving a delegate.

89

90. The apron of a "Frère à talent", featuring the insignia of that office (see *No. 84*). It is a Dutch apron of the eighteenth century, probably from a lodge in Amsterdam.

91. The apron of the Master of the Dutch lodge "La vertu" in Leyden. It dates from 1801 and its dominant motif is the column, a recurrent feature in previous illustrations *(Nos. 79, 81, 83, 85 and 87)*. The three virtues on which any lodge should rest were considered to be Strength, Wisdom, and Beauty, symbolised by the Ionic, Doric, and Corinthian columns respectively.

90

91

(48)

VIII

The last year

Mozart as Mason
Approach to Death
"The Magic Flute"
Requiem aeternam
Envoi

66. *Sketch by Joseph and Peter Schaffer of Act II stage-setting possibly for the first performance of "The Magic Flute," 1791. The characters are (left to right) Tamino, Pamina, and Papageno.*

Mozart as Mason

Did Mozart meet his suffering and death as a Freemason or as a Catholic? The question would not have occurred to him. Most of his local brothers in the craft were Catholics, many of them punctilious Catholics; priests belonged to the Vienna lodges, and to Mozart the practices and teachings of Freemasonry were an exciting extension of religion. Note the deliberate word "exciting." A creature sensitive to the snubs of society, and most happy in the company of people who forgot rank, at least during the making and enjoyment of music, was naturally drawn to the Masonic ideals of brotherhood and philanthropy. But it was not only the ethical and philosophic aspects of Masonry which interested him: he was obviously drawn to the mystery and ceremony. In a devout Catholic this may need explanation.

Freemasons nowadays being most numerous in non-Catholic countries, the conclusion has been drawn that their lodges minister to the natural craving for symbolism, colour, and mystery in man – "a being darkly wise and rudely great." The craving, it is supposed, is supplied by the Catholic enactment of sacramental worship and constant reference to the supernatural, saints, and an unseen life, more than by religions which are primarily didactic, ethical, and rationalistic. This is no doubt true, but nothing written by the Mozarts (and little written by other people of their time) suggests that Catholic worship *impressed* them. Confession and communion, prayers, fasting and feasting, observance of days of obligation – the duties of the Catholic are mentioned often enough; but they do not write with delight or awe about the high masses and vespers for which their

67. The earliest illustration of a Masonic initiation ceremony. Engraving published by Jacques Chéreau in Paris probably in 1744.

grand music was purveyed. When daily dress and manners were ceremonious, there may have been more of convention and pomp than of awe and mystery in church, even where rationalist clerics did not treat the familiar words and acts perfunctorily. However much the paintings and sculptures of Baroque and Rococo churches depict anthropomorphic deity and the saints, patriarchs, and angels, these grand theatrical buildings do not suggest mystery as medieval churches do; instead they are like the finest halls of royal palaces, conceived for the Supreme Prince. Their very theatricality was pious, for the church was often called *theatrum sacrum*, the sacred theatre where the holy sacrifice, the mass, was enacted. There can be solemnity, even severity, in parts of Mozart's church music, but very little composed for the *theatrum sacrum* would have been out of place in serious or even comic operas for the secular theatre.

When we remember that in Mozart's time priests belonged to lodges and celebrated "Corporate Communion of Brothers," we must suppose that Catholics aware of the papal measures against Masonry felt their situation precarious. For the Mozarts this feeling may well have been attractive, for their strong churchmanship did not alter their contempt for unworthy clerics nor their enjoyment of defiance. They were fortunate that the ability to be both Catholic and Freemason in Vienna just outlasted their lives. It was exactly during Mozart's short life in Vienna that Masonry most flourished there and "enlightened" Catholics joined the lodges – not all with Mozart's deep feelings. Mozart was the only great musician of his time to write Masonic music; Haydn wrote none at all, and possibly saw no more reason to think of Masonry profoundly than he did to study theology and the intellectual defence of the religion he loved so naïvely.

For his happy conscience as Freemason and Catholic Mozart could thank the Pope's supposed supporter, the Holy Roman Emperor! Franz of Lorraine, Maria Theresa's consort, became a Mason in 1731 through Lord Chesterfield. The papal bulls against Masonry were promulgated in 1738 and 1751 but their enforcement depended upon heads of state. Maria Theresa suppressed the lodges in 1764 but they continued in secret. When she died in 1780 there came the great revival which attracted so many intellectuals and artists. Freemasonry was a token of enlightenment.

The enlightened Joseph II did not become a Mason. His private letters reveal some ridicule of the esoteric elements in Masonry, but there is no question of the fact that he was responsible for the freedom and prosperity of the order in Vienna during his reign. From Prague he brought Ignaz Born, whom he was to ennoble, ostensibly to catalogue the imperial geology and natural history collection. The more important position was as master of the oldest lodge, "Crowned Hope," for under Born it became a "Society of Science, and Academy for the Furtherance of the Freedom of Conscience and Thought." Joseph recognised both the idealism and the social usefulness of a popular secret society under a man like Born, not merely loyal to the court but in sympathy with the emperor in a restless, revolutionary epoch.

Maria Theresa had rid Austria of the Jesuits who would have exerted most pressure for the legal enforcement of papal bulls. Joseph therefore managed to issue a compromising edict at the end of 1785. It required the eight lodges of the capital to amalgamate into two, "Truth" and "New Crowned Hope." The name of the latter preserved the old famous one which absorbed "Three Fires" and "Benevolence," the lodge to which the Mozarts had belonged. Born was certainly consulted about the mergers, which gave Masonry certain safeguards. In some German states, especially where members of secret societies included state officials in corrupt or despotic governments, Masonry had its heretics and schismatics. It was imitated by charlatan societies under founders with a demagogic love of leadership and conceit of their own expression and thought. One of these rival societies, the "Illuminati," was numerous and powerful in Bavaria; it came under suspicion of state and church, and in 1784 caused Karl Theodor's ban upon all secret societies in Bavaria and the Palatinate.

Before he died Mozart saw signs of similar repression in Austria, for the enemies of Masonry in church and state renewed attack as soon as Joseph was succeeded by Leopold in 1790. Applauding "The Magic Flute" Freemasons enjoyed a corporate demonstration, for the fate of the Bavarian lodges led them to identify the Queen of Night's hostility with that of Karl Theodor rather than of Maria Theresa and the church. The owner of the theatre and librettist of the opera, Emanuel Schikaneder, also wrote the words for Mozart's last Masonic cantata, "Eine kleine Freimaurer-Kantate," K.623. When the sick composer was hard at work on the opera and the Requiem during the summer of 1791, this joyful cantata

68. *Ignaz von Born. Engraving by Jakob Adam after a painting by Gabrielle Bertrand, 1782.*

was expected from him for the dedication of a new Masonic temple in November. The event saw Mozart's last public appearance, for soon after it he took to his bed. He was delighted with the congratulations of his brother Masons, saying to Constanze, "If I did not know that I had written better music their enthusiasm would make me believe it to be my finest work."

We have devoted much comment to Mozart's wholehearted allegiance to Freemasonry because it reveals so much of the man and checks those who would present him to us as a potential revolutionary. Just as not every advocate of reforms towards the "left" envisages a totalitarian ideal, so not every hater of arrogant privilege and cruelty in decaying feudalism approved of the work of the French revolutionaries. Yet the enemies of Freemasonry made use of the European scare caused by "Jacobinism," and not even men of Born's stamp could prevent the suppression by Franz II in Vienna in 1794, soon after Mozart's death. Only one of many letters about Freemasonry which passed between the Mozarts, father and son, is known to exist, for the cautious Leopold destroyed the rest. Possibly the best summary of the reasons for Mozart's devotion to the craft is in an essay by Dr. Bernhard Paumgartner, a composer and musicologist who in 1945 reorganised the Mozarteum at Salzburg and brought new vitality to the Mozart festivals there:

> The benevolent and liberal efforts of Freemasonry, its fight against superstition and narrow-mindedness, the idealistic principles of mutual assistance and fraternal equality of rights had a strong effect on Mozart's sensitive mind. His fondness for cheerful society, the need he felt for conversation among intimate friends . . . must have made him appreciate the fraternity as a revelation after the repressing confines of his Salzburg environment. The mysterious ceremonial of the order and the important part played by solemn music . . . completed the hold of Freemasonry on Mozart's artistic imagination.

Approach to Death

Mozart deliberately approached his death. No other composer aware of his diseased body, not even Berlioz, was as clear and calm about it. The letter to his father of April 4, 1787 has already provided evidence of his private views on death – ". . . the true goal of our lives . . . this best friend of men . . ." were his words. And even then he could say: "I never go to sleep without remembering that . . . I may never see the following day."

Another letter, of September 1791, supposedly addressed (in Italian) to Da Ponte is in similar vein and it is quoted below although its authenticity has been seriously questioned (but not completely disproved) on circumstantial grounds. Evidently Mozart had seen Da Ponte on the eve of the latter's exile from Vienna

69. Emanuel (Johann Joseph) Schikaneder. Engraving by Philipp Richter.

for, wrote Da Ponte, "I tried to persuade Mozart to go with me to London, but he was then setting a German opera, 'The Magic Flute,' to music and asked me to give him six months for his decision." The letter following in September says:

> I should like to take your advice but how can I? My head is in a whirl. Only with difficulty can I think at all, and I cannot free my thought from the image of the unknown. I constantly see him before me; he pleads, urges, and impatiently demands work from me. I go on because composition is less tiring than doing nothing. Moreover I have nothing more to fear. I can tell from my present condition that my hour is striking. I am on the point of death. My end has come before I could profit from my talent. And yet life has been so beautiful! My career began under such lucky stars! But no man can control his destiny; none can number his days; he must accept. What Providence ordains will come. I must stop now, for before me lies my swan song. I must not leave it unfinished.

What lay before him, if he did indeed write this letter, was the Requiem, but we cannot say for certain that the "image of the unknown" was the gaunt messenger who came to his house in July 1791 with an anonymous commission for the work. The most important sentence is "composition is less tiring than doing nothing"; we should not regard as other than merciful the fact that Mozart's last months superimposed upon his other troubles the anxiety of three commissions, one of which even he could not fulfil in time. Apart from the Requiem, which remained unfinished, there were two operas. First was "The Magic Flute," his true swan song, his final commentary on life. The other opera was "La clemenza di Tito" (Titus's Magnanimity), commissioned during July through the Prague National Theatre. The work was to be given early in September as a *festa teatrale* during the celebration of Leopold II's coronation as king of Bohemia.

"La clemenza di Tito" was written in 18 days, some of it in the carriage on the way to Prague, Süssmayr probably composing the recitatives and helping with the copying. He had by then been Mozart's pupil for about two years, and was evidently a poor, ungainly or naïve youth, somehow managing to live by teaching and by work in the theatres or with orchestras, probably doing much copying and chorus-singing. He has been denied his due, both as a modestly competent musician and as a help to Mozart, probably because the Mozarts seem to have made fun of him, e.g. "Tell that idiot of a boy Süssmayr to send me the scores of . . ."

It is unlikely that much more than sketching of items could be done in the carriage and during the night at various inns. Much had to be done after Mozart knew exactly who the cast were. He left on August 18. On September 2, when Leopold II arrived, Mozart directed a performance of "Don Giovanni" to an enthusiastic audience. It is doubtful if many of them could get into the theatre, crowded by courtiers from Vienna, for "Tito" on September 6. We lack much information about the performance or its reception, which is generally supposed to have been merely polite. As usual the opening was held up for over an hour because the royal party arrived late, and the opera was but one conventional affair in the coronation festivities. Had Mozart time or inclination for dining out? Did he go to Bertramka or Count Thun's? Did he enjoy the street circuses and pageants, or go to the cathedral for the coronation mass? We do not know. He was invited to a lodge where the cantata he had composed to honour Born, K.471, was given in his own honour. Nissen, probably quoting Constanze, says that when Mozart left Prague in September "He was sick and taking medicine continually. His complexion was pale, and his eyes dull and sad, but cheerful moods occurred, when he showed a kind of gay seriousness." As he bade farewell to his friends he was moved to tears.

"The Magic Flute"

As soon as he was back in Vienna Mozart worked at "The Magic Flute" with more urgency than when he first felt drawn to it, for his concept of it had changed. The colourful and extravagant Schikaneder himself is thought to have supplied the words, giving them to Mozart in instalments, for those who speak German recognise them as naïve, not the work of an educated writer; yet some of the passages are in a dignified, almost liturgical style which would have been crudely parodied by an unskilled hand. His helper was probably Johann Georg Metzler, better known as Karl Ludwig Giesecke, who actually claimed, after Mozart's death, to have been the librettist.

Mozart had the advantage of knowing some of the singers and players and the exact conditions of performance. Schikaneder had taken over in 1789 the "Theater im Starhembergschen Freihause auf der Wieden." The Freihaus is still the name of a complex of buildings in the Wieden suburb, then just outside the city ramparts from the gate called the Kärntnerthor, and on land formerly an estate of Prince Starhemberg. The buildings included a number of courtyards, and a wooden theatre had been put up to fill one of the larger ones. In another courtyard Schikaneder fitted up a little summer-house for Mozart, hoping that he could speed his work when so near the theatre. This little shack has been in the garden of the Mozarteum at Salzburg since 1950, having previously been on view on the Kapuzinerberg.

Schikaneder and his theatrical company were highly sociable creatures and Mozart, who often slept away from home during the dreary weeks when Constanze was away in Baden for the cure, seemed glad to spend evenings with them. Association with his librettist and the other loose-living rascals led to the suggestion in one of the obituary notices that Mozart himself hastened his end by "excesses"; there is no justification whatever for this reflection of Vienna's delight in scandal. Mozart was glad to eat with them rather than in his wretched house, but his letters during this period show that he never worked harder. His state of health precluded even heavy drinking. He was fond of going in the afternoons to the quiet grounds of a religious house at Josephsstadt, and probably did more mental composition (which was more important than the scoring) out there in the country than at home or in the Freihaus shack.

"The Magic Flute" was first presented on September 30, 1791 and by a gracious delay of fate Mozart was enabled to witness the first few productions. He was physically weak but his spirits were roused to feverish excitement as he saw the audiences grow larger and more enthusiastic with each performance. Characteristically he loved all the mechanics of the stage. His mood is reflected in letters to his wife, still in Baden:

> At half past five I went out for my favourite walk beyond the ramparts towards the theatre. What do I see? Don Primus [the manservant] with cutlets. *Che gusto*! Now I am eating to your health. The clock has now struck 11 and perhaps you are already asleep. Sh! I must not wake you.
>
> . . . The hairdresser arrived promptly at six and Primus lit the fire and woke me at a quarter to six. Oh why does it have to keep raining? I hoped you would be having fine weather. Keep warm so that you do not catch cold.
>
> Tomorrow [October 9] I shall take your mother to the theatre. Hofer has already given her the libretto to read . . . I went backstage for Papageno's song with the glockenspiel because I was in the mood to play it myself. Once when Schikaneder

70. An unauthenticated Mozart miniature painted on porcelain by Joseph Grassi, 1785.

had a pause I played an *arpeggio*. He was surprised, looked into the wings and spotted me. When the pause came a second time I did not do it. At this he stopped and would not go on. I guessed what he wanted and struck a few notes. Then he banged the glockenspiel and shouted "Shut up!" Everybody laughed, for many of them realised for the first time that he was not playing the thing himself! On October 13 he took Salieri and Madame Cavalieri to the theatre.

> You cannot imagine how kind they were and how much they liked not only my music but also the story and the whole show. They both said it was an *operone*, worthy to be given at the greatest festival before the greatest of monarchs. They declared they were going to see it often for they had never beheld a more enjoyable spectacle. Salieri listened with the utmost attention from overture to final chorus, and every item elicited from him a "Bravo!" or a "Bello!" . . . Karl was very pleased at being taken to the opera.

So much for the story that Salieri poisoned Mozart! Two days later Mozart went to Baden to bring his wife home. He was worried about Karl's education. He had written to Constanze complaining that his school kept the boy in good health and spirits but that his speech and manners were those of a peasant. Karl had confessed to enjoying most of his time running around the grounds of the school but seemed not at all interested in studies. They must seek a good monastic school for him. (An answer to those who would like to paint Mozart as a humanist freethinker!)

Requiem aeternam

Before the end of October Mozart's condition worsened. One evening, while out with Constanze on the Prater, he burst into tears. He said he felt he must have been poisoned and feared he would not live to complete the Requiem. He recovered sufficiently to finish the Masonic cantata, K.623, and direct it at the opening of the temple for the "New Crowned Hope" lodge on November 18. But two days later he took to his bed, having "swellings on the hands and feet and an almost complete inability to move his limbs. Later he had fits of vomiting."

During this final illness his mind continually reverted to the unfinished Requiem, ordered by he knew not whom. Such anonymous commissions were sometimes placed by amateurs who would secure a performance of the professional's work. Since the music would be copied out by the amateur recipient, his guests would suppose it to be his own composition. He would not claim it, yet neither would he deny it. A smile and a bow would acknowledge their flattery. The identity of the commissioner in this case was not discovered until after

Mozart's death. To Mozart in July he was simply "The messenger," "The mysterious caller." But when the messenger called again in August to find if the commission was accepted the effect on the sick composer became awe-inspiring. He was "a gaunt, tall man in a grey cloak." Naturally romantic Mozart literature abounds in legends that Mozart thought him to be death personified and that he set Mozart to compose his own Requiem. Nothing reported from Mozart, his wife, or his friends gives us authority for supposing that he regarded the commission as other than symbolical of his approaching death. He was not naïvely superstitious. Moreover we now know the unknown messenger really had an appearance to strike solemn anyone whom he approached for the first time, for his portrait in oils was found in 1954. He was Anton Leitgeb, son of the mayor of Vienna. (Not to be confused with Ignaz Leutgeb, the Salzburg horn-player, for whom Mozart wrote his horn concertos and who later kept a cheesemonger's shop in Vienna.) He had a face to choose for that of a "hanging judge" in a play; how must it have looked below a black tricorne and above the grey cloak of a tall man? Leitgeb, who played several instruments, frequented music-makings arranged by another amateur musician, Count Walsegg-Stuppach, who had estates in Styria but owned the town house in which Puchberg had apartments. Puchberg, too, arranged musical evenings in which Leitgeb participated. When the countess died in February 1791 her husband wished to direct "his" Requiem, and it is most likely that Puchberg, knowing Mozart's need of money, recommended him as the "ghost" composer and Leitgeb as the safest and most taciturn messenger. We should not be shocked at a form of deceit for which wealthy amateurs were willing to pay high money. Earlier that very year Beethoven had "ghosted" for Count Waldstein with the "Ritterballett."

More urgent than any romantic reasons for Mozart working on the Requiem are those put forward by Professor Schenk. Earlier in the year Mozart had received a reply to an application for the post of musical director at St. Stephen's. He was appointed unpaid assistant to the holder, Leopold Hofmann, with the expectation of succeeding him if the post fell vacant. The old *Kapellmeister* died two years after Mozart, who heard on his death-bed that he was offered the post on Hofmann's retirement. Since the C minor mass of thanks for his marriage, Mozart had composed no important church music. The Requiem recalled him to the style he thought fitting.

As usual and despite his condition Mozart composed all details mentally. He could therefore tell Süssmayr all the major points of instrumentation and accompaniment. Moreover he had a piano in the room which he or Süssmayr could use, the more to impress what he wanted upon Süssmayr's memory. He held little rehearsals of choral passages, the singers including himself, Süssmayr, Franz Hofer, the Bohemian tenor Schack, the bass Franz Gerl, and sometimes Joseph

Eybler, a very able musician still in his twenties but destined to become imperial *Kapellmeister*. It was to Eybler that Constanze first turned for help with the Requiem after her husband's death. She was anxious to secure the fee for it. For an unknown reason Eybler declined after starting work, possibly because Süssmayr's manuscript was more like Mozart's, and the patron would have no suspicions.

A week before Mozart died Dr. Closset and a consultant from the Vienna hospital whom he called in gave no hope of recovery. On December 4, the day before he died, Mozart was still working at the Requiem, with his faithful friends gathered to rehearse it in the afternoon. One Johann Roser is known to have been at the piano and to have cheered Mozart by singing Papageno's "I am a jolly birdcatcher." During a rehearsal of the Lacrimosa Mozart broke down weeping. Constanze herself was ill at the time and had sent for her sister Sophie, who declared that on her arrival Mozart said: "Ah, dear Sophie, I am glad you have come. You must stay overnight with me and see me die." He disregarded her attempt to cheer him: "I already have the taste of death on my tongue, and who can support my dearest Constanze if you do not stay?" She was sent to St. Peter's for a priest. He needed persuasion, probably because of Mozart's prominent association with Freemasonry, but also because the wintry weather made him wonder if he could not wait until morning. He came that night. Sophie said that when she returned Mozart was still giving Süssmayr instruction about the Requiem. He then told Constanze that she must tell nobody about his death before she had told Albrechtsberger, because the cathedral appointment which he could not accept belonged by rights to Albrechtsberger (who was in fact given it).

Dr. Closset was at the theatre and returned to hear that he was needed. He ordered "cold compresses to be placed on Mozart's burning head, which were such a shock to the sick man that he did not regain consciousness until he passed away." He remained in coma until he died an hour after midnight, that is to say early on December 5, 1791.

Envoi

Because of the gross exaggeration that the most naturally gifted of all great musicians was "thrown into a pauper's grave" and "deserted by all those whom he so richly served," it is necessary to finish our story with details of the days just after his death. As soon as it was known, despite the bad weather, Count Deym came with his plaster to make a cast of the composer's face. Mozart became one of the Count's waxworks dressed in his own clothing! The death mask is lost. We have already told how Constanze smashed her copy "accidentally." She had thrown herself on the bed in a paroxysm of grief and could not be calmed until Baron van Swieten comforted her and persuaded her to stay with friends for a few days. Van Swieten is blamed by some for ordering the cheapest obsequies, but even this fact needs explanation.

> Among the pet phobias of Joseph II were the superstitious notions his subjects entertained about tombs and graveyards. On August 23, 1784, he made burial in church crypts illegal. Remains . . . were dug up and, to the amazement and mortification of the lower classes, transported to cemeteries amid all signs of disrespect . . . It was decreed that the dead should not be buried in coffins but merely sewn into sacks and covered with quicklime before being interred. Most of the ceremonial customary at funerals was abolished . . . It is true that he had to repeal the law after a riot against its enforcement had led to bloodshed . . . but the spirit of the decree persisted among "enlightened" people. For many years after Joseph's death ceremonious funerals were scorned . . . The priest was no longer allowed to go along to the grave.

This information comes from Erich Schenk and consists of quotations from various historians. Van Swieten and most of the Masonic brotherhood were among the "enlightened" admirers of Joseph's ideas.

A tablet in St. Stephen's marks the chapel in the north aisle where the short funeral was conducted. As well as male members of the family there were present Salieri, Albrechtsberger, several Freemasons, Van Swieten, and other members of the nobility. Others, including Schikaneder, were deterred by dreadful blizzards of snow and sleet. None of the mourners accompanied the body to the cemetery of St. Marx which was some way outside the city. Though the body was put in a coffin no cross marked the grave and the authenticity of remains exhumed in 1801 could not be established. Constanze later blamed herself for this, but mentioned the weather, her illness at the time, and her belief that others would have seen to the marking of the grave. Sophie spoke of crowds of people who walked by the house and loudly wept for him – the sound effects can be taken with a pinch of salt. More important is the fact that the emperor came to Constanze's help with a pension and a benefit concert. In addition Frederick William of Prussia bought some of the manuscripts at an inflated price and, when "Tito" was given at the Burgtheater, one of Mozart's concertos was played by Beethoven.

Only two of Mozart's children survived him. The younger was Franz Xaver, who was born about four months before his father's death. He sought a musical career, studied in Vienna with Hummel, Salieri, and Albrechtsberger, and became known by his father's name Wolfgang. He composed a few pretty social pieces and achieved some reputation as a pianist, being for a few years popular at concerts. He spent most of his adult life in Lemberg (Lvov) where he was music-master to several families. He was 53 when he died. The other was Karl, whose speech and manners were deplored by his father as not being up to Mozartian standards of gentility. Schenk discovered that he became a fine and beloved gentleman when he retired from his civil-service appointment in Milan and bought a country estate near Lake Como. "His name still lives in the memory of grateful local residents, for his lavish bequests testified to the deep attachment he felt towards the district in which he spent his closing years. His donations also provided for the Mozart collections of the Salzburg museums. He seems to have been a sensitive, tactful, and lovable man." He died in 1858. And what was the source of his money? Royalties from his father's operas! He bought his estate with his receipts from "Figaro" in Paris.

How futile are the "ifs" of history! Foolish though it would be not to deplore Mozart's early death, as we do Purcell's and Schubert's, we should be even more foolish to try to guess what we have lost. We should be foolish, too, to deny the misery he suffered, yet utterly mistaken not to recognise that many more fortunate and "successful" artists have lacked his ebullient overcoming of despair. Few who died aged over 60 have known the supreme pleasure of powerful artistic creation right to their last days. His short life was far happier than that of most men for all its strain and misfortune, for he never lost his dreams, so to speak – of a cloud-cuckoo Italy of opera, of the real Italy which his son Karl so loved, of a Vienna which he expected to exalt him and which might have done so, after all, but for his disease, of wonderful performances and productions, of little celebrations at home, of good company, and of the brotherhood of men in Catholic Freemasonry. When knowledge that he must soon die made him aware that his dreams could not come true, he could still make them realities, with undimmed brilliance, in his compositions.

Acknowledgements

Material from Adrien Fauchier-Magnan's book "Les Petites Cours d'Allemagne au XVIIIème Siècle," which appears on Pages 10 and 11, is used by kind permission of the original publishers, Flammarion et Cie, Paris, and the publishers of the English translation (by Mervyn Savill), Methuen and Co., Ltd., London.

In the following acknowledgements of sources of illustrative material the figures represent illustration numbers, *not* page numbers. Those in parentheses refer to illustrations in the inset colour sections.

Archiv für Kunst und Geschichte, Berlin, *57*
Bayerisches Nationalmuseum, Munich, *(49)*
Bibliothèque-Musée de l'Opéra de Paris, *6, 7*
Bundespostmuseum, Frankfurt -am- Main, *10, (35, 36)*
Bundesverwaltung der Staatlichen Schlösser, Gärten und Seen, Schloß Nymphenburg, Munich, *38*
Civico Museo Bibliografico Musicale, Bologna, *(11)*
Colección Montellano, Madrid, *(46)*
Deutsches Freimaurer-Museum, Bayreuth, *67, (81, 86, 87, 89)*
Mary Evans Picture Library, London, *25*
Collection of Dr. Erich Fiala, Vienna, *(10)*
Foto Robert Häuser, Munich, *(61)*
Foto Steinkopf, Berlin, *(53)*
Gemeentelijke Archiefdienst, Rotterdam, *27,*
Germanisches Nationalmuseum, Nuremberg, *(39, 40)*
Gesellschaft der Musikfreunde, Vienna, *49, 61, 62, 64, 65, (15)*
Graphische Sammlung Albertina, Vienna, *44*
Adolf Hahnl, Salzburg, *34*
Herzog-August Bibliothek, Wolfenbüttel, *(28, 29, 30, 31, 32, 41, 44, 45)*
Historisches Museum der Stadt Wien, Vienna *35, 46, 50, 52, 53, 54, 58, 59 (33, 34, 42, 43, 55, 56, 68, 69, 70, 71, 72, 73, 74, 75, 76, 77, 78, 83)*
Historisches Museum, Frankfurt -am- Main, *63*
Hunterian Museum, University of Glasgow, *(21)*
Interfoto, Munich, *(59)*
Kunsthistorisches Museum, Vienna, *(48)*
Les Editions d'Arts Yvon, Arcueil, *(65)*
Lord Chamberlain's Office, London, *(62, 63)*
Ivo Moretti, Rome, *(67)*
Mozart-Gedenkstätte, Augsburg, *8, 36, 42, 45, (9, 38)*
Mozart-Museum der Internationalen Stiftung Mozarteum, Salzburg, *4, 5, 12, 17, 21, 33, 37, 40, 47, 48, 55, 70, (1, 2, 7, 8, 12, 13, 14, 16, 17, 18, 19, 20, 22, 23, 24, 25, 26)*
Musée Condé, Chantilly, *23, (4)*

Musée National du Château de Versailles et des Trianons, Palais de Versailles, Versailles, *(51)*
Musée National du Louvre, Paris, *(5, 27, 50)*
Nationalgalerie, Berlin, *(53)*
National Portrait Gallery, London, *(52)*
Novello & Co., Ltd., Sevenoaks, Kent, *2, 3*
Österreichische Nationalbibliothek, Vienna, *9, 20, 34, 41, 43, 56, 60, 66, 68, 69*
Orde van het Groot-Oosten, The Hague, *(79, 80, 82, 84, 85, 88, 90, 91)*
Phonogram International/R. Nooy, Baarn, *(3, 79, 80, 82, 84, 85, 88, 90, 91)*
Photo Erwin Meyer, Wien, *(48, 58)*
Photographie Giraudon, Paris, *(4, 5, 27, 46, 50, 51, 64)*
Residenzmuseum, Munich, *(59)*
Rijksmuseum Amsterdam, Rijksprentenkabinet, Amsterdam, *24, 26, 29, 30*
Abbey of St. Peter, Salzburg, *34*
Salzburger Museum Carolino Augusteum, Salzburg, *1, 13, 14, 15, 22, 32, (47, 54)*
Staatsbibliothek Preussischer Kulturbesitz, Berlin, *11*
Fürst Thurn und Taxis – Zentralarchiv, Regensburg, *18, 19, 28, 31, (37)*
Vatican Museum, Rome, *(66)*
Westermann-Foto/H. Buresch, *1, 4, 5, 8, 10, 12, 13, 14, 15, 16, 17, 18, 19, 21, 22, 28, 31, 32, 33, 35, 36, 37, 40, 42, 45, 46, 47, 48, 49, 50, 55, 58, 59, 61, 62, 64, 65, 67, 70, (1, 2, 7, 8, 9, 10, 12, 13, 14, 15, 16, 17, 18, 19, 20, 22, 23, 24, 25, 26, 28, 29, 30, 31, 32, 33, 34, 35, 36, 37, 38, 39, 40, 41, 42, 43, 44, 45, 47, 54, 55, 56, 57, 60, 68, 69, 70, 71, 72, 73, 74, 75, 76, 77, 78, 81, 83, 86, 87, 89)*
Yale University, Collection of Musical Instruments, New Haven, Connecticut, *(6)*

General Index

For references to original executants of illustrative material readers are referred to the separate index of artists and engravers. Both there and here figures in italic are illustration numbers and *not* page numbers. Figures in parentheses refer to the inset colour sections. Major references are indicated in bold type.

Aachen – See Aix-la-Chapelle
Académie royale de musique, 27
Academies – See Concerts (general) and Mozart: Public concerts
Academy of Antient Music, 27
Adlgasser, Anton Cajetan (1729–1777), 15, 55
Adolf Fredrik of Sweden (1710–1771), (47)
Affligio, Giuseppe, 33, 38
Agujari, Lucrezia (1743–1783), 34
Aix-la-Chapelle (Aachen), 20, 24
Albrechtsberger, Johann Georg (1736–1809), 103, 104, (34)
Allegri, Gregorio (1582–1652), 35
Allegro in G for clavier (K. 72a), (3, 7)
Amalia, Princess – See Anna Amalia
Amsterdam, 30, (3, 48)
Ancaster, Peregrine, Duke of (1714-1778), 35
Anderson, Emily (1891-1962), 43-44
André, Johann (1741–1799), 95, 64
André, Johann Anton (1775–1842), 2
Anna Amalia, Princess (1723–1787), 24
Ante-chambering, 59
Antiphons, 36
Antwerp, 30
Arco, Franz Eugen, Count (1707–1780), 34
Arco, Georg Anton Felix, Count (1705–1792), 26, 55, 59, 61
Arco, Karl, Count (son of Georg Anton Felix), 59, 60, **61–63**
Arias, Concert, 48, 58, 71, 73, 86, 91
Arrangements, 89
Artaria & Co., 65, 67, 73, 96
Aschaffenburg, 94
Attwood, Thomas (1765–1838), 76, 84, 85
Auersperg, Prince Karl (1720–1800), (40)
Augsburg, 10, 11, 13, 14, 20, 24, 27, 31, **44, 46**, 51, 64, *11 (5, 21, 22)*
    Holy Cross, 13, 24, 46; St. Ulrich, 13, 24
Aurnhammer family, 65
Aurnhammer, Josephine, 65, 69, 76, 91
Austria, 10–11, 20–23, 32–33, 46, 69, 99, *10*
Austrian National Calendar, 6, 8

Bach, Carl Philipp Emanuel (1714–1788), 89
Bach, Johann Christian (1735–1782), 27, 29, 34, 55

Bach, Johann Sebastian (1685–1750) 11, 32, 41, 91
Baden-bei-Wien, 17, 71, 81, 91, 92, 93, 94, 101, 102, *58*
Baiæ, 35
Balls, 36, 81, 83, 85, 86, *52*
Banquets, 22, 26, 83, (1)
    Freemasons' "banquet," (43, 47)
Baranius, Henriette, born Husen (1768–1853), 91
Barcelona, 33
Barisani, Dr. Siegmund (Sigmund) (1758–1787), 76, 92
Barisani, Dr. Silvester (1719–1810), 17, 38, 76, *17*
Barrington, The Hon. Daines (1727–1800), 20, **27–29**, *25*
"Bäsle" – See Mozart, Maria Anna Thekla
Bath, 72
Battoni (Batoni), Pompeo (1708–1787), 5
Bavaria, 10, 11, 20, 47, 99, (21, 37)
Beaumarchais, Pierre Augustin Caron de (1733–1799), 81, 84
Beck, Franz (1723–1809), 46
Becke, Johann Baptist, 58
Bedford, John Russell, Duke of (1710-1771), 26
Beecke, Ignaz von (1733–1803), 42
Beethoven, Ludwig van (1770–1827), 32, 47, 51, 63, 64, 65, 72, 74, 80, 81, **85**, 88, 103
Benda, (Georg) Jiří Antonín (1722–1795), 56
Benucci, Francesco (1745–1825), *54*
Berchtold zu Sonnenburg, Johann Baptiste, Baron von (1736–1801), 76, (12)
Berchtold zu Sonnenburg, Baroness von – See Mozart, Maria Anna
Berchtold zu Sonnenburg, Leopold von, (12)
Berger, Ludwig (1777–1839), 66
Berlin, 6, 24, 80, 89, **91**, (7)
Berlioz, Louis Hector (1803–1869), 99
Berne, 31
Bernhard, Dr. Johann Anton von, 22
Bertati, Giovanni Giuseppe (1735–1815), 83, 85
Bertramka's Vineyard – See Prague
Biberach, 24
Billiards, 5–6, 81
Boccherini, Luigi (1743–1805), 89
Bologna, 8, **34**, 36, 44, *29*, (5)
    Accademia Filarmonica, 34, 36, 43, 44; San Francesco, 34; San Petronio, 34
Bolzano, 33
Bondini, Pasquale (died 1789), 84, 86
Bonn, 24, 96
Bonno, Giuseppe (1711–1788), 75
Born, Ignaz von (1742–1791), 78, 80, 98–99, *68*
Bory, Robert (1891–1960), 5
Breitkopf (pseudonym of an unknown artist), 5

Brenner Pass, 33
Bridi, Giuseppe Antonio (1763–1836), 67
British Museum, 29
Broschi, Carlo (alias Farinelli) (1705–1782), 34
Brunetti, Antonio, 59–60
Brünn (Brno), 32
Brussels, 20, **24**, 30, *18*
Bullinger, Joseph, Abbé, 54, 55
Burney, Charles (1726–1814), 11, 24, 30
Bussani, Dorotea, born Sardi (c.1763–1808), *54*
Byron, George Gordon Noel, Baron (1788–1824), 93

Calais, 27, 29
Cambrai, 30
Cannabich family, 47, 56, 58
Cannabich, Johann Christian (1731–1798), 46, 47, 51, 56
Cannabich, Martin Friedrich (fl. 1723–58), 46
Cantatas:
    "Die Maurerfreude" (K. 471), 78, 101
    "Eine kleine Freimaurer-Kantate" (K. 623), 99, 102
Canterbury, 29
Caroline, Princess of Nassau-Weilburg, 29, 30, **48**, 50
Casanova, Giovanni Giacomo, Chevalier de Seingalt (1725–1798), 33, 86
Casti, Giovanni Battista (1721–1803), 83, 84
Catholicism (see also Jesuits), 11, 13, 14, **98**
Cavalieri, Caterina (1761–1801), 102
Ceccarelli, Francesco (1752–1814), 59, 60
Čermáková, Anna (died 1931), (14)
Chabot, Duchesse de, 53
Chabot-Rohan, Count, (3, 5)
Chantilly, (2)
Charles I of Gt. Britain (1600–1649), 15, 39
Charles Alexander, Prince of Lorraine (1712–1780), 24
Charlotte Sophia, wife of George III (1744–1818), 27, 29, (30, 52)
Chesterfield, Philip Dormer Stanhope, Earl of (1694–1773), 98
Church music (general), 38, 42, 58, 93, **98**, 103
Cignaroli, Fra Felice, 33
Clement XII, Pope (1652–1740), (32)
Clement XIV, Pope (1705–1774), 35, *31*, (5, *66*)
Clementi, Muzio (1752–1832), 66–67
Closset, Dr. Nikolaus, 61, 92, 103
Coaches – See Travel
"Cobenzl" – See "Reisenberg"
Cobenzl, Countess – See Rumbeck
Cobenzl, (Johann) Philipp, Count (1741–1810), 65, 66
Coblenz, 24
Colloredo, Hieronymus Joseph Franz de Paula, Count (1732–1812), 11, 14, 20, 35–36, **38–43**, 44, 48, 50, 55,

111

Index of artists and engravers

Listed here separately are the original executants of illustrative material. As in the general index figures in italic refer to illustration numbers. Those in parentheses refer to the inset colour sections.

Aa, Pieter van der, *11*
Adam, Jakob (1748?–1811), *68*
Alphen, Eusebius Ernst (Alf, Alfen, Alwen) (1741–1772), *(16)*

Balzer, Johann (1738–1799), *57*
Beauvarlet, Jacques-Firmin (1731–1765), *26*
Benedicti, H. (fl. 1800), *(35)*
Berger, Daniel (1744–1824), *45, 64*
Bertrand, Gabrielle (1730–1790), *68*
Bettelini, Pietro (1763–1829), *49*
Bosio, G. B., 5, *7*

Canal (Canaletto), Giovanni Antonio (1697–1768), *30*
Carmontelle, Louis Carrogis de (1717–1806), *23, (3, 4)*
Chéreau, Jacques (1689–1776), *67*
Cignaroli, Felice (Giuseppe) (1726–1796), *33, (7)*
Corvinus, Johann August (1683–1738), *36*
Croce, Johann Nepomuk della (1736–1819), 5, *17 (8, 8, 10)*
Cunego, Domenico (1726–1803), *31*
Czichna, C., *15*

Danreiter, Franz Anton (died 1760), *13, 14, 32, 36*
Degle, Franz Joseph (1724–1812), *(9)*
Delsenbach, Johann Adam (1687–1765), *42*
Demarne – see Marne
Dröhmer, Hermann (1820–1890), *20*
Ducreux, Joseph (1735–1802), *28*
Duplessis, Joseph-Siffrein (Siffred) (1725–1802), 5, *(64)*

Ender, Eduard (1822–1883), *20*
Engelbrecht, Martin (1684–1756), *(38)*

Facius, Georg Siegmund (1750–after 1813), *65*
Firmian, Franz Lactanz Count (1712–1786), *12 (see also general index)*
Fischer von Erlach, Johann Bernhard (1656–1723), *42 (see also general index)*
Frisch, Johann Christoph (1738–1815), *64*

Gödel, F., *60*
Goya y Lucientes, Francisco de (1746–1828), *(46)*
Grassi, Joseph (c. 1758–1838), 5, *70*
Greiter (Greitner), Johann Michael (c. 1735–1786), *(54)*
Greuze, Jean-Baptiste (1725–1805), 4, 5, *(6)*

Grooth, Johann Nikolaus (1723–1797), *(59)*
Guttenbrunn, Ludwig (fl. 1770–1813), *51*

Hansen, Hans (1769–1828), *(22, 25)*
Hardy, Thomas (fl. 1778–1798), *65*
Hickel (Hickl, Hikl), Anton (1745–1798), *38*
Hickel (Hickl, Hikl), Joseph (1736–1807), *(56)*
Hummel, Christiane Luise, born Duttenhofer (1776–1829), *46*

Janscha, Lorenz (1749–1812), *58 (68)*
Jagemann, Ferdinand (1780–1820), *(23)*

Kändler, Johann Joachim (c. 1706–1775) *(86, 87, 89)*
Kinninger (Kininger), Vincenz Georg (1767–1851), *56*
Klinger, Johann Georg (1765–after 1830) *53*
Knight, Charles (1743–c. 1826), *25*
Knoller, Martin (1725–1804), *(8, 12)*
König, Franz Xaver (1711–1782), *34*
Krafft, Maria Barbara (1764–1825), 8, *(1, 15)*
Kügelgen, Gerhard von (1762–1820), *39*

Lakner, J. C. de, *59*
Lange, Joseph (1751–1831) 5, *6, 45, (1, 5, 8, 22, 14, 21) (see also general index)*
Lanzadelly (Lancedelli, Lancedelly), Joseph (1774–1832), *56*
Latour (La Tour), Maurice Quentin de (1704–1788), *(50)*
Lehmann, Edvard (1815–1892), *6*
Lorenzoni, Pietro Antonio (Peter Anton) (1721–1782), *(1, 17, 18, 19)*
Löschenkohl, Hieronymus (died 1807), 6, *9, 54, (1)*

Mansfeld, Johann Ernst (1739–1796), *59*
Mansfeld, Johann Georg (1764–1817), *5, 6*
Marne (Demarne, Marnette), Jean Louis de (1754–1829), *(18, 27)*
Medland, Thomas (died after 1822), *29*
Meruielle, Maria Anna, born Torricella, *35*
Meyer, *23*
Meytens (Mytens) Martin van, (1695–1770), *(48, 55)*

Nijmegen, Gerard van (1735–1808), *26*
Nilson, Johannes Esaias (1721–1788), *40*
Novello, Edward Petre *2, 3*

Ollivier (Olivier), Michel Barthélemy (1712–1784), *(5)*

Palser, Thomas (fl. 1805), *(81)*
Pekenino, Michele (fl. 1820), *55*
Perelle, Gabriel (1603–1677), *24*
Piringer, Benedikt (1780–1826), *(68)*
Porta, Giovanni Domenico, *31*

Posch, Leonhard (1750–1831), 6, 8, *4, 5, (13)*

Rähmel, Achaz Gottlieb (1732–1810), *53*
Ramsay, Allan (1713–1784), *(52)*
Remshard (Rembshart), Karl (1678–1735), *13, 32*
Richter, Philipp, *69*
Rogers, Nathaniel (1788–1844), *55*
Rosa, Saverio dalla (1745–1821), 33, *(7)*

Sasso, Giovanni Antonio (fl. 1809–1816), *7*
Schaffer, Joseph (fl. 1780–1810), *66*
Schenker, Nicolas (1760–1848), *39*
Schiavonetti, Luigi (1765–1810), *51*
Schindler, Johann Joseph (1777–1836), *46*
Schmutzer (Schmuzer), Jacob Matthias (1733–1811), *28*
Schütz, Carl (1745–1800), *44 (33, 69, 71, 72, 75, 76, 77)*
Schweikart (Schweikert), Karl Gottlieb (1772–1855), *(26)*
Scotti, di Cassano, J. A. *57*
Slater, Joseph (fl. 1750), *25*
Smith, John (1717–1764), *29*
Spitzer, Thomas (born 1779), *(24)*
Stief, Sebastian (1811–1889), *16*
Stock, Doris (Dorothea, Dora) (1760–1832), 6, *8, 81, 95, (1)*

Touchemolin, G. F., *41*

Vigée-Lebrun, Marie Louise Elisabeth (1755-1842), *(51)*

Wenzl, J. A., *15*
Wölff, Jeremias, *19*

Ziegler, Johann (1750–1812), *50, 58 (34, 43, 70, 73, 74, 78)*
Ziesenis, Johann Georg (1717–1777), *(49)*
Zoffany, Johann (1733–1810), 5, *(2, 62)*

MOZART
The Musician

I

The creative process

"Unusual Power of Detachment"
The Enigma
Developing the Gift

1. A page from the autograph manuscript of the "Jupiter" Symphony, K. 551.

"Unusual Power of Detachment"

The phrase "unusual power of detachment" comes from Otto Jahn, Mozart's first important biographer. The key word is "unusual"; any composer of rank (even one held to have wasted time in playing music instead of composing it, or in diverting himself with company) must have had the ability to concentrate whenever he chose. Therefore it is not entirely naïve to speak separately of Mozart "the man" and Mozart "the musician," especially when they seem to have different personalities. The difficulty comes from the fact that both native and acquired power as an artist is stored in the *subconscious* mind, and can be brought into play more easily by one man than another. Hence our difficulty in knowing if we do right to praise or blame a particular composer for producing much or little of high quality. Can anyone by taking thought (i.e. using the *conscious* mind and trying to concentrate for great lengths of time and study) add one cubit to his stature as an artist? If so, such men as Rimsky-Korsakov, Saint-Saëns, and other famous teachers would be the greatest of musical artists.

Mozart had "unusual" powers of concentration which we should discuss now lest, without being foolish enough to regard him as a facile composing machine, we under-·estimate the labour to which he himself confessed (in connexion with the quartets he dedicated to Haydn) and the sheer merit he deserves for not remaining during his short life the purveyor of popular and pleasing music that could enrich him financially. We are fortunate to know from Mozart's pupil Attwood and from others that often "the artist" could be seen taking dominion over "the man." Mozart was observed at the end of a meal to begin folding and unfolding his napkin; with polite excuses he left the room and returned to the company an hour or so later in good spirits. Often when this happened he had completely scored a lengthy work that would never be altered by so much as an accent, bow mark, or staccato dot. The implied "detachment" is rarer than the concentration. Surely no composer was capable of greater concentration than Beethoven; his notebooks show very different procedures from Mozart's, but do they show different procedures of the mind? The Abbé Stadler, who helped to put Mozart's musical affairs in order after his death, certainly thought so. He told Vincent Novello, founder of the British music-publishing business which still bears his name: "Beethoven began before he knew his own mind, and altered passages backwards and forwards as fancy directed; but Mozart never began to write until he had arranged the whole design in his mind just as he wished it; it then stood without change." Surely Stadler's understanding was limited. Unless Mozart, too, had begun "before he knew his own mind" he would not have confessed to "great labour" in composition; as for Beethoven, he declared to Ries that though he changed so much in detail and tried so many developments before

fixing upon the one he wanted, "insomuch as I know exactly what I want when I discover it, the fundamental idea never escapes me."

Mozart's detachment probably owed more to natural temperament than to discipline. Mathematics and billiards both demand foresight. How will the calculation or the game stand after certain moves are taken? How will it stand if others are taken instead? Similar prediction is required by all composers, who must imagine sounds ahead of those they are actually putting into notation; but Mozart was "unusually" endowed, in that he could imagine all details exactly and store a long and complex work in his memory while he attended superficially to other people and other business which might have enraged Beethoven while planning a work.

Novello and his wife Mary, in a Continental tour they undertook in 1829, visited Constanze Nissen, Mozart's widow. She told them: "Mozart seldom went to the instrument when he composed . . . He walked about the room and knew not what was passing around him. When all was arranged in his mind he took inkstand and paper and said: 'Now, dear wife, let's hear what people are talking about'." He continued to write while being entertained by gossip, and that was more, she said, than she could have done with the writing of the commonest letter.

2. Abbé Maximilian Stadler. Engraving by Johann Balthasar Pfister, 1818.

The Enigma

In our previous study of "Mozart, the Man," we tried to imagine Mozart simply as he appeared and sounded, with little deduction of his inner psyche. Is not the inner Mozart the more important, and is he not to be deduced chiefly from his music? Yes: yet we should not expect works to reflect the conditions in which they were conceived. This widespread error needs discussion.

Though by definition a prodigy will always elicit wonder, yet infant prodigies are no more enigmatic than supremely great adult musicians. Genetic and other theories explain Mozart's or Mendelssohn's youthful precocity, and if Mozart had died at 18 his work, though marvellous, would not have aligned him with the enigmatic great artist. (Young Mendelssohn matured earlier.) Modern exegesis of the workings of our subconscious minds cannot remove the enigma, cannot prevent our asking how X, who never travelled outside a small area, or Y, a simple, meek, domestic creature, produced music that moves us deeply precisely because it implies experiences which he cannot have known except by hearing or reading about them. There may be a direct, even a temporal correspondence between music and conscious life. Berlioz, Schumann, Liszt, Mendelssohn, and other Romantics were not the only musicians to declare what stimulated them to musical expression; for centuries musicians had responded convincingly to words about heroic, amorous, or pathetic experiences not their own. Two points about the fact need emphasis. First, the music would not be treasured if the ability to produce it had not existed *before* the composers made their response to the words or other stimuli. Hamlet said of the actor moved to tears by his own expression of Hecuba's grief – "What's Hecuba to him or he to Hecuba?" What was Ariadne to Monteverdi, who made thousands weep and lament with her? What was Don Giovanni's guilt and fate to Mozart? The second point is that most music by Haydn, Mozart, Beethoven, and Schubert – the "Big Four" of the Viennese Classical school – defies correspondence of its mood and character with the concomitant moods or circumstances of its composers. Beethoven's happiest symphony, which he called "My little Eighth," engaged his mind when his spirits were greatly depressed by suffering. Mozart's last three symphonies were produced when his distress had begun, the first begging letters to Puchberg had been written, his health was declining, and he was worried about paying for his wife's cure at Baden; yet the nickname of the last symphony, "Jupiter," is a tribute to its Olympian poise and vigour.

Though obviously an artist's work reveals his character, it does not necessarily reveal the character he presented to other men in his daily life. Sometimes the contrast reaches paradox, as it did in Borodin. His music suggests a fierce and colourful personality, Asiatic voluptuousness and cruelty. Yet nothing about the *man* suggests anything but an over-worked scientist, intellectual, and philanthropist. Borodin ranks higher among scientists than among musicians (he was the first professor to train women students and his discoveries led to the manufacture of benzine, plastics, disinfectants, fixatives, fertilisers, and a number of other things that have altered our lives), but more people value him as a composer than as a biochemist because others build upon and cover a scientist's discoveries (we do not use Faraday's electric lamps!) whereas the songs, poems, plays, and carvings of men long dead may move us more strongly than those of the living. But where in Borodin's alternately aggressive and luxurious, brilliantly colourful music is that big, bovine, gently-spoken doctor and chemist, incapable of anger, overworked for charitable causes, and so exploited that he could write music only when he and his wife escaped into the country during the summer vacation? That music reveals as much of Borodin as did the professor who "always looked harassed." The vigour and sensuousness, the barbaric splendour was "in his blood" as our forbears would say, or in his subconscious as many of us would say, for Borodin was the natural son of a Caucasian prince from the magnificent wild country of the Cossacks. No wonder that the antidote to his muddled and drab surroundings, to his persistent research, teaching, and concern for the poor and sick, came in his music.

The Mozart that would be hidden but for his music is less easily explained. No evidence shows him to have been pitifully unhappy until the very last years of his life, and then, though the causes of his unhappiness became aggravated, he was incurably disposed to forget them at every temporary relief. Yet some of his finest music is in a minor key; indeed it might be proved that most of his greatest music tends to be serious or poignantly tender – but not all of it. To call Mozart an essentially tragic artist is grossly to exaggerate, but "tragic" happens to be a word popularly accepted as commendatory. Even Haydn whose hilarious finales are the most brilliantly organised of his movements, was for many years neglected and unexplored; with the revived interest in his work has come the unnecessary assurance that he could be tragic, though with no satisfactory definition of the term.

If two people respond to Mozart's great G minor symphony and find more to admire about it every time they listen to it, surely it matters not at all that one calls it tragic while the other contradicts – "How can it be tragic with those rhythms? The finale especially is deliberately comic, and includes a piece of unprecedented humour just at the beginning of the development." Unless music is ancillary to words, stage action, films, etc. it is none the better because we can describe it in words or say what it conveys.

As we savour Mozart's various great works we bear in mind that even such an innocuous phrase as "the tender *Andante* which comes next" limits rather than extols the music, for it must be a very poor movement that conveys only tenderness in one shade of that quality. Music is

3

powerful because, from the composer's subconscious to ours, it conveys moods, feelings, shades of experience and character for which there are no words. It is powerful in alliance with words because it can heighten and colour ideas expressed by them, such as triumph, hope, despair, desire; but even in opera, music would be contemptible if it did no more than heighten and colour what is already expressed by other means. Fine programme music is that which conveys its own effects – multifarious experiences – to a listener who may not know the programme. In Mozart's supreme achievement, opera, the scenes, characters, events, and situations were catalysts for music that measures far more of our common humanity and exercises far more of our imagination than would a presentation of the words and action without the passage through Mozart's own humanity and imagination. The rest of his music is to be cherished inasmuch as it achieves the same result without his knowing (or our trying to guess) its catalysts, for they cannot be named.

Developing the Gift

From the Salzburg trumpeter Andreas Schachtner, in letters to Mozart's sister Nannerl after the composer's death, we learn something about the child's extraordinary ear. When he was not yet five he began to call Schachtner's violin a "butter-fiddle" because to him its tone seemed fat, soft, and smooth; but one day he surprised its owner by saying: "Herr Schachtner, your violin is tuned an eighth of a tone lower than mine unless it has been altered since you last came." His father Leopold asked for a test and found the boy to have been right. "Until almost his tenth year he had an insurmountable fear of the trumpet. If one merely held a trumpet towards him, it was like pointing a pistol at his heart. Papa wanted to cure this childish fear and asked me to sound the trumpet towards him. My God! I wish I had never let myself be persuaded! As soon as Wolfgang heard the piercing tone he turned pale and began to reel." Still more remarkable is the child's first attempt at ambitious composition. "Once I accompanied your father home after the Thursday service and found the four-year-old Wolfgang busy with a pen." He said he was writing a clavier concerto. After their amusement at the smears and blots, Leopold and Schachtner studied the paper carefully and could see that he understood the style and shape of such an undertaking, but added: "It is so difficult that nobody could play it." The child replied: "That's why it is a concerto; you have to practise until you can play it. See, this is how it should go" . . . and at least he could show what he intended.

Sometimes the pupils of famous musicians are brought to the microphone to explain how the great ones taught them – what was distinctive about their teaching; and often they find their task difficult. During their times with the masters they have been so engrossed in the music performed or discussed that they are unable to specify the difference between these sessions and previous ones with musicians of inferior calibre. It is therefore dangerously easy to assume, from what we know of Bach's teaching, that all eighteenth-century teaching was better than nineteenth-century teaching, or our own. It had certain advantages for the really musical pupil. For instance, there was no prescribed syllabus leading to some examination in performance upon an instrument, or some test of singing. Leopold Mozart, like Bach, might give what would now be called piano, violin, or singing lessons, or tutor students in harmony, counterpoint, and composition; but whatever we should call the lessons, what he really taught was "Music as I know it and as it is required." Lessons in clavier-playing included the harmonising of basses with or without figures, adding other parts to melodies, the elementary composition called extemporisation, and acquaintance with other instruments than the one specially studied.

In our times there has been much advocacy of this wide and liberal music teaching, but its effectiveness depends on the musical experience and calibre of the teacher, to say nothing of the pupil's capabilities. To work from a printed "Violin Method" or "Pianoforte Tutor," a standard book of exercises and scales with pieces graded in stages, each of which can be tested by a national examining body if necessary – this has its merits; it makes the merely average teacher feel safe and gives the pupils (or their parents) assurance that they have reached a prescribed and accepted stage of progress. Such printed instruction books and collections of graded pieces were not available in the eighteenth century. (The fact may explain the enormous demand for a treatise on violin technique which Leopold Mozart wrote – popularly known as the "Violin School" – and also the composition of sonatas known in England as "Lessons" and of facile sets of variations on popular songs and tunes from operas.) A teacher of Leopold's standing compiled a book himself, as Bach did for his second wife, Anna Magdalena, and for one of his sons. Such books are valuable to us when they contain evidence like Bach's list of ornaments or details of fingering. The pupil often took over the manuscript book and added to it, and the mere copying of pieces, maybe the harmonising, transposing, or arranging, was itself valuable experience.

The method had one great advantage (with the right teacher and pupil) over some later methods. From the very first the pupils dealt with complete pieces of music – dances, songs, variations, etc. Furthermore theoretical instruction was not divorced from the playing or singing of real music; it was not "paper" work or merely verbal, but related to sounds. That is why little Wolfgang learnt much while hearing his sister Nannerl taking lessons and practising, and naturally the book compiled for Nannerl would be used later for his instruction. Fortunately we know what it contained, for it is preserved. Leopold wrote on it: "Pour le clavecin, ce livre appartient a Mlle. Marie-Anne Mozart, 1759." It contains a large number

GRADUS
AD
PARNASSUM,
Sive
MANUDUCTIO
AD
COMPOSITIONEM MUSICÆ
REGULAREM,
Methodo novâ, ac certâ, nondum antè
tam exacto ordine in lucem edita :

Conotus Vienn. Fi. Exen Elaborata à difcaf. S. P. Augustin

JOANNE JOSEPHO FUX,
Sacræ Cæfareæ, ac Regiæ Ca-
tholicæ Majeftatis CAROLI VI. Ro-
manorum Imperatoris
SUPREMO CHORI PRÆFECTO.

VIENNÆ AUSTRIÆ,
Typis Joannis Petri Van Ghelen , Sac. Cæf. Regiæque Catholicæ Majeftatis Aulæ-Typographi , 1725.

---

3. Frontispiece and title page of Fux's "Gradus ad Parnassum," Vienna, 1725. The illustration, by Jacob van Schuppen, is engraved by Gustav Adrian Meiller.

4. Ludwig Köchel. Anonymous oil portrait.

quite accurately called folk-songs) and Protestant chorales with which Leopold became well acquainted as a boy in Augsburg. (Wolfgang's first public performance seems to have been as a singer, a child's part being required in Eberlin's opera "Sigismund, King of Hungary" performed before the prince-archbishop of Salzburg.)

The items for singing may have been intended as religious devotions; the items designed to bring full control of the keyboard were grouped into 25 suites covering the different major and minor keys and including such points of technique as hand-crossing, contrapuntal overlap of phrases between the hands, *arpeggio* figurations with *cantabile* melody, toccata-like pieces, etc. Not all the composers have been identified but it is not surprising that most are of north-German provenance and many from an older generation than Leopold's. Like Haydn, Leopold Mozart was young while Bach, Handel, Rameau, Domenico Scarlatti, and other great Baroque artists were still composing. He retained something of their styles, notably a tread of harmony that points to the old *basso-continuo* practice; his own music therefore has a certain sturdiness by which we can tell it from the more Rococo, Italianate music of J. C. Bach, Wagenseil, Dittersdorf, and the Italians favoured in Salzburg and Vienna, as well as the music of his own son who was influenced by them.

Early in 1767, during the months at home after Leopold and his children had returned from a grand exhibition tour of Europe, Leopold paid particular attention to Wolfgang's further musical education. We know this from a notebook of the period filled with counterpoint exercises based on Fux's "Gradus ad Parnassum." The childish indication of the voices as "Signor d'Alto," "Marchese Tenore," and "Duca Basso" suggests that a little humour was incurred as sugar to the pill, for there are frequent corrections on the worked exercises. Without going into technical discussion we may safely declare that today "strict" counterpoint is widely disapproved because its rules cannot be verified from great music, such as Palestrina's or Bach's. The authority is the writer of the text-book (who often trims Fux) or some examining body. Today most reputable examiners ask for the continuation or completion of a genuine period piece. Fux and his followers claimed to take rules from Palestrina, but enforced many which Palestrina seems not to have known, and on the other hand relaxed many which he strictly observed; but it was for that very reason that Fux was valued in an age which knew little Palestrina and no Bach. Fux adapted much in the practice of the older masters to suit the style of his own time. (He died in 1741 aged 81.) Unlike so many teachers, he was respected as a composer, and rightly. His operas and oratorios, still more his church music, show a sound grasp of polyphony that is lacking in most work by his contemporaries. Moreover he was the Emperor's *Kapellmeister* and widely famed for his kindness and fatherly dealings with the musicians who worked under him as well as many who consulted him.

of minuets, marches, and sets of variations, and then less symmetrical and more extended compositions by Wagenseil, J. Fischer of Augsburg, Schobert, and others, with some by Leopold himself. Against some of them are such entries as "Wolfgangerl learnt this in his fourth year," and "Wolfgangerl learnt this minuet and trio on January 26, in half an hour at half past nine in the evening, one day before his fifth year."

Later in the book come the first specimens of the boy's own essays in composition, minuets preponderating; they are in Leopold's hand, but they cover the first five items in the Köchel catalogue,* and purport to belong to the period from January to July 1762. Leopold then compiled a second book for Wolfgang, its pieces being in rhythms other than that of the minuet. They come from works by Telemann, C. P. E. Bach, J. Fischer, and J. G. Graun. Evidently the boy was to sing as well as play some of the items, which include both German *Volkslieder* (not

---

* Ludwig Köchel (1800–1877), an Austrian geologist and botanist, who lived in Salzburg and Vienna, devoted much time to compiling a thematic and chronological catalogue of Mozart's works, including lost and spurious ones. Alfred Einstein revised it in 1937 and 1947, but throughout this book we shall use the old "K." numbering.

II
The travelling composer

Early Works and Influences
Milan, Bologna, and Rome
An Opera for Munich
Mannheim
Paris

5. *Title page of the Sonatas K.6 and K.7, published in Paris, 1764, and dedicated to Princess Victoire.*

SONATES
POUR LE CLAVECIN
Qui peuvent se jouer avec l'Accompagnement de Violon
DEDIÉES
A MADAME VICTOIRE
DE FRANCE
Par J. G. Wolfgang Mozart de Salzbourg
Agé de Sept ans.
OEUVRE PREMIERE.
Prix 4 Liv: 4 S.
Gravées par Mme Vendóme Ci-devant rue St. Jacques
à present rue St. Honoré Vis-à-vis le Palais Royal.
A PARIS
aux adresses ordinaires
AVEC PRIVILEGE DU ROI.

imprimé par petit blé

The chief value of the "exhibition" tours undertaken by Leopold Mozart with his children lay in Wolfgang's hearing the work of others and meeting important performers and composers of his day, many of whom exerted a positive influence on him. Leopold's main concern was to secure the favour of rulers and aristocrats with whom Wolfgang might later find employment. Yet in Vienna during their very first tour in 1762 contact with such people as Dr. Mesmer, the notorious "magnetiser," and Dr. Bernhard, the professor of medicine at the university, proved ultimately of more value. Public concerts there depended largely upon the intelligent middle classes, and these two friends in particular may have done more than any to swell Mozart's later Vienna audiences.

More important than the aristocrats they met in Paris in the winter of 1763–64 during the "Grand Tour" of Europe were leading French musicians such as François-Joseph Gossec, symphonist and opera composer, and Jean Pierre Duport, one of the first great cello soloists; particularly important were migrant German musicians employed in Paris, notably Johann Eckard from Augsburg, held to be the most brilliant keyboard player at that time, Johann Schobert from Strasbourg, composer of clavier works and former organist at Versailles, Leonzi Honauer, whose chamber music, including harpsichord sonatas, were popular in London as well as in Paris, and Hermann Raupach, who had been in Russia and returned there in 1768 to become second *Kapellmeister* at St. Petersburg. The Germans in Paris must have had some influence on young Mozart, for nearly every movement of his first written essays in concerto design has been traced to a sonata by one of the four. These four concertos (in F, K.37; in B flat, K.39; in D, K.40; and in G, K.41) were not performed until 1767 in Salzburg, as far as we know, but may have been composed in London or Paris or while travelling. The sonatas from which the boy took the materials were probably given to him by his father or by the composers themselves. Two movements have not been traced to them. Mozart's French biographer Saint-Foix suggested that the slow movement of the first concerto was entirely Mozart's, and Einstein that the finale of the third was taken from a sonata by C. P. E. Bach. Some earlier "K." items represent works claimed to be original and written in Paris – four sonatas for harpsichord and violin, K.6–K.9. Leopold had them engraved, two with a dedication to a French princess whom the Mozarts had met at Versailles.

In London, as in Paris, they encountered many German-speaking musicians. The most popular (in the sense of "fashionable") composer and performer was Johann Christian Bach, youngest and most beloved son of the great J. S. Bach, who left him three of his harpsichords. When his father died he was under the care and tuition of his elder brother, C. P. E. Bach, at Berlin, but went to Italy at the outbreak of the Seven Years' War. He studied under Padre Martini, became a Roman Catholic, and delighted connoisseurs first by his church music, then by his operas. Officially organist at Milan Cathedral, he was too often absent to supervise his operas at Naples, and was glad to go to London at the invitation of the manager of the King's Theatre, Haymarket, chief home of Italian opera in England. His success there was enormous, the king and queen attending performances on successive nights.

When the Mozarts arrived in London in April 1764, J.C. Bach had just begun collaborating with a former pupil of his father, C. F. Abel, a string player and virtuoso on the gamba and cello. For 17 subsequent years they ran concerts at Spring Gardens, Almack's, the Hanover Square Rooms, and elsewhere. Bach was a champion of the new fortepiano and it was at his concerts that the pre-Classical piano concerto became the most fashionable of genres. His influence on Mozart was such that nobody has yet claimed to be able to tell at a first hearing certain works by young Mozart from some by J. C. Bach. The two were deeply interested in each other's work, and Mozart evidently found an ideal style in Bach's combination of Italianate melody with northern harmonic and textural thoroughness. After Leopold had fallen seriously ill in London in the summer of 1764 and was ordered rest and quiet, Wolfgang probably seized the chance to emulate this style in his first symphonies (K.16 and K.19) though it has not been established which of the movements as they now stand are exactly as he first produced them. (K.18 is now known to have been taken from Abel.) It is possible that Bach or Leopold revised what London heard as the boy's "overtures" – a title used as late as 1790 to advertise Haydn's new symphonies. Their transitions and textures are suspiciously more secure than those of much easier pieces for keyboard in a manuscript book of the same period. Other works produced during the visit to London included the first vocal composition in the record of Mozart's works (K.20 – the four-voice motet "God is our refuge"), written for a visit to the British Museum in what Wolfgang thought the "antient" or Baroque style of Anglican church music. His father also published the six sonatas for harpsichord and violin, K.10–K.15, labelling them as Op.3 and dedicating them to Queen Charlotte.

Returning to the Continent the Mozarts visited Holland where most members of the court orchestra at The Hague were Germans. Foremost amongst them were the *Kapellmeister* Ernst Graf, whose compositions were fine but "old-fashioned," and the oboist J. C. Fischer, of Dresden, a minuet by whom provided the theme for Wolfgang's set of variations, K.179. In Amsterdam the publisher Hummel engraved Wolfgang's latest works (assisted or wholly original, we are not quite sure), which included the six sonatas for harpsichord and violin, K.26–K.31 dedicated to Princess Caroline of Nassau-Weilburg. Performed in Amsterdam were the new B flat Symphony,

6. *Interior of the Rotunda at Ranelagh Gardens, London. Drawing and engraving by John Bowles.*

K. 22, and two sets of keyboard variations, one on a song by Graf (K. 24), the other on the national air "William of Nassau" (K. 25); but these were transcended in popularity by a work of the kind now known as a "switch" or "pot-pourri" (Bach called it a "quodlibet"), being loosely built on melodies known to the audience. Mozart's, for orchestra and piano and entitled "Galimathias Musicum," K. 32, began with a Handel quotation and ended with a fugue on "William of Nassau." Surely Leopold had a hand in this, for his own most popular pieces were of similar character – "Sleigh Ride," "Village Wedding," and so on. The "Galimathias" piece was obviously written for the return to The Hague, which was *en fête* for the coming-of-age of the Prince of Orange. As Graf was in charge of the music, both sets of keyboard variations turned compliments.

A return visit to Paris and Versailles was paid in May 1766 and Mozart's first known church music (discounting K. 20) dates from this period – a "Kyrie" for four voices

and strings, K. 33. An article in Baron Melchior Grimm's "Correspondance littéraire," which appeared during the visit, laid much emphasis on the boy's progress as a composer.

When the family finally reached Salzburg again at the end of November 1766, Leopold's employer Archbishop Schrattenbach was cunning enough to find out if Wolfgang was the composer whom others declared him to be, or if he was helped at home. He tested young Wolfgang by having him shut up in the Residenz to compose the first part of a Lent cantata, "Die Schuldigkeit des ersten und fürnehmsten Gebotes" (The Lesson of the First and Foremost Commandment), the two other parts to be by Michael Haydn, who had been *Konzertmeister** at Salzburg since 1763, and the court organist Anton Adlgasser.

---

* Short dictionaries describe the *Konzertmeister* as the leader or principal violin of a court orchestra and the *Kapellmeister* as the director who normally sat at the harpsichord. In fact there might be more than one *Konzertmeister* (or even *Kapellmeister*) since only by

9

It had two performances and showed astounding competence. In neither this, K.35, nor the Passion cantata, "Grabmusik," K.42, can we see without considerable and possibly unreliable exercise of the imagination much that distinguishes Mozart from his father, or from Eberlin or Adlgasser; still fewer signs of originality are traced in the Latin intermezzo "Apollo et Hyacinthus," K.38, immediately commissioned for the university graduation ceremony. No doubt the audiences were large and enthusiastic because they, too, wanted to see for themselves if Wolfgang's international reputation was deserved, and because he remained for hours after the performance playing to them.

During this short period at home in Salzburg they heard the concertos he had arranged from sonatas by the Germans in Paris. He also wrote three "epistle" sonatas (K.67–K.69) for two violins, bass, and organ continuo. These are certainly in a more light, Italianate style than similar works by Michael Haydn, whom we are now getting to know as a composer not to be passed over because his older brother was such a giant. If it were not for our hindsight in the light of Joseph Haydn's great advances we should regard Michael as the better composer of the two, as judged only on what the brothers produced before 1770.

The family had been at home for little more than nine months before Leopold decided to leave again in September 1767. They stayed away until January 1769, a year longer than they should have, mainly because of Leopold's wish that his son should shine as an opera composer. In Vienna they saw Hasse's "Partenope" and Gluck's "Alceste," and Leopold shrewdly decided that Wolfgang would be better served by some of the very good *opera buffa* performers in the capital than by inviting comparisons with admired masters of *opera seria* and using singers whom he thought poor. He secured from a librettist recently arrived, Coltellini, the libretto of "La finta semplice" (The Pretended Simpleton) and, with assent from the imperial office, signed a contract for its production. Neither the opera nor the two symphonies in D (K.45 and K.48), which Wolfgang composed while waiting, received performance during their stay and neither of them is very highly treasured today.

A charming little treasure, however, is Mozart's first setting of German for the stage, "Bastien und Bastienne," K.50. It was commissioned by Dr. Mesmer who had married a wealthy woman and had a fine country house near the Prater with a large garden and a little theatre and, of course, his laboratories. The text was taken from a Viennese translation of a parody on Rousseau's "Le devin du village." The story shows the course of rustic true-love going awry when the feudal masters of the young lovers try to thwart it, but reaching a happy end-

ing by the help of the village fortune-teller. Without making too much of the "revolutionary" element (which at the time might have made a "Figaro" or a "Don Giovanni" into a delicate undertaking) we can assert that this work appealed to the boy; he spoke its language, he understood the human emotions and the humorous element in the pretty pastoral, and he could maintain quality on the smaller scale of this *Singspiel* better than throughout a full opera.

One other success came his way before he went home. Ignaz Parhamer, a Jesuit mission priest who could always draw crowds to his sermons, had been appointed supervisor of parish schools. (He dressed as a pilgrim with beard, staff, and cloak.) He took particular interest in a big orphanage in the city where the syllabus of reading, writing, and arithmetic was expanded to prepare the boys for trades and crafts and the girls for "domestic economy" – at least dressmaking, cooking, and household usefulness; still more, Parhamer took a leaf from the

7. *Portrait of Leopold Mozart engraved by Jacob Andreas Fridrich for the "Violin School."*

8. *The Christiaan Müller organ in the St. Bavokerk, Haarlem, on which Mozart played in 1766 during his visit to Holland. Engraving by Jan Caspar Philips after a drawing by Gerrit, Toorenburgh, 1762.*

book of the Italian conservatory system and prescribed good instruction in singing and playing. The uniformed orphans marched with a band and had both choral and instrumental music for their church services. Parhamer was present when the emperor asked Wolfgang about his opera. He invited the Mozarts to dinner, showed them his children on parade, and included a firework display. He then invited the boy to write the mass for the consecration of a new chapel at the orphanage, the music to include an offertorium and a trumpet concerto. It was long thought that the offertorium was "Veni Sancte Spiritus" (K.47) but it is now believed to have been another, lost together with the trumpet concerto. The mass is now thought to have been the one in C minor, K.139. The court and archbishop were present at the performance on December 7, 1768, which, Leopold wrote, "restored the reputation our enemies thought to destroy . . . the throng was amazing."

Archbishop Schrattenbach, far from reproaching the Mozarts on their return to Salzburg, wanted to hear "La finta semplice" on his nameday early in May 1769. Mozart added a *licenza* (a gratulatory offering to a patron) in the recitative and aria "Sol nascente," K.70. The Mozarts' landlord and friend, Johann Hagenauer, had a son, Kajetan, who became a priest and took the name Dominicus. Kajetan's diary records that when he celebrated his first mass in St. Peter's the 13-year-old Mozart provided and directed the music. The bright Italianate style of this Mass in C, K.66, was "considered by all to be most elegant. After dinner he played the organ for half an hour to the delight and astonishment of the guests." The Mozarts were invited to dinner the following day at old Hagenauer's suburban house and gave a splendid concert there.

After returning to Salzburg Wolfgang had composed another mass before the "Pater Dominicus" one – the Missa brevis in D minor, K.65. For the carnival season he wrote several minuets and other pieces, including two cassations, K.63 and K.99, and a serenade, K.100. As *gassationen* is a dialect word for dalliance and serenading, "cassation" is almost synonymous with "serenade"; but Mozart's cassations make prominent use of wind instruments and include marches. It is noteworthy that he wrote few of these suite-like works after his Salzburg days. The main items for public concerts in the capital were overtures, symphonies, and concertos, whereas serenades and cassations were associated with provincial courts.

Milan, Bologna, and Rome

When Leopold was in London, J. C. Bach and others had convinced him that there were few better musical centres than Milan, where Wolfgang might secure commissions for composition, especially opera. Armed with enthusiastic recommendations from new Viennese friends, Baron van Swieten and Count Sporck, to influential

people in various Italian cities, the Mozarts set off early in December 1769.

In Milan Count Firmian, Governor of Lombardy, not only paid handsomely for the musical entertainment provided by the Mozarts but also secured for Wolfgang a contract on excellent terms for the first opera of the following season. The music was to arrive during October and the composer to be in Milan early in November, to meet the cast and follow rehearsals. His board and lodging would be provided. Eric Blom gives us the useful reminder that in eighteenth-century opera houses "novelties, not revivals, were the main repertory," so that the practice by which the composer himself worked with a cast, instead of trusting a *regisseur*, was normal and sensible; he notes that even today ideal performers are not always available for parts which Mozart intended for particular occasions and actors. The second important fact about the stay in Milan was Mozart's hearing of music which was attractive but somewhat different in style from pre-Classical German work, such as that by Stamitz or Wagenseil or the Salzburg musicians. He was specially impressed by Sammartini, who proved his admirer. Several arias he wrote for concerts in Milan, as well as his first string quartet, K.80, composed during his onward journey, show distinct influences of Sammartini.

Before going on to Rome for Holy Week and Easter, Leopold visited Bologna in the hope of securing for Wolfgang the commendation of the savants there, particularly Padre Martini, doyen of Italian musicians and Europe's oracle upon the theory and science of music. They called at S. Francesco to which the aging padre had retired as *parroco* and there he gave Wolfgang a subject upon which he bade him write a fugue. They left with presents of Martini's "Esemplare di contrappunto" and the first volume of his "Storia della musica" but no written testimonial. Calling at a country house near Bologna they met the greatest male soprano of his day, Farinelli, and then continued their journey through Florence. Wolfgang played at court and met the violinist Nardini and the Marquis de Ligniville whose hobby was devising vocal canons to liturgical texts. Needless to say Wolfgang, at an age that often inclines towards artifice rather than art, had to emulate these ingenuities. Some of the results are the Kyrie for five voices, K.89, and the six riddle canons, K.89a, in which the entries of the voices have to be guessed.

The Mozarts arrived in Rome in time for the ceremony which included the singing of Allegri's "Miserere mei Deus," a work in which five-voice and four-voice choirs alternate until a short final section uses all nine voices. The piece was regarded as sacrosanct, the exclusive property of the Sistine Choir, and the making of copies was supposed to incur punishment by excommunication. It is difficult to know why, despite its solemn beauty, Allegri's "Miserere" was so highly regarded when finer Passiontide settings were sung elsewhere. It was certainly guarded from copyists for many years after its priest-composer, who joined the Sistine Choir in 1629, wrote it

9. Carlo Broschi, known as Farinelli, Engraving after a painting by Jacopo Amigoni, 1735.

for that body. Without actually declaring that Wolfgang wrote it *all* down after once hearing it, Leopold tried to suggest the feat. His letters to Salzburg say that Cristofori, one of the singers, perused the transcription and found it accurate. Was this merely assurance that the boy's act was not scandalous? Mozart's biographers have never questioned Leopold's account, or rather the impression he tried to convey. The matter is worth our consideration here, being of more interest than the usual performances before astonished grandees.

The beauty of such Passiontide settings as Palestrina's "Improperia," Victoria's "Tenebrae" Responds, or the short *turba* choruses in their settings of the various Passion gospels, lies in their simple modal chords, the direct homophony used for the solemn occasions as compared with the elaborate polyphony of their festal works. The bare structure of Allegri's psalm is little more complex than that of a slow hymn, made rich by the many-voiced outlay. It was also enriched by *appoggiature* and other unwritten ornaments – a fact that has been supposed to account for the disappointment of connoisseurs in Vienna when they heard the work performed there. Metastasio especially said that it did not sound at all like the piece he heard in Rome. So the jealously guarded "Miserere" was sung in Vienna? Yes, and probably elsewhere. There may have been no score at the Sistine; a copy normally meant a set of parts, from which a score was made only by someone who wished to study the work rather than have it performed. An authorised copy had been sent to the Emperor Leopold I at Vienna; a score was made by Padre Martini; and Burney quoted from the piece in his "History of Music." Therefore at least three copies existed outside the Sistine while Mozart was still a boy, and obviously there were more. One might therefore ask the following questions:

1. Is it likely that Mozart was totally unacquainted with the general shape and harmonic tread of the piece, having been in Vienna and also having been at least three times with Padre Martini?
2. How, during the time taken by one performance, could anyone have jotted down enough notes of the nine-part texture to complete the score later?
3. Why was Leopold so anxious to reach Rome on the Wednesday when other days of Holy Week offered much more interesting ceremonies and liturgies? Was it because the "Miserere" would be sung again on the Thursday and Friday, and so Wolfgang could, if necessary, hear it three times?
4. Why the checking of the parts by Cristofori? The important point was the accuracy of the parts. Was the singer previously notified so that he could substantiate the claim?

It is significant that nobody but Cristofori seems to have been shown the score, for presumably it recorded the "gracings" missing in the Vienna performance, and would have been a godsend to later scholars. (Frankly one cannot accept the conscientious attempts made by two excellent German musicologists to compare the

10. *Joseph Mysliveček. Engraving by A. Hiderhofer.*

written and the conjecturally "graced" versions of works by Palestrina and others, nor their suggested example of the likely treatment of Allegri's "Miserere.") Perhaps it was not a complete score. If it had to be handed back or destroyed on the spot, it is hardly credible that the Mozarts did not keep another copy to show Martini on their return journey. Without actually lying, Leopold had learnt the art of *suggestio falsi*, for the papal diary covering this visit to Rome refers to the "little German boy" as "aged 12." It is almost certain that Mozart was advised beforehand to cause special notice by applying his feat of memory to this particular composition of legendary "secrecy"; and it is likely that he already knew its general outline. This does not negate an ability probably not possessed even by musicians with extraordinary hearing, such as Debussy and Ravel. From a gramophone record, armed with a bass already sketched, many musicians could jot down the chords of a work as slow-moving as that "Miserere"; but it is unlikely that in the known history of harmonised music anybody except Mozart could have either spaced the chords accurately or remembered their outlay without actually writing them down fully during the performance. Mozart "remembered" this outlay, though he probably checked it by a second hearing on the Thursday.

Less than a fortnight in all was spent in Rome before the Mozarts returned to Bologna. As a guest at the country house of Count Pallavicini, Wolfgang probably began work on his opera for Milan, "Mitridate, rè di Ponto" (Mithridates, King of Pontus). The libretto, an Italian version of Racine's tragedy by the Turin poet, Cignasanti, had been supplied by Mysliveček, the Bohemian composer of many successful Italian operas and symphonies.

Naturally Padre Martini had to be revisited, for he had fascinated Wolfgang with the vital and not merely archaic artifice of counterpoint. For Martini it was more than demonstration, the solving of problems, the performance of exercises proposed by book or teacher; it was more than the imitation of older music, archaism to parallel that of the landscape gardener with his temples and grottoes or the architect restoring Gothic churches. Counterpoint for Martini was an imperishable art which could vitalise most kinds of contemporary music, giving texture variety and inexplicable interest for the naïve listener and enormous delight for the connoisseur. In his time there were particular reasons for its study; it had to be *learnt*, observed – hence the phrase *stile osservato* or learned style. What is admired by our period-fancying ears as the pre-Classical style, that of Bach's sons and the Mannheimers, which young Mozart inherited, covered an unprecedented purveying of some of the shallowest musical gossip ever kept murmuring for the idle pleasure of the titled, rich, and fashionable. The more musical amongst them were no more satisfied than were the better composers. Their minds could hardly be stayed in assessing rival performers of work which could not be admired for its own ideas and designs. Mozart's better patrons, not only antiquarians like Baron van Swieten, found music more enjoyable, even worth repeated hearings in days when music was expected to be new, when it engaged the mind as well as the senses. Whatever retrospect thinks mistaken in Fux's "Gradus ad Parnassum," the enormous demand for that little manual of counterpoint shows it to have been the only work of its kind that then satisfied a felt need in a musician's training. Of course the deliberate conservatism of church music and the desire to compensate for the absence of the colouristic effects used in theatre music made liturgical settings the chief medium for contrapuntal devices; but Martini used them for the immediate adornment of mass and vespers, not as museum pieces.

Young Mozart eagerly responded to him by attempting motets in the *stile osservato*, at first somewhat stiff and archaic. His antiphon "Quaerite primum regnum Dei" (Seek ye first the kingdom of God), K.86, was thought good enough to qualify him as a candidate for member-

ship of the Accademia Filarmonica although he had not reached the prescribed age of 20. His examination consisted of setting a given text and *cantus firmus* in *stile osservato* employing the theme and a four-voice texture. The result, produced, according to Leopold, in half an hour, won enthusiastic applause and the testamur of membership.

On October 13 they left for Milan where, despite expected hitches and intrigues, "Mitridate" had its first performance on Boxing Day, 1770. Such was its success that Wolfgang was asked to compose another opera for 1773.

Almost immediately after Mozart returned home to Salzburg in 1771 he heard that he would be asked to supply a "serenata" for the wedding of the Archduke Ferdinand to Princess Beatrice of Modena in Milan during October. He also had to compose an oratorio for Padua ("La Betulia liberata") and, furthermore, since he now held the office of *Konzertmeister* at Salzburg, he had to justify his stipend and produce church music – the "Litany of Loretto," K.109, the Missa brevis in F, K.116, two Kyries, and some psalm settings influenced by Martini's tutoring. He also produced four more symphonies during this short period at home, but much of their mental composition may have been done earlier.

The Milan wedding was on October 15. On the third evening of the festivities the court attended Mozart's *azione teatrale*, a two-act pastoral serenata entitled "Ascanio in Alba" to a libretto written by Giuseppe Parini, one of the Milan university men. The application of the allegory was obvious. Sylvia's dreams of a noble youth come true, after a few pretty misunderstandings, when Venus brings her son Ascanio to be the nymph's husband. Because the ballet music was wanted for rehearsals Mozart wrote it first. Then came a prelude, 14 arias and 3 trios, and lastly 8 choruses. The work won tumultuous acclaim and eclipsed Hasse's "Ruggiero" which had been performed the night before. Hasse generously said later: "This boy will consign us all to oblivion."

Father and son were back in Salzburg before Christmas 1771. On December 16 Archbishop Schrattenbach died and by March the following year it was known that his successor would be Hieronymus Joseph Franz de Paula, Count of Colloredo, who commissioned an *azione teatrale* to mark his accession. The libretto, Metastasio's "Il sogno di Scipione," which had served similar occasions before, was taken from the shelves. (His ancestors appear in a dream to Scipio, along with the goddesses Constancy and Fortune.) The work was given on April 29 and before the end of May Mozart produced three more symphonies (K.128–K.130) and the "Regina coeli," K.127.

This exemplary industry was perhaps to obviate trouble in obtaining leave to go to Milan at the end of October for the production of his opera "Lucio Silla," K.135. It contains fine pages which are still performed, for they reveal the "pre-Romantic" expression of the darker emotions which is also found in some of Haydn's music of the 1770's and betokens a wide movement. These portions were probably more to German than Italian taste. Mozart learnt directly how difficult the weeks before an operatic production could be, for the *prima donna*, Anna Lucia de Amicis, arrived later than expected from Venice and demanded more brilliant and showy music than she was originally given. For various reasons singers had to be replaced at the eleventh hour, and on the night itself the audience was kept waiting for hours because the royal guests were late; the excuse was that the archduke had to write important letters. Yet "Lucio Silla" triumphed on the first night and had to be repeated on 20 successive nights. It must be remembered that the original promoters were seeking what would please Vienna-come-to-Milan; Milan itself never commissioned another opera from Mozart. Wolfgang was delighted by de Amicis, still more by Rauzzini, the *primo uomo*; as a superb tribute to him he wrote the now very popular "Exsultate, jubilate," K.165. The runs and high notes suggest that, even for a castrato of international fame, Rauzzini had an exceptional voice.

Leopold lingered in Milan, outstaying his leave in the hope that his son would be engaged by the Grand Duke of Tuscany, but when he heard that no appointment was forthcoming he took Wolfgang back to Salzburg in March 1773. To the end of his life Italy, nursery of opera, remained Mozart's El Dorado. Although his distaste for servitude at Salzburg was strong while the recollection of his triumphs in Italy was vivid, only one feature of the vast amount of Salzburg music he composed gives us any hint that he was dissatisfied. That feature is the extra quality, even the stylistic advance, of works composed for artists away from Salzburg, or visiting it, since they represented international instead of provincial and conservative taste – the superb E flat piano concerto, K.271, for Mlle. Jeunehomme is a fine example; yet we should be cautious even with this deduction, because a fine artist nearly always spurred Mozart to work of specially enduring vitality, as is proved by the "Exsultate" motet for Rauzzini or the *scena* "Ah, lo previdi," K.272, which he was to compose in 1777 for Josephine Duschek; moreover there are no more splendid Salzburg works than two which seem to have been composed primarily for court performance – the Sinfonia concertante for violin and viola, K.364, in which the soloists may have been Leopold and Wolfgang, and the C major symphony, K.338, sometimes called "without minuet" and sometimes, amongst older orchestral players in England, "Beecham's favourite," for nobody since Sir Thomas seems to have so relished the "heavenly length" of that work's middle movement.

It is a romantic fallacy to connect all the emotions expressed in an artist's work with those he may have experienced at the time of producing the work. A beautiful yearning sentiment suffuses some of the lyrical ideas in Mozart's Salzburg works, especially during slow movements and arias, and if any listener enjoys it more by imagining it to be yearning for a real or idealised lover, for Italy (real or idealised), for escape from Salzburg, or just for fine weather, let him do so; but let us also remember that such sentiment is endemic to sexually mature youth. (Alas that happy marriage so often cures it!) Since it is sometimes found in the quartets of Haydn, who was happy in servitude, we may doubt its particular association with Mozart's dissatisfaction with Salzburg. Most of his Salzburg music is *galant*, gay, self-confident, and not very serious, and most of it is distinguished (and that not by ears seeking the "great" Mozart before his years of greatness) by unrivalled beauty of texture and sense of medium. But it is best to consider such aspects of the music after we have traced the events of the Salzburg period.

Colloredo was absent from Salzburg in the summer of 1773 and Mozart, ever hopeful of a better appointment, took the opportunity to visit Vienna in July. He was back in Salzburg in October richer only by the D major Serenade, K.185, the Divertimento in D, K.205, and the six string quartets K.168–K.173. At home in what remained of the year and in the course of 1774 he wrote his first string quintet (in B flat, K.174), his first original piano concerto K.175, a brave piece of *galanterie* with the trumpets and drums that were to serve him for many years when he wanted to win audiences, a bassoon concerto, and several symphonies, including the earlier G minor, K.183, still often valued for the fire and passion that surprised and probably offended some of its first hearers.

An Opera for Munich

Then came a commission from the Elector of Bavaria for a comic opera, "La finta giardiniera" (the unknown librettist was possibly Calzabigi, who collaborated with Gluck) for the carnival of 1775. He wished Mozart to be in Munich to rehearse and direct the performance, and Colloredo could hardly refuse as his own presence was expected. The work was a tremendous success at its performance on January 13 and most arias had to be repeated. Beautiful though they are it is ensemble items, especially the two brilliant act-finales, and the vivid touches of wit from the orchestra which most clearly foretell the composer of "Figaro," "Così fan tutte," and "Don Giovanni." Here is the opera most likely to surprise those whose acquaintance with Mozart's dramatic works begins with "Idomeneo," and who expect an "early" opera that is a little more mature than "La finta semplice." Fortunately a recording can prove that, in his favourite genre, the youth of 18 commanded greater vitality than that of men twice his age, not excluding Haydn. The wit, dramatic pace, and human feelings are not thwarted by the highly artificial story.

The garden-girl is (of course) a young countess who secures her true love (of course a count) despite her elders

11. Cover of the piano score of "La finta giardiniera," published by Karl Ferdinand Heckel, Mannheim, 1829.

and the rich old roué (of course no aristocrat, but merely a mayor) who desires her, and (of course) after mistaken intentions and identities are cleared two other couples are united to live happily ever after. There is one more "of course" – the city is in Italy, just as the vague locale of "Figaro" and "Don Giovanni" is in Spain: the censors did not allow misbehaviour or folly by aristocrats to be represented as occurring in the imperial domains or German-speaking states. Munich was then much smaller than Milan and Mozart's opera had only a few performances in its original language, but the Mozarts themselves are known to have written some of the words in a German version and, as "Die Gärtnerin aus Liebe," the opera was performed in south-German states for at least a decade.

The Mozarts stayed on in Munich until March 1775. The piano sonatas, K.279–K.284, were commissioned by Baron Dürnitz after he had heard Mozart play in a contest with Ignaz von Beeke. The elector himself was so impressed by two masses and other church pieces given in Munich that he asked Mozart for an offertorium, the "Misericordias Domini," K.222. He did not request another opera. However, for a visit to Salzburg in April by the Archduke Maximilian, who was on his way back from France, Wolfgang was ordered by Colloredo to compose a *festa teatrale* to Metastasio's "Il rè pastore," a text which had often been set before and of which the poet himself had a high opinion.

It concerns Alexander the Great's discovery that the noble son of a vanquished king is living as a shepherd. He is restored to his throne and love, and the equally noble daughter of the usurping king secures her own lover. The moral reflections and noble sentiments give it more poetic than dramatico-musical worth. Because the Mozarts were at home, there is nothing about its reception in their letters, but even we, who know Mozart of the great operas, cannot fail to notice music more beautiful than that of Mozart's previous stage works in "Il rè pastore," K.208. Instead of trying to make drama where it did not exist he hung upon .the limpid words the same kind of beautiful melody as was soon to pour from him in the violin concertos. Much in the 14 numbers is concerto-like. "L'amerò, sarò costante," with its violin *obbligato*, is fairly well known, but the pastoral arias with flute *obbligato* are quite as fine, and so is the duet for the re-united lovers. The overture, too, is worth notice. Mozart no longer composes a *sinfonia avanti l'opera* of three movements, which can be used as a concert symphony when the work for which it was originally composed has finished its run. Henceforward he uses single-movement overtures, with or without slow introductions. Probably at Mozart's request a fine castrato and a solo flautist were borrowed from the Munich *Kapelle* for the performance on April 23.

That Wolfgang was well enough appreciated in Salzburg is made plain by several works of 1775–76, such as the "Serenata notturna" for double orchestra, K.239, the three-piano concerto for the Countess Lodron and her daughters, K.242, the solo piano concerto, K.246, for Colloredo's niece, Countess Lützow, and the music for the wedding of the daughter of Sigmund Haffner, burgomaster of Salzburg, most of it known to us as gathered into the D major Serenade, K.250 and the later symphony in the same key, K.385. Add to these the church music, the lovely violin concertos and divertimenti, and above all his first really great piano concerto, the E flat "Jeunehomme" of January 1777 and we have the fruits of activity which seem to have precluded any notable unhappiness.

Signs of discontent did come, however, in September 1776 in a now famous letter sent to Padre Martini with some motets for his scrutiny. Amongst complaints about Salzburg and the lack of singers was the information that "A mass with Kyrie, Gloria, Credo, epistle sonata, offertorium or motet, Sanctus, and Agnus Dei must not last longer than three-quarters of an hour. This holds good even for the most solemn mass celebrated by the prince himself. Special study is necessary for such conditions of composition, since the mass must still use all the instruments, including trumpets and drums."

In March 1777 an application for leave to undertake a concert tour was refused and in August Wolfgang petitioned for discharge. His request was granted and he was at last free to undertake his last extensive tour in search of better employment, accompanied this time only by his mother. It did not produce a very rich harvest of music and nothing at all in the way of appointments. When no result seemed to follow an interview with the elector in Munich, Leopold's letters directed Wolfgang to Mannheim via his native Augsburg, where the chief attraction for young Mozart proved to be his gay, tomboyish cousin, Maria Anna Thekla, nicknamed "The Bäsle." Another was his admiration of Andreas Stein's pianos, the reason for which we shall give later.

Mannheim

Before Karl Theodor took his court to Munich in 1778, Mannheim had been Germany's most enviable artistic Mecca. It is foolish to alter such labels as "Baroque," "pre-Classical," "Classical," and "Romantic" when they are widely accepted not for their aesthetic accuracy but their useful indication of a period style; otherwise the Mannheim court orchestra could be said to have brought Romantic features into pre-Classical composition and performance – the famous long *crescendo*, explosive *tutti*, the charming phrase or figure which draws attention to this or that wind instrument, contrast of texture and colour. They elicited rapturous tributes from phlegmatic British travellers.

Mozart effortlessly absorbed whatever he admired. He has been called a "musical chameleon" because the whole character, not just the mood of his expression, can change between one of his great works and another. The last three symphonies illustrate the fact, but perhaps it is shown most remarkably by comparing his music for an Italian comedy, such as "Figaro," with that of his last great German opera, "The Magic Flute." It was natural for him to write one or two very Mannheim-like works which fascinate us more by their texture than by the appeal of their musical ideas. Therefore many people who go about humming snatches of some of his early works, which owe much to J. C. Bach, may less easily remember fragments from the brilliant "Paris" Symphony, produced just after his stay in Mannheim; yet its composition and scoring are virtuosic. A similar comment might be made upon the Piano Sonata in D, K.311, which is by no means a favourite but can be greatly admired if compared with other sonatas, even those of Haydn, composed before 1778. Indeed it is shaped so much like a Mannheim orchestral work that Mozart could have translated its keyboard figurations to make an overture-symphony of three movements with trumpets and drums. This does not mean that any work by the Mannheim composers, even those of Austrian origin, could long be mistaken for Mozart's; nor could the *whole* of any by Haydn. The only musicians whose styles sometimes resemble Mozart's are J. C. Bach, Dittersdorf, and Schubert in very early symphonies.

The Mannheim influence is not adequately shown by the few works in which Mozart seems deliberately to have imitated Stamitz, Holzbauer, or Cannabich. It remained in his fondness for the clarinet. He himself was the first composer to give us really superb works for the clarinet, and it was at Mannheim that he first found clarinets regularly used in the orchestra. His experience of "the Mannheim sound" even affected the texture of works for the piano or string quartet, not just his scoring for orchestra. It has been necessary to emphasise this fact because we might otherwise be tempted to accept his father's opinion that his stay in Mannheim was a waste of time.

As in early tours, Wolfgang's important contacts in Mannheim were not with the aristocracy but with musicians and the Weber family, to which his future wife belonged. He was well aware of the elector's attempts to promote opera in the vernacular and raise the *Singspiel*, or popular German musical play, to a high level (Mozart himself was destined to achieve that ideal) and while in Mannheim he heard some examples of German opera. He thought poorly of Anton Schweitzer's music to an "Alceste" by Wieland, but highly of Holzbauer's more Italianate "Günter von Schwarzburg," and he actually directed the music of Schweitzer's "Rosemunde" during its composer's illness. Mozart could not have been active in the theatre unless welcomed there by the musicians, whom Leopold thought "loose-living" rogues. The fine oboist Ramm and the flute-player Wendling were indeed bohemian types but their artistry elicited from Mozart music that is still treasured and regularly performed.

The musician most greatly favoured in Mannheim at the time was probably the Abbé Vogler. He had come from Würzburg and been sent at Karl Theodor's expense to Italy, where Martini declared that he had ability but lacked patience and perseverance. This, and his publication of Bach's chorales with their harmony "improved," has made posterity regard him as a charlatan, but a fine symphony, some overtures to his operas, and church music, including an outstanding Requiem, disprove this summary judgment. His weakness was temperamental rather than musical, and Martini perceived it. His restlessness and impatience made him work brilliantly in Mannheim, Stockholm, Darmstadt, Frankfurt-am-Main, and Munich as performer, composer, and above all teacher, for wherever he settled (if that is the correct word) he set up valuable schools of music; after a few years, however, neither honours nor salaries and gifts could hold him. (He travelled to London, Russia, Greece, Portugal, Africa, and even Greenland!) This restless impatience made him immediately put to use whatever skill or knowledge he had acquired. The few fine works amongst his large number of compositions are those to which he gave time. Having learnt the elements of counterpoint in the treatment of a motive or a phrase or *cantus firmus*, he had to go about the world giving organ and piano recitals in which even good musicians were impressed by his powers of extemporisation on a theme — the kind of composition which may seem less valuable when written down, and therefore submitted for

12. Ignaz Jakob Holzbauer. Anonymous ink drawing.

consideration by repeated hearing, than it is when heard only once. We know of no coolness between Vogler and Mozart, yet Wolfgang wrote in somewhat deprecatory terms about Vogler's playing and extemporising, perhaps because Leopold had told his son to cultivate the Abbé for his high standing in the elector's favour.

Paris

Leopold's greatest fears, however, lay in Wolfgang's interest in the Weber girls, and he urged his wife and son on to Paris. Mozart's tragic stay there, from March to September 1778, proved to be the least productive period in his life. One of the few works he did write was a sinfonia concertante for flute, oboe, horn, and bassoon for the Mannheim players who had also travelled to Paris – Wendling, Ramm, Punto, and Ritter. When the day of performance arrived the score was "mislaid" by the conductor. The players were furious; Mozart was merely amused. Like his father he had learnt to expect intrigue, but unlike his father he did not put Gluck, then triumphing in Paris, amongst his enemies. Why should Gluck, by then 64, wish to intrigue against a 22-year-old in a kind of music in which he was no competitor? Like Haydn, Gluck was of humble origins and had a similar bluff good nature that could not easily be hurt by the contempt of social butterflies. He was quite aware that he made his way with a talent by no means outstanding until it was inspired by tragedy of the dignified kind cultivated by the French lyric dramatists. Only in France was Gluck's triumph complete, and he staged his new-style operas there regularly after his allies, Count Durazzo, the intendant of theatres, and Calzabigi, his librettist, had left Vienna.

When Mozart arrived in Paris the pamphlet battle between supporters of Gluck and his French-style *tragédie lyrique* and the supporters of Niccolò Piccinni and his Italian-style *opera seria* was at its stupid height. Its skirmishings had incurred little judgment of music. It revived a long-smouldering controversy about the rival merits of French and Italian as languages for lyric drama. This had begun between 1645 and 1662 when Mazarin brought Italian opera companies to Paris. Delighted with the scenic machinery and lavish use of chorus and ballet but puzzled by recitative, French audiences conceded that a classical story could be presented musically but, unlike audiences elsewhere, determined to rival the Italians, not to import their product. They were proud of their own drama, their leadership in both ballet (meaning gesture and crowd-management as well as dancing), and above all of their own language which the Academy subjected to minute examination in order to secure fine declamation and correct musical setting. Lully's *tragédies lyriques* realised their ideals during the Grand Epoch. After Louis XIV's death they were carried on by Rameau, an exact contemporary of Bach and Handel; his genius for orchestral colour gave special musical interest to the *divertissements*, during which the dignified unrolling of the classical story was in abeyance while the audience enjoyed a hunting scene, a storm or shipwreck, a pastoral ballet, invocations of witches, even the discovery of monsters or Red Indians! They are mentioned lest it be thought that only the Italian form of opera, with its strings of arias to repeated lines of verse, held up the drama for music.

French travellers were aware of the attractions of Italian opera and its scope for splendid singing, for arias were really concerto movements for solo voices, framed by orchestral *ritornelli* that were sometimes as delightful as the singing. Moreover one did not need to visit Italy to sample the operatic stars. Naples had become to Italian opera what Hollywood became to the first widely popular films, and ran the export industry as far as Russia and England. France alone resisted it, and under the royal absolutism a monopoly of her own products was possible, though not rigidly applied. Between 1752 and 1754 an Italian troupe visited Paris and performed a dozen samples of *opera buffa*, including Pergolesi's "La serva padrona" (The Maid Become Mistress), a short and amusing work for two characters which had been a great favourite in other cities from its first appearance in 1733. The old partisanship of Italian opera was revived against the partisanship of French, and the controversy raged amongst the pamphleteers in the *Guerre des bouffons* (War about the comics). Skirmishes continued almost until the end of the century, but flared up into another pitched battle when the presence of Gluck and Piccinni in Paris enabled the literary combatants to appeal to the public and judge rival settings of the Iphigenia story – Gluck's in the French tradition of *tragédie lyrique*, Piccinni's in the Italian tradition of *opera seria*.

Why make these historical and critical observations about a quarrel in which young Mozart took no part? Who were Gluck and Piccinni to him, unhappy and yearning for Aloysia Weber, except as composers commissioned to produce what he most longed to produce – music for the stage? Our justification lies in that very fact. Mozart was to prove himself the greatest musical dramatist and, though yet even less accomplished than Piccinni, must have judged other composers of opera far more perceptively than did the literary squabblers in whom he probably took no interest at all. He observed Gluck with a shrewdness not generally admitted. Details in Mozart's music prove that he knew "Alceste" and other works by Gluck very well indeed. For instance the climbing chromatic scales on woodwinds, rising eerily in the orchestral texture of "Don Giovanni" to suggest the presence of the ghostly statue (they occur first in the overture), are incontrovertibly taken, no doubt unconsciously, from Gluck's "Don Juan" ballet. We must wait until we examine "Idomeneo" to recognise the extent to which Mozart could use Gluck's methods. Neither he nor any great composer before Berlioz was wholly Gluck's disciple as regards the shaping of an opera, but Blom's belief that

Mozart was "if anything a Piccinnist" is sometimes dangerously repeated without Blom's qualifying comments. Piccinni was a splendid professional musician who conceived it his work to provide the right treatment of the libretto *as he received it*; the shape of the drama was the poet's business. This was not Gluck's or Mozart's opinion in the years of their great operas. They regarded the shape and the characterisation as being the musician's business, and they tried to work in alliance with their poets. Dramatic interest was not negated by Mozart's love of virtuoso singing in arias. Contrary to popular belief, Gluck also used arias, including *da capo* arias, in his famous last operas; but he used them less to display vocal agility than powers of expression, for he put them (as Mozart did) at those junctures of the drama which in spoken tragedy might have used soliloquies. Gluck had less room for them than Mozart because he fertilised the moribund Italian *opera seria* with elements from French lyric tragedy – persistent participation of the chorus, orchestrally accompanied solo declamation and *arioso*, evocative incidental music for the instruments. Mozart's dramaturgy must be examined later. He may not have read the literary sallies when he was in Paris, but we may be certain that no alliance of music and drama escaped his observation.

France dragged far behind England in the provision of *public* concerts, but there were two royally licensed series – the *Concert spirituel* (a title not used in the plural), founded

13. François Joseph Gossec. Engraving by Julien Léopold Boilly, 1820.

in 1725 by Anne Philidor for the performance of instrumental and religious music only, and the *Concert des amateurs*, directed by Gossec, who had made his name as an opera composer and been in the service of the Prince de Conti. Gossec had also at one time directed the *Concert spirituel* and incurred trouble during his attempt to re-organise it. He was supplanted by Joseph Le Gros, whose name did not belie his big size and paunch. Mozart frequently dined with Le Gros and reaped no other reward for complying with his request to supply eight choruses for a "Miserere" by Holzbauer. We have mentioned the "mislaid" sinfonia concertante for wind instruments, but the "Paris" Symphony in D, K. 297, given on Corpus Christi Day, was such a resounding success that it had to be repeated later. About K. 297 Mozart wrote:

> At the rehearsal I was frightfully worried ... You cannot imagine how they stumbled and scraped through the symphony twice in succession. I should have liked another rehearsal ... but there was no time, and next day I resolved not to attend the concert. Then the evening happened to be fine, and I went, resolving that if it went as badly as the rehearsal I should rush to the platform and seize the violin from La Houssaye, the leader ... The whole audience was carried away, and there was great applause. I knew as I wrote it the effect it would produce ... I had heard that here finales begin, like first movements, with all instruments together and usually in unison. I began with two violins only, softly for eight bars. Then came the sudden *forte*. As I expected, the audience whispered "Hush" during the quiet part. Then the loud crash. They clapped at once. I was so happy that I went straight to the Palais Royal and drank a large sherbet,* then said the Rosary as I had promised.

No doubt Le Gros had told him of the Parisian admiration for a *coup d'archet* or uniform stroke of the bow by every player at the opening of an *allegro*.

> I can be sure that it will please the few intelligent French listeners; as for the stupid ones ... I hope the asses will find something to enjoy, for I have not forgotten the *premier coup d'archet* ... these animals make such a fuss about that. Good heavens I see nothing wonderful about it – they merely begin all together with uniform attack as they do in other places. It gives me the giggles!

According to Mozart he let Le Gros have another symphony to follow up the success of the D major one. Unless this is the work now listed as K. App. 8 and called "Overture in B flat" the second Paris symphony has not been traced. Mozart was also asked to supply an oratorio, since choral works were a feature of the *Concert spirituel*. No such work has survived, nor does Mozart seem to have

---

* Mozart writes the French word "sorbet." It has been translated "ice," which would not be questioned if its usage were modern.

14. Jean Georges Noverre. Engraving by Barthélemy Joseph Fulcran Roger after a drawing by Pierre Narcisse Guérin.

written any for Gossec's concerts although Gossec was his friend and admirer. He may have helped Mozart through others, such as Noverre. That ambitious master of Marie Antoinette's ballet was unhappy, despite his good salary. He had greatly increased the *corps de ballet* at the Opéra but was the victim of intrigues, squabbles, and rebellions. Mozart supplied him with new music for "Les petits riens," K. App. 10, which was not discovered until 1872 in the archives of the Opéra. Noverre had produced a mime with this name some years earlier in Vienna. This explains Mozart's comment: "He wants just half a ballet . . . Six pieces will be by others. They are nothing but wretched old French airs." Mozart's name did not appear on the programmes or advertisements, but the music was enthusiastically applauded, as indeed it deserved. The ballet was originally sandwiched within a performance of Piccinni's "Le finte gemelle" (The Pretended Twin Sisters) but was later given with Anfossi's "Il curioso indiscreto" (The Rash Intruder).

Little came of introductions to the aristocracy, although Mozart made some money by giving lessons. Amongst his pupils was the daughter of the Duc de Guines whose talents lay in harp-playing and not in composition as the father had hoped. He himself played the flute and the Concerto for Flute and Harp, K. 299 was written for them to play together.

The important experience Mozart had in Paris in seeing many operas of various types is reflected in the piano variations he wrote on several of their favourite airs, probably as teaching as well as performing pieces. They include those on a march from Grétry's "Les Mariages samnites," K. 352, on "Lison dormait," from "Julie," a popular opera by Nicolas Dezède, K. 264, on the well-known song which some have attributed to Dezède though it seems to be of folk origin, "Ah, vous dirai-je, Maman," K. 265, and on "Je suis Lindor," said to have been written by Beaumarchais himself for his "Le Barbier de Seville," K. 354. He finished the six violin sonatas, K. 301–K. 306, which he began at Mannheim, and amongst the piano sonatas associated with Paris (even if composed on the way there) is the splendid one in A minor, K. 310.

In the meantime Mozart's mother had fallen victim to an illness that had been recurrent since she left home. After she had been bled her condition steadily declined into delirium and coma, and on July 3 she died.

Leopold enticed his son back to Salzburg by assuring him that the archbishop was prepared to take him back into the court *Kapelle* on favourable terms. Wolfgang, however, dallied on the way – first in Mannheim, where he was asked to compose for the Mannheim theatre, now taken over by a well-known troupe which achieved popular success with a form of lyric play then called "duodrama" but later "melodrama." Like *Singspiel* it was in German and used spoken dialogue, but like opera it took its stories from classical mythology and ancient history. Mozart admired two examples, a "Medea" and an "Ariadne auf Naxos" by the Bohemian composer Georg Benda, and began to set a "Semiramis" which was shown to him by Baron Dalberg, who became manager of the theatre. There was another extended stop in Munich, where Mozart proposed to Aloysia Weber and was rejected, and it was not until January 1779 that he finally reached home. He was destined to stay in Salzburg for nearly two years and during that period he produced the first examples of his really great and original works. Whether they flatter or flaunt convention, we cannot conceive any other authorship; and they are in a separate class amongst Mozart's works because no music of his written after those Salzburg years shares their peculiar atmosphere of ardent youthfulness. The actual output was not large, nor is it all accurately described as written *in* Salzburg. In October 1780 he began work on an opera he had been invited to write for the Munich carnival and when he left for Munich on November 5 he was never to compose in Salzburg again – at least under his own name. When he made his only return visit to the city in July 1783, he wrote two duets for violin and viola as a kindness for his former colleague Michael Haydn, who had been unwell when they were commissioned by the archbishop. Several composers have left us skilful instrumental duos, notably Telemann with his pieces for two recorders or two oboes, but these two by Mozart outshine anything of their class and it is a pity that they are not sometimes played as extras when the sinfonia concertante for violin and viola is given.

Pictorial Essay:
Journeys at a Glance

1. The Nymphenburg palace, Munich. Oil painting (detail) by Bernardo Bellotto, 1761.

Few eighteenth-century children, however rich, can have seen as much of the world as Mozart did before the age of 15. His father's ultimate aim was security for his son in the service of the great. The hope was never fulfilled, and from that point of view the "exhibition" tours he undertook were probably self-defeating. So much travel may have engendered in the child a restless spirit ill-suited to servitude, particularly under the conditions obtaining at Salzburg. They certainly made Mozart cosmopolitan enough to value his own freedom and independence above participation in the petty artistic rivalries of local princes.

The most obvious advantages of his journeyings were musical and Professor Hutchings discusses them fully in Chapter II. Here we are concerned solely with what Mozart saw. We do not know what impression the scenes illustrated here made on him, but we do know from the family's letters that both he and his father were not oblivious to the art and architecture of the cities they visited.

The child made his first major appearance outside Salzburg at the Nymphenburg palace in Munich. Appropriately it is there that we begin these glances at the world, geographically speaking, as Mozart saw it.

1. A year after this picture was painted Mozart played here for the elector of Bavaria, Maximilian Joseph III. The original palace, designed by Agostino Barelli and dating from 1664, was considerably enlarged in the eighteenth century. The gardens were designed in 1701 by Carbonet, a pupil of André Le Nôtre, who laid out the gardens of Versailles.

2. View of Brussels. Mid-eighteenth century engraving on copper by Francis Garden.

The Mozarts first visited Brussels in 1763 on the way to Paris during the Grand Tour. Here Leopold Mozart spent much time touring the fine Gothic and Italo-Flemish churches and admiring the art of Rubens. The engraving, however, provides a grim reminder in the boarhunt and the wayside corpses, a sight common in those days, that Wolfgang encountered more on his travels than grace and refinement.

3. The port of Calais. Optica (reversed) print published by Daumont of Paris, c. 1760.

After the first stay in Paris, which we shall visit on the Grand Tour's return route, the Mozarts embarked here for England in April 1764. The notoriously choppy Channel, apparent in the engraving, was none to Leopold's liking.

2

(2)

3

4

4. St. Paul's Cathedral from the Thames. Oil painting by Canaletto (Giovanni Antonio Canal), c. 1747.

The Mozarts stayed more than a year in London, and Nannerl's diary tells us that "St. Paul's Kirch" was one of the sight-seeing attractions. The cathedral, redesigned by Sir Christopher Wren, whose church architecture dominated the city after the Great Fire of 1666, was begun in 1675. As seen by Canaletto it still had an air of freshness for it was not completed until 1711. Whether the Mozarts saw Venetian barges rowed by British sailors is open to question. While Canaletto and his nephew Bellotto (see *No. 1*) were almost photographically faithful as topographical artists, they gave their imaginations freer play in peopling the waterways they painted.

5. The Buitenhof in The Hague. Engraving (detail) by La Fargue, 1764, published by Fouquet, Amsterdam.

After travelling via Dunkirk, Lille, Ghent, and Antwerp, the family reached The Hague on September 11, 1765. They must certainly have been familiar with the Buitenhof, or Outer Court buildings, which originally housed the workshops and stables of Count William II. Behind

7

8

9

10

11

is the Binnenhof (Inner Court), now the Parliamentary buildings of the Netherlands, centred on the thirteenth-century Ridderzaal (Knights' Hall).

6. The Dam in Amsterdam. Oil painting by Jan Ekels the Elder, c. 1760.

Illness prolonged the Mozarts' stay in the Netherlands to seven months and one of those was spent in Amsterdam. Dam Square, as they saw it has changed little. On the left is the city hall (now the royal palace), dating from 1648 and designed in Palladian style by Jacob van Campen; in the centre is the Nieuwe Kerk, dating from 1408 and rebuilt in 1645. The weigh-house on the right has since disappeared.

7. The Pont Neuf, Paris. Oil painting by Jean Baptiste and Nicolas Raguenet, 1777.

Mozart arrived on the second of his three visits to Paris in May 1766. The first had been in the winter of 1763–64. The sad and frustrating third, during which his mother died, came the year after this sombre picture was painted. Actually the massive Pont Neuf begun in 1578, and seen here from the Right Bank, was much more cheerful in Mozart's time than is suggested here. It was, in fact, the centre of Paris life and in the outward curves of the parapet between the piers street-vendors and medicinal quacks set up their shops. The market-fair of the Pont Neuf continued till the rule of Napoleon III and the Mozarts must have seen it often. At the tip of the Ile de la Cité can be seen the bronze equestrian statue of Henry IV erected in 1614 (it was replaced by a copy in 1818).

8. The Grotto of "Les Bains d'Apollon," Versailles. Oil painting by Hubert Robert, 1774–75.

The courtly glitter of Christmas 1763 spent at Versailles and the return visit in 1766 must have remained long in the memory of the child Mozart. Just as the palace (begun by Louis le Vau under Louis XIV in 1661 and continued by Jules Hardouin Mansart) became the architectural symbol of monarchical power, so in the reign of Louis XV the grounds and gardens became the epitome of courtly indolence and extravagance. It is unlikely that Mozart ever saw the grotto of "Les Bains d'Apollon" (pictured here under construction by the artist who designed it), for it was not completed until 1781. He may, however, have seen this seventeenth-century sculptural group, "The Horses of the Sun" by Gaspard Marsy, which was previously in the famous Grotto of Thetis, demolished to make way for the palace's north wing in the 1770's.

Italy remained, as Professor Hutchings points out, "El Dorado" for Mozart throughout his life, but the attractions for him, as for many travellers and artists of his time, must have been more than purely musical. His first impressions of the country were gained as a child in the tour of 1770–71 which took him as far as Naples, but he returned often and was never disillusioned as he was later with France.

9. The Piazza Navona in Rome. Hand-coloured copper engraving, 1750, by Thomas Bowles after a drawing by Le Geuy.

Mozart first saw Rome during Holy Week, 1770, and in July he returned to receive from the Pope the Order of the Golden Spur. In the Piazza Navona, about half a mile from the Quirinal, where the investiture took place, the family probably saw two famous products of the two great Italian Baroque masters whose work dominated the city – Francesco Borromini, whose Church of S. Agnese (1653–55) is on the left, and Gian Lorenzo Bernini, whose Fountain of the Four Rivers (1648–51) with its Egyptian obelisk stands before it.

10. The Piazza dell'Arno, Florence. Optica (reversed) print from an engraving by Balthasar Friedrich Leizelt, circa 1750.

On the way to Rome in 1770 the Mozarts passed through Florence. Many faces were known to them for the hereditary rule of the city-state had passed, on the extinction of the Medici line in 1737, to the Dukes of Lorraine – in other words to the family of the emperor in Vienna. The change was to bring economic and industrial progress, but at the expense of much of the city's historic architecture. Fortunately its unique monuments still include the Tuscan Gothic Palazzo Vecchio (its 308ft. tower is this engraving's focal point), built between 1299 and 1344 and attributed to Arnolfo di Cambio, and the cathedral, whose dome (also visible) was designed by Filippo Brunelleschi around 1420.

11. The Doge's Palace and Basin of San Marco, Venice. Optica (reversed) print from an anonymous hand-coloured etching, first half of the eighteenth century.

The Mozarts spent the carnival season of 1771 in Venice. The festivities were almost certainly centred on the Piazza San Marco, the corner of which is in the right foreground. The Doge's Palace, dating from 841, took its present style in the early fourteenth century after a succession of fires. The huge granite column (one of two on the Piazza) was brought from the Levant in the twelfth century and bears the Lion of St. Mark's.

12

12. The house of Johann Andreas Stein, Augsburg. Anonymous eighteenth-century engraving.

Mozart was familiar with but not overfond of Augsburg, where his father was born. His earliest memories of it were probably of stops made there on the Grand Tour in June 1763 and November 1766. This illustration, however, concerns his visit there with his mother in October 1777. Both were grateful for the hospitality of Stein, the piano-maker (whose house is in the left foreground). Mozart was much impressed by Stein's fortepianos and it was these rather than the city's attractions that prolonged his stay.

Some two and a half years before Mozart's death, when he was poor in pocket and in spirit, he welcomed the chance to accompany his friend Prince Lichnowsky on a business trip to Berlin. Performing for the admiring Frederick William II of Prussia at Potsdam must have brought back memories of his triumphs as a child at the grandest courts of Europe. The last two pictures portray Berlin as he must have seen it in 1789.

13. The palace and cathedral, Berlin. Oil painting (detail) by Carl Traugott Fechhelm, c. 1780.

The royal palace in Berlin took the form seen here during the rebuilding by Andreas Schlüter between 1698 and 1706. It was destroyed during the Second World War and the remains cleared in 1950 to form the site of East Berlin's Marx-Engels-Platz. The cathedral was also severely damaged and by the mid-1970's had not been rebuilt.

14. The Kurfürstenbrücke, Berlin. Oil painting (detail) by Johann Friedrich Fechhelm, c. 1780.

The Kurfürstenbrücke (Electoral Bridge) over the Spree still stands in East Berlin beside the site of the old palace (see No. 13) but Schlüter's famous equestrian statue of the Great Elector of Brandenburg, Frederick William, has since been moved to the West and now stands before the Charlottenburg.

III
The Salzburg music

History and Heritage

Composer and Master

Church Music

Symphonies

Serenades and Divertimenti

Concertos

Music for Dancing

15. Hohensalzburg seen from the east. Engraving by Johann August Corvinus after a drawing by Franz Anton Danreiter, first half of the eighteenth century.

Salzburg presents such a perfect fusion of Italian and South German art, and therefore such a counterpart of Mozart's music, that we need more than the behaviour of Colloredo, its last feudal ruler, to explain Mozart's earnest desire to leave it and not return. He did not feel that desire until he had reached musical maturity, for he can hardly have known a better training-ground for his art. Salzburg court music had been outstandingly fine under previous princes to those known by the Mozarts, and it should not be forgotten that Colloredo, villain of Mozart's story, considered himself a connoisseur of music as well as one of the more intellectual ecclesiastics of the Enlightenment, and indeed he was a competent enough violinist to participate in chamber music on occasions when the company was grand enough for the condescension to be admired properly.

The consecration of the cathedral, much advertised as capable of holding 10,000 persons (surely well packed!), gives Salzburg its first notoriety in music history as the venue of a classic example of music in the Italian "heavy Baroque" style – a Benevoli mass, which requires 12 four-part choirs (*spezzati*, i.e. spread around in galleries) and their associated instruments. Greater honour than this pretentious and inflated work could bestow came later in the seventeenth century when Heinrich Biber was enrolled in the Salzburg *Kapelle* and became *Kapellmeister* – a position which Leopold Mozart was never to secure because of his frequent absences on tour with his son. A royal or aristocratic *Kapelle* was simply the employer's musical establishment, and the *Meister* was normally the orchestral director and chief composer, not "chapel master," as in medieval times. The names were retained from appointments chiefly concerned with directing and composing for choirs, but by the eighteenth century, although the orchestra was used in royal chapels, cathedrals, and greater churches, the *Kapellmeister*, like Jommelli at Stuttgart, might be concerned chiefly with opera or, like Fux at Vienna, chiefly with the chamber music, i.e. orchestral concerts. Biber was a Bohemian violinist of unrivalled virtuosity, some of whose demands in multiple stopping and *scordatura* (unusual tuning of strings) are still taxing; more important, however, is his transformation of the suave Italianate manner of the Baroque sonata by German thematic interest and emotional seriousness. Of nearly 60 sonatas by Biber very few are trios; nearly half are what are called multi-voice (like English viol consorts) and were played, or could be and are played, by a string orchestra, thus being the precursors of the "sonata-concerto" known to us best through Corelli.

Biber's almost exact contemporary, Georg Muffat, actually knew Corelli though he had previously studied with Lully. Appointed organist at Salzburg for the 11 years 1678–89, it was he who brought the standard of

16. *Coat of arms of Hieronymus Joseph Franz de Paula, Count Colloredo.*

string-playing at the court to the pitch it retained until Mozart's time. He moved to the episcopal court at Passau to serve as *Kapellmeister* to an outstandingly musical ruler, and from there published his concertos with a preface in four languages explaining the effective antiphony of *concertino* and *tutti*, how to conduct rehearsals, etc.; but most of Muffat's work was actually composed while he was at Salzburg, and these concertos are largely arrangements in Corelli style of his former "chamber sonatas" (i.e. orchestral suites) called "Armonico tributo" and "Florilegium." If Salzburg music was so good for a century before Mozart knew it, why is it rarely mentioned in histories of music except in connexion with composers' names – Benevoli, Biber, Muffat? The answer is relevant to a study of Mozart, since it incurs reference to at least four courts in which Leopold hoped to see his son as a "famous *Kapellmeister*" (his actual expression) and at least two, other than the coveted imperial post at Vienna, which Wolfgang himself visited in hope of appointments.

Histories of music are expected to give space in their sections covering the seventeenth and eighteenth centuries to the two genres that were both ascendant during that period and also destined to leave us a rich musical inheritance – opera and orchestral music. To deal with opera first, we must admit that Salzburg is not specially important in the history of the lyric theatre. Until modern times Salzburg lacked public opera, though even while Monteverdi was still living productions were privately mounted on grand occasions, and musico-dramatic entertainments, sometimes in the cathedral square, were given by the scholars at the Benedictine university. In Mozart's time there were operas on special occasions, such as the welcome of distinguished visitors or the archbishop's nameday, in the hall of the winter palace. One cause of the adolescent Mozart's dissatisfaction was the absence of a public opera theatre, which also helps to account for the long delay before Salzburg was recognised as the ideal place for a Mozart or any other music festival. The first Mozart Festival was in 1877 and only seven more were held in the next 33 years. The famous "Figaro" conducted by Mahler was in the small Municipal Theatre. In 1925 the old riding-school was converted but soon superseded by the fine Festspielhaus.

As for the personnel and status of the Salzburg orchestral *Kapelle*, they do receive notice in histories of music, but only sporadically. Historians cannot be expected to follow closely the growth and prowess of more than a hundred princely musical establishments maintained in German-speaking states alone before Mozart was born. Their accounts begin with the first famous orchestra, Lully's, and the first orchestral repertory of "ouvertures" or French suites beloved by the German court orchestras; attention is then focused on Italy's instrument-makers and the rise of the Italian concerto, which became the second orchestral repertory and ousted the suite; so mention is made of Bologna, where Corelli was trained, and of its Accademia Filarmonica, then of Corelli's Rome, Vivaldi's Venice, and the three-movement Venetian concerto which conquered the German orchestras and encouraged fine solo performers as well as brilliant ensemble. This brings us right into the eighteenth century when most orchestral establishments were being enlarged to swell princely pride, and no one-volume history can spare pages for accounts of other orchestras than those associated with important names (Biber's and Muffat's Salzburg, Bach's Cöthen, Handel's Hanover) and those, usually of the greater states though not necessarily so, of largest size and repute – the imperial one at Vienna; the one at Dresden called "The King of Poland's Orchestra" after Frederick Augustus of Saxony, as an Austrian protégé, had been given Poland as well; the one at Stuttgart (Württemberg) associated with Jommelli; the one at Potsdam owned by the flute-playing Frederick the Great of Prussia and served by Quantz and C. P. E. Bach; the Bavarian court orchestra at Munich (for the Wittelsbachs were the most musical of German royal families and Mozart badly wanted the elector's patronage when he visited Munich); and finally the most famous of them all at Mannheim, owned by the pleasure-loving Karl Theodor of the Rhine Palatinate and called by Burney "an army of generals." It employed many Bohemian, i.e. Czech, musicians whose brilliant compositions and performances sped the advance of the pre-Classical symphony and sinfonia concertante and hastened the passing of the Baroque concerto and suite.

Composer and Master

The ruler and court of Salzburg certainly wanted Mozart to return. They knew him to be a musician of rare ability. Did they recognise his *genius* in composition as well as performance? The question is not easily answered. It is not safe to use "genius" instead of "great talent" of a composer aged only 23. Even today the point at which a young living composer's talent seems to reach genius is not decided unanimously even when several other composers, as well as writers about music, hail him as a genius. Few eighteenth-century patrons were careful about the distinction. Composers who were fluent in supplying what was enjoyed were all said to have genius by their admirers, not many of whom compared composers except those locally employed. The historical culture of music, unlike that of architecture and painting, was in its infancy; but in the half-century before the musical flowering of the Romantic movement people applied "genius" to composers who deeply stirred their feelings rather than to those who purveyed elegance in quantity. Many years before Beethoven was admired as an unpredictable genius, creatures of the Enlightenment could speak of "divine madness" in a complimentary way, as when they considered this attribute of genius to have produced Gluck's tragedies.

Did Colloredo himself recognise genius in such works as the "Jeunehomme" piano concerto or the sinfonia concertante for violin and viola? It is often supposed that he did not, though he was a violinist himself. His final treatment of Mozart was probably motivated by pride in possessing a musician who might live to be classed with Haydn. "Possession" is the right word to describe his attitude. Haydn had remained his prince's servant; if this young Mozart wanted to do well instead of dissipating his energies and abilities, let him be schooled in obedience. With the utmost deference to the most perceptive writer about Mozart's music, one may differ from Alfred Einstein's suggestion in "Mozart – His Character, His Work":

> . . . he voiced the fear that Colloredo would take revenge on him [for leaving Salzburg]. It is another point in the archbishop's favour that he never thought of such a thing, as well that he never made Leopold suffer for the behaviour of his son.

Colloredo lived to know the world-fame of his former court organist. In 1803, after the secularisation of the diocese of Salzburg, he moved to Vienna. He lived until 1812, reaching the age of 80. In all probability the memory of his relation to his former servant, Wolfgang Amadeus Mozart, never gave him a moment's concern. But it is a misfortune for his reputation that he ever had anything to do with the Mozarts.

Most of that passage is admirably fair to a sour authoritarian who, had he not been a cleric, might have greatly benefited from marriage. (Not the slightest suspicion has been cast upon his sexual morality, and one cannot stifle the private thought that if, like Karl Theodor, he had held a mistress and illegitimate offspring in great affection, his subjects would have had a happier time.) He lived into the age of Beethoven. Let us suppose that he could not "understand" (which, applied to the arts, means "enjoy") the expression of the younger generation any more than their manners, nor lose hope that the Corsican upstart would be crushed and something of the *ancien régime* restored. Is it not possible that a man of his culture *did* reproach himself for his mishandling of a man whom all came to call "genius" – a man whose music, moreover, retained in its most disturbing pathos so much of the graciousness of days that had gone?

He lost Mozart when he gave him leave to direct the opera "Idomeneo" as the Munich carnival opera for 1781. We therefore regard as Salzburg works whatever Mozart composed before his first great opera. They can be divided into the following categories:

1. Music for the piano or harpsichord, including concertos for keyboard instruments. They will be discussed in a later chapter since some of them were used in Vienna, and Mozart's continuous development in both solo and concerted piano music merits separate examination.
2. Church music.
3. Chamber music, including orchestral music and dances.

Throughout the eighteenth century, music was classified into only three types, according to its place of performance – theatre, church, or chamber; thus orchestral symphonies and concertos were called chamber music, not concert music. We shall consider first the Salzburg church music, as nothing need be added to what has already been said on Mozart's theatre music before the first of the great operas, "Idomeneo."

Church Music

Some of Mozart's church music is of permanent interest, musical as well as historical, but to say that he wrote church music throughout his life is to exaggerate. In Vienna he held no post which required church music from him. The two great masses which he did not complete were that in C minor, K.427, in fulfilment of a vow, and the Requiem, K.626, in fulfilment of a commission. They stand as distinct as do his compositions for Masonic rites from the church music required by his service at Salzburg. So also does the Kyrie in D minor, K.341, written early in 1781. Though Mozart was then still enrolled as a Salzburg musician he had gone to Munich,

and both the key and the solemnity of the piece (unchanged *Andante maestoso* throughout) prefigure the Requiem. The inclusion of parts for clarinets and violas, to say nothing of four horns, banishes thought of its use in Salzburg. Wolfgang wanted the highly musical Karl Theodor and the court at Munich to know the sort of church music the composer of "Idomeneo" could supply. He had written home: "Please send me the scores of the two masses I took with me as well as the Mass in B flat, for Count Seeau will say something to the elector about them." Count Seeau was not given the chance, for Mozart evidently decided that these works would not impress Munich. Since, however, they were his own selection from his Salzburg masses, we may take them to represent his best achievement in work which was not quite to his liking, for he was not entirely free to choose its form and style. Indeed the church music is the least distinctive of Mozart's early work – so much so that for many years the most popular example of it was "Mozart's Twelfth Mass" (in Novello's edition) which is known to be spurious, and may have been by one of the Reutters or by Eberlin. It was sung by choral societies and even played by brass bands, the Kyrie becoming the tune of a hymn still used in Protestant churches. Young Mozart so easily absorbed the styles and methods of other composers, chiefly his father's friends and former Salzburg musicians whose works were still used at the cathedral, that it is quite unsafe to note points of musical vocabulary and style in his later works and then discover them in early works as proof that these early works are his. Excellent scholars have been deceived by subjective and internal evidence, and works formerly listed as Mozart's in Köchel's catalogue are now known to be copies he made from other musicians.

The B flat mass, K.275, composed in the autumn of 1777, is unmistakably Mozart, and lyrical Mozart too. No wonder he took it to Munich in case he had no time to write new church music there, for it is rich in the kind of music which could be used in operas if it had room to expand! This is true of the C major "Coronation" Mass, K.317, of March 1779 (which may be one of the others taken to Munich), wherein there is just a little more room for expansion, since it was intended for the pilgrimage church at Maria Plain, near Salzburg, and not for the cathedral. Even the "Coronation" Mass has many features of a *missa brevis*, about which there seems to be some misunderstanding. When Colloredo arrived in 1772, as Mozart explained to Martini, long masses were disliked even on high festivals, and though Salzburg masses are as short as any of their kind and period they were so before Colloredo's advent. It was just that ungracious man's habit to promulgate his wishes on the subject, as on any other. Long before Mozart was born *missae breves* were required at Vienna, where Maria Theresa regarded the imperial *Kapellmeister*, Johann Reutter, as setting a model for others. Reutter used the orchestra too colourfully for us to call his masses utterly dull, but without the instrumental dressing their music is somewhat empty and

17. *The pilgrimage church of Maria Plain, near Salzburg. Engraving by Johann Bernhard Hattinger, after a drawing by Franz Anton Danreiter, first half of the eighteenth century.*

often inept in its treatment of the text. It is not easy to admire either the music or the man who was so harsh towards young Joseph Haydn, and turned him into the streets as soon as his voice had broken. Haydn's brother Michael, however, learnt the technique of short-setting lengthy texts (which lack symmetry or verbal repetitions) while he served at St. Stephen's under Reutter, and Michael Haydn was Salzburg's best composer of church music. We know that Mozart liked him and admired his work.

Without commending Reutter's, Eberlin's, or Adlgasser's masses, and without excusing Colloredo's unpleasant orders, we may note the good reasons for avoiding musical impediments to the progress of the liturgy during the sacrificial action – from the offertory of the Host to the consecration. The three ministers would be kept standing and everybody else kneeling during a long Sanctus, Benedictus, and Agnus Dei, while

the meaning of the words, which should pass *through* those items and form one long prayer of consecration and oblation, is halted and chopped up. At a concert these pieces of music make vivid their own words; in the liturgy they are incidental, and one does not align oneself with any school or period by recognising the ideal treatment – unaccompanied plainchant by which the celebrant's solo singing of the prayer is carried on and passed back by the choir without any breaks but the breaths taken at punctuation marks in the text. The two long items of music, Gloria and Credo, make least disturbance of the rite, being both outside the canon in the preparatory material, and both occurring at junctures. This is proved by their being shifted to various places in different modern revisions of the mass, and by their frequent total omission in the traditional mass. Thus Gloria was not and is not used in Advent, Lent, and penitential seasons, and Credo is not used in the Requiem or whenever it is desired to gain time. A lengthy Gloria and Credo also cause no physical discomfort, for it is customary to sit and listen to them as soon as the celebrants have said them mentally and gone to the sedilia; yet their florid development would be incongruous in a *missa brevis*, and that is one reason why Mozart's C major mass of May 1776, K.262, is not wholly satisfactory. It has sometimes been called *missa longa*. Composed for St. Peter's Church, not the cathedral, it did not incur the obligation of brevity; yet Mozart followed his normal practice and made the three items within the canon as short as in a *missa brevis*.

The mention of this C major work is deliberate. It shows a strong contrast with the B flat mass we have selected for comment. It is less distinctively Mozartean because it is less operatic, more consistently in a solid church-like style. We may postulate two extremes in the unique musical amalgam called "Mozart," and his immature church music is precisely that in which they do not always amalgamate. At one extreme is music so German that it is influenced by north-German composers such as Telemann, Graupner, and J. F. Fasch, though it reached Haydn through C. P. E. Bach. It reached Mozart chiefly through musicians engaged in the south, including his father's friends. Its merits are fine part-writing (not necessarily in formal counterpoint) and thematicism. It is music of good, solid texture, admirable for choral and church music. It is not unmelodious, for the Italian opera and concerto greatly influenced German composers of the age of Bach and Handel. Moreover, especially in Austria and Bavaria, folk-music which did not wait to be "collected" went into the movements of orchestral and instrumental music. The other extreme was Italian opera, both as a direct influence and through such composers as J. C. Bach. Its supreme characteristic, of course, was extended melody, deployed at its loveliest in *bel canto* arias, and there was no room for arias in a *missa brevis*, no opportunity for the kind of music Wolfgang composed for Rauzzini in the "Exsultate, jubilate" motet.

One of the older composers who was most friendly towards Mozart was the extremely facile Johann Adolph Hasse, "Faustina's" husband, who settled in Vienna after a long and highly successful career and died there in 1783. He was musically utterly Italianate rather than German, and no doubt Mozart would have liked to write masses like his rather than like old Eberlin's or even Michael Haydn's. Now, without pretending that the B flat mass, or even the brilliant "Coronation" Mass, are to be ranked amongst Mozart's major works, we can recognise in them a marvellous feat. Like most of Mozart's masses they have the compression of *missae breves*, yet they manage to use efficient German texture in symphonic style as well as Italianate melody in beautiful flights that do not suggest still-born arias. This is more remarkable in the B flat work (and others which are not quite so appealing) than in the "Coronation" which allows more room and specifies soloists. In most *missae breves* there are only passing solo flights which soon rejoin

18. *Johann Adolph Hasse. Engraving by Lorenzo Zucchi after a painting by Pietro Antonio Rotari.*

the chorus. This fusion of traditions was of enormous value to young Mozart purely as training in composition. Let any musician who fails to wonder at its success try setting just a little of one of the long proses of the mass, following the Classical key-scheme for symphonic pieces, never repeating words, ensuring thematic interest, yet providing attractive melody. The symphonic coherence in itself Mozart could command, and it gave no difficulty in a Kyrie or Agnus Dei with the text neatly divided into three parts of equal length; a little more difficult was Gloria, in which the triple form of the text does not easily allow the music of the first part to fit the rhythms and phrase-lengths of the third, while the Credo defies reliance on the text as a vehicle for symphonic themes. Mozart's ways of overcoming his task were, even if he used lengths of lyrical melody, to devise short motives. When voices could not use them without maltreating words, they could sound from instruments, often in little flights of contrapuntal imitation; when, to compensate for the time taken by some beautiful "et incarnatus est" or any other words, the text had to be sung swiftly in ensuing passages, Mozart was capable of negating an effect of rushing or perfunctoriness by moving the harmony slowly, with a symphonic tread, and ensuring that the organ or violins overrode with a line of decent melodic interest.

Excluding the great C minor mass and the Requiem, Mozart wrote at least 16 settings of the mass, of which 10 are in the key of C major. Since many of them are described as "for four-part choir, organ, and strings" (without violas), the choice of key cannot have been suggested, as either C or D was to composers before Mozart, by convenience for trumpets. Most of these works are *missae breves*, including some of those not supplied for Colloredo at the cathedral, and it is remarkable that so many of them can be commended in terms already used towards that one in B flat. Einstein speaks of those "still found in church libraries," suggesting with some justification that they rarely leave the shelves to adorn the mass since the advent of liturgical experiments, though they may occasionally be used for a pontifical ceremony or the Midnight Mass of Christmas Eve. It may be worth reminding musical holiday-makers that in some countries church notices need careful searching, and that in Prague, Salzburg, Linz, Vienna, Munich, and several other cities the Latin mass is still regularly performed on Sunday with Classical musical settings, and that some of the churches in these cities have orchestral players at their disposal. It is also worth mentioning that the "musical" church is not always the cathedral, nor the time of service always that expected. In 1971 masses by Mozart and Haydn were used on Sundays during August and September in St. Michael's Church, Munich, at 9.30 a.m. (This was once the court church where, no doubt, Mozart heard some of his music.) Though none of the Sundays was a festival, some of these masses used wind instruments. An hour later High Mass was sung at St. Peter's with string orchestra. In Salzburg Mozart's masses are naturally to be heard both at the cathedral and at St. Peter's.

Since the times and places just mentioned may be changed, the information is not offered as a tourist guide but to support Einstein's remark about works to be found in "church libraries," for the settings favoured in central Europe are those favoured before the war in high Anglican churches (where they were given with organ only) and amongst the local choral societies which were then still fairly numerous. Some of them are quite early Mozart, for instance the very concise pair of masses in F and D, K. 192 and K. 194, written in 1774. It is not proposed to go through the rest as if awarding marks of popularity. Those with most appeal are those most reminiscent of opera in the Italianate "Exsultate, jubilate" vein, and the wonder is that it could seem prevalent when there was no room for proper arias even in Benedictus or Agnus Dei. Often the listener is directly reminded of opera. An obvious instance may be quoted from the Salzburg mass that is most often heard in the concert room, the "Coronation" C major, in which the melody of the Kyrie, recurring at the end of the work for "Dona nobis pacem," is found in Fiordiligi's aria "Come scoglio" in "Così fan tutte" while the opening of Agnus Dei recalls the Countess's "Dove sono" in "Figaro." Even in the little passages of formal counterpoint, Mozart

never seems ponderous and for this very reason was until recently thought "irreverent," a word equated with "theatrical." Ecclesiastical taste, considerably changed since about 1920, no longer thinks lightness and gaiety to be incompatible with reverence; rather does the "dim religious light" of medieval and pseudo-medieval churches need elucidation of older ideals. We know from Mozart's contemptuous remarks about the cathedral at Ulm that he did not appreciate Gothic, yet he no more anticipated modern religious thought than he composed operatic masses to annoy Colloredo (who liked Italianate music) or to show disregard for the ritual he set or the ceremonial he watched.

No apology is made for taking space here to discuss eighteenth-century religion, lest we misunderstand not only Mozart but Haydn, J. C. Bach, Martini, and other musicians as well as their ecclesiastical and noble patrons. Whether theist or atheist first made the epigram "God made man in his own image and man faithfully returned the compliment," those who cannot accept the first of its sentences cannot deny the second. What cannot be apprehended by the physical senses must be conveyed by symbol, and symbol must come from material known through the senses. A well-known example occurs in the aria "Quoniam tu solus sanctus, tu solus Dominus" in Bach's B minor mass – "For Thou only art holy, Thou only art the Lord." The chief characteristic of this piece is the splendid but difficult horn *obbligato*, for Bach's image of "the Lord" was that of the supreme feudal lord, the seigneur, and he was seen amongst his peasantry chiefly when he was taking his pleasure in the hunt, the horn announcing his presence. To gaze at the interior of Salzburg Cathedral, still more at the gay pilasters and Rococo ornamentation of St. Peter's, should be enough to tell us how "men of reason," children of the Enlightenment, conceived the abode of deity as a palace in the best taste – not dim, but bright and richly coloured and ornamented. Because of what was enacted there it was called *teatrum sacrum*, the holy theatre, and was not the theatre the most splendid room in a lord's palace? Moreover in the theatre or grand salon subjects saw and heard their seigneur, so the church had to be designed with minimum obstruction of altar and pulpit from the eye and ear.

Of Mozart's orthodoxy there is no doubt. Indeed it is remarkable that one so rebellious against entrenched arrogance, one so rational and critical, should persist in using objects and procedures of devotion which modern Catholics regard as superstitious or naïve. The artist, however, may cherish a tradition or a legend because it symbolises greater truth than historical accuracy. The rational side of Mozart found in Masonry the moral expression of Catholic belief, but it is not true to say that he was unmoved by formal religion and its music. That error is a false conclusion to two observations about his church music – that much of it is conservative, and that (at least in the "duty" masses) little of it is personal in the sense of subjectively pathetic. Church music tends to be conservative not out of reverence for deity but because the main Sunday services of all denominations are public and formal. To honour a public occasion, the performers at concerts or the officials at inaugurations and commemorations don formal attire that is "out of date." Similarly, in Lutheran as much as Catholic churches, subjective piety was excluded from the fixed liturgy, and private expression, with the word "I" and the phrase "my Saviour," confined to the changeable chorales and cantatas. Always a personal touch intrudes – the right word when the general aim is to exclude – when composers who have often said the words suddenly think of their meaning, the best known example of this being Beethoven's addition of "O" to the phrase "miserere nobis" in Gloria, or his giving stress to "et" in Credo, as if it meant "even this I believe" rather than simply "and this."

The intrusion of the personal and subjective in Mozart's settings is more subtle. Mozart's most intensely personal expression is put into the mouths of his opera characters, and it fertilises symphonies and concertos and works without words. It is most characteristic (as in the two famous arias for the Countess in "Figaro") when it is in a major key yet wistful. Another kind of expression not exactly paralleled by other composers, despite the much-mentioned *Sturm und Drang* trend, requires a minor key, a chorus, and wind instruments which smoulder rather than flare; public solemnity and private passion seem both to inform it.

Now one or both of these uniquely personal veins can always be found in church music which Mozart did *not* write for his sovereign. The finest examples are the incredibly beautiful and long "Et incarnatus est" solo and the "Qui tollis peccata mundi" double chorus with trombones in the C minor mass composed after Mozart had finished writing for Salzburg; but both are anticipated in some of his earliest church music. K.139, the mass the 12-year-old boy is thought to have provided in 1768 for the consecration of Parhamer's *Waisenhaus* chapel, is a lengthy work with soloists and an orchestra that included no less than four trumpets as well as the usual three trombones and timpani. No doubt Leopold supervised, but the two veins are not found in work by Leopold, and they are evident at the very opening – a solemn orchestral prelude in C minor, then the alternation of soloists and chorus in an Italianate "Kyrie eleison" reminiscent of Hasse and J.C. Bach. In the "Christe eleison" the soloists touch, in a major key, the wistful vein just mentioned. No wonder that the "Waisenhaus" Mass was once thought to have been written in 1771–72 and associated with public mourning for Archbishop Schrattenbach, though not a Requiem. The two veins appear again in parts of the C major "Dominicus" Mass, K.66, for Hagenauer's son Kajetan. We find them even in some *missae breves*, for instance the "Credo" Mass in C, K.257, so called because of the thematic use of the reiterated opening four-note motive associated with the first word of the creed. (Incidentally the opening four-note motive of the Sanctus also opens the finale of

Mozart's last symphony. He was fond of four-note motives announced like *canti fermi* when a work could be well served by counterpoint. We shall not yet discuss Mozart's command of counterpoint because we are now concerned with features of his music which are distinctive and personal. He was neither wholly fluent nor wholly personal in manipulation of counterpoint until his experiences with Van Swieten's society in Vienna.) Earlier we mentioned the solemn personal vein in Mozart's D minor Kyrie for Munich, and we may regret that he did not complete a mass in E flat as he intended to do at Mannheim in 1778. The major key does not prevent the "solemn personal vein" from appearing in the Kyrie, K.322, completed by Abbé Stadler. Of the Sanctus only a fragment remains.

Though an instructive concert could be given with the best selected pieces from Mozart's Salzburg masses, it is understandable that only one mass is heard in our concert halls, apart from the later C minor and the Requiem. In this "Coronation" Mass we find neither the solemn vein nor passages of formal counterpoint. It was composed for an occasion during which a crown was placed on the image of Mary at the church of Maria Plain. A bright and efficient *missa brevis* texture, made the brighter by Rococo trumpets and drums, is relieved by beautiful operatic solo work. None of the Salzburg church music gives a full revelation of genius; yet not to enjoy some of it is to miss evidence of the labour by which the budding genius overcame tasks that were later presented by his own purposes, not his employer's. Splendid examples of this fact are amongst the 17 epistle sonatas, mostly for organ and strings. Such pieces came to replace lengthier movements of Baroque church sonatas and concertos in a part of the service where they were not necessary. The prose, chiefly of psalm verses, called the gradual was formerly chanted between the readings of epistle and gospel, and was said by the priests during the sonatas, which became obsolete almost before Mozart died. The reading of the gradual and the little procession to the place where the gospel was chanted took less than the two minutes which Colloredo thought enough for the delightful usurpation. Wolfgang might complain to Martini but he marvellously achieved the required brevity in epistle sonatas, which are of more than documentary or technical interest; for though musicians may be fascinated as they follow their compression of "first movement" design, recordings of these works are bought by listeners who respond simply to their musical appeal. The analyst cannot easily explain this; he can but observe that themes are concise but have attractive and athletic rhythms with room for seemingly spontaneous development, sometimes even miniature "development sections." The hidden instructors were certainly the Haydns – Joseph in many a harpsichord sonata or quartet, Michael in his own Salzburg epistle sonatas.

We have two Salzburg settings of vespers from Mozart, the "Vesperae de Dominica" (Lent Vespers), K.321, of 1779 and the "Vesperae de confessore," K.339, of a year

19. The Benedictine Abbey of St. Peter, Salzburg. Engraving by Karl Remshard after a drawing by Franz Anton Danreiter, first half of the eighteenth century.

later, for a saint's day, but who the "confessor" was we do not know. Nor do we know in what church they were used. They both have an oratorio-like spread, the psalms and canticles being set in different keys, though both services begin and end in C major. Moreover there is deliberate contrast between successive items. In each, for instance, a choral "Laudate pueri" in contrapuntal motet style (in the second setting it begins with a strict canon) is followed by a "Laudate Dominum" in the style of a florid solo aria. The "solemn personal vein," with reminiscences of Gregorian chant, yet with menacing diminished seventh chords, comes in the settings of the first psalm, "Dixit Dominus"; and in each service is a brilliantly symphonic Magnificat. The second service, belonging to the same year as the "Coronation" Mass, is the finer, and should be more often heard. It was Mozart's last piece of church music for Salzburg, since the D minor Kyrie (K. 341) was for Munich.

Equally interesting, however, are some of the items in Mozart's settings of litanies. Most churchfolk regard litanies as does the Oxford Dictionary – "series of petitions recited by clergy and responded to in repeated formulae." It is not easy to see how the quiet devotion normally represented by this type of service was served by the brilliant cantatas called litanies by Mozart. We have yet to discover where and on what occasions most of them were performed, for "performed" they must have been. No congregation was "led" in such music. It is useful to know that the second of them, a Litany of the Blessed Sacrament, K. 125, of 1772, which is florid but not very personal or distinguished, was performed on New Year's Day at one of the Munich churches, probably the gorgeous and huge court chapel, St. Michael's, now the Jesuit church. Mozart may therefore have composed them for occasions which were as special as the festivals fixed by the church calendar.

We have four of these litanies. Two, including the one just mentioned, are each entitled "Litaniae de venerabili altaris sacramento," and the other two "Litaniae Lauretanae de B.M.V." (Lorettan Litany of Blessed Mary the Virgin). A legend that Mary's house at Nazareth, or parts of it, were transported to the Italian town of Loretto, south of Ancona, led to the building of a pilgrimage church there named after the Santa Casa or Holy House. A teaching order of Lorettan nuns was founded in 1609 and may have had a convent with a big school which Mozart honoured by his two litanies. (The famous Scottish school called Loretto is an early nineteenth-century foundation.) Naturally the last two of the four litanies are much the finer works, and they are more prophetic of Mozart's really great music, choral and solo, than are the Salzburg masses. Einstein points out that many of their solo items could with little alteration have been rescued to make concerto movements with solo clarinet, violin, or cello, and many items have *obbligato* parts for solo instruments with the solo voices. This is particularly true of the second Litany of the Blessed Sacrament, K.243, of 1776. The first of the Lorettan litanies, K.109, of 1771, contains much tender and beautiful music, but is overshadowed by the second, K.195, of 1774, which is worthy to stand beside Mozart's post-Salzburg work, for no Agnus Dei in any Salzburg mass is the equal of the setting included in this litany. We possess three of Mozart's settings of "Regina coeli," written in 1771, 1772, and 1779 respectively. This Marian antiphon is sung only during the festal weeks from Easter to Ascensiontide, and all the settings tend to be brilliant throughout. The last one, K.276, is very much the best, and may have been used with the "Coronation" Mass. Whereas the previous settings are sectional, the last one is conceived with the integrity that would serve a choral movement in a symphony, its advance unchecked by the interplay between voices and orchestra, soloists and chorus; this work also should be kept in our concert repertory.

(A setting of the psalm "De profundis," K.93 relegated to App. A22 in the 1964 edition of Köchel, is now generally accepted as a piece by K. G. Reutter copied by Mozart.)

Symphonies

What the eighteenth century called chamber music, meaning that played in palace or public concert room, not a church or theatre, is now regarded as reaching its apogee in the best symphonies. For this fact Haydn and Mozart were responsible. While they were purveying symphonies in quantity they can hardly have imagined that their attitude to the genre would prevent their successors from purveying them in quantity – from publishing symphonies in batches of six or 12. Programmes still call Haydn's last symphony "No. 104" and Mozart's "No. 41," though we happen to have more symphonies left by them than those numbers suggest. But how many of Mozart's 40 to 50 justify the responsibility we have mentioned – responsibility for the fact that future symphonists would rarely achieve the most famous tally of nine? How many are so rich in whatever we mean by "musical thought and emotional depth" (which we need not define) to hold our attention after a lifetime's acquaintance, or after as many consecutive listenings as would make simple music sound stale? How many justify pride of place so that orchestral programmes are built round them as the main items?

Forced to give no other answer to these questions than a number, most musicians would say "seven" – two less than the Beethoven number. (If the question had referred to concertos, Mozart would greatly have exceeded Beethoven.) Only one of the seven, K.338 in C, of 1780, would lie within the Salzburg period, and all seven were composed within eight years – not quite Mozart's last eight years, for he wrote no symphony after 1788. Alas that there are no "London" Symphonies by Mozart to delight not only us but the composer of the famous 12 "London" Symphonies, for Mozart did not live to undertake the visit to England which Haydn strongly recommended! In fact some listeners, probably most, treasure the last three or four Mozart symphonies even above Haydn's, and it is unprofitable to question or commend the validity of their opinion. It may change, but not the opinion that Haydn left *more* symphonies worth frequent performance, which is worth examining in an account of Mozart's orchestral music. Mozart's purely orchestral works do not continue as a fairly regular output spanning his life as Haydn's did. They therefore do not show a comparable advance from shallow to deep musical thought, despite the fact that we could name a handful of Mozart's early symphonies which are better as sheer essays in composition than any which other composers, including Haydn, produced at the same age; but these do not immediately precede the great symphonies. A fine work of 1773 may be followed by two or three inferior ones until we reach the best of 1774, and so on. Moreover there are huge gaps such as the four years between K.202 in D and the "Paris" Symphony requested by Le Gros, or the five years which separate the "Linz" C major from the famous last three symphonies – or would do so but for the "Prague" D major of 1786.

Mozart is certainly not to be blamed for this. On the contrary we should regard ourselves as most fortunate in possessing the last three symphonies, for evidently Vienna made no demand for them comparable with the previous demand for piano concertos. Because, unlike Haydn, he was not in regular employment where symphonies were wanted, nothing distracted him from his great musical love, the composition of opera. If there is any value in asking which of the great classical composers most fully measured our humanity and, thinking of symphonies, we are inclined to say "Beethoven," we should pause and think of chamber music, the theatre, and the concerto. Nothing from other composers is comparable with Mozart's string quintets, his operas, or his concertos. Still more important – and this we should constantly bear in mind when deciding what is great or merely well-composed Mozart – those symphonies and other works which are supremely treasured are precisely those in which is reflected the humanity of the operas, where indeed the singing instruments actually seem to be eloquent dramatic characters or the ensemble sounds as if transferable to a dramatic situation.

If we could suddenly effect a metempsychosis to the 1770's some of the symphonies which we now accord only historical interest might strike us as more operatic than, say, Haydn's or Stamitz's. The origin of the title "symphony" is operatic, but to say "The symphony came from the Italian opera overture called *sinfonia avanti l'opera*" is an over-simplification. The first repertory of the court orchestras, increased to equal the famous one under Lully, was of suites or "ouvertures," imitated by the Germans until first the concerto grosso and then the solo concerto spread from Venice after 1715. German composers were already Italianised in the concert room as well as the opera theatre. The repertory of concertos and concerto-like suites lasted until nearly the middle of the century to be joined by the new symphonies which they influenced. Even if Italian overtures had been unknown outside Italy the *style* of the pre-Classical symphony would have been what it is; but the Italian overture is perhaps its most important parent because it imparted the *design* rather than the style. In C. P. E. Bach's symphonies we see the style in a man who never went to Italy and had little to do with opera.

Without going into technicalities we should note the difference between style and design; for although Mozart from childhood knew and imitated the Italian overture design, we may sometimes find movements which we cannot readily recognise as following the subject-and-key scheme of so-called "sonata form." To understand the design of extended movements before the rise of the symphony we need only to consider some long chorus in "Messiah," for instance the well-known "For unto us a child is born." The text takes three distinguishable types of music or ideas: (*a*) "For unto us, etc." (*b*) "And the government, etc." (*c*) "Wonderful, Counsellor, etc." There is some contrast between their rhythms but they hold together in one long paragraph and may be regarded as a main idea with attendants, not as discrete first and second subjects. This paragraph is presented four times as it passes through the normal Baroque "cycle of keys," sometimes not quite accurately called the "cycle of fifths." The principle behind it is best described as "out on the sharp side (dominant) and back by the flat side (subdominant)," so that this particular chorus runs through the keys G–D–G–C–G. The same sort of design will be noticed in, say, the first movements of the "Brandenburg" Concertos, and as regards the order of keys many early symphonies (including Mozart's first three)

had no fixed design but only the principle "out by the sharp side, etc."; disregarding design, however, and observing only style, we see an enormous difference between pre-Classical symphonies and their predecessors. Long before the Mannheim symphonies became famous, symphonies (or Italian overtures) had dynamic marks running through all movements, beginning usually *f–p–f–p*–etc., but sometimes *p–f–p–f*–etc. In contrast, not a single *f* or *p* will be seen in the outer movements of the "Brandenburg" Concertos; there are dynamic marks within Handel's concerti grossi but never at the opening of a movement; presumably one began *forte* unless one saw that direction ahead!

Next we notice the fondness for patterns of repeated notes, especially in the bass, and of chords repeated (rather than held as in vocal music), sometimes with rests between the repetitions; for in the pre-Classical style a stolid progression of changing chords was thought inelegant, to be associated with the old-fashioned wig, the *Zopf*. (Bach's sons irreverently called their father *Zopf*, greatly though they respected him.) Texture and variety of texture mattered more than originality in the harmony. Formerly composers had been forced to variety of texture whenever they used trumpets, horns, and drums, for these instruments could be used only with the main ideas specially written to suit their limited range of notes and keys. We may note, too, that the Venetian opera overture was specially known for its employment of trumpets. More and more during Haydn's and Mozart's lifetime the symphony was to show other contrasts of texture, even within portions requiring only the instruments of the string quartet. Above all – and this applies very much to Mozart – the growth in command of materials, style, and design, which in one sense is a growth in the complexity that defies analysis, accompanied a growth in memorability and appeal to which the dramatic tensions and contrasts contributed.

The reader may wonder why so little has yet been said about Mannheim, since Karl Theodor began to employ the famous Bohemian players and composers, who were to make his orchestra the most splendid of any, as early as 1743; by 1750 their symphonies were being imitated, but until Mozart stayed in Mannheim on the way to Paris the Mannheim influence on him was only indirect, as it seems to have been on Haydn. Before the Leipzig professor, Hugo Riemann, revealed the number, quality, and influence of this Mannheim school, which he rightly called a Bohemian school, histories of music hardly mentioned the Mannheim symphonies. Riemann's work was not widely known until the beginning of our own century; eighteenth-century praises of the Mannheimers concern not their compositions but their attack, drilled bowing, unanimous attention to expression, and other qualities of performance. It was not from the Mannheimers but from the most Italianate of Germans, J. C. Bach, that the boy Mozart first took his models of symphonies. Bach himself may have known little about the Mannheim symphonies but much about those applauded

33

in Milan, Turin, Naples, Rome, and then Paris – the cities in which he himself was applauded. The child Mozart composed his first symphonies, K. 16 and K. 19, almost under J. C. Bach's supervision in London during the winter 1764–65. The Bach–Abel concerts had just been inaugurated, and a symphony by Abel which little Mozart copied was until recently catalogued as K. 18. Today we know that K. 17 and K. 98 are also wrongly attributed to Mozart and that only the introduction of what was once known as the Symphony No. 37, K. 444, is his (the rest is by Michael Haydn).

If it were not known to be by Mozart, aged only eight, his first symphony, made from the small change of music then fashionable, would attract little attention apart from the fact that its middle movement is in C minor, the others being in E flat major; by thus using the relative minor he was simply following a practice of J. C. Bach and Abel. His second symphony, K. 19, though showing no greater originality, is so much better a composition that nobody could take it for the work of a child only just nine. With the Symphony in B flat, K. 22, written at The Hague in 1765, he showed himself an expert, competent to purvey symphonies by the dozen if any employer wanted them. From connoisseurship of his later music we may even recognise the appearance of personal characteristics, for instance the chromatics in the G minor middle movement, or the *crescendo* in the first, which may come indirectly from Mannheim but is more reminiscent of a conspiratorial scene or an imbroglio in a Mozart comic opera.

Until K. 45 of 1768, no Mozart symphony has more than three movements, and many of those composed later are without the minuet although the third and final movement may be in minuet tempo. Stamitz at Mannheim has been named (Grove's Dictionary) as the first composer to introduce the minuet into a symphony as a fourth movement; but having done so Stamitz did not make four movements his normal practice. The minuet was adopted because it was so much enjoyed in divertimenti and in serenades, which had an enormous influence on symphonies and quartets, particularly Haydn's. In Austria generally, though first in Vienna, the inclusion of a minuet became common during the 1760's. Most of Mozart's symphonies have four movements, despite the fact that the last composed at Salzburg, the magnificent K. 338 in C, is known generally as "ohne Menuett," unless a conductor decides to add one from another work, as Mozart himself did to several symphonies which were originally of only three movements. (Though Mozart began a minuet for K. 338, another minuet composed in 1792, K. 409, is often played with this Salzburg symphony, and Einstein claimed that it was expressly composed for its performance in Vienna. Whatever was expected in 1792, K. 338 is satisfactory without the minuet, and gains little by the addition.)

Undoubtedly Mozart's adoption of the minuet movement, as indeed most other advances in symphonic composition that were not prompted by his own ingenuity,

came from his admiration of Haydn. If "corrective" is not an unfortunate word, we may regard the influence of Haydn as a corrective of the influence of J. C. Bach and the Italian overture model. It is particularly remarkable in the first of Mozart's really arresting symphonies, which happens to be the first now frequently played.

Other symphonies cannot be said to "lead up" to that arresting K. 183 in G minor. Within Mozart's broad advance as a symphonist there are halts and withdrawals both of style and invention. In one symphony, e.g. K. 132 in E flat, there may be an advance to which acquaintance with Haydn's work has contributed, while in its successor the conventions of the Italian overture are resumed, and the advance is only in brilliant instrumental interplay. Mozart's slowness in making the symphony a more ambitious essay is evident in the fact that right up to 1779 he was using opera overtures and symphonies interchangeably. Köchel's list of the symphonies includes the overtures to "Il rè pastore," "Ascanio in Alba," "La finta giardiniera," and "Il sogno di Scipione" (all with added finales). It is important to note that *opera buffa* had become popular before Mozart began composing, and that the musical vocabulary and phraseology of *opera buffa* was uppermost in Classical symphonies before Beethoven's, especially those written by Austrians. It persisted even when expression was tragic or passionate, as we can prove by simply tapping the rhythms of the two outside movements in Mozart's most "serious" symphony the great G minor, or of the first movement in the still more poignant G minor string quintet. The most frequently happy-sounding of symphonists, Haydn, is oddly enough among those whose music least shows the debt to Italian comic opera, for it owes much to the songs and dances he heard as a boy, as well as to the Baroque composers with whom he became acquainted as an imperial chorister and the serenade music in which he participated to earn money after his voice broke. Mozart, on the other hand, having from birth lived in musical sophistication, is among the most Italianate of symphonists except when under the influence of Haydn.

It was certainly that influence which led to his first offering Salzburg a symphony in a minor key. It is ridiculous to say that K. 183 in G minor "points to" the great G minor symphony or one of those disturbingly pathetic works by Mozart in minor keys which suggest suffering "too deep for tears." By 1773, the date of K. 183, Haydn had composed some 50 symphonies of which no less than six were in minor keys, for the appreciation shown by his employers gave him greater artistic freedom than Mozart enjoyed. If we omit the Bachs and Haydn, we shall find the number of minor-key chamber works composed between 1750 and 1775 to be small. Despite the *Sturm und Drang* movement, Salzburg may have wondered why emotions normally reserved for the setting of solemn words in church should be offered in chamber music, that to them meant music for social pleasure by musicians who were paid to supply it. There is no reason to suppose that Mozart intended a public catharsis of troubled thoughts, but once he had embarked on the adventure of the minor key (and for him at Salzburg it *was* an adventure) he responded to its stimulus. People who regard all works in minor keys as the equivalents of psychiatric case-books forget a simple technical point – that the notes of the ascending minor scale differ from those used in the descending form, so that the minor mode offers a richer range of pathetic harmonies than the major. There is little of subjective pain or pathos in this somewhat severe K.183; nor is there in Haydn's G minor symphony, No. 39, which certainly led Mozart to emulation. What has been said about *opera buffa* rhythms still holds true, yet only the tender slow movement reminds us of opera. Compared with previous Mozart symphonies this one is better described by the epithet *ernst* than *kläglich*, for not even the minuet suggests dancing or *galanterie*.

A fusion of Italian and Haydnesque elements is found in some of the other very good symphonies of late 1773 and 1774, and fortunately several of them are beginning to appear in our programmes. The C major, K.200, is as finely expanded and developed as the G minor, and has a brilliant *buffo* finale. The most understandably popular of this group is the delicious and lightly scored A major, K.201; it is in Mozart's favourite sunny key and – a feature not always found in Mozart's very great works – all four movements maintain the standard set by the first. Here are ingenious growths from memorable ideas, some in fine codas; and with them are telling orchestral effects. Mozart himself thought well of these 1773–74 symphonies, for he used them at his own concerts after he had left Salzburg. Apparently he did not so honour the "Paris" Symphony, which has been called his first "great" one instead of the first to display his delight in a big orchestra. The A major is a finer work. Its small orchestra and smiling mood have beguiled good scholars into thinking that it resembles chamber music in the later sense of the term. They are forgiven if they never submitted to a teacher who forced them to arrange orchestral works for string quartet. That questionable exercise would have led them to discover that the first movement of Beethoven's "Eroica" could have been accepted as the first movement of a splendid Beethoven quartet, whereas the corresponding movement in this K.201, containing pages that *look* like those of a Haydn quartet, baffles the attempt at translation. Technical demands account partly for the difficulty; it must have violins and violas in the plural, must have a double-bass, must have wind instruments to hold chords while the strings are engaged in their little figurations; but technical demands do not account for the whole difficulty. The conception is orchestral and symphonic. That opening could lead to a grandiose trumpet and drum passage before proceeding to its "second-group" Tyrolean lilt, and so initiate an ambitious movement comparable with one in the "Prague" or "Linz" symphonies, although it so perfectly suits its own work.

To treat K.201 as if it were a divertimento is to perpetrate a travesty. The work is often spoilt by taking three of the movements too fast and dragging the *Andante* sentimentally. A particular snare is provided by the dotted rhythms of the unique minuet, for careless players will unconsciously increase speed and even make the figures into triplets. Musical boxes tell us the speed at which the "Don Giovanni" minuet and also the minuet in the great E flat symphony were taken soon after Mozart's death; the minuet in the symphony is not much faster than the one used for dancing. Two swallows do not make a summer, and two minuets should not lead us to suppose that all Mozart's minuet movements went at the same speed; but to rush a symphonic minuet is not merely to spoil one movement – it may spoil the effect of a finale, making it seem too staid unless it also is rushed. Good rhythm does not depend upon speed, and if the spirited finale to K.201 goes too fast we lose the pacing of the repeated "accompanimental" chords, the nuances of bowing, and the brilliant interplay of that virtuosic development section. In this, young Mozart's finest finale, he has caught up with Haydn (at his most brilliant in a hilarious finale) without even reminding us of Haydn's earthiness and bluffness of humour. Scale and mood are deceptive. This A major symphony is a finer achievement than its immediate successor in D with trumpets, and, as already pointed out, finer than the still

20. *Jean (Joseph) Le Gros. Engraving by Charles François Macret after a drawing by Philippe Leclerc.*

35

more grandiose "Paris" Symphony in D, K.297, of four years later, which has a disappointing slow movement. For many years this piece, in a context which leads one to expect a more ambitious design, was thought to be the original slow movement. It is now known to be the simpler one supplied because the conductor Le Gros thought the original too complex.

One does not wish to belittle the "Paris" Symphony just because Mozart himself, in the course of his sour letters about the French generally, wrote as if he merely gave the fools what they wanted. He was on tenterhooks to ensure that it went well after those disappointing rehearsals. Could he have been worrying merely about his popularity? No; despite Leopold's advice, Wolfgang was unable to "write down" once he had begun a work. He had just come from Mannheim and the "Paris" Symphony is the most Mannheim-like in the whole series. The fact that he had composed no new symphonies for four years is not of great significance. During that time he was providing for a Salzburg which wanted less demanding entertainment than symphonies but liked the superficial attractions of concertos, divertimenti, and serenades. These did not turn Mozart from symphonic processes of composition: one of his great symphonies had its origins in serenade music for Burgomaster Haffner.

The Paris commission reawakened Mozart's interest in symphonies, for he composed two soon after reaching home in 1779, and both are worth keeping in repertory. The first, K.318 in G, which needs four horns, two trumpets, and drums, may have been intended as an overture to "Zaïde." Different analysts have regarded it as being in three movements or two. It seems to be in one! A splendidly expansive opening *Allegro* is interrupted. Just where we expect a development or middle section the martial tempo is changed to slow triple metre and the trumpets and drums are silenced for what seems to be a slow movement. It proves to be an insertion shorter than most slow movements in symphonies, for the *Allegro* is resumed without a break as a finale. After some new music it recapitulates materials from the opening section and gives them a fine coda. The other symphony of 1779, K.319 in B flat, is for the small orchestra normally available under the parsimonious Colloredo. It is full of warm sentiment and sounds very Viennese, as if pointing to Schubert's early symphonies. Mozart added a delightful Viennese minuet to it when he used it for his concerts in the capital.

"Its heavenly length," wrote Schumann, referring to the slow movement of Schubert's "Great" C major symphony. The description is aptly applied to the middle movement, *Andante di molto*, in the superb Mozart symphony of 1780, K.338 in C. That long outpouring of melody is without peer or parallel. The movement is scored for strings and two bassoons, which Köchel does not mention, and one wonders why Mozart added flutes to all movements in Vienna. One shrinks from "describing" the music, but each movement calls for comment because it offers so little comparison with any correspond-

ing movement in a later symphony. The finale, for instance, is the last in the symphonies of the sublimely heightened gigues of the kind previously enjoyed in K.201 and K.319. There are plenty of first movements in the pompous style which musicians of the time called *Prunk und Pracht*, and Mozart frequently turned to it right up to his last symphony; but in no other symphony nor in any concerto does such a movement open with the courtly swagger and, without altering the martial rhythm, proceed with ideas that actually seem to mock the magnificent strut, as if playing the part of a court jester. The two outside movements of K.338 have another marked feature. The fully scored passages in each seem to act like *ritornello* sections in concertos towards small groups of instruments. The development section of the first movement is like a concerto episode, and the finale actually reaches a held six-four chord without an ensuing cadenza but *with* the shake on the cadential chord that we associate with the end of a cadenza! The supreme jewel of all Mozart's Salzburg music must be for many music-lovers, as it was for Beecham, the *Andante di molto* written in such short notes that the *di molto* applies only to the beat of two crotchets per bar. (Many conductors use a quaver beat lest the slightest slackness should mar this taut and lithe marvel.) Heaven knows there are plenty of lovely singing andantes in Mozart's instrumental works, but nowhere else such big paragraphs of melody so marvellously articulated. They are not punctuated merely by cadences but also by harmonies which, whether diatonic or chromatic, have the effect of that excellent counterpoint which uses the mild discords – suspensions, passing notes, leaning notes, etc. Not even the big flight of melody that opens the middle movement of the Piano Sonata in F, K.332, is extended with the brilliance of this movement. To do it justice the interpreter must not only hit the exact speed and keep it; he must also command several gradations of climax and approach to climax, none violent.

Serenades and Divertimenti

The most popular of Mozart's serenades was composed in 1787, and so lies well outside Salzburg music; yet there are two reasons for referring to it here. First, this "Eine kleine Nachtmusik," K.525, is so well known that we can recall its music without the help of music quotations; second, Mozart wrote so little music of its kind after leaving Salzburg that we can include it all within one survey. We do not know for whom or what occasion K.525 was written while Mozart was strenuously engaged in finishing "Don Giovanni," nor why it has lost the extra minuet and trio mentioned as its second movement in the notebook catalogue which Mozart began to keep in Vienna. It is important to know for what instruments such a work could be designed without any difference in size and type of constituent movements.

The score looks like that of a string quartet except that against the bass clef is printed "Violoncello e basso." Like many such works by Haydn, Mozart, and others, it could have been played (without the double-bass) as a string quartet, and so it probably was sometimes played. Most of the thousands who know it, but may not even know the meaning of its German title, associate it with a bigger string orchestra than is ideal for the music. They may even know it only from some arrangement for brass band, or a small group such as a dance band. (Mozart might not have been horrified as we are by the treatment, for he wrote at least one fine serenade for "poor devils" of wind-players, as we shall see.) For our present purpose we may also notice that, even without transposition to C or D major, it could be scored for a festive symphony orchestra. Let us hear the opening in our minds' ears – first the full ensemble with trumpets and drums in the unison, then an almost "Mannheim" *crescendo*, chiefly for strings, over the repeated bass notes ("The Mannheim road-roller"), and at the mark *p* some concertante between woodwind and strings. Why this exercise in imagination? The object is to remind ourselves that, before Haydn and Mozart had given symphonies an exalted status as the most ambitious and comprehensive essays for orchestra, the style and scale of quartet, symphony, serenade, cassation, and divertimento were not sharply distinguished. The last three designations normally incurred more than one minuet, perhaps an initial or final march, and at least one movement in which a solo violin or other instrument behaved as in a concerto. Sometimes, too, the sequence of movements kept to one key, as in the older suites. This did not make them tedious if they were spaced out during a wedding or garden party as dances are separated for conversation, refreshment, and changes of partners.

Mozart wrote serenades and divertimenti for orchestra, small groups of instruments (as small as a trio), wind instruments, and string instruments. Let us begin with those for the largest forces. D major is one of the festive keys for trumpets and drums, and it is noteworthy that four of the serenades which Mozart wrote for orchestra in that key were for many years sold with four movements only, like "Eine kleine Nachtmusik," and called symphonies. The most famous of them is the "Haffner" Serenade, K. 250, which many people regard as Mozart's first great orchestral work. Certainly a good performance gives one a surprise if one has forgotten its date, 1776. It comprises no less than nine movements – an introductory *Allegro maestoso*, leading to a brisker *Allegro* in "first-movement" style; a beautiful *Andante* like a concerto movement for the solo violin, framed by a *ritornello*; a minuet in G minor, with a trio in G major wherein wind instruments support the solo violin (this is the first movement not in D major); another concerto-like movement, this time a lively rondo, the solo violin much featured in the main theme; a return to key D for a minuet with trumpets; a luxurious *Andante* in A, *rondeau*-shaped with varied instrumentation at recurrences of the main idea –

a favourite design of Haydn's; another minuet with two trios, one for wind instruments; a short slow introduction and a gay finale in triple tempo and sonata design.

Elizabeth Haffner's wedding was richly honoured, but was this music served during the festive meal? Was the orchestra stationed in the square, street, garden, or house? Or did the guests sit and listen to it somewhere after the meal – treat it as a concert? We do not know. Much of the original suite would seem to be second-class listening at a concert if it were immediately preceded by the "Haffner" Symphony, for it is not easy to believe that the symphony was only another serenade. In spirit it was no Salzburg serenade. Critics can be very perceptive of style when they know the circumstances of composition. The "Haffner" Symphony, K. 385, lacks the second minuet which was sent in 1782 when Mozart heard from his father that the Haffners wanted a second serenade similar to that of 1776 because the son of the family, Sigmund, had been ennobled. Mozart also sent along the march, K. 408 (No. 2), with the four movements we know and the minuet which we have either lost or failed to identify. When a copy of the whole work came back to Vienna in 1783 Mozart called it by a significant name, here italicised – "My new 'Haffner' *symphony* has quite amazed me, for I had forgotten every single note. It must have a fine effect indeed." It was Wolfgang himself who discarded the march and the second minuet, letting Vienna hear it as a symphony. And thus surely it should remain, however serenade-like critics think the slow movement to be. The description does not belittle a delicious movement, less highly organised than corresponding movements in Mozart's later symphonies but much more interesting than the slow movement of the "Paris" Symphony.

During Mozart's Vienna years his serenades become increasingly serious. They gradually shed movements which an older generation called *galanteries* and become like symphonies of four movements. In Salzburg days the lightest of serenades were for wind-players, regarded as socially lower than string-players, so that unless they were in court uniforms they were merely town waits. Don Giovanni's supper, with wind-players as waits playing snatches from popular operas, was for its first beholders a contemporary scene. Yet the greatest of all Mozart's serenades, K. 361 and K. 388, were two of his last three for wind band. The three are each worth special notice.

K. 361 in B flat, of 1781, called "Gran Partita" (a phrase used for suites, especially outdoor ones) in Mozart's notebook, is usually referred to as the Serenade for thirteen wind instruments. It is scored for two oboes, two clarinets, two basset horns, two bassoons, four horns, and a double-bass which could, of course, be replaced by a double-bassoon. (A version for a smaller band, K. App. 182, may be Mozart's but the arrangement of four movements as a string quintet, K. 46, is not.) This splendid work was begun while Mozart was still "under" Salzburg but in Munich for "Idomeneo." It is a true serenade with two minuets (each with two trios), two slow movements, the first a love-lorn Notturno, the second a song-like Romanza, a set of light variations, and a bright rondo finale. It may have been heard in Vienna but was plainly for the fine Munich players, no doubt intended also to impress Karl Theodor. Maybe "Notturno" indicates the intention of an outdoor performance by torchlight. The temptation to make miniature concerto movements for the oboes or clarinets was resisted. Instead the work presents an unparalleled diversity of orderly ensembles. The score is so much more effective than it looks that only a student who has tried to write a movement for the same band, maintaining the serenade spirit, and who has then *heard* his work, can fully appreciate Mozart's "ear."

K. 375 in E flat of the same year, written in Vienna, is also a true serenade, not a wind symphony. We know that the portable instruments – two clarinets, two horns, and two bassoons – were played by waits, for Mozart's letter of November 3, 1781, tells the circumstances. The serenade was ordered by "the sister of Herr von Hickel, court painter," and the six players "at her house were poor devils who, however, play well together . . . It gained much applause, and on St. Theresa's night was played in three different places; for as soon as they had finished performing in one place they were paid to take it somewhere else." The grateful waits gave Mozart a pleasant surprise on the night of his own nameday (St. Wolfgang) for, just as he was undressing for bed, they struck up outside his house, asking "that the street door could be opened so that they could march into the courtyard." As in the older outdoor suites, all the movements are in the one key, relieved by the C minor and A flat trios of the two minuets which flank the central *Adagio*. (Mozart later rescored the work, adding two oboes, and it is this version which is usually heard today.)

K. 388 in C minor, of 1782, called "Nacht Musique" in the notebook, is one of Mozart's supreme creations. It is scored for two each of oboes, clarinets, bassoons, and horns, but is frequently heard as arranged by Mozart in 1787 for string quintet, K. 406 – a translation incurring rather more loss than gain. The four movements are those of a particularly fine symphony. The level of musical thought is indeed higher than that of most symphonies composed before 1782, even by Haydn, and higher than that of the "Haffner" Symphony, fine work though it is. Without omitting the first word we could not aptly give K. 388 the title of Gounod's charming "Petite symphonie à vents." The sheer composition of K. 388 is so serious and brilliant that it could be deprived of the sombre tone-colour which is admittedly part of its glory and still be impressive as a piano duet, as indeed it is as a string quintet. Can a work with only the *Andante* in a major key, with a finale made of variations which do not relax C minor until almost the end, with solemn and ingenious canons in the C minor minuet of all movements – can this virtuosic wind symphony be a commissioned serenade? In fact it was, but surely for a very musical patron. According to the composer's letter of July 27,

1782, it was wanted "in a great hurry." The Mozarts were already aware of the need for money, and he would hardly refuse any reasonable commission; but what prompted his personal best in so non-festive a mood remains a mystery. Soon afterwards at the end of 1782 Mozart finished the G major quartet, the first of the great set of six quartets dedicated to Haydn. One can hardly accord the C minor serenade greater honour than by declaring it the equal in depth of the D minor quartet, K. 421, in that "Haydn" set.

Mozart himself is thus responsible for our sitting solemnly in the concert hall, or by the gramophone or radio, and sampling serenades, divertimenti, and cassations with the alert ears given to important concertos and symphonies. Obviously they reached some alert ears, and witty entries of horns or other instruments suggest that Mozart hoped to attract attention during music that was commanded or commissioned to accompany eating, promenading, conversing, or enamouring. Mozart is also responsible for unwillingness to hear or record those works which nowhere foreshadow the features which delight us in operas, concertos, and symphonies of the Vienna period.

The presence of a minuet (later scherzo) in classical symphonies points to their origin in less demanding music. A similar survival is that of marches in serenades and divertimenti when these movements were no longer used for marching, any more than the symphonic minuet for dancing. Now most of Mozart's music for wind instruments was composed very early in his career and the marches were probably functional. The march signalised the approach of the waits and covered their entry to the square, courtyard, dining-hall, garden arbour, or wherever they were stationed. For the two C major divertimenti, K. 187 and K. 188 (the first an arrangement of music by Starzer and Gluck), the marchers seem actually to have been militia, and the music may have been for a military occasion such as an event in the riding-school; the unusual scoring is for five trumpets, two flutes, and four drums.

Most of the 22 works rightly or wrongly called divertimenti by Köchel (some were certainly commissioned serenades) are light, facile pieces which not even Mozart's authorship can make most listeners wish to hear one after another. Many have probably been used only at the place and time for which they were written. From the six scored for oboes, bassoons, and horns, and composed between 1775 and 1777, the best example (probably K. 270 in B flat) could be used to illustrate the simple music which evolved towards the tremendous K. 388; but some of Mozart's later wind divertimenti, though still in short, unpretentious movements, reveal invention and skill worth at least the attention of students – whether of composition or of ensemble performance. Indeed they probably *were* for users who may be called the best of students, for we have no evidence that they were commissioned to be played by waits at weddings or social gatherings. They were probably for

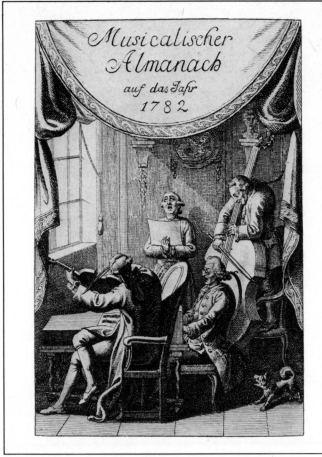

21. *Frontispiece of the "Musical Almanack" for 1782. Engraving by Johann Rudolf Schellenberg.*

home players amongst Mozart's friends, such as the Jacquins. They have the customary two minuets but no marches. After Mozart's death five divertimenti for two clarinets and a bassoon disappeared until Simrock issued them with two added horns in 1800. They are thought to have been written in 1783 and intended for three basset horns – instruments featured in Mozart's Masonic music. The players may have been Masonic friends. Particularly worth hearing are the canon for two basset horns and a bassoon, K.410, and a solemn Adagio for two clarinets and three basset horns, K.411.

More likely to be heard at concerts are works which associate strings with wind instruments, beginning with the D major divertimento, K.251, which requires an oboe and two horns and has a march "alla francese." Two horns play with the strings in K.247, K.287, and K.334, none of which is nearly as witty and interesting as the earlier K.131 in D, which uses four horns and has seven movements. So has the "Andretter" music, labelled "Finalmusik" by Mozart but usually known as the D major serenade of 1773, K.185. This was required, like the "Haffner" music, for a Salzburg wedding. The Andretters were family friends of the Mozarts, and as Wolfgang was in Vienna we must either suppose that he was well paid for the serenade or that Leopold asked him to send it as a present. Old Andretter was the court

councillor who dealt with the militia and the riding-school, and possibly the martial rhythms in some of the movements are a sly compliment to him rather than to his son, the bridegroom. The first violin is given concerto-like prominence in the movements (one fast and one slow) which are in keys other than the tonic D, and also in the trio of one of the minuets.

It remains to mention only two or three works which, like the "Haffner" Serenade, secure fairly regular performance. One is the four-movement Divertimento in E flat, K.113, which Mozart composed during his stay in Milan in 1771, and called "Concerto ò sia divertimento." It seems to be his first orchestral score with clarinets, and he uses the word "concerto" in its older sense, referring not to solo display but the interplay of strings and wind. He might have used the same term for the better-known "Serenata notturna," K.239, of January 1776, which recalls the Baroque concerto grosso in its recourse to a string *concertino* – a quartet, but with double-bass instead of cello. Another unusual feature is the use of timpani with the string orchestra. This work maintains its charm in all movements. There are really more movements than the three into which it seems to be divided. The first is a march, followed by a minuet with a trio for the *concertino* only; but the third movement, an enchanting rondo, incorporates an *Adagio*, in the mocking style of a very slow and pompous minuet, and a rustic-sounding *Allegro*. A "Notturno," K.286, for New Year's Day 1777, employing strings and horns, is euphemistically described as being written for four orchestras. In fact it merely forms a pattern of "echoes" which become rather tedious repetitions after the novelty has become familiar. This work is not to be compared with its beautiful predecessor.

Worth more frequent airing is the festive work in D, K.320, in the style of the "Haffner" Serenade, but often called the "Posthorn" Serenade after the instrument introduced in a way Haydn would have enjoyed during one of the trios to the second minuet. The work might also have been called the "Piccolo" Serenade, for a piccolo is also introduced in one of the minuet-trios, playing two octaves above the violins. This work was written soon after Mozart's return from Paris and seems to have been intended simply for the Salzburg court; we cannot assign any particular reason for what seem to be humorous intentions in other movements than the minuets – for instance in strong dynamic contrasts. There are no miniature violin concertos as in the "Haffner" Serenade, but in their place come two movements for flutes, oboes, and bassoons each of which could be labelled "sinfonia concertante."

Ronald Knox made the epigram "No parody can be less vulgar than what it parodies," and indeed most long parodies, musical or literary, are tedious, reminiscent of amateurish contributions to college magazines. Mozart seems never to have crossed the division between wit and crude humour even for stage action which would tempt most composers to do so. His nearest approaches to a feeble order of musical humour occur in the serenade or

22. *Cover illustration from a copy of the first edition of "Ein Musikalischer Spass," K.522, published by Johann André, Offenbach-am-Main, 1802, sold by L. Plattner, Rotterdam.*

divertimento for string quartet and two horns called "Ein musikalischer Spass" (A Musical Joke), K.522. The work was also known as "Die Dorfmusikanten" (The Village Musicians) and no doubt amused contemporary ears who were familiar with serenades by incompetent but ambitious amateurs. The trouble is that the exquisite Mozart was unwilling to poke us in the ribs and overdo the bungling, as no doubt Beethoven or Richard Strauss would have done. The listener who has never actually studied composition merely supposes that there are a few wrong notes and that the music is conventional and undistinguished. Having heard much modern music in which he would not know if "wrong" things were played, he misses the point of the horns that miss their transposition, the violinist who strays out of key in a cadenza and sounds an "open" string to test his intonation, or the village composer's naïve attempt at a fugue, which jerks forward by full stops.

Concertos

Whereas in the Salzburg symphonies and serenades we trace the promise of greater music, in many Salzburg concertos we treasure music of unique intrinsic value. In those for solo string instruments Mozart enshrined what could never be recaptured. Summer shows its riches only by losing the spring tenderness of the meadows and woodlands. Mozart's instruments went on singing, but only at Salzburg did they sing with the rapture and smiling melancholy of youth that dreams of an unattainable love or an ideal country where Goethe imagined the citrons in bloom but Mozart imagined his beloved flowers of the lyric stage. The land of his dreams was an idealised Italy.

The five violin concertos (K.207, K.211, K.216,

40

K.218, and K.219) composed during 1775 in rapid succession require soloists as sensitively musical as the greatest singers, although they will meet no technical demands more difficult than those in divertimenti. We judge their performances by beauty of tone, moulding of phrases, judgment of major and minor climaxes, interplay with the orchestra, sense of "build" and paragraph. In short, we want to hear these works as if the composer were playing. He took the viola in quartets but was a good enough violinist to have been the soloist when these works were heard at the Salzburg court. No doubt he sometimes was so, and no doubt he played one of the solo instruments in the great Sinfonia concertante, K.364; but we read Leopold Mozart's comment about a new slow movement for K.219 – "Adagio for Brunetti, as the old one was too complex for him." We may assume that Brunetti, who succeeded Mozart as *Konzertmeister* in 1777, had privileges as a soloist.

Two years before the five violin concertos of 1775 Wolfgang composed a pleasant, graceful three-movement work with two solo violins and solo parts also for oboe and cello, K.190, for which the title "Concerto" was incongruously swollen to "Concertone" – a word missing from most dictionaries. It means no more than "Grand concerto," which this delightful hybrid is not. It resembles one of those leisurely and attractive orchestral works by J. C. Bach which have several solo instruments. One or two writers openly call it a "sinfonia concertante" – another euphemism. We mention this work only because Mozart was for a time fond of it. He took it with him to Mannheim in 1777 and Wendling advised him to get it played in Paris when he moved on there. These facts provoke a few questions. During the 1770's violin concertos were enormously popular in Paris; at first the conceited Giornovichi was all the rage, and when he riled so many influential musicians that he thought it advisable to leave, Paris was even more charmed by its admirable Pierre Gaviniès who showed himself willing to help young Mozart. (The finest of the Paris violinists was Viotti, but he did not arrive there until Mozart had left.) Why, then, did not Mozart get Le Gros, or Gossec, or Gaviniès to secure a performance of one of his violin concertos?

Although until the end of his stay Mozart was anxious to leave France, he must have heard violin concertos there and studied them. Perhaps the *rondeau* (rather than "sonata rondo") shape of the finales he used in the violin concertos shows that he was already familiar with French models. It is not proposed, however, to compete with the many learned inquiries about Mozart's borrowing of ideas and even reworking of materials from Boccherini, Nardini, Pugnani, Gaviniès, or anyone else. The son of Leopold Mozart stored in his memory more violin concertos and sonatas, old and new, than most of his contemporaries got into their heads before they died. We are concerned only with the quality of the result, not the "influence," and cannot but regard concert-givers, performers, and the musical public justified in their greater

affection for the last three than for the first two of the five violin concertos and for their rating them according to their order of composition, the last the favourite. The first two hardly sound Mozartean, for we expect lengths of singing melody, less obvious and formal solo entries, and finales with witty episodes. (In 1776 Mozart changed the sonata finale of K.207 in B flat for a rondo, K.269, which is more personal and attractive.) His authorship is betrayed chiefly by the wealth of materials which, at this apprentice stage, actually hinders appeal and memorability.

Suddenly the third concerto, the one in G, blossoms with a spontaneity and vitality so remarkable that, forced to hear it immediately after the second, we might find ourselves exclaiming "Ah! Mozart!" as though its predecessors had been early Haydn or Dittersdorf, or as if years had separated the third concerto from the second. In fact the third followed after a mere three months, from June 14 to September 12. During that time Mozart achieved not only the technical advance which would require at least three years from other composers but also an artistic growth comparable with the sudden glorious bursting of a flower that had long delayed its opening. To the question "When did Mozart turn from a young prodigy to a great artist?" some people would answer: "During his last Salzburg years." The caution is unnecessary. Wolfgang became "Il Mozart" in the late summer of 1775, his twentieth year.

The last three violin concertos of the five of 1775 are too well known to warrant much comment here. The first of them, in G, is deliciously youthful rather than actually child-like, yet sometimes sounds as if the wish to dance were tempered by the wish to sing, so that the singing goes with movement. The next, in D, has been called the most sensuous, probably because it is more sonorous than the G major and has a slow movement which might be called *amoroso* and given to an operatic heroine, mezzo rather than high soprano. The presence of ideas shaped suspiciously like some in Boccherini's D major violin concerto does not detract from this work's originality. Several musicologists were asked to suggest which materials were improvements of Boccherini's. Their answers were hesitant, diverse, and inaccurate! The passages most of them mentioned were the contredanse and gavotte inserted into the rondo finale. These are meant to sound old-fashioned and may have been popular dances or French dances known in Salzburg; but neither came from Boccherini's concerto.

The fifth concerto, the A major, for all its period size, is one of the greatest of all violin concertos. The masterly organisation of its first movement excels even that of some of the Vienna piano concertos; its slow movement has a loveliness that draws tears; its finale is a masterpiece of that rare humour which never betrays the perpetrator's preparation. This finale is also meant to suggest an old-time dance, so that its sedateness shall be upset by the "Turkish" contredanse and chromatic slither retrieved from his Milan ballet, "Le gelosie del serraglio" (The

Jealous Harem-women) of 1772. The new middle movement of 1776, K.261, does not suit the rest of the witty concerto as well as the original with which we are familiar; but one can hardly accept Leopold's malicious explanation that Brunetti wanted something less complex. The extra movement is indeed *Adagio* and very dignified, but it is not technically easier than the other slow movement, which must have been well within the technique of the Salzburg violinist. The muting of the violins of the orchestra and the reticent writing for a mere two flutes and two horns are complimentary to the aria-like solo part, which was plainly intended to give Brunetti the opportunity to show a rich range of lyricism, less articulated than in the former movement. The piece is worth hearing. So is another rondo, K.373 in C, for Brunetti to play in Vienna early in 1781 when the Salzburg musicians were there with their master. Einstein believes that the lost "Andante for a concerto" in A, K.470, composed in 1785, was a substitute for the middle movement of Viotti's E minor concerto to please Mozart's friend the violinist Anton Janitsch. Mozart also added trumpets and drums to the outside movements of the Viotti concerto which had its original middle movement in E major.

Before the Second World War there were frequent performances of three other concertos thought to be Mozart's. K.271a in D, which has the best claim to authenticity, is not contemptible, but it cannot be classed with the last three violin concertos of 1775. When its authenticity was questioned, Tovey made the perceptive comment that if the work were a forgery "then it was a very clever one" which did not "make the mistake of imitating a generalised Mozart of no particular period." The E flat concerto, K.268, he said, seemed to be based on "genuine material" but could not be genuine "in the form known to us." In fact the material was amplified by J. F. Eck, a violinist only 10 years older than Mozart. He was born in Mannheim and became first a member of the court orchestra, then opera conductor at Munich before marrying a wealthy woman. He was considered a magnificent performer and a fine musician. Obviously he had a thorough knowledge of Mozart's style in the violin concertos, but seems to have supplied an unconvincing middle movement. Mozart often made short scores, arrangements of orchestral works on two staves from which the composer could give some account of the music at the piano. In 1933 Marius Casadesus published through Schott a D major concerto transcribed from such a score (with the upper stave in D and the lower one in E!). The original of this work, known as the "Adélaide" Concerto (from an alleged dedication to Louis XV's daughter) is in a private collection in France and, apart from Casadesus, no one has been allowed to examine it.

It was an established custom by the time Mozart's music was in request that only the first movement of a concerto should require very attentive listening. The designs of *both* following movements were many – "sonata without development," rondo or *rondeau* (the latter the simpler, with interpolations rather than developed episodes), variations, extended arias, extended minuets, various types of ternary or binary structure – but they had to be easy on the ear and mind. They might be surprising and, as when one of them used the minor key, emotionally arresting; but while Mozart was still young it was almost an affront to society (whether in a palace or at a public concert) to serve second and third movements demanding the concentration of the first. Those movements were interchangeable with some in divertimenti, for concertos were "fashionable" music. To say this without qualification is to omit the gradual change from Mozart's audiences to Beethoven's and the enormous growth of musical perception and intelligence in the most musically favoured of cities – Vienna, Munich, and other places in Germany where public concerts and opera flourished and where there was a sensitive musical intelligentsia. Even so, Mozart was forced throughout his adult life to make retreats and advances, and modern listeners must find it hard to recognise the very daring advance made by his most beautiful Salzburg work, the Sinfonia concertante in E flat for violin and viola, K.364, of 1779. (A similar work of the same year, in A major, including a cello with the soloists, K.App. 104, was not finished, but its fragments show that it also was mature, symphonic, and splendid in conception.)

23. *Johann Baptist Vanhall. Engraving by Karl Hermann Pfeiffer after a painting by Johann Adamek.*

The Sinfonia concertante, K.364, is a more advanced work than the earlier but splendid and equally surprising piano concerto in the same key, K.271. That work still uses the *galant* style in parts of its outer movements; and it is all the better for doing so. The rhythms and figurations of the piano, or rather the fortepiano, would have lost much of their sparkle and vitality if they had not incorporated *galant* formulae. What sense would there be in a concerto which required the piano only to sing like a violin or viola? In K.271 and later piano concertos the piano often assumes a rhythmic or ornamental function which falls to the horns and oboes in the sinfonia concertante. Features of *galant* concertos by J. C. Bach, Wagenseil, Vanhall, and many others, maybe wonderfully transformed, survive to the last of Mozart's piano concertos but are completely absent from his very last concerto, that for clarinet. They are also almost entirely absent from this sinfonia concertante, for even the gay finale, which gives us a mild surprise when the soloists in turn play the same flight of melody, lies in fine paragraphs rather than little figurations. The eloquent pathos of the middle movement cannot but have struck any contemporary audience as new and daring, its C minor seriousness being as far from fashionable music as would be a dialogue between two heroines in a Gluck tragedy – not that Gluck commanded such melody. The orchestral

24. *Title page from the first edition of the Horn Concerto, K.412, published by Johann André, Offenbach-am-Main.*

virtuosity, the rich sonority, and the maturity of expression is without contemporary parallel except in parts of "Idomeneo." A particularly remarkable feature is the unexpected heightening of interest, time after time, when a solo instrument repeats (without variation in the melody itself) what the other solo instrument has just played. Because the viola soloist must sound through the rest of the strings, the part is written in D and the instrument must be screwed up half a tone. Though we do not know the circumstances of the first performance or how it was received, Mozart's own valuation is evident from his writing out of the cadenzas – models of brevity, forward urge despite their purpose, and effectiveness. To lengthen or alter them seems inexcusable.

The concertos for wind instruments derive extra value because of the dearth of such works from other composers of rank. One only amongst those highly esteemed dates from long after the composer's close association with players in the Salzburg, Mannheim, or Munich orchestras. This is K.622 of his last year, the A major clarinet concerto, exceptional indeed amongst all concertos, being Mozart's last, and the only great one for the instrument. (Its history is discussed in Chapter IX.) He had previously delighted his friend Anton Stadler with the beautiful Clarinet Quintet in A, and it is almost safe to say that he never wrote a concerto for a wind instrument except for a particular performer or patron – Stadler, Leutgeb, Baron Dürnitz, or the Duc de Guines. All good musicians should be familiar with the capabilities of a solo instrument, but of nobody except Mozart have generations of critics made trite the opinion that he had a "feeling" for the character, not just the characteristics, of individual instruments both in solo and in ensemble.

Ignaz Leutgeb seems to have been a very fine horn-player – Paris thought so when he played there – though not a man of cultivated tastes, musical or otherwise. Music for him was simply good horn-playing. He left the Salzburg orchestra but continued playing in Vienna where he kept a cheesemonger's shop and became prosperous in trade. A jolly fellow, his social position gave him no qualms, and he seems to have been delighted with Mozart's crude name-calling – "ox," "ass," "fool," "poor old pig." The last of the horn concertos, written after Leutgeb had come round to Mozart's house begging for it, had to be pieced together from papers scattered on the floor, some belonging to other works, while Mozart finished what was wanted. The concerto was headed "Das Leitgebische," for the player also spelt his name "Leitgeb." It is written in inks of various colours, supposedly referring to types of cheese. On the horn part of the D major rondo for horn and orchestra, K.514, occurs a series of comic directions and remarks, e.g. "Oh, what a swerve [*stonatura*]! . . . Careful! . . . Lucky little man! . . . Specially for you, Mr. Donkey," ending with "Thank God this is the end!" We can safely say of the horn concertos, as of the violin concertos, that they are not as difficult as they sound, though they are brilliantly effective, especially because the first movements are less complex than those of piano concertos, so that there seems to be no falling from seriousness to divertimento level for the poetic, short slow movements and "hunting" finales. All three of the complete horn concertos, K.417 and K.447 of 1783 along with K.495 of 1786, are well known and enjoyed, and all are in E flat. (Movements from incomplete concertos are listed by Köchel and have been put together to make concert items.) The middle one of the three needs a better player than the other two and, as it uses clarinets in the orchestra, it was possibly for a Mannheim or Munich player, not Leutgeb. It is likely that Mozart heard at Salzburg and benefited from the wind concertos of Rosetti, an Austrian whose real name was F. A. Rössler and who also influenced young Schubert in Vienna.

We should be more impressed with Mozart's concertos for wind instruments if he himself had not left us the great piano concertos and the work for clarinet. The earliest wind concerto we have from him is K.191 of 1774 for bassoon, which may be one of three which he is said to have supplied to Baron Dürnitz. It is so admirably idiomatic that cellists, regretting that Mozart left them no concerto, have also to regret that an arrangement of the bassoon concerto merely betrays the transcription. The same comment holds true for the Flute Concerto in G,

K.313, of 1778. This was for De Jean, Mozart's Dutch patron in Mannheim, who asked for a simpler slow movement, the Andante, K.315. Fortunately he did not ask for an easier finale as a substitute for the delightful *Tempo di minuetto*. At a time when Mozart was hard pressed De Jean wanted a second concerto and was supplied with K.314 in D, also known as the "Ferlendis" Concerto for oboe. Giuseppe Ferlendis, oboist at Salzburg and a friend of the Mozarts, is often mentioned in their letters. For De Jean Mozart is thought to have transposed from C to D a concerto he had written for Ferlendis. The finale later provided material for Blonde's aria "Welche Wonne, welche Lust" in "Die Entführung aus dem Serail." Ferlendis and De Jean were not the only recipients of this work, for a letter from Wolfgang to his father of February 15, 1783 asks him to "send immediately the little book which contains the oboe concerto I wrote for Ramm, or rather Ferlendis. Prince Esterházy's oboist is offering me three ducats for it, and promises six if I will compose a new concerto for him." We possess no such "new concerto" for oboe, only beginnings of two others.

Music for Dancing

Brahms paid a sincere compliment to the younger Johann Strauss when he wrote down the opening bars of "The Blue Danube" Waltz and added "Unfortunately not by J. Brahms." It might have been by Brahms if he had not been living when, for some years, a division of labour had taken place between composers dedicated to the supply of "serious" music, or music for attentive listening, and composers ready to give the public what it wanted. One of the regrettable popular beliefs of the last century or so has been that "Art" (whatever that means) does not include work for entertainment. Mozart no more believed that than did Aristophanes or Shakespeare, for you may know the quality of an age by the quality of its entertainment. Even today it is possible that an artist capable of the entertainment offered by Haydn or Mozart might sweep shoddy musicals off the boards. Mozart therefore supplied music for dances.

Such music is at a great disadvantage when used purely for listening unless it is played in very short sessions. Haydn's cunning minuets in quartet and symphony, with phrases that do not keep to multiples of two and four bars, would merely perplex dancers, who need regular rhythms and well-marked accents. A chain of dances in similar tempo can soon hang fire as music for listening, even when served with the variety and cunning of Mozart's "German Dances," or of Schubert's "Valses nobles," or Brahms's "Liebeslieder" Waltzes. Circumstances forced Mozart to supply most of his dances in triple time and at a pace between that of the courtly minuet, inherited from the early years of his century, and that of the waltz, which was not admitted into court circles until

25. Franz Anton Rössler, known as Rosetti. Anonymous silhouette.

26. *The Prater, Vienna. Engraving by Johann Ziegler, c. 1780.*

Schubert was an adult. It was popularised during the Congress years in Vienna, that is to say from about 1815 to 1825, when high and low society mixed in dances on the illuminated Prater. The waltzes of Lanner, then the elder Strauss, became popular at the end of this period.

There was a premonition of their popularity back in 1786 when audiences wildly applauded a waltz in Martín y Soler's "Una cosa rara" which Mozart duly used as one of the popular "hits" to be played by the waits at Don Giovanni's supper, eliciting sarcasm from Leporello. To Don Giovanni's "Isn't this a pretty tune?" the servant answers: "Very appropriate, sir," which we can take to mean "You are a rare case yourself." In "Don Giovanni" the tune is given in six-eight but not to be played fast, like a gigue. Mozart thought of it as a Teutsch (German dance) or Ländler. The difference in pace between his minuets and his "German Dances," or even between differing minuets, is much affected by

harmony. The point can be illustrated from his best-known minuet apart from the one in "Don Giovanni." The opening of the minuet in his great E flat symphony has a different bass note to each crotchet, and has to be marked *Allegretto* lest the pace and manner be too stolid. The trio, however, has a bass note only on the first crotchet of each bar – a light touch on cellos and basses. The tune is played by the clarinet and suggests a Ländler rather than a minuet. This contrast between minuet and trio is sensible on purely musical grounds, but in some of Haydn's and Mozart's works it incurs a social commentary. The "second minuet" (or trio) at provincial balls was for servants and people on the estate. (English readers may recall the ballad "When Grandpapa met Grandmama in the second minuet".) Minuet-trios often sound rustic, but this may come from the imitation of bagpipe drones in the "musette" trios of Baroque composers, such as Bach. Not until Mozart's part of the eighteenth century did the bagpipe or countrified trio become more frequent in music for listening. It was natural for Haydn's contemporaries to use oboes and bassoons in trios, not only as the most obvious contrast with the full orchestra, but also as suggesting pastoral and open-air dancing; moreover the harmony was often thinned to three parts – the feature from which the trio got its name. The contrast was possible without the change of instruments. Compare, for instance, the stately minuet in "Eine kleine Nachtmusik" with its hurdy-gurdy trio, or notice the waltz-like accompaniment to what is almost an angelic yodel in the second trio of the clarinet quintet. Naturally the most happy hunting-ground for the contrast between the courtly and the simple is in the minuets of serenades and divertimenti, but the contrast exists, softened by refinement and lyricism, in many a symphony and chamber work for strings.

It is not proposed to give an account of every separate set of minuets and "German Dances" (which may be called, as is the last set but one, K.606, "Ländlerische Tänze") but merely to point out that the minuets remain courtly, like square, equal-phrased symphony-minuets, whereas the "German Dances" are more easy-going and bourgeois, if not actually countrified. This is not always easy to recognise because Mozart was the least countrified, most urbane and sophisticated of musicians, yet even his muse was fertilised by the parent plants of music from the hills and plains of villagers. His father was largely his mentor in this matter; for Leopold, so anxious for his son to be the supreme courtly musician, was himself popular at Schrattenbach's court and far beyond the Salzburg area for his "novelty" music, imitations of sleigh-bells, rustic weddings, yodelling songs, etc. (We now know the most familiar of "toy" symphonies, once attributed to Haydn, was Leopold Mozart's.) The last of the K.605 "German Dances" is actually labelled "Die Schlittenfahrt" (The Sleigh Ride) and evokes posthorn and jingles passing into the distance at the end.

Mozart called more than 30 of his dances "Contredanses." There have been learned explanations of the name, which is most likely a simple corruption of "country dance," for John Playford's "The English Dancing Master or Rules for Country Dances" was still being reprinted and copied by other publishers well into the eighteenth century and was well known on the Continent. We know that contredanses were danced chain-wise or "longways" by the couples, for Leopold wrote home from Italy on April 14, 1770:

> Wolfgang ... sends a contredanse. He wants Herr Cyrillus Hofmann to invent the steps for it; when the two violins lead off, only two people should step out; but whenever the orchestra comes in with all the instruments the whole company should join in. The best arrangement by far would be a dance of five couples ... as there are five solo and five ensemble passages. The first couple should lead with the first solo, the next with the second, and so on.

This contredanse, K.123, like the others, is in eight-bar

sections – eight for the two violins and eight *tutti*. Most such sets of dances begin with one in six-eight and end with a brisk two-four. Moreover the suites use dances in different keys, not necessarily ending in the key of the first dance. The best sets are those of K.267 for the Salzburg carnival of 1777, those of K.462 and K.463 of 1784, and the set written towards the end of his life, K.609, which includes a dance called "The Hurdy-gurdy Men" and also a dance arrangement of his most popular aria, Figaro's "Non più andrai."* It is known from other than musical sources that, during most of the eighteenth century, social classes were mixed at palace dances, still more in carnival or gala balls, especially in Austria and south-German states. Mozart reflects this.

* For a full treatment of this subject see Hans Engel's contribution "Der Tanz in Mozarts Kompositionen," to the "Mozart-Jahrbuch" for 1953.

Pictorial Essay:
Salzburg Then and Now

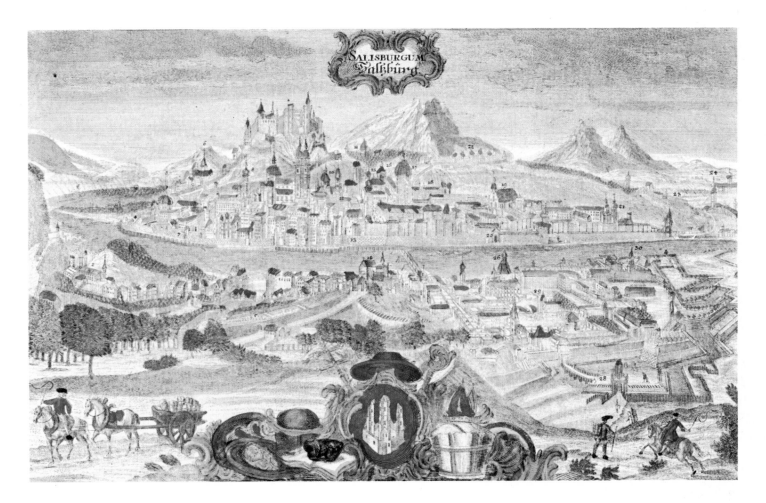

15. Salzburg, c. 1730. Engraving by Martin Engelbrecht after a drawing by Friedrich Bernhard Werner. The view is from the Kapuzinerberg, over the river Salzach towards the Hohensalzburg fortress which breaks the skyline atop the Mönchsberg. The blue dome and twin spires beneath it are of the cathedral and in the wood to its right is the Franciscan Church. To the left on the slope, numbered 6 on the print, is the spire of the Nonnberg Nunnery. To the right of the cathedral, numbered 10, is the Benedictine Church of St. Peter. Further right is the dome of the University Church, numbered 17. On the near bank of the Salzach points of interest are (left to right) the orphanage (No. 2), the Capuchin Friary (No. 14, beside the bridge at St. Michael's Gate), and Holy Trinity Church (No. 26). The spire immediately below Holy Trinity is that of St. Sebastian's Church in whose cemetery Mozart's wife and father are buried. No. 29 is the palace of the Lodron family and by the river on the right is the Mirabell palace and gardens (No. 30).

16

17

(10)

Salzburg, with its rare combination of natural splendour and superb architecture, is one of the world's most beautiful cities. It was so in the eighteenth century and it remains so now.

Demolition and rebuilding have made it difficult to imagine Vienna as the Mozarts knew it. Salzburg, on the other hand, is so well spread over its slopes and squares that nineteenth-century builders would have had more trouble and expense in pulling up cobbles and putting new buildings among the old than in using the flatter land across the river. Compared with Vienna little has changed (see *Nos. 21–26*) and the accurate eye of the twentieth-century camera can tell us just as much about the Salzburg Mozart knew as a naïve eighteenth-century print, however charming. Both have therefore been used in this pictorial section, each complementing the other.

Among the earliest institutions known to Mozart in the city of his birth, were probably those founded by St. Rupert in the seventh century – the Nonnberg Nunnery and the Benedictine Abbey of St. Peter, though most of the existing buildings at the abbey are from the seventeenth and eighteenth centuries and the twelfth-century church was remodelled and "improved" in Rococo style (see *Nos. 20 and 39*). Medieval remains are also to be found in the nave of the Franciscan Church dating from 1221. The fortress of Hohensalzburg (see *No. 20*) dates from 1077 but was rebuilt around 1500. In 798 Salzburg, originally a Celtic settlement and later the Roman town of Juvavum, became an archbishopric and in 1278 its archbishops were recognised as princes of the Holy Roman Empire. This meant that the Salzburg of Mozart's day was not only a city but also a sovereign state, and it remained so until 1803, when Napoleon dethroned the last prince-archbishop, Count Colloredo, Mozart's little-loved master.

The fact that the rulers of the sovereign state of Salzburg were not hereditary, for ecclesiastics could not beget legal heirs, was fortunate for the city and the Mozarts. Unable to perpetuate their pride and names by founding families, the prince-archbishops were almost more anxious than other rulers to leave buildings as their memorials and to gain fame while they lived for their patronage of the arts. While the city's medieval heritage suffered from the rebuilding and "Baroquing," the long-term result for Salzburg was a rich architectural legacy in a rare combination of Italian Renaissance and Austrian Baroque styles.

It was Wolf Dietrich von Raitenau, archbishop from 1587 to 1612, who brought the Renaissance style to the city and his plans were furthered by his successors, Marcus Sitticus (1612–19) and Count Lodron (1619–53). Salzburg Cathedral (see *Nos. 20 and 21*), designed by Vincenzo Scamozzi and built in 1614–28 on the site of a medieval basilica, was one of the first churches in Italian style built in Austria and the German states. The archbishop's official residence (see *No. 21*), begun in 1595, was completed in 1619, though improvements, such as the alteration of the façade in 1710 and the addition of a new wing, continued until 1792, the year after Mozart's death. The shape these buildings took together in the centre of the old town was so thoroughly Italianate as to show a marked contrast with the flamboyant buildings of Bavaria, through which travellers usually approached this Austrian monument of feudalism.

16. View of the Salzburg suburb Mülln. Eighteenth-century print by Louis Vallet.

17. View of Salzburg from the Convent of Maria Plain by Johann Christian Wirsing, after a drawing by Johann Gottfried, Count Lützow.

18. A glimpse of Fischer von Erlach's University Church from the Mozart Geburtshaus.

19. Getreidegasse, the street in which Mozart was born, as it is today.

18

19

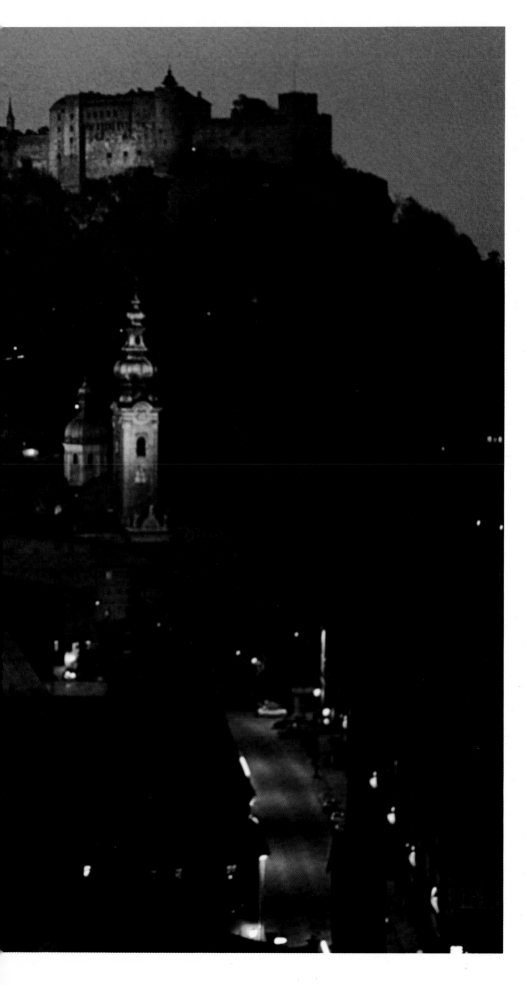

20

Though the architects of this first stage of Salzburg's present splendour were Italian, greater glories were to come when the Austrian Johann Bernhard Fischer von Erlach became architect to Archbishop Johann Ernst, Count Thun (ruled 1687–1709). His inspired synthesis of Roman, Renaissance, and international Baroque styles, which came to be known as Austrian Baroque, helped to transform Salzburg in the 1690's. Among masterpieces still to be seen are the University Church (*Nos. 18 and 20*), 1694–1707, and Holy Trinity Church, 1694–1702. Fortunately one facet of his genius was integration of his designs within existing architecture (see *No. 20*), and the result in Salzburg has been wonderful homogeneity. It is perhaps not too fanciful to imagine that Mozart, who could see the University Church from his window (see *No. 18*), found in Vienna in later years a comforting reminder of home in the many examples there of Fischer von Erlach's distinctive and enduring art.

20. Salzburg at dusk. (Photograph by Werner Neumeister.) The floodlit buildings on Page 12 are the cathedral (see also *No. 21*) and, nearer the camera, the University Church. The juxtaposition here reveals particularly well the skill with which Fischer von Erlach matched the church's form with the already existing Italianate cathedral without compromising his very individual style. Floodlit on Page 13 are the Hohensalzburg fortress and, below it, the remodelled Benedictine Church of St. Peter, where the C minor Mass, K. 427, was first performed.

21

23

24

The eighteenth-century prints and modern photographs comprising *Nos. 21–26* present three comparisons of Salzburg then and now which suggest that, at least as far as fountains are concerned, little has changed since Mozart's day.

21 and 23. No. *21,* an engraving by F. Müller after a drawing by Franz von Naumann, shows the Residenzplatz with the cathedral (see also *No. 20*), part of the archbishop's residence on the right, and (left) the "Neubau (New Building) mit dem Glockenspiel," which, far from being new, dates from 1588 and was built for Archbishop Wolf Dietrich. *No. 23* shows the square from another angle, looking towards the Neubau with the cathedral on the right. The fountain, despite the exaggerated proportions in the engraving, is the same; built between 1656 and 1661, it is attributed to Tommaso di Garona.

22 and 24. Salzburg's famous "Horse" fountain. *No. 22,* again an engraving by Müller after Franz von Naumann, shows the fountain in its proper context, fronting Fischer von Erlach's façade for the archbishop's stables. The sculpture (1695) is by Michael Bernhard Mandl, and the frescoes by Joseph Ebner.

25 and 26. The gardens of the Mirabell palace, the archbishop's summer residence. The palace dates from 1606 but was remodelled by Johann Lukas von Hildebrandt in 1721. The panoramic view of *No. 25,* an etching by Probst of Augsburg after a drawing by M. Diesel, is interrupted in the photograph by a new building added after the palace was damaged by fire in 1818 – a change it is true, but, typically of Salzburg, a tasteful one in keeping with the past.

(15)

25.

26.

IV
The first great opera

"Opera seria"
"Tragédie lyrique"
The Plot of "Idomeneo"
Comparison with Gluck
Musical Vitality

27. *View of Munich from the west. Engraving after a painting by Bernardo Bellotto, 1761.*

"Opera seria"

Mozart was to return to Salzburg only once after he left in November 1780 but there is nothing to suggest that he had determined or even hoped never to return when he went to Munich to finish and supervise "Idomeneo" for the carnival there. The libretto had been commissioned from the Salzburg court chaplain Giambattista Varesco, who took his plot from a lyric tragedy written by Danchet and set to music by Campra in 1712; though the customary French five acts were converted into the three of a Metastasian *opera seria*, the work retained some of those French features which add to the interest of Gluck's tragedies – ballet, incidental, and "scenic" music, and choruses that are not merely short introductions or endings to the acts. Bearing in mind the claims of Cherubini's "Medea" or Berlioz's "The Trojans," to say nothing of the best of Gluck's works, many people regard "Idomeneo" as the last and greatest example of true *opera seria*.

It is not affectation of foreign languages that maintains the terms *opera seria*, *tragédie lyrique*, *opera buffa*, *opéra-comique*, and *Singspiel*. They denote distinctive ways of allying music with stage action, and misjudgment could come from failure to distinguish them; for instance "The Magic Flute," because its music does not delineate real, warm human characters on the same scale as "The Marriage of Figaro," might be regarded as an inferior opera. The sub-titles *Singspiel* and *opera buffa* not only told eighteenth-century audiences not to expect comparable ideals and music in these works, but also reminded them of other works of the same type by which to judge each.

No composition gave Mozart greater delight than that for the theatre. To whatever type each of his great operas belonged, he modified it – though he allied himself with no dramatic theories as to the direction in which that type should advance. His unprecedented originality and daring in the treatment of each type is not negated by Gluck's treatment of *opera seria*. This fact is not easily recognised today by those of us who know the types chiefly or only by Mozart's operas. To relish their originality as much as did their first audiences we may be helped by a brief survey of the lyric stage as it was before Mozart proved himself its greatest artist. We begin with *opera seria* and shall consider other types as we reach Mozart's dealings with them.

In the older histories of music *opera seria* of the eighteenth century (before Gluck's last examples) receives more execration than any other form of music. It was "undramatic," "artificial," arranged chiefly as a series of arias for the display of stars who "dictated" to composers; it was a mere concert in costume. Unfortunately many people who love the magnificent music in, say, Handel's operas deny these charges instead of questioning them. What is the meaning of "dramatic"? Should opera move at the pace of a spoken play and take as many words? If a fine aria, without the attentions of a fussy producer, halts stage action, does it halt the drama or does the drama continue within the music? How much stage action is there in "Tristan and Isolde," rightly called one of the greatest of dramas, but by its composer a music-drama? Spoken drama is available for those who do not relish what music can do more powerfully than words. For ears which love music and its processes a splendid concert in dramatic format is preferable to a play declaimed in recitative or presented so that speech and background music are mutually obscured and encumbered.

Before Mozart was dead *opera seria* was dying, not because it was originally contemptible but because, like the madrigal, the concerto grosso, and every other art form it had its ascendance and decadence and was no longer vital. Its day was over, and a mighty long day at that! Musical forms are decadent when hundreds of minor composers can fill them with a facility that engages only their craft and not their aspiration to original human expression. The moribund condition of *opera seria* by 1770 is manifest by the fact that a boy prodigy could supply it for Milan or Salzburg while established composers approached it with "flagging inspiration." Dr. Michael Robinson has written:

> Very noticeable is the contraction in the number of musical idioms employed. A study of Mozart's "Mitridate, rè di Ponto" will reveal the severely limited, hedged-in styles common in *opera seria* of the year 1770. Mozart was far too young at that time – he was only 14 – to do more than parody current musical conventions, but he did it well enough to receive approbation and other commissions. ("Opera Before Mozart": Oxford University Press, London, 1966.)

In Mozart's day few composers offered *opera seria* except by commission for a court solemnity, receiving instructions as to which libretto they should set.

In a non-feudal society this entertainment would have passed away earlier. British composers shunned it after Handel's final attempt to establish it, for Londoners could enjoy its musical contents in oratorios which gave them the advantage of knowing the stories and understanding the language, while they gave Handel the advantage of less expense in the theatre. The Viennese no longer wanted it after they had sampled Mozart's German operas, then such works as Weber's "Der Freischütz" and Beethoven's "Fidelio" – in their own language with stories and characters of (or near) their own times instead of the remote ages of classical mythology and ancient history. The characters of *opera seria* were divine, royal, or otherwise exalted, and the hero so exalted that his voice was not a man's but a castrato's. The language was literary Italian like Dryden's or Milton's English. (Verses from operas by Zeno and Metastasio, imperial poets laureate, are still rightly admired in Italian anthologies.) First imported by courts late in the seventeenth century, this type of opera lingered until Mozart's day because courts still considered it right for

28. *Niccolò Piccinni. Engraving by Johann Friedrich Schröter.*

grand occasions such as royal weddings, visits of heads of state, and coronations. Mozart could not persuade Vienna to hear "Idomeneo" when there was no court occasion similar to that of its original production; moreover it needed the splendour, expenditure, and musical resources forthcoming in Munich. Even the esteemed Gluck found that his Italian operas were not wanted in Vienna and, after "Alceste," produced each new one in French and in Paris, mounted under royal licence.

Mozart himself wrote only one more *opera seria* after "Idomeneo." For the Emperor Leopold's coronation as King of Bohemia in 1791 he was asked to set a libretto of 1734 which had been used by many previous composers – Metastasio's "La clemenza di Tito." The locale was Prague, of all places! Prague, where "Figaro" and "Don Giovanni" had triumphed with their vital characters and contemporary settings! The work was no more than politely received as a *festa teatrale* financed from the imperial exchequer. It would not have succeeded commercially even in Prague, let alone Vienna, which was flocking to "The Magic Flute."

Unlike Gluck, Mozart voiced no public condemnation of the old type of Italian opera. There is very clear evidence that he studied Gluck's tragedies and benefited from them. The aesthetes may or may not have interested him while he was in Paris with their controversy about the rival merits of Piccinni's old and Gluck's new way of treating a classical libretto, but it is dangerous to say "Mozart was Piccinnist rather than Gluckist." All we dare say is that, within his treatment of a libretto, he saw the advantages of the traditional treatment of a story by the poet, but would disregard him when his words (especially moral and philosophical reflections or crowded images) were not vehicles for powerful musical expression. Advantages? Yes, we must recognise them because Mozart did. The poet provided short sections of alternating prose and verse. Accompanied by the harpsichord and a cello or bassoon, a character declaimed the prose in swift recitative which took the plot from one situation to another, and therefore from one mood or passion to another – anger to tenderness, despair to revenge. At each new situation the verse couplets were sung to an aria with orchestra, after which the character left the stage, and another took over the next recitative and aria. Though the stage scenery might remain unchanged, each sequence of recitative and aria was called a scene. The libretto also indicated places where a duet should replace an aria, where a short chorus should begin or conclude an act, where there should be a march, a trumpet call, a pastoral symphony, or other incidental music. The composer who did no more than was indicated by the libretto could at least compose splendid arias with *obbligato* instruments and elaborate *ritornelli*, others of more simple beauty, and all of them concerto movements for voice and orchestra. Supplying only six or so he might prove his wide versatility in a range of emotions and styles. Unlike the movements of symphonies, however, the contents of *opera seria* dealt with one emotion at a time and, to composers with their own dramatic sense, the desire to show a conflict of emotion, or even strong contrasts, seemed thwarted. By disregarding the poet's intentions Handel and others declined to chop intense parts of the story into "scenes." They integrated two or three of them into a complex called a *scena*. Participant characters were kept on stage instead of leaving after an aria, the orchestra was retained throughout, and the rapid *recitativo secco* ("dry" declamation) changed to a free but melodious dialogue called *arioso*. Gluck used both *secco* recitative and *da capo* aria but declared in a preface to "Alceste" that he would not interrupt the drama – "I did not wish to arrest an actor in the full heat of declamation in order to wait for a tiresome *ritornello*, nor halt him in the middle of a word or vowel favourable to his voice so that he could display agility in a lengthy ornamented passage."

"*Tragédie lyrique*"

We inherit the word "reform" to describe Gluck's special type of *opera seria* because it was used by the first British historians of music, Burney and Hawkins, as a mistranslation of the German *Umgestaltung*, a reshaping.

Gluck did not make something bad into something good. Gluck himself, who is said to have been the victim of Handel's sour tongue in London, kept Handel's portrait prominently in his best room and almost worshipped its subject. If anybody had suggested that he could improve upon Handel's music he would not have been flattered. He would not accept the shape of traditional *opera seria*, as chopped up into scenes, but he went much farther than Handel, reshaping the whole, not just impressive parts. Notice, therefore, that a musician found himself dissatisfied with poets and so in alliance with several philosophers and literary men who objected to the operatic treatment of classical stories. A widely-read attack on the Metastasian libretto by Francesco Algarotti, a friend of Voltaire, led several composers to please "enlightened" courts (notably Parma and Stuttgart) by breaking the conventional chain of "scenes." Gluck achieved fame with a thorough reshaping, first by "Orfeo ed Euridice" (produced in 1762), because he and his poet, Calzabigi, had the backing of the imperial director of theatres, Count Durazzo, and because Vienna was Europe's musical as well as imperial capital.

He was influenced by his observation of opera in the one country which had resisted the Italian product – France. Between 1670 and 1770 Naples was to Italian opera what Hollywood became to American films in our

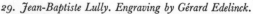

29. *Jean-Baptiste Lully. Engraving by Gérard Edelinck.*

50

own century, though the films were at least "dubbed" into the languages of importing countries. France of the Grand Epoch regarded herself as the leader of all civilised fashions and arts, and she was also too proud of her own drama and her language to cede anything to Italy. When Paris first sampled the Italian export, audiences were impressed by the idea in general and by the scenic machinery in particular, but thought the recitative insulting to elevated dramatic speech.

France would have her own opera, and ironically a Florentine who first spelt his name "Lulli" produced the royal and national *tragédie lyrique*. Lully studied carefully the great French tragic actors and sought to echo their declamation, its accents, emphases, and pitch variations, by a slow-rolling and orchestrally accompanied *récit* in which the time-signature could be changed as often as was necessary to secure exactitude of speech inflection. There was no chopping of the story into a chain of "scenes" for soloists taking turns. A tragedy was set to music, but the services of a librettist were needed because a sung tragedy which used the whole of a spoken one would be excessively long and lack the distinctive attractions of music in its own right. These could be secured partly by very thorough use of incidental music, choruses, and ballet – not always dancing, but grouped and gesturing (for Greek tragedy had, after all, been communal). Moreover characters in tragedy shared the stage. "The recitative loads the gun: the aria fires it," J. C. Bach is reputed to have said; but the epigram did not apply to French opera, wherein *récit* and *air* were both orchestrally accompanied and not distinguished by pace or floridity. There was provision for solo *airs*, often strophic with choruses, because tragedy provided soliloquies at certain junctures.

Though French singers could earn distinction with their compatriots for their dramatic intelligence, clear articulation, and even vocal tone, none could acquire international fame purely as a singer. French opera did not require the purely technical training and splendid range of voice sought in Naples, nor had it room for the castrato. Without lavish scenery, choruses, ballet, and much incidental music even France might soon have wearied of the unbroken dignity of tragic *récit*, the slow unrolling of a mythological or classical story. By Rameau's time French opera was, in its own way, quite as "unnatural" as Italian, for the tragedies were so filled with *divertissements* that they, rather than the story proper, engaged the main attention both of audiences and composers. These and their choruses are what chiefly support Rameau's claim to be the first really brilliant orchestral genius. They were not merely survivals of the masque, as were the hunt scene, the witches' scenes, and the sailors' dances in Purcell's "Dido and Aeneas." Purcell does not make the chorus-ballet occupy most of the tragedy, nor does he open it with a balletic prologue (of Diana's votaries, of Venus subduing Mars with "Loves" representing the arts and pleasures, of the Furies – to cite the openings of Rameau's first three tragedies) for he has no need to enliven his main tragic material. France, on the other hand, actually produced a form called *opéra-ballet*.

Gluck "reformed" French tragedy in "reforming" *opera seria*. As seen on a score the components of an act in one of Gluck's operas are still numbered, e.g. sinfonia – chorus – recitative – air with chorus – dance – recitative and aria – march – recitative and chorus. None is inserted for its own interest alone. All spring from the action, which does not mean that all cause stage incident but that they seem inevitable in the slow unfolding of the drama. The music of an act may be attractive or dull, but it achieves an effect of dramatic integration rarely exceeded by Mozart himself, and does so where there is no evidence of conscious repetition or development of musical ideas. This effect would have been impossible if Gluck's poets had not supplied stories in shorter and simpler forms than had been customary. Mozart's tussles with Varesco show how well he understood this. Incidents and emotions as numerous as in some acts of "Idomeneo" would have been unacceptable to Gluck. Before we examine the affinities and disparities between Mozart and Gluck, it is useful to know the plot of "Idomeneo" in the simplest possible summary that covers the musical treatment.

The Plot of "Idomeneo"

The characters are: Idomeneo, King of Crete (sung by the tenor Anton Raaff); Idamante, his son (for soprano and sung by the castrato Vincenzo dal Prato); Ilia, daughter of Priam of Troy (sung by the soprano Dorothea Wendling); Electra, a Greek princess (again for soprano, sung by Elisabeth Wendling); Arbace, confidant of Idomeneo (sung by the tenor Domenico de Panzacchi); the High Priest of Neptune (for tenor) and the Voice of Neptune (for bass). There is a chorus representing Cretan people, Trojan prisoners, sailors, soldiers, priests, and dancers.

The whole action takes place on the island of Crete. Returning from the sack of Troy, Idomeneo has sent on in advance a batch of prisoners, including Ilia, who falls in love with Idamante.

Act I: Ilia's recitative and aria – her conflict between love of Troy and love for Idamante. Idamante's recitative and aria of love for Ilia. There is an announcement that the Trojans are to be set free and a chorus of rejoicing. Arbace announces the sinking of Idomeneo's ship. Electra's recitative and aria – she passionately loves Idamante and vents her fury at the thought that Idomeneo's death will bring the marriage of Idamante and Ilia as king and queen. Chorus of prayer for Idomeneo. Idomeneo enters, dismisses his retinue and tells how Neptune quelled the storm on hearing the vow that Idomeneo would sacrifice the first living being he met on landing. He sees Idamante and in horror orders him from his presence, despite the son's bewildered pleading. The

act ends with a brilliant march, followed by a (French) chaconne chorus praising Neptune and honouring the returning Cretans.

Act II: Arbace advises that Idamante be sent to a distant land. Aria by Idomeneo suggesting he be sent to Greece as escort to Electra. Idomeneo, realising from an aria by Ilia that she loves Idamante, expresses his despair. Aria for the happy Electra. March. Embarkation – a chorus of farewell with interspersed solo by Electra. A trio, in which Idamante and Electra take leave of the king, passes to storm music betokening Neptune's wrath at the evasion of the vow. Appearance of a sea-monster sent to plague the island. Idomeneo confesses his guilt. Chorus – the crowd terrified.

Act III: Ilia and Idamante in a love scene, ending in a duet. Idamante tells Ilia he will go and fight the monster. Idomeneo and Electra join them in the famous quartet. Recitative and aria for Arbace, usually omitted. There is a change of scene to the temple of Neptune. The people hear that Idamante must be sacrificed. March of priests and beginning of ceremony, interrupted by a shout of triumph and Arbace's announcement that Idamante has slain the monster. Idamante now knows of the vow and offers himself for sacrifice. Ilia demands to take his place. The voice of Neptune declares that the crime will be expiated if Idomeneo will abdicate in favour of his son. Short expressions of relief and thanks give place to Electra's recitative and aria of violent rage and despair. She rushes off, presumably to kill herself. After Idomeneo's beautiful aria in which he presents the new ruler to the people (omitted at the first performance), the accession of the new king and queen is celebrated with chorus and dance.

30. Front of the piano score (by Wenzel) of "Idomeneo," published by Schmidt and Rau, Leipzig, 1796/97 with an engraving by C. Scipp.

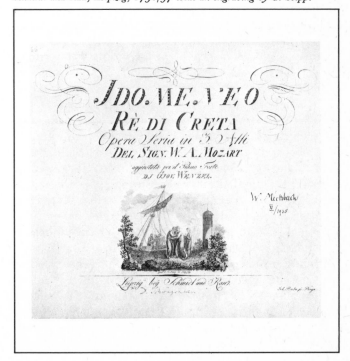

31. Anton Raaff as Idomeneo. Anonymous water-colour, 1781.

Comparison with Gluck

Anyone familiar with Gluck's operas will see in the synopsis just given many of their frequent ingredients – the choruses, the voice of an unseen supernatural being or an oracle, the march of priests and solemn ritual, subjects for recitative that could not be treated tragically without recourse to the orchestra and passages of *arioso*. Yet it would be an exaggeration to call "Idomeneo" a Gluckist opera. Mozart's music admits both of the features which Gluck regarded as malpractices – the Italian chopping up of the text into "scenes," each ending with an aria and the singer's exit ("Idomeneo" begins with two of them), and the French introduction of *divertissements*. Mozart is careful to avoid far-fetched diversions. We have no carousings and dances of sailors before Neptune sends the storm, no military drill for the soldiers at the embarkation, no intruding ballet of sea-nymphs or fishes in a grotto of shells! Mozart's storm, his marches and choruses and dances can all be said not only to belong to the story but to seem a realistic part of its unfolding. Some of them are more desirable than necessary; they are there for musical rather than dramatic reasons, and who is not glad of that? Where they cannot spoil the

action at the end of Act I Mozart introduces a march and chaconne chorus of rejoicing immediately after the main story has dealt with the king's horror at meeting his son. Gluck would have ended the act with this encounter, and would have begun the second act with the king's despatching of Idamante to Greece, with farewells between the lovers. Gluck would probably have omitted the character of Arbace. He might also have omitted Electra, the virago whose brilliant rantings and florid arias are amongst the chief delights of Mozart's work; for she is not essential to the story; as Professor Dent says: "What on earth was Electra doing in Crete?"

Gluck could justify arias of principal characters because there were soliloquies in spoken tragedy and they powerfully assisted Greek drama; so did choruses with expressive groupings. Mozart was not bothered by precedents, nor by other justifications than those of good theatre and music. He surely thought, as do many people still, that some of Gluck's finest tragedies (they include "Alceste") lacked stage incident and scope for great singing. Some of Gluck's most splendid items, notably his short declamatory choruses, could seem dull and heavy outside their dramatic contexts. Certainly Dr. Burney could not have written of Mozart as he did of Gluck: "It seldom happens that a single air can be taken out of its niche, and sung singly, with much effect; the whole is a chain, of which a detached single link is but of small importance." After all, Gluck wrote no supremely great music for the concert room. Yet Mozart, who was a persistent theatre-goer, not just for opera, knew "Alceste" extremely well, and must also have known that it maintained a consistent unfolding of the drama that he himself never achieved in tragedy, not only because (after "Mitridate") he never had the right libretto for it, but also because he had no intention of paying the musical price.

Mozart was never presented with a superb libretto like that of Gluck's finest opera, "Iphigénie en Tauride," and it is quite relevant to our present considerations to say that, as far as we can judge, he would have treated it as Gluck did, that is to say used short airs, brilliant arias, *arioso* or "developed" recitative, quick and "functional" recitative, choruses, ballet, and incidental music exactly where Gluck did. "Would have" is, of course, as weak an assertion as its denial, and it is justified only by the fact that this opera, which to anyone with musical as well as dramatic ears justifies all Gluck's previous efforts,

> returns to long-breathed, purely musical, even lyrical forms in the arias. It is as though the extreme of revolt against the dominance of music over poetry had passed, and the two were coming together again on equal terms. It is an example of the final stage of revolutions which usually end by taking over much which at first they reject . . .

The quotation is from D. J. Grout's "Short History of Opera" (Oxford University Press, 1947) and it proceeds to note how Monteverdi and Wagner illustrate the same point.

32. Christoph Willibald von Gluck. Lithograph by François Séraphin Delpech.

Mozart cannot have witnessed those final Gluck tragedies in Paris, and we are not justified in saying that "Idomeneo" puts him on the side of the Gluckists who welcomed "Alceste," only that he knew how to emulate Gluck in the kind of expression which Gluck achieved superbly. It comes especially in solemn ceremonial scenes such as sacrifices, *tombeaux* or funeral rites, the descent of deities, the appearance of ghosts, the pronouncements of oracles, the appeals of heroes or heroines to their folk. Very rarely does Mozart's actual music sound like Gluck's. He was so much the younger man that style had changed and become more ornamental and Rococo, less solid, though Haydn's kept abreast of change and showed very clearly the influence of Mozart. Even if Gluck and Mozart had been exact contemporaries their musical personalities would have been distinct. No single piece by Mozart sounds more like one of Gluck's than does the priests' march in "Idomeneo." Two other passages, both

more complex than this march and both in "Don Giovanni," show Gluck's influence strongly. The first, near the beginning of the opera, is the *scena* between Anna and Don Ottavio as they discover that the Commendatore has actually been murdered. The recitative and *arioso*, leading to the duet promising vengeance, are the very stuff of a Gluck tragedy. Then, near the end of the opera, the chorus of demons, heard while Giovanni makes his last defiance and Leporello expresses shaking terror, directly recalls the Furies in "Orfeo"; still more, Mozart's rising chromatics on the woodwind, eerie and sulphurous, are actually taken (deliberately or unconsciously) from Gluck's own "Don Juan" ballet. We may imagine that Gluck would have enjoyed the temple scenes in "The Magic Flute," but not a bar of the music, not even the opening march for the priests, can be mistaken for anybody's but Mozart's in his last year. This does not negate the likelihood that solemnities in Gluck's operas inspired

53

music in "The Magic Flute" as well as much else that Mozart wrote for Freemasons.

Musical Vitality

It is not necessary for a great artist to have himself undergone every experience he conveys. He need not have been physically tortured to express excruciating pain nor have been incarcerated to convey the bewildered rapture of the prisoners in "Fidelio" when brought out into the light. Parallel experiences are known to his subconscious and the capacity to imagine others is implanted as a pre-natal attribute of mankind. A Shakespeare or a Mozart brings our wonder because his art can even mirror the emotions of the sex to which he does not belong. Even so, there has never yet been an artist who, in middle or old age, although he could command the brilliant vitality of Verdi's old age, could recapture or plausibly imitate the first rapture of his full power. We have already pointed out that though music in many ways more admirable than the Salzburg violin concertos came from Mozart in Vienna, their peculiar beauty, or rather their intense aspiration for an even greater beauty than theirs, could not be credibly imitated by a Mozart turned 21. Implicit in the power and loveliness of spring is the glory of summer – a greater glory perhaps, but it cannot co-exist with that of spring.

The thought that "Idomeneo" dates from "before Vienna" may have done less harm than the very phrase most often used to praise it – "the greatest of *opere serie*." This compliment seems at once to put it into history, make it a museum piece with which we should sometimes acquaint ourselves as part of our education and culture. This attitude is partly fostered by the male soprano part for Idamante, most of which can be read without alteration of a single note as if it were written for a tenor. The characterisation is so well defined that nothing sung by Idamante can be mistaken for music from the mouth of Idomeneo or Arbace, any more than anything sung by Electra can be mistaken for music from Ilia. Indeed the power of characterisation by music (not to be confused with appropriate treatment of characters already well distinguished in the words), for which Mozart is so much extolled in writings about the comic operas, first shows itself brilliantly in "Idomeneo," so much so that to cite examples from the arias and solo parts is almost insulting. More marvellous is the first development of a feature of characterisation never notably used by opera composers before Mozart and never used by those after him with his facility. This is the ensemble item for several characters, each retaining its musical personality in a piece as thoroughly constructed as a movement or series of movements in a symphony. Nothing in previous operas can touch the trio at the end of the second act between the barcarolle chorus "Placido è il mar" and the storm music and chorus of the Cretan people; few ensembles by Mozart are more beautiful than the famous quartet before Idamante's parting from his father and the two women who love him.

The use of the orchestra is a primary contributor to the unique brilliance and originality of "Idomeneo." Previously Mozart had consistently shown his apparently innate understanding of instruments in combination. Here, with the wonderful resources of Munich in mind, he was able to exult in his strength. We may assert that he had never produced a better score. Wonderful scores like those of "Così fan tutte" and "The Magic Flute" are entirely different in character, and in picking the one we call the best we merely pick the opera we like most. Did Mozart's contemporaries marvel as we do at his handling of the theatre orchestra, or did they share Joseph II's opinion that the scoring for wind instruments was too rich for such singers as were available? Can we believe that any part of the work revealed its orchestral beauty when Mozart gave it privately in 1786, presumably with few strings? Could even he reduce from four to two the marvellously interlocked horn parts in the storm scenes?

The fact that Mozart wanted to revive "Idomeneo" shows the value he himself set upon it; but it is no chamber work. One of the grandest of grand operas, it is a perfect choice for the modern successor of the royal *festa teatrale* – the entertainment to be chosen to celebrate some international gathering or national time of rejoicing. Even during an excellent Glyndebourne performance one felt that it needed a great national theatre and a large cast and setting. It is greatly to be hoped that familiarity with its music by records or broadcasting will incline great opera houses to mount it sumptuously, with magnificent singers, as often as they mount "The Magic Flute."

V

Freedom and fame

Break with Colloredo
"The Seraglio"
Contest with Clementi
Concert Life
C minor Mass
Years of Popularity

33. Costume sketches for the first performance of "The Seraglio" (Die Entführung aus dem Serail).

Break with Colloredo

After the success of "Idomeneo" Mozart threw himself into the pleasures of the Munich carnival. We should not forget that, despite the heavy preparatory work for "Idomeneo" he found time to compose in addition the wind serenade K.361 and the quartet K.370, which uses an oboe instead of the first violin, as well as several concert arias and the Kyrie in D minor, discussed earlier. His leave of six weeks had become four months when he was summoned in March 1781 by Colloredo, who was in Vienna. Mozart objected particularly to the instructions that he was to be quartered in the archbishop's residence, for he believed that if he had been free to give public and private concerts in Vienna he could have earned a year's salary in two months. He did, however, greatly impress the concert-goers of Vienna when Colloredo, having first forbidden Mozart's participation in a charity concert organised by Starzer, president of the Vienna Society of Musicians, was forced to relent under pressure from others. The concert on April 3 at the Kärntnerthor Theatre, scene of later triumphs, was an enormous personal success. The programme included the C major symphony, K.338 and Mozart's piano-playing was wildly applauded. What Mozart regarded as the humiliations he suffered at his employer's hand in Vienna – the limits on his freedom and being forced to eat with the servants – together with his success at this concert helped to precipitate the climax of his relationship with Colloredo. Having decided not to return to Salzburg with the court, he had a stormy audience with his master on May 9. The following day he tried to hand his resignation to the archbishop's steward, Count Arco, but it was not accepted. In a further interview a week or so later Arco again refused to accept Mozart's petition for dismissal and gave him some friendly advice about the fickleness of the Viennese public. On June 8 the count finally lost his temper in yet another interview and pushed Mozart from his presence with a now notorious kick. Mozart in the meantime had taken up lodgings with the Weber family, who had moved to Vienna, and there he was soon to become engaged to Constanze, sister of his former love Aloysia. He moved to new quarters in the Graben early in September 1781 and in August 1782 he was married with his father's grudging consent.

Mozart's years as a free and successful artist in the imperial capital take us into a new chapter of his story. What did he himself envisage as its summit? The imperial *Kapellmeister*-ship? Not the office itself, considered merely as a grander appointment than that of orchestral director or chief of cathedral music to the archbishop. Possibly he hoped for the honour and salary. His dreams were chiefly of Italy, but Italy in Vienna – in short of opera. How fine to become Vienna's and the emperor's provider of the most humanly moving of music, that in which the listeners identified themselves with the loving, suffering,

raging, complaining, laughing, teasing, intriguing, boasting, or yielding characters in the microcosm of a drama! He had already proved his capability to be this musician, and not surprisingly during the summer and autumn of 1781 it was a new opera, "Die Entführung aus dem Serail," which occupied his mind. German operettas and opera-like *Singspiele* were in favour with the emperor and had proved popular at the Burgtheater as soon as they were sampled there in the 1770's. Translations of French comic operas were at first the staple repertory, and Gluck ingratiated himself with impresarios and audiences by sending home from Paris his versions of French comedies. (The best known, because of Mozart's piano variations K.455 on the rascal dervishes' song, is "Die Pilger von Mekka" from Dancourt's French play "La Rencontre imprévue.") The astute Salieri, later imperial *Kapellmeister* and opera director, had a notable success at the Burgtheater with "Der Rauchfangkehrer" (The Chimneysweep), which Mozart must have seen. Although Gluck named Salieri as the composer most in sympathy with his own tastes, he showed Mozart admiration and friendship too and it was undoubtedly his recommendation which ultimately brought "Die Entführung" (to a libretto by Gottlieb Stephanie, an actor and official at the Burgtheater) to production in 1782.

Eric Blom's is the best translation of the opera's title – "The Elopement from the Harem" – but for convenience we shall follow general custom and call it hereafter simply "The Seraglio." The Turkish setting and escape plot are foreshadowed in a German opera which Mozart wrote at Salzburg. It was left unfinished because Salzburg had no opera house and there was no immediate prospect of its performance. Amongst the missing parts are an overture

34. Gottlieb Stephanie. Engraving by Johann Ernst Mansfeld after a painting by Joseph Lange.

and the ending. But it brought some fine music which was garnered after Mozart's death by the publisher André, who called the work "Zaïde" after the heroine's name.

"The Seraglio"

"The Seraglio" is important as the first of the operas for which a free and adult Mozart must take full responsibility. He was limited neither by the traditions of Italian *opera seria* nor the need to accept what was provided by a librettist commissioned to supply his work for a prince. He could, and did, tell his librettist what he wanted. Indeed Stephanie was asked to write and to alter verses for music already composed:

> In the original, Osmin has only this short song and no other music to sing except his part in the trio and finale; so he has been given an aria in Act I and must have another in Act II. I have explained to Stephanie the words I want for this – indeed I had finished composing most of the music before Stephanie knew anything about it.

As far as conventions and mythological characters allowed, Mozart expressed human feelings in "Idomeneo" to a degree that imbued several characters, such as Electra, with distinct personality. He was now free to make all characters "come alive," though the comic ones, especially the malevolent major-domo Osmin, are caricatures, just as are Dr. Bartolo and the scandalmongering music-teacher Don Basilio in "Figaro"; but the two lovers and the pasha are serious, noble, and human. The lovers' faithful servants, who assist them in their attempt at an elopement from captivity, are not of noble origins, and therefore supply both comedy (which wilfully freezes emotion) and human passion which is taken seriously.

The story is simple. Belmonte loses Constanze when she is captured by Turkish pirates and prepared for the harem of the pasha Selim; her maid, Blonde, is with her. Belmonte comes to rescue her but is noisily told to get packing by Osmin who, like Belmonte's man Pedrillo, is interested in Blonde. Pedrillo introduces Belmonte to the pasha as an architect – evidently princes in Turkey, as in the German states, were expected to have a craze for building and laying out pleasances. The pasha Selim is portrayed as both noble – he will not take Constanze except she also love him – and Turkishly cruel, for he threatens death and torture. Osmin, the chief obstacle, is made drunk by Pedrillo. The attempt at an escape takes place at midnight, with a ladder, as in "The Barber of Seville," and with a similar discovery. Osmin and the guards bring the plotters and the ladies before Selim, who recognises Belmonte as the son of his bitterest enemy; this makes his pronouncement of pardon and freedom all the more magnanimous.

Apart from stage business and comedy, it is obvious that the last act needs fine music if it is not to appear

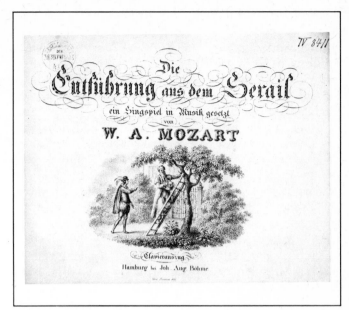

35. *Cover of the piano score of "The Seraglio," published by Johann August Böhme, Hamburg, 1823.*

weak, and it gave Mozart a good deal of trouble. Late in 1781, Gluck's "Iphigénie en Tauride" and "Alceste" were produced, and naturally Leopold Mozart supposed Gluck to have schemed to push aside his son's opera. In fact Mozart's opera would have been hastily and badly finished unless it had waited until July 16, 1782, for its first performance. Despite two nights during which a *claque* tried to hiss the first act, it proved an enormous popular success – "the theatre was again packed out despite the dreadful heat . . . , people are mad about this opera, and it does me good to hear such applause." At Gluck's request it was given beyond the proposed run. "Gluck paid me a great many compliments and I am going to dine with him tomorrow." Before the end of the year "The Seraglio" was produced in Berlin and then other northern cities, yet a composer who was not "in management" received only the money agreed for the original commission, and was well advised to collect his music sheets before copies could be pirated. He could then at least charge another theatre for use of his own copy, though he could not prevent piracy away from his surveillance. We shall see later that we have a clue to the spread of copies in north Germany. After telling his father about the success of the first six performances in Vienna, Mozart mentions the sum taken per night by the box office and sarcastically adds "for the theatre, of course!"

A rescue from Moorish, Turkish, or other dark-faced pirates, with or without lubricious references to a harem, must have been the subject of entertainments in European countries long before Shakespeare's time, and there would be no point in mentioning previous treatments to Stephanie's but for an amusing protest from a Leipzig businessman. German versions of the story may have come from French ones, like the one we have mentioned by Dancourt to music by Gluck. The English form of *Singspiel* is usually called ballad opera, of which the eighteenth century produced two very popular examples on the "Turkish escape" theme as presented by Dryden in his "Don Sebastian." One of these musical plays was Dibdin's "The Captive" of 1769, the other was Bicker-staffe's "The Sultan, or a Peep into the Seraglio" of 1775. Yet the following appeared in November 1782 in the "Leipziger Zeitung":

> A certain Mozart in Vienna has had the impudence to misuse my drama "Belmont und Constanze" as the text of an opera. I hereby protest most strongly against the infringement of my rights, and claim the right to take further action. Christoph Friedrich Bretzner, author of "Das Räuschchen."

Bretzner's text, written for a *Singspiel* with music by Johann André, was certainly Stephanie's source-book.

The Prussian ambassador ("a most charming man"), who had witnessed the opera's triumph in Vienna, asked for a copy, which Mozart had made in Salzburg to lessen risk of piracy. (The work eventually had outstanding success in Berlin.) Thus no less a person than Goethe came to provide us with the most interesting comment on Mozart's success. Goethe himself supplied words to encourage *Singspiele* at Weimar. He felt that for most people the cultivation of Italian opera, with its elaborate arias and mythological or classical stories, was an affected taste imitating that of courts. He championed words in the vernacular and music that expressed their sentiments as directly as did popular songs. These German pieces were popular north of Vienna for many years before the emperor fostered them in his capital, for the Viennese lyric stage had been a "little Italy" since the seventeenth century, when Monteverdi's disciples mounted their sumptuous operas at the imperial court and the Bavarian. Goethe's compliment to Mozart took the form of a regret: "All our efforts to keep (German opera) simple were nullified when Mozart appeared on the scene. 'Die Entführung aus dem Serail' put every other work in the shade."

It does contain *Singspiel* items, though Mozart was also to fertilise Italian comic operas with materials of popular origin. Possibly Don Giovanni's famous serenade is no less popular (rather than courtly) in effect than Pedrillo's verses which serenade Blonde, but no Italian comedy by Mozart has an item quite as rollicking as the "Vivat Bacchus!" duet as Pedrillo gets Osmin drunk, and no other work by Mozart finishes with a *vaudeville* – a popular chorus to which each character in turn contributes a verse. None, of course, has the local colour of the "Turkish battery" (bass drum, cymbals, triangle) which always enters *forte*. What was called Janissary music (the Janissaries being the Turkish military bodyguard) was so popular in Europe during the eighteenth century that harpsichords and fortepianos were often furnished with a *Janitzscharenzug*, a stop which rattled like a snare drum. Mozart's audiences must have been delighted when the orchestral Turkishness was augmented by the Janissary choruses. If Mozart had not written those great arias, he would have had enough music and comedy of popular

36. *Playbill for the first performance of "The Seraglio" at the Burgtheater, Vienna, on July 16, 1782.*

appeal to ensure success with patrons of the Burgtheater. Osmin is as outrageous yet as realistic a comic character in music as Shakespeare's Falstaff was without music. Yet Goethe was right, for "The Seraglio" is no *Singspiel* in the traditional meaning of the term. It is a German opera, the first to make greater musical demands than most Italian operas, and the first landmark in the rise of German opera that rivalled, and for a time almost ousted in Germany itself, creditable Italian works. It is not simply an Italian form set to German words.

Today does anyone think of it as a *Singspiel*, or imagine it (as one can "The Magic Flute") as composed for a theatre that produced popular operettas? That enormous first success belongs to history, for the work must now compete with great German operas and translated operas from Italy, France, Russia, and other countries. Audiences tend to be shy of operas which they cannot put into categories. With what can "The Seraglio" be compared – with comic operas, romantic operas, or serious operas? With what other work by its composer can it be compared? The principals are serious, real, warm-blooded characters, and their musical expressions of fear, love, and anguish are so beautiful as to be recalcitrant to a comic setting; we switch from comic conspiracy, teasing, or malice to tragic pathos and tenderness. The original performers seem to have been outstandingly good, and so Mozart honoured them with exacting parts. Unlike Mozart's Italian comedies and "The Magic Flute," this beautiful work may nowadays miss a production in most of the famous opera theatres for several years running. Even the period conventions of "Idomeneo" are less daunting than the sheer musical demands of "The Seraglio." It is so much a "singer's opera" that even international music festivals rarely produce it with a cast of which every member can do his or her part at the required standard. Transpositions, cuts, and other alterations have often to be made. Most performances by repertory and local companies make one wish that they had not been undertaken, for they merely give audiences a poor opinion of the work; and when the principals must all be great, not just good singers, they are normally artists of such experience that they cannot easily appear youthful. It is not merely that few sopranos can do justice to Constanze; few basses can sing Osmin's part as well as they can act it. Without the first-class performers, both in the orchestra and on the stage, some of the arias seem too long and parts of the work remind us that the stage is momentarily static.

The most notable example of this is the most famous item in the opera. Having repudiated Selim, Constanze is threatened with "Martern aller Arten" – tortures by all devices; by any ideal of realistic drama her defiance should be immediate. Surely Stephanie intended that, for her aria takes those last three of the pasha's words and flings them back at him – "All refinements of torture may be in store for me but I scorn them all." Dramatically effective would be an aria without preliminary *ritornello* like "Or sai chi l'onore" in "Don Giovanni"; but Selim has to await Constanze's first word for 60 bars, during a *ritornello* resembling a sinfonia concertante with solo parts for flute, oboe, violin, and cello. Unfortunately we are plagued by producers who think us incapable of enjoying great music for its own sake, and all too frequently the two are asked to indulge in gestures and the pretence of dialogue while the orchestra is playing – an absurd procedure when their altercation has reached its period and climax; still worse is the custom of moving about the stage and striking attitudes. Since we are about to hear one of the most splendid of concert pieces, let the stage be still and expectant like the concert platform and let the aria be regarded as dramatic only in the sense that we call a symphonic movement or an overture dramatic.

To judge this or any other opera chiefly by the pace of its action or the way in which its words unfold the story seems as absurd as to compare Gilbert's offerings to Sullivan with English comedies. Mozart himself leads us into the error because, until the middle of the second act, there are sections in which he sweeps along through solo and ensemble music with the dramatic *élan* so superbly characteristic of his next great opera; and, as in "Figaro" too, he presents human emotions, makes us find our own selves, in characters which at times take us out of the heartless world of wit and humour (in Horace Walpole's words "Life is a comedy to him who thinks, a tragedy to him who feels"). Many good musicians seriously believe that Mozart's very best operatic music and also passages of his most brilliant management of the stage are to be found in "The Seraglio"; others agree with Dent that its limitation lies in its "jumble of incompatible styles." Most of us depend upon production and singing of a quality that makes us forget Dent's undoubtedly justifiable opinion. The work gives opportunity for enchanting costumes and stage sets in "eastern Rococo," like the fantasies by Oliver Messel for a production which is

remembered by the mind's eye after more than 20 years. When to these delights is added splendid singing, one hardly notices changes from real drama-in-music (the many items which spring directly from situation and action) to concert drama.

Mozart himself was well aware of the contrast, which he tried to justify more than once in the many letters he wrote while tussling with the text:

> The poetry must be the obedient servant of the music. For why do Italian comedies succeed everywhere with their silly libretti, even in Paris, as I saw for myself? Because the music is sovereign and audiences forget everything else. An opera will be most effective when the plot has been worked out [by the composer, Mozart means] and *the words are written for the music* [our italics] with no need to insert words and whole stanzas which destroy the composer's designs for the sake of a wretched rime.

Curiously enough this doctrinal opposition to Gluck's or Wagner's theories does not cause any contradiction of their practice. What they wrote suggests that they wished to set a good spoken play with the utmost respect for its words; what they composed shows that they rejected any words which failed to elicit their own kind of music, so that Gluck also made his librettist the obedient servant of his music without acknowledging the fact and Wagner wrote his own words. It is wise to judge composers by what they do rather than what they say. Lacking space to quote every interesting comment in Mozart's letters about "The Seraglio" we must be content with a selection:

> Originally the opera began with a soliloquy for Belmonte, and I asked Herr Stephanie to make it

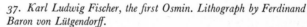

37. Karl Ludwig Fischer, the first Osmin. Lithograph by Ferdinand Baron von Lütgendorff.

into an arietta and then, instead of leaving the two chattering after Osmin's song, to write a duet. We have given Osmin's part to Herr Fischer who has a fine voice indeed (despite the fact that the archbishop said he sang too low for a bass, when I assured him that next time he would sing higher!) and we must avail ourselves of it, for he has a following from everybody in Vienna.

As Osmin's rage grows, just when the song seems to be finishing, there comes the *allegro assai* which is in a different tempo and key; this is sure to be effective for, just as a man in such a frenzy of anger goes beyond the bounds of good behaviour and control, and quite forgets himself, so the music must seem to forget itself; yet as passion, whether violent or not, should never be expressed in a way to excite disgust, so music even in the most terrifying situations should never offend the ear.

Now let me turn to Belmonte's "O wie ängstlich o wie feurig." Would you like to know how I have expressed it – even to show his heart-throbs? By two violins playing in octaves . . . I wrote it expressly to suit Adamberger's voice. You feel the trembling, the hesitating, and see his beating heart swelling in a *crescendo*. You hear the sighing and whispers which I show by first violins, muted, playing in unison with a flute.

The most interesting admission concerns the most brilliant of the singers, a young lady born in Vienna despite her Italian name, Caterina Cavalieri.

I have sacrificed a little to the agile throat of Mlle. Cavalieri . . . as far as an Italian-style *bravura* aria allows I have tried to express Constanze's feelings.

38. Valentin Adamberger and Caterina Cavalieri, who created the roles of Belmonte and Constanze. Silhouettes by Hieronymus Löschenkohl.

I have changed "hui" to "schnell," so that it goes "Doch wie schnell schwand meine Freude." I just do not know what our German poets are coming to . . . they need not make their characters talk as if they were addressing a herd of swine. Hui, sow! [Unless there is an Austrian dialect meaning of "hui," specially connected with pigs, the word is simply an interjection like "Ho, there!" or "Whoa!" It is also used in the phrase "im hui," meaning "in a flash," and could therefore be replaced by "schnell."]

The first act was finished over three weeks ago, along with an aria in Act II and my drunk duet (*per li signori viennesi*) which is made entirely of my Turkish tattoo . . . I cannot compose any more because the whole story has to be altered, and at my request. There is a charming quintet, or rather finale, at the beginning of Act III, but I would rather have it at the end of Act II . . . Stephanie is up to his eyes in work, so one must have a little patience with him . . . After all he is arranging the text for me exactly as I want it and, by Heaven, I don't ask anything more from him.

"Exactly as I want it." Not with Mozart can be found from now on the excuse that he was forced by a librettist or patron to do this or that. Whatever criticism is made of his operas, he must be held responsible because he was determined to be so. Our only caution must be the thought that he was composing for immediate success with a known cast and a known audience. "Would be effective," "would be sure to bring applause," and so on are the recurrent reasons for what he does. They may sound banausic to modern composers who prefer to speak of "my creative work" rather than "my music." Mozart was no less a believer in the divine afflatus than other artists, but possibly Bach was the only eighteenth-century musician who wilfully wrote for posterity, and he did so because he was less widely esteemed as a composer than he was as a teacher.

Contest with Clementi

Mozart finished the first act of "The Seraglio" fairly quickly but took an unusually long time with the rest. Apart from his courtship of Constanze one of the distractions was a piano-playing contest with Muzio Clementi at court on Christmas Eve, 1781. Such contests were common in the eighteenth century and well into the nineteenth. Beethoven participated in several, and on one occasion Liszt was matched with Thalberg. It must be remembered that the piano was a comparatively new instrument, providing imagination with the relish of greater musical forces than its singing strings actually provided. For those who merely wanted to admire dexterity it had its attractions, but its expressiveness enabled finer tastes to tell a musician from what Bach had called a

39. *Muzio Clementi. From a painting by Thomas Hardy engraved by the artist.*

pianist, and the verdict would not have been unfair to Mozart. Clementi was the more virtuosic technician of the keyboard, as distinct from the greater musician. It seems plain that Mozart was disturbed by Clementi's brilliance, and in criticising his opponent wilfully failed to mention a distinctive feature which was taken over by Beethoven and almost all great pianists of the future – the holding down of a note for its full length unless the composer directed otherwise. This demolished the style of piano-playing that followed upon harpsichord-playing, whereby *legato* was exceptional for, as C. P. E. Bach wrote, "notes which are marked neither *staccato* nor *legato* require the finger to be lifted before the following note is played, and are normally held for half their value."

Clementi was an educated man with a mechanical bent. From about the time of Mozart's death until his own death in 1832 he grew rich as the owner of a piano-manufacturing and music-publishing firm in London. He had been "discovered" in Rome by the Hon. Peter Beckford (cousin of the author of "Vathek") and brought to England at the age of 14 to be educated and trained at Beckford's Wiltshire mansion. He astounded London when first exhibited in 1773. By 1780 he had far outstripped other pianists in such matters as velocity of shakes and scales, range of tone, and evenness of accompanimental figuration; and his music for the instrument was up to that time the most idiomatic – for the piano, not the harpsichord – and the "most" is a superlative over Mozart's better music as much as over most composers' poorer. As a composer Clementi has recently received the admiration he deserves, both for some of his 20 symphonies and the finest of some 60 piano sonatas which are not to be confused with the sonatinas in his "Gradus ad Parnassum." His compositions for piano are (even in modulations) nearer to those of the nineteenth century, including young Beethoven's, than is any of Mozart's – a fact which does not make it finer than Mozart's but different.

In his correspondence Mozart dismissed Clementi as "a mere *mechanicus*" and his sonatas as "worthless," but we can hardly regard his opinions as unbiased. Fortunately there was a reliable witness to the contest, the composer Karl Ditters von Dittersdorf. He was first popular as a superb violinist and his symphonies and chamber works show a style very similar to Mozart's without the originality and unexpected turns of harmony and melody. At the time of the contest it was supposed that the emperor, with whom he was in good standing and who had admired some oratorios he had written for charity concerts, would give him an appointment; but he is said not to have applied.

In the contest Clementi played first. He began with his Sonata in B flat, Op. 47 No. 2, the opening idea of which Mozart used, consciously or not, in his overture to "The Magic Flute" – so much for Clementi's worthlessness! Mozart then improvised a prelude and set of variations, possibly including materials prepared for the demonstration. Some sonatas by Paisiello were produced (according

"keyboard cavalier." We must not imagine any event similar to our piano recital. The pianist gave an exhibition, usually by items sandwiched between vocal solos and instrumental ensemble, and he was expected to appear as a performer or extemporiser of his own compositions. The concerto combined all attractions of the exhibition; a contest between two performers was almost the only alternative form of display, except in private concerts. Nor must we imagine that Mozart was considered to be Europe's greatest virtuoso of the ascendant instrument. His fame as a performer was chiefly local, for Vienna was "the city of the piano" according to him. Elsewhere he was remembered as the boy prodigy, a composer and performer who had been in hiding, so to speak, and was not known yet as we know him – as a great mature artist. Clementi, on the other hand, four years older than Mozart, would probably have been named soon after this contest as Europe's most brilliant to Mozart "wretchedly copied in his own writing") and Mozart sight-read the first movements, Clementi the slow movements and rondo finales. From these sonatas the theme was selected for the competitive variations. Dittersdorf later reported the following conversation:

Emperor: Have you heard Mozart play?

Dittersdorf: Three times so far.

E.: What do you think of him?

D.: As any connoisseur must, I admire him.

E.: Have you heard Clementi?

D.: Yes, I have.

E.: Some people put him above Mozart, amongst them Bigwig [a nickname for Kreibich, director of the imperial orchestra]. What do you say? Be quite frank about it.

D.: Clementi plays with art: Mozart plays with both art and taste.

E.: That is exactly what I said.

Those words "art" and "taste" come from A. D. Coleridge's translation of Dittersdorf. The original distinction is between *Kunst* and *Geschmack*, and without knowing what force that distinction carried in critical parlance at the time we are not much more enlightened than by the English words. However, *Kunst* could mean great skill, and *Geschmack* could imply musical feeling. Certainly Clementi himself avowed himself "overwhelmed" by Mozart's slow movement and had "never before heard anyone play with such intelligence and grace." It must be remembered that the Viennese instruments and style of playing in general were a revelation to him, for he had used the more brilliant and metallic English pianos.

Inordinate coverage of the contest is justified because Mozart's brief years as "the favourite of society" in Vienna – Professor Schenk's phrase is no exaggeration – were gained by him as a pianist-composer. By no means most of the people who heard his piano concertos

40. Ticket of admission to a concert at the Augarten, Vienna, 1782.

responded fully to their riches, but they recognised the first major poet of the new instrument. It had reached a stage in its growth that enabled it to satisfy demands that were not made from harpsichords. Mozart was not just a brilliant harpsichordist turned pianist, nor does any harpsichord do justice to his best piano music. The wave of enthusiasm on which he rose to popularity was shared by the instrument, which was wanted in people's houses, not just in the houses of musicians and wealthy connoisseurs. It was soon to be ready for Schubert's song accompaniments and sociable pieces; but we defer its further discussion until we deal collectively with Mozart's famous concertos for it.

Concert Life

The real music-lovers of Vienna, like the real music-lovers of any city today, were those who made music in their homes – amateurs in the best sense of the word. They included rich and poor, those employed as musicians (who had time for home performance during the summer months) and those otherwise employed, some of potentially professional ability, for the making of music has always minimised the rift between people caused by rank and wealth. The "amateurs" whose houses Mozart sought formed the backbone of his public support, and at least one of the meetings, on Sundays at Baron van Swieten's, considerably influenced his composition.

Mozart was fortunate in taking up life in Vienna just as a young amusement caterer from Regensburg, one P. J. Martin, had secured both permission and promise of patronage from the emperor for "amateur" concerts in the public park called the Augarten, summer serenade concerts on fine evenings in the main squares of the city, which travellers thought extremely "solemn and beautiful" as night came on, and winter concerts in the Mehlgrube, a building in the New Market which was the chief locale of the concerts for which Mozart composed his greatest piano concertos. The name "Mehlgrube" suggests a store for flour or meal, but the building known to Mozart had always been for balls, concerts, and similar gatherings; probably it was on the site of a former granary, for it was preferred to other halls during the winter as being less cold.

On May 26, 1782, Mozart made his first appearance at the Augarten, which had a concert pavilion with adjacent restaurant. The programme included the Concerto in E flat for two pianos, K. 365, which Mozart played with the talented Josephine Aurnhammer, one of a select number of pupils he had taken on in 1781 "to make ends meet" until he achieved security. It also included a symphony by Mozart (probably the C major, K. 338), one by Van Swieten, and performances by "amateur" singers and instrumentalists.

It was in 1783 that Mozart initiated his greatest triumphs in the concert room. Three notable concerts

41. *The café in the Augarten. Engraving by Leopold Poratzky, published by Artaria, Vienna, c. 1820.*

swept him to popularity during March. At the first, in "the theatre," probably the Kärntnerthor, he directed his "Paris" Symphony and played his Salzburg D major concerto, K.175, with its Vienna rondo finale, K.382. On the 23rd Vienna heard the latest of the three new concertos he had completed since settling in the city, K.413–415. Both this concert and the third, on March 30, which included a repeat performance of K.415, were attended by the emperor.

It should be said now (though the comment applies to the whole of Mozart's career from marriage to death) that though the compositions assigned to a period because performed then may be excellent, even more important are those works not immediately made public – those written for personal satisfaction and not to please immediate concert listeners or to make money, like the great six string quartets dedicated to Haydn, the first of which was completed before the end of 1782, or those

marking self-tuition in unfamiliar ventures. This does not apply only to Mozart. Purcell's most wonderful achievement, according to most who have themselves tried to compose, was the collection of string fantasias which were no doubt for the delight of himself and his friends in their homes, for they were in a style no longer fashionable in public music; Handel achieved nothing finer than his Op.6 concerti grossi, which he cannot have needed for public occasions – he had plenty of concertos and suites to play during the intervals of oratorios and could easily rabbet movements together. So for Mozart possibly the most important compositional work produced between December 1782 and the summer of 1783 was the arrangement for strings of fugues by J.S. Bach and the movements of the unfinished C minor mass, K.427, a work he had vowed to compose for performance in Salzburg when he brought Constanze there as his wife.

C minor Mass

Why Mozart's grandest and most exacting piece of choral composition (which quite excels the Requiem in ambition and in diversity of interest) remained incomplete is hard to understand, for when Mozart made his only return visit to Salzburg with Constanze in July 1783 he surely had time to finish it there. In January he had written to his father reiterating his intention to have it performed during his visit and mentioning that "the score of half of it" was to hand; moreover the absence of clarinets shows that he remembered the limited Salzburg resources. When he eventually arrived he had finished only a few items of the long Credo, and no clear proof is forthcoming to support the accusation that he finished it from movements in earlier works. He originally intended that Constanze should sing the first soprano part, including the difficult and extremely beautiful "Et incarnatus est," and tradition has it that in fact she did so. The work was performed at St. Peter's on August 25, by which time Mozart had composed no original music for the Agnus Dei; he repeated music from the Kyrie eleison – a procedure his pupil Xaver Süssmayr was later to adopt to complete the Requiem.

The brilliant counterpoint and the superb writing for double chorus with independent orchestra in the C minor mass have naturally led many people to regard it as the most obvious consequence of Mozart's study of works by Bach and Handel for concerts at the home of Baron van Swieten; it has even been asked if he could possibly have known parts of the Bach Passions or the B minor mass. To achieve what is formidably demonstrated in the C minor mass, or in the finales of the first (G major) quartet of the "Haydn" set or of his last symphony, or in the Recordare of the Requiem, the overture to "The Magic Flute," and a dozen other brilliant displays of counterpoint it was not necessary for Mozart to have seen Bach's masterworks. All we know is that the music he met through Van Swieten's enthusiasm excited and inspired him. But the technique which we are discussing, without his own special application to the rhythms and harmonies of his own style, he could have studied (and most certainly first came to know) through Italian Baroque composers such as Leo, Caldara, Durante, and Alessandro Scarlatti, some of whose works were known in Salzburg. They, rather than music by the Renaissance polyphonists, were the models for exercises set by Padre Martini and Fux, who sought the application of counterpoint to what they regarded as modern music. The church musicians of Salzburg, including Michael Haydn, had been well schooled in Italian counterpoint. Masters of Baroque counterpoint had served there (Muffat), at the neighbouring bishopric of Passau (Aufschnaiter and Pez), and at the court of Munich to which Salzburg musicians looked with envy. The desire to use Baroque-style counterpoint was what mattered in Haydn (who was born early enough to inherit some of it at an impressionable age), in Mozart, and ultimately in Beethoven; of the three, Mozart was the most able absorber or parodist, and there were plenty of models for him to study without the supreme ones by Bach.

Nobody in his senses wishes to deny the effect of the acquaintance with Bach and Handel; but only in the sequence of four "numbers" (5 to 8) in the Gloria does Mozart actually remind us of Bach – not that the music can be taken for Bach's after we have heard a few bars. The first and third items of that sequence are the duet "Domine Deus" and the trio "Quoniam tu solus sanctus," both cast in the shape of *ritornello* arias with invertible and imitative counterpoint, vocal and instrumental. Just the opening bars of each might be passed off as Bach's (or Scarlatti's or Handel's) after which the melodies take on sequences and cadential ornaments that deliciously proclaim the Rococo rather than the Baroque. Instead of the stolid, regular chord-change of Baroque continuo harmony comes the light and shade of texture belonging to Mozart's own age; no Baroque composer made the strings thus quiver with life. Moreover the nervous play of tonality ("nervous" is used in a laudatory sense) comes after decades of what may be called sonata ideals. Mozart does not spread his motivic developments with unchanged texture and tonality into Bachian paragraphs which are led round the Baroque cycle of keys. He makes the best, and that a wonderful best, of two musical worlds, the old and the new.

The other two items in that sequence of four are even more likely to make non-specialist listeners wonder if Mozart had seen any of Bach's greater church compositions. The six-bar chorus, sung loudly like an exclamation to "Jesu Christe," ends on the dominant chord, the incomplete effect making it an introduction to the long fugue "Cum Sancto Spiritu." The music is not at all like any of Bach's but people recall the short, dramatic choruses in the Passions, not knowing that "Jesu Christe" in the Gloria was often treated reverently as if it were a choral interpolation halting the general forward sweep of Gloria. The great "Qui tollis peccata mundi," Mozart's most impressive choral piece, brings two reminders of Bach; first the fact that it is a double chorus stirs the memory, which is further assisted by its inexorable orchestral rhythm, used more than once by Bach to suggest the blows of scourging or the throbbing of pain. The actual harmony is not at all Bachian. It could come from only one composer. There is no precedent for the marvellous effect of the trombones in this double chorus, nor for the syncopations that stress the anguished "miserere nobis." Technically this piece is superb; expressively it is unique, sublime, and tragic.

Sublime in a different way, that is to say without hint of terror, is the section at the opening in which Christe eleison is enclosed by the two similar versions of Kyrie eleison. Apart from the famous "Et incarnatus est" aria, this is the most appealing section for its sheer beauty. The appeal is powerful for ears that do not recognise or

42. Autograph manuscript of the opening of the Kyrie from the Mass in C minor, K. 427.

analyse the triple counterpoint of the Kyrie sections. The loveliest effect of all, unimaginable in the age of Bach and Handel, is the contrast between the solemnity of the first Kyrie as it yields to the entrancing but difficult soprano solo in the Christe, which floats in as though bliss were attained by the previous struggle. Part of the effect in both sections comes from Mozart's unerring sense of the right places in which to use mild discords such as suspensions and appoggiaturas. They yearn towards concord and thus impart a forward thrust without which contrapuntal texture is stodgy. Beethoven took time to discover this, and for some years published only fugues with a pace and accentual rhythm that disguised the weakness. Textbooks of the period did not impress the point upon students, nor did the exercises Beethoven worked for Albrechtsberger. Mozart acquired the art of discord because sheer musical perception led to it.

No fugues by Mozart and Beethoven are like Bach's.

The best of them are so effective in their contexts that we rejoice at the inspiration that prompted their use, though all betray the labour that went to their making, as Bach's never do. The title "Fugue" on the cover of a textbook implies an attitude which Bach would have ridiculed. Does anyone publish a textbook entitled "Sonata"? Bach made fugues the vehicles of a wide range of expression, as Beethoven did sonatas, and therefore they are even more varied in design and structure than Beethoven's sonatas. (It is interesting to compare extremes from the "Forty-eight" – for instance No. 7 in E flat, a limpid, short piece which ends quietly, is continued chiefly by episodes; the portentous following work in the minor key cannot be said to have any episodes, so determinedly is it concerned with presentations of the subject in the devices of *stretto* i.e. overlap, inversion, augmentation, diminution, and even variation.) The Viennese masters composed only cumulative fugues, normally sounding severe. They were not "masters of fugue," for in that case they would have been masters of fugues, as they were of symphonies and sonatas. We should no more expect them to be masters of fugues than expect Bach to be a master of Palestrinian polyphonic forms. He benefited from their study and the benefit went into his live expression. The same could be said of Mozart's and Beethoven's study of Baroque fugues. Possibly Mozart's best fugue – a very tough one too, heavily packed for its length with entries and devices – is the one in C minor for two pianos, K.426, usually heard (and made to sound less tough) in its arrangement for strings. The Italian-style fugues in the C minor mass work splendidly and are well placed, but they certainly do not "point back to Bach."

Years of Popularity

Mozart returned from Salzburg to the two peak years of his incredible public activity and understandable popularity in Vienna. Fortunately for us he began his *Verzeichnis* or "Catalogue of all my works from the month of February 1784," which he maintained faithfully to the end of his life. The first entry is highly significant – that of the Piano Concerto in E flat, K.449, the first of his last 14 piano concertos. All but two were composed in the following two years, and all but one (the "Coronation") rank with the greatest of their genre. Much as we value Mozart's last three symphonies, along with the "Linz," "Prague," and "Haffner," it should be remembered that they are luxuries in the biological growth of music, as are his splendid string quartets. Despite their intrinsic worth, the history of music would be unchanged if they had never been composed and if the years of Mozart's life were represented in symphony and quartet only by the works of Haydn. Mozart's rise to fame was made by opera and concerto – the two genres in which Haydn failed to reveal his full genius.

There was in Mozart's personality a connexion between his excellence in opera and in the type of concerto which he brought to a glory that even Beethoven did not excel. ("He is the master of us all in this art," said Beethoven to Ries as they heard Mozart's great C minor concerto, K.491.) For the moment we must be content to notice something of that connexion in the mere orchestral opening of K.449, the first "Vienna" concerto listed in Mozart's catalogue. One can imagine stage action corresponding with the contrasted sections marked *p–f–p–f–p–f–p* before the piano enters. For Mozart's audience the opposition of ideas was almost violent, but they also met it in his great operatic finales and ensembles, with characters and moods brilliantly opposed. The elaborate organisation of many ideas was not usual in first movements of symphonies before Beethoven's Third. Even Mozart's most richly thematic movement, which opens his last E flat symphony, uses only four themes of marked personality. On the other hand many ideas were essential to a good operatic imbroglio and, in Mozart's mature conception, essential to the first movement and the rondo finale of a good piano concerto.

Mozart was not the only interpreter of the great Vienna concertos. In the heavy round of concerts in 1784 it was his pupil Babette Ployer, daughter of the Salzburg agent at the imperial court, who first performed K.449 in February and proved as great a credit to him as Josephine Aurnhammer had been. Soon she was to have specially written for her another work, K.453 in G, one of the finest, with a lovely "aria" slow movement followed by delightful variations on a tune suggested by the chirpings of Mozart's pet starling. But before that came K.450 in B flat, which is considered one of the most difficult of the concertos, especially the syncopations and cross-hand work of the finale. The cadenzas are written out as if to be ready for a pupil, but they too are not easy, and it is likely that both K.450 and K.451 in D, completed a week later in March, were played by Mozart himself.

The next concerto in the sequence was K.456, finished at the end of September 1784 and written, it is believed, at the request of Maria Theresa Paradis, a blind pianist, singer, and composer, whom Mozart met while she was in Salzburg in 1783 on a concert tour with her mother. Her compositions were chiefly for the theatre but towards the end of her life she devoted her time to teaching and founded a music school for girls in Vienna. There is no evidence that Mozart ever heard her play K.456 or that she did so. But he certainly made good use of it himself. When Leopold was staying with his son in Vienna in 1785 he wrote home to Nannerl on February 14: "On Sunday your brother played a magnificent concerto which he had written for the Paradis from Paris" (his phrase "nach Paris" meant that she had returned from a tour of 1784 in Paris and London). All the other concertos of the Vienna period were for Mozart's own performance and at this point we should consider how they may have been played.

Pictorial Essay: Contemporary Composers and Instruments

In discussing Mozart's musical development it is easy to forget that the composers and instrumentalists he met on his many travels were real people of considerable reputation and that in many cases their relegation to passing references in modern musical history books was entirely due to the sheer magnitude of Mozart's genius.

Of those portrayed here only J. C. Bach (*No. 27*), Gluck (*No. 30*), and Joseph Haydn (*No. 34*) achieved anything like Mozart's lasting fame, but it is as well to remember that the young Beethoven thought well enough of Albrechtsberger (*No. 37*) and Salieri (*No. 31*) to prefer them to Haydn as teachers. If character can be judged from a face then Albrechtsberger probably had the qualities of firmness and fatherly understanding which the young Beethoven needed and which made him a friend of Mozart's close enough to be remembered in his last wishes. Similarly, one might see in the face of Salieri something of the scheming nature which kept him longer in royal favour than was to Mozart's advantage.

Added to these portraits are examples of instruments of the period. Many of them required skills and techniques quite different from those of the modern orchestral player and for those who consider Mozart's works for wind, for instance, demanding enough nowadays, a glimpse of the kind of instruments for which he originally wrote is enough to inspire new respect for musicians like the flautist Wendling, the oboist Ramm, the clarinettist Stadler, and Punto, the horn-player.

27

27. Johann Christian Bach (1735–1782). Oil portrait by Thomas Gainsborough, 1776. J. C. Bach exerted probably the greatest single influence on the young Mozart apart from the boy's father. The two met first in London in 1764 when Mozart was eight and the deep impression Bach's music made upon him was soon apparent in his early symphonies and concertos. Bach's interest seems to have been genuine and it was his recommendation that led the Mozarts to Italy where he had studied under Padre Martini (*No. 28*).

28. Giovanni Battista ("Padre") Martini (1706–1784). Anonymous oil painting. Martini was, in Professor Hutchings's words, "the doyen of Italian musicians and Europe's oracle upon the theory and science of music." He was also Europe's most sought-after teacher and apart from Mozart his pupils included J.C. Bach (*No. 27*) and Gluck (*No. 30*).

29. Mozart's Walter clavier which now stands in the Geburtshaus, Salzburg. The instrument, built by the Viennese maker Anton Walter in 1780, was purchased by Mozart in 1784 and fitted with a special sustaining device. The attraction for Mozart was the "Viennese" escapement – also a feature of the pianos made by Andreas Stein of Augsburg (see *No. 12*).

30. Christoph Willibald von Gluck (1714–1787). Oil portrait by Étienne Aubry, 1772. Mozart's musical relationships with Gluck, whom he succeeded as imperial court composer in 1787, are fully discussed by Professor Hutchings in Chapter IV. His international reputation in opera had been firmly established long before Mozart sought recognition in that field, and Leopold's suspicions of intrigues by Gluck against his son were probably groundless.

31. Antonio Salieri (1750–1825). Anonymous oil portrait.

Leopold Mozart's assessment of Joseph II's *Kapellmeister,* Salieri, as "a scheming egoist" probably had more foundation than his suspicions of Gluck (who was Salieri's close friend), but there is no truth in the legend that he poisoned Mozart. In fact the two became quite friendly towards the end of Mozart's life. Salieri was highly regarded as a teacher, his pupils including Hummel (*No. 44*), Beethoven, Schubert, and Liszt.

32. Wind instruments from Mozart's time (for clarinets see *No. 41*). Top to bottom: (a) A natural horn by J. G. Haltenhof, Hanau-am-Main, 1798. There were no valves in Mozart's day and the central crook was interchangeable, making harmonic series in different tonalities available. In addition the hand was used in the bell to alter pitch and obtain additional notes. (b) A bassoon by J. H. Grenser of Dresden, c. 1800, with nine palmwood keys. Mozart's bassoon did not have the upper range of the modern instrument and for much of his lifetime only four keys were standard, necessitating much cross-fingering to obtain the semitones. (c) An oboe (maker unknown), c. 1820 (owned by the Royal Archaeological Society, Amsterdam), with five copper keys. Below it is one more typical of Mozart's music – an anonymous Dutch three-keyed instrument with silver mountings, dated 1785. (d) A transverse flute (privately owned by R. J. M. van Acht of The Hague), made in boxwood by F. G. A. Kirst of Potsdam, c. 1780, with three interchangeable upper joints for tuning. This is the traditional one-keyed instrument known to Mozart, but from around 1760 a flute with three additional chromatic keys was available.

30

31

32
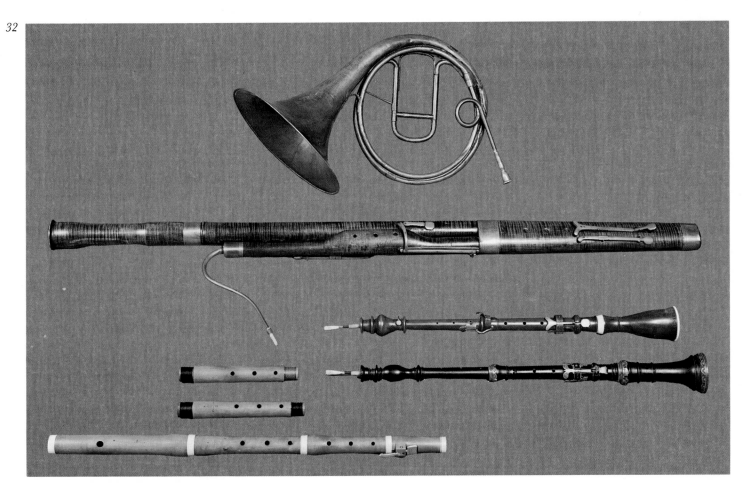

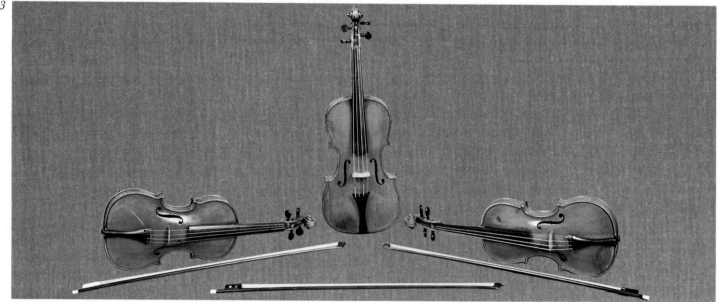

34

33 and 35. A quartet of string instruments by the eighteenth-century Dutch maker, Johann Cuypers of The Hague. *No. 33* shows (left to right) a violin (1791), a viola (1805), and another violin (1798). The cello (*No. 35*) is from 1793. The bows, which are French from the end of the eighteenth century, and the instruments are from the Carel van Leeuwen Boomkamp Collection.

34. Joseph Haydn (1732–1809). Oil portrait by Thomas Hardy, 1791. No more appropriate instruments could accompany a portrait of Joseph Haydn, affectionately known to Mozart and his friends as "Papa." He was the true father of the string quartet and it was in this medium that Mozart chose to honour him in the 1780's with six quartets which remain today among the finest ever written. The two, who were also Masonic brothers, often played in quartets together in Vienna and the respect they had for each other was mutual. "The greatest composer I know in person or by name" was how Leopold Mozart heard his son described on one such occasion by the man he himself regarded as the greatest composer then living.

36. Michael Haydn (1737–1806). Anonymous oil portrait. Joseph Haydn's younger brother Michael, *Konzertmeister* at Salzburg for more than 40 years and organist at St. Peter's (see *No. 39*), where both he and Mozart's sister lie buried, had the misfortune to work directly in the shadow of two musical giants. Yet both his brother and Mozart (and later Schubert) had the greatest respect for his ability as a composer and his music was fine enough for one of his symphonies to be mistaken for Mozart's "No. 37" for over a century. Conversely Mozart's fine

36

duos for violin and viola were once thought to be by Haydn.

37. Johann Georg Albrechtsberger (1736-1809). Anonymous oil portrait. Albrechtsberger, appointed court organist by Joseph II in 1772, was a highly esteemed teacher of counterpoint. Beethoven thought highly of him and his other pupils included Eybler (*No. 38*) and Hummel (*No. 44*). He and Mozart were good friends in Vienna – so much so that in his last hours Mozart urgently requested that Albrechtsberger be the first to know of his death so that he might secure the post of director of music at St. Stephen's Cathedral to which Mozart had just been appointed but which he knew he could never take up.

38. Joseph von Eybler (1765–1846). Anonymous oil portrait. Eybler's stature as a composer is indicated by the fact that his teacher Albrechtsberger (*No. 37*) officially ranked him second only to Mozart himself and testimonials from both Mozart and Beethoven enabled him to attain the position of imperial *Kapellmeister*. He was a close and helpful friend during Mozart's last days and it was to him that Constanze first turned after her husband's death for help in the completion of the Requiem.

39. The organ at St. Peter's, Salzburg. Dating from 1620, it took its present form in 1763 and must have been played by Mozart on many occasions.

37

38

40. Georg Joseph ("Abbé") Vogler (1749–1814). Anonymous oil portrait with a psaltery. Vogler, court chaplain at Mannheim when Mozart met him in 1778, was a noted teacher and organist who had studied briefly under Padre Martini (*No. 28*), to the satisfaction of neither. His pupils included Carl Maria von Weber and Aloysia Weber, later Mozart's sister-in-law, whose singing benefited much from his coaching. Mozart wrote deprecatingly about Vogler's abilities probably, as Professor Hutchings suggests, because his father insisted that he cultivate this "very clever man." Perhaps another reason was Vogler's interest in Aloysia, albeit purely musical, for Mozart was in love with her at that time.

39

40

41. Four clarinets and a basset horn from the eighteenth and early nineteenth centuries.

Clarinets are illustrated separately from other wind instruments of Mozart's time (see *No. 32*) because they were relatively new. Although Mozart was certainly not the first great composer to employ the instrument he was the first to write great music for it which fully exploited its expressive capabilities, particularly in the lowest register, still called the chalumeau after the open keyless pipe from which the clarinet descended.

The mechanical refinement which turned a rude folk instrument into one of the most versatile, colourful, and complex components of the modern orchestra was the "speaker" key which opened up a whole new brilliant range of harmonics above the chalumeau. This development is attributed to Johann Christoph Denner, a German flute-maker (1655–1707), and an example of the kind of two-key instrument he made standard can be seen in the lower of the two boxwood examples in *No. 41*, which is by an unknown maker and dates from around 1750.

Mozart could have heard clarinets in London as early as 1764, for J. C. Bach used them the previous year in his "Orione." He certainly heard them in Milan in 1771, but in Italy their main function initially was to take over clarino parts when the art of high trumpet-playing was in decline. Writing for the clarinet was further limited by the lack of skilled instrumentalists who could control by embouchure the intonation problems early clarinets presented. Initially oboists were persuaded to take clarinet parts but the instruments and techniques differed so radically that music had to be of the simplest.

41

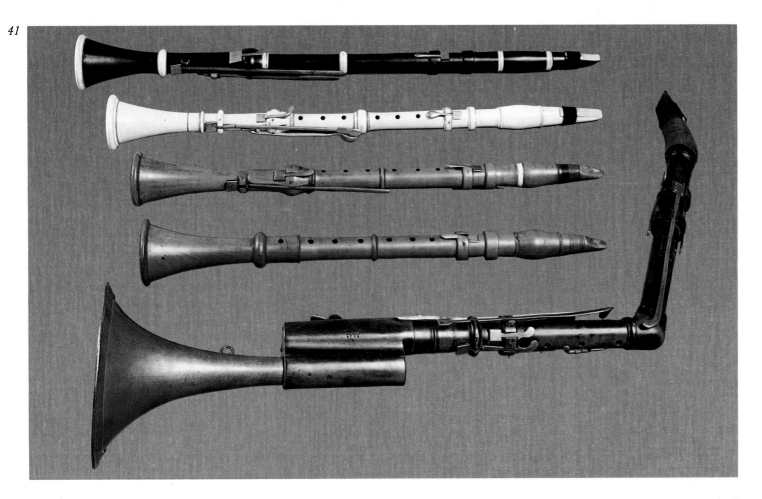

The first German clarinet specialists were at Mannheim and it was there in 1778 that Mozart probably first heard the instrument's true expressive qualities. Once there were players, technical development speeded up and the treble orchestral instrument most often available to Mozart had four keys – similar to the second boxwood example illustrated, which dates from around 1780 (maker unknown).

The early clarinet was usually pitched in C but to lessen technical difficulties it very soon became a transposing instrument, usually in B flat like the ivory clarinet illustrated, which has five silver keys and was made in Germany at the end of the eighteenth century. The other standard version, in A, became general a little later (illustrated is a five-keyed example by J. Winnen, cadet, of Paris, c. 1835, in

the African blackwood which is now the universal basic material).

It is in a published version for clarinet in A that Mozart's Clarinet Concerto, written for Anton Stadler, is now generally performed but it seems to have been intended for a deeper instrument (extending to a third below the usual range) in which Stadler then specialised (nowadays referred to as a basset-clarinet).

The other instrument illustrated in *No. 41* is the basset horn, on which Stadler also specialised (and which Mozart used extensively in his Masonic music). The basset horn emerged around 1770, became obsolete in 1850, and was resuscitated in the early twentieth century. The example illustrated is by Johann Heinrich Grenser of Dresden, c. 1800.

42. Joseph Starzer (1726–1787). Anonymous oil portrait. Starzer, *Konzertmeister* at the Vienna court *Kapelle,* was a fine violinist and composer who became enormously popular at the St. Petersburg court during an extended stay in Russia in the 1760's. After he had resumed his duties in Vienna Mozart and he met frequently at Baron van Swieten's. where Starzer was a regular and valued performer.

43. A violin dated 1766 by the Florentine maker Giovanni Gabrielli – a rare example, still in its original state, of his later work (Carel van Leeuwen Boomkamp Collection). With it is an eighteenth-century Italian bow (privately owned by W. Bouman of The Hague). While such instruments are treasured now as much for their rarity as their craftsmanship, stringed instruments by the great Italian makers, particularly those of Cremona, were highly prized even in Mozart's day for their excellence of tone.

44. Johann Nepomuk Hummel (1778–1837). Anonymous oil portrait. Mozart first encountered Hummel when the child's father became conductor at Schikaneder's theatre in Vienna. Teaching was not one of Mozart's favourite occupations but he was so struck by the boy's piano-playing that he offered to train him. As a result Hummel lived for two years with Mozart in his house in the Schulerstrasse before his father took him on tour as a prodigy, as Mozart's had done. On his return to Vienna in 1793 he studied, like his friend Beethoven, under Haydn (*No. 34*), Albrechtsberger (*No. 37*), and Salieri (*No. 31*), and for a time he held Haydn's old post as *Kapellmeister* to Prince Esterházy.

45. Johann Wenzel Tomašek (1774–1850). Anonymous oil portrait. The Czech composer and teacher Tomašek, whose reflective piano pieces were to influence Schubert and Schumann, was still a student of 17 in Prague when Mozart paid his last visit to that city. He probably never met or even saw Mozart then, but complete familiarity with Mozart's works was something he regarded as essential to his own development as a composer.

42

43
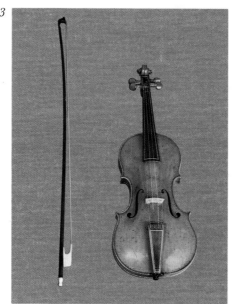

44

45

VI
Mozart and the piano

His Playing
The Instrument
The Concertos
Solo and Duet

43. A fortepiano by Anton Walter, Vienna, c. 1780, similar in construction to Mozart's instrument (see No. 47).

His Playing

Harold C. Schonberg of the "New York Times" in his book "The Great Pianists" (Victor Gollancz, London, 1964) collected reports on Mozart's playing by several people who heard it but, because they were not eminent composers or writers, are not well known. Their testimony concurs in a way that makes it credible, especially when they compare Mozart's playing with Clementi's or Beethoven's. In parts of his concertos he played more than the notes we see in print, not just by insertion of conventional ornaments but by enrichment of textures which appear in our scores as of only two parts – single notes for each hand. He allowed himself no dramatic fluctuation of rhythm, no extreme of dynamic, no bodily or facial movements by which musicians before him (even Corelli playing the violin or C. P. E. Bach the clavichord or harpsichord) enabled onlookers to see the emotional interpretation they heard. If Clementi and Beethoven, who did to some extent make visible their emotional reactions, had indulged in the hand-liftings, hip-squirmings, eye-rollings and closings, mouth-pullings, and pretended communications with conductor and orchestra which modern soloists affect when they are aware of a camera, we should most certainly have heard of their antics; but Mozart's remarkable stillness and poise impressed all who watched him.

Two accounts mention his sitting tensely waiting until there was not the slightest noise or whisper in the room, his requiring "near perfect" playing from the orchestra, and, when one of his pupils played, from the pianist. Schonberg points out the number of letters and conversations in which he used the phrase "flow like oil." He also makes the following remarks upon another of Mozart's favourite phrases:

> As a pianist Mozart was not the fiery kind of virtuoso that his competitor Clementi was. Before the public . . . Mozart was musician first, pianist second. He insisted on naturalness – in playing, in interpretation, in posture . . . When he heard the daughter of one Hamm in Augsburg he was greatly disturbed by the way she held her hand. "She undoubtedly must have a gift for music, as she has been studying only three years and yet can play several pieces really well. But . . . she seems so curiously affected. She stalks over the clavier with her long fingers in such an odd way. She has made me laugh a great deal . . ." That refrain in Mozart's letters, "laugh a great deal," or "I could have died of laughing," comes up again and again, more and more unpleasantly each time.

We have seen that he did not "die laughing" after the encounter with Clementi; but the important matter is that the virtuoso who so disturbed Mozart actually wrote, "I have never before heard anyone play with such intelligence and grace." So Mozart *was* the first great pianist in the eyes of the very man who did not share his style.

The technical difference between the styles was not related entirely to difference between instruments, for they used the same type in front of the emperor. It lay in Mozart's extraordinary development of all fingers on a very light hand. It is generally recognised, for instance, that a *crescendo* or the "bringing out" of a *cantabile* melody engages weight. Consciously or otherwise the mind makes the hand, the wrist, the forearm or the rest of the arm add or withdraw "pressure," which means weight. Mozart taught that, as far as possible, expression should be controlled by the muscles of the fingers. Obviously it did not do so in his own playing, but he produced the illusion that it did by the sheer technical development of the fingers. His comment on Maria Anna Stein, daughter of the admired Augsburg piano-maker, is particularly interesting. He makes play on the name Stein by saying that anyone who can keep from laughing on seeing her play "must be made of stone (*Stein*)." He proceeds:

> She sits towards the treble instead of the middle of the instrument as this gives her more chance of moving about and making grimaces. She rolls her eyes and smirks. When a passage is repeated she plays it slower . . . when notes are emphasised it is done with the arm, not the fingers . . . The most amusing thing of all is that when she reaches a passage that should flow like oil but needs finger-change, she does not bother about it but just raises her hand and leaves notes out . . . She has great musical talent but she will never show it if she goes on in this way, and she will never achieve rapidity, for all she does tends to make her hands heavy. Moreover she will never acquire *the most essential and most difficult requisite, which is rhythm* [our italics] for from her earliest years she has not played in time. Herr Stein and I have discussed the matter for at least two hours . . . and now he asks my advice on everything. He used to be enthusiastic about Beecke but he now sees that I am a better player, that I do not pull faces and yet play with such expression that, he admits, no one else gets such good effect from his pianos. Everyone is amazed that I keep strict time. What these folk cannot grasp is that in *tempo rubato* during an *adagio* the left hand should continue in strict tempo. With them the left hand always follows suit. Count Wolfegg and several other keen admirers of Beecke openly admitted at a concert the other day that I quite excelled him.

That tells so much about Mozart's ideals of playing that we need consider only one sentence. It is very doubtful if his left hand always maintained tempo with mathematical exactitude when the right played *rubato*; but Mozart wanted an illusion of its doing so, as he wanted the illusion that an increase or diminution of tone was controlled entirely from the fingers.

He could play at great speed with astonishing evenness of touch and perfect control of expression, yet he detested unauthorised excessive speed, still more what is

44. The Church of Holy Cross, Augsburg. From an engraving published by Jeremias Wölff, c. 1790. The church, where Mozart played the organ during his visit to Augsburg in 1777, is seen from the east with the entrance to the monastery and the guest rooms.

now called "getting away with it" – taking music fast so that imperfect mastery of detail will not be noticed. For him perfect accuracy meant also accurate expression, though the word he used is usually translated "precision." He said that if he had been Rosa Cannabich's teacher he would have made her practise "nothing but scales, trills, mordents, turns, and so forth very slowly until each hand was properly trained, first the right hand alone, then the left." His harshest remarks about a player of repute were passed on Vogler in 1778, whom he heard trying one of his concertos and using speed and dash to "get away with it."

> He took the first movement *prestissimo*; the *andante* he played *allegro*, and the rondo even more *prestissimo*. He often got the left hand parts wrong . . . Nothing else is possible at such a tempo, for the eyes cannot follow the music [Vogler was sight-reading] nor the hands perform it. What good is it? To me sight-reading of that kind is no different from shitting . . . It is much easier to play a thing quickly than slowly.

He went on to say that a reputation for playing at sight was hollow unless there was, first, complete accuracy of notes and rhythm and, second, taste. The last word was an eighteenth-century touchstone. It was not used quite as *gusto* is today though it carried a little of its present meaning. As Mozart's words show, "taste" was the comple-

mentary virtue to accuracy, the musicianship or musical experience that added vitality of expression to accuracy. Two centuries after Mozart we know how even a fine conductor or player may sometimes fail to invest a movement with the "grace" that undoubtedly exists in Mozart's conception of it; and, as in Mozart's time, the greatest danger is with slow movements. For instance the slow movement of Beethoven's last symphony, given after most careful rehearsal with excellent players and all points of expression, cannot survive the ruin that follows the first two strokes of a baton if the conductor has misjudged the tempo by beginning before he has mentally tried both the opening bars and those of several passages to come later. The same disservice is often done to Mozart's slow movements, usually by making *andante* lose its forward movement by taking it a shade too slowly. As we heard from Clementi, it was in slow movements that Mozart astonished other musicians by his "taste" and his command of expressive *cantabile*.

He astonished audiences in general by his improvisations, which were asked for at most of his concerts. Of course cadenzas to concertos were regarded as improvised though they rarely were wholly so. Even if we lacked the cadenzas written out by Mozart for most of his concertos, presumably for the use of pupils, we should know that such a perfectionist did not approach a movement which included a cadenza unless he had ideas and

69

schemes for it in his head. The cadenzas he left us bear out what has been said about his superb restraint and taste. All are short. None vaunts the vulgar exhibitionism of latter-day cadenzas, rivalling previous treatments of a main theme; indeed they usually deal lightly with ideas not heavily worked in preceding texture, and they never take on a virtuosity incongruous with context. They were meant as models: they remain so.

Cadenzas may not have been entirely extempore, but how did Mozart treat themes chosen by members of the audience, as by the emperor at the contest with Clementi? Literally extempore music, like extempore speech, may engage us by subject matter which it must perforce present loosely. Daily conversation inures us to hesitant, repetitious, ill-connected, interrupted, incomplete, and ugly sentences, full of reach-me-down words and periphrastic phrases; but we do not listen to speech as we do to music. All we seek from a talker is what he or she means, knowing that we respond, maybe to interrupt a sentence. In music the sound and the meaning are united. What does not sound well is not conveyed well, perhaps not conveyed at all. Ill-composed music becomes empty music. By its very nature music aspires to perfection of expression and form, and form is linked with design – the planned shape. Literally extempore music must therefore be contemptible. Admired extempore music has been rapidly composed before it is heard, if only minutes or seconds before. It is not malicious to counter "He extemporises splendidly" with "Then where are his written works?"

These reflections are not intended to condemn extemporisation or to deny the merit of extempore performances one has heard, chiefly from French organists; for in France rigorous training is given in this art. It is needed, for instance, during ceremonies in cathedrals when the organ must play versets on plainchant so that a canticle or hymn may outlast a procession, the preparation of the elements and the lavabo at the offertory, censing, etc. We may well understand Mozart's impressiveness (and Beethoven's) in extempore playing by noticing the tactics of French organists when, at their recitals, they are handed a theme for extempore treatment. They rarely present it more than once or twice as they receive it, spreading it out as a melody, lest their piece should become a sprawling line with progressions of chords lacking phrase and sentence and paragraph. Either immediately, or soon after presenting the whole theme, they derive from it a short motive to a pregnant rhythm. This enables them to build paragraphs from "bricks." (The most famous example of the procedure is the opening of Beethoven's Fifth Symphony.) They may then be more leisurely, perhaps playing a meditative section at a pace slow enough to be genuinely extempore, with wayward modulations and recourse to the colours of various stops and chords; this can be followed by "fireworks," with brilliant toccata-like figurations or display material such as a solo on the pedals, the whole clinched by some grandiose treatment of the given theme; but nothing

impresses audiences more than a final section in which some version of the theme is presented *fugato*, and this was so when Mozart played. Now not the cleverest improviser can present a fugue upon a theme he has not seen before if the fugue is to bear inspection like a written one. Its texture cannot include phrased countersubjects in all parts or simultaneous presentations of the subject by overlapping, inversion, or augmentation. The improviser is not required to give us a fugue that bears inspection but music that is impressive, broadly logical, and integrated as it passes our ears. It therefore follows the externals of fugal artifice – the characteristic opening entries, the thick and thin variations of texture, effective middle entries made telling after episodes, and the cumulation to a final section.

There have come down to us several pieces by Mozart which seem to tell us that his improvisations followed similar principles to those of admired organ recitalists. Nearly all of them are called fantasias, and they are sectional. Two of them are fine, carefully prepared compositions in what, to Mozart, was an archaic style used by organists before and after church services. These are the two fantasias for what is not quite accurately described as a mechanical organ, for Mozart wished they had been for such an instrument. We know them best in piano-duet form, and very fine they sound for one or two pianos and two players; they are also enjoyed by organists in arrangements which Mozart would have liked, for they make thrilling recital pieces. They worried him precisely because, as he said of the first of them:

> If it were for a large instrument so that it sounded like an organ piece I could get some enjoyment out of it; but the mechanism employs only tiny pipes which are too high-pitched and childish.

He wrote this piece on the way to Frankfurt in 1790 and finished the work at odd moments while he was there. It bored him, but the result does not suggest the fact. He had to write it on three soprano staves "for the watchmaker, so that I can put a few ducats into the hand of my dear little wife." The work was commissioned by Count Deym, who showed a collection of curiosities that was soon to include Mozart's death mask. Deym wanted it to go inside a clock beneath a waxwork figure of Marshal Laudon set in a model mausoleum. The original title of K. 594 was not "Fantasia" but "Adagio and Allegro." It is an A–B–A design, the repeated *Adagio* enclosing a brilliant *Allegro* so reminiscent of movements in Handel's organ concertos that scholars are sure that Mozart must have known them. Better known is a second fantasia supplied in the following March (K. 608) and entitled simply "Organ Piece for a Clock Mechanism." It is a more elaborate affair of four sections, two of them fugal, and it is normally called the Fantasia in F minor. Though these works are far from improvisations they are made in the same way and of the same kind of materials as improvisations. A fragment circulated in manuscript at teaching institutions purports to be someone's recollection of Mozart's improvisation at St. Thomas's,

Leipzig, which, as we shall see later, delighted Bach's pupil Doles. The "brick" from which it expands is very similar to the motive with the *gruppetto* or "turn" in K.608.

More likely to have been actually used as improvisations are three piano fantasias – K.394, preceding a fugue in C; K.396 in C minor; and K.397 in D minor. They are as interesting but not as fine as the much later one in C minor, K.475, which is played before the C minor sonata, K.457, for Frau von Trattner. This passionate piece could stand alone, though it suggests the introductory use to which it is put. It has been called Beethovenian – quite wrongly. Wonderful though Beethoven's modulations were, he would not and never did use the particular enharmonic modulations in this piece; nor, though he made the piano suggest orchestral ranges of tone, did he ever employ the same sort of hand technique for his effects. Yet naïve ears invoke Beethoven precisely because in these fantasias – all of them – Mozart indulges in "orchestral" sonorities, octave doublings, full chords, and arpeggios (notably of the stormy diminished seventh beloved by Liszt) that run the full length of the keyboard. It is most likely that when improvising he was willing to exploit the sonority and compass of the piano in a way which he shunned when using it in concertos as the participant with orchestral instruments in a large musical

45. Beethoven at the age of 16. Silhouette by van Neesen, 1786. It was about this time that Beethoven visited Mozart in Vienna.

conception, transcending the virtuosic display of one instrument. This was an ideal quite foreign to the "show" pianists of the following century. Maybe some of these fantasias were considered as introductions to sonatas, suites, or fugues; but as they come down to us they are more like prepared improvisations owing much to the impassioned styles of C. P. E. Bach.

The Instrument

In 1825 Karl Holz jotted on a writing pad "Was Mozart a good pianist?" and handed it to the deaf Beethoven. It is often said that Beethoven's answer was evasive – "Well, the piano was still in its cradle then"; but Beethoven had himself greatly admired Mozart's playing, and his answer was shrewd. Mozart was the greatest performer on a certain kind of instrument, and that was not Beethoven's instrument; nor would Mozart's playing have fully employed the musical resources of that instrument. If he had lived longer (so the fantasias suggest) Mozart would have expanded his style and bought the latest in pianos. There is a far greater difference between Mozart's piano by Walter and Beethoven's Broadwood than there is between Beethoven's piano and instruments known to Chopin, Liszt, or even Schumann and Brahms. That piano by Anton Walter of Vienna was obviously thought by Mozart to be an improvement upon those he had so admired when passing through Augsburg, where he had spent much time with Andreas Stein. Let us therefore note what he wrote home about Stein's instruments, no doubt hoping that his father would buy one for him to use in Salzburg. The letter is dated October 17, 1777.

> I shall begin at once with Stein's pianofortes. Before I saw any of his make, Späth's had always been my favourites. I now prefer Stein's because they damp very much better than the Regensburg ones. When I strike hard, I can keep the note down or raise my finger, but the reverberation stops ... the tone is always even ... it never jars ... His instruments have a special advantage over others in being made with escapement action. Only one maker in a hundred cares about this; without escapement it is impossible to prevent jangling and vibration after a note is struck ... When Stein has made one of these claviers he sits down to it and tries all kinds of passages, jumps and runs, and refines his work until it can do anything; for he works in the interest of music and not just for profit – otherwise he would be finished at once ... He guarantees that the sound-board will not break or split. When he has finished one he exposes it to the open air – to rain, snow, the sun and all hell to make it crack ... The device you control with your knee is better than on other pianos. I have only to touch it and it works.

The knee device was the sustaining "pedal" which removed the dampers. Only in England were pedals

46. *Beethoven's last piano, made by Thomas Broadwood. Anonymous drawing.*

already really pedals, worked by the foot. Mozart's piano by Walter had no sustaining device when he bought it in 1784, but as Leopold noted in a letter to Nannerl, Mozart got Walter to add the pedal attachment – "very heavy." Because it is not seen with the piano in the museum at Salzburg it has been erroneously suggested that it was a pedalier, or set of bass keys worked by the feet, as on an organ. The other technicality mentioned – escapement or "freedom from blocking" – will be understood by anyone who finds a note on the home piano that cannot be repeated rapidly. It sounds when the key is struck; then the hammer takes too long to fall back, or it may stick near the strings until the instrument is opened and it is knocked back. The defect is often attributed to damp, but nearly always the escapement and other mechanism needs overhaul.

Leopold wrote that Stein's piano sounded excellent but very expensive. Home in Salzburg Wolfgang had to be content with the family Späth. In his day of triumph in Vienna he could have bought a Stein; yet he bought the Walter and had the pedal added instead of Stein's knee device. How did this instrument so differ from Beethoven's as to make Beethoven suggest that it limited performing style? Those in love with new capabilities rarely see that they normally incur the sacrifice of other capabilities. A modern orchestral horn is easier to play than

the French horn still used by some great soloists; rapid and chromatic notes in difficult scores can be managed with security, but at the sacrifice of the beautiful characteristic tone of the classical instrument. Let us therefore consider an example of a texture which cannot easily sound well on a fine modern piano, nor on Beethoven's, but makes one wish to have a fortepiano of Mozart's time. One of the finest movements in Mozart's sonatas is the first of the work in A minor, K.310. For much of its texture the left hand repeats a close three-note chord *en bloc* and in quavers, that is to say eight times per bar. The opening is marked *forte*, but even played quietly, with the music's vigour falsified, these close and repeated chords sound unpleasant on a modern piano – unpleasant in this work. Beethoven knew quite well what he was doing when he asked for the same kind of texture, or wrote a grumpy fistful instead of a sonorously spread chord-cum-pedal. On Mozart's piano these repeated chords did not (*do* not, for the instrument can sometimes be heard) sound crude and thick; the slight knock of their three hammers gives the kind of metrical pacing to the melody that Wagner seeks with the repeated wind tonguings in the brilliant Act III prelude to "Lohengrin."

Another advantage of the shallow key-fall and light action was that the hands did not easily tire, and that small hands could more easily execute rapid scale and

47. Mozart's fortepiano, built by Anton Walter of Vienna in 1780 and now in the Geburtshaus, Salzburg. (See also colour illustration No. 29.)

arpeggio passages than on later instruments. In fact the fortepiano combined the qualities of both harpsichord and clavichord, but added some of its own, including a compass of more than five octaves. The first pianos owned by Beethoven had the same number of keys, though the present white ones had become white; on Mozart's piano the present whites were black and only the sharps and flats were white. During Mozart's childhood the clavichord enjoyed a period of special favour in Germany, being specially commended by C. P. E. Bach for the instruction of the young. It was intimate and expressive and, as anyone knows who has played it, very "tell-tale." If the finger released a key in the middle of what should be a joined phrase, the note sounded *staccato*. On its very quiet level it enabled pressure and release of pressure to impart *crescendo* and *diminuendo* to the moulding of phrases. The harpsichord was, of course, needed in the concert room where the clavichord could not be heard. Just when Mozart was making even more brilliant the concerto style of his friend J. C. Bach, his father wrote in April 1778: "If you can find a good clavichord in Paris, such as we have, you would no doubt prefer it, and it would suit you better than a harpsichord." The clavichord was also much less costly than the harpsichord and easy to maintain and tune; but that fact would not have affected the extravagant young man. He loved the piano because he could get from it the expressiveness and *cantabile* of the clavichord with the brilliance (in an *allegro*) of the harpsichord.

It can be reasonably argued that a modern piano gives an even finer and richer singing tone than Mozart's, along with a very much greater range between the extremes of loud and soft. Although to say "Mozart would have loved it" is not history but speculation, we are honest when we say that, as far as we can imagine, a few of his keyboard works gain nothing by our seeking a reconditioned fortepiano and much by using a modern piano. They include some of the splendid duets, such as the F major sonata, K. 497, the G major variations, K. 501, and the fantasias arranged for two pianos; but they do not include the D major sonata for two pianos, K. 448, wherein the modern piano makes the left-hand broken chords too resonant. His finest piece for solo piano, the Adagio in B minor, K. 540, as well as that C minor fantasia played before the sonata, K. 457, call for the later piano and gain nothing by transfer to the older instrument, yet the playing of any music by Mozart on a modern piano needs an adjustment (of the mind as much as of the fingers) not quite demanded by Beethoven's music. On the one hand it is stupid to use a modern piano and try to make it sound like a different instrument. Nowadays harpsichords are common enough to leave no excuse for playing the piano as if it were a harpsichord, though we still occasionally hear wooden sham-historical Bach playing; but fortepianos are not common and the short period of their vogue hardly justifies their manufacture on a large scale.

Solo playing demands more consideration than concerto playing. In the concert room, with the present size of what is now called a smallish orchestra, which would have seemed large to Mozart, and with the present size of most halls used for concerts, the modern piano can be used for what it is. We need a make that gives brightness rather than heavy bass resonance, and if necessary we can use one of less than full concert-grand length. It is pretentious to observe one or two historical conditions while suppressing others – for instance to play a "Brandenburg" Concerto with a small number of instruments but to omit the clavier continuo or make it inaudible. Similarly there is little sense in shutting the lid of the piano or playing very quietly in a large hall with an orchestra of 40 or more. Beethoven wrote to the Archduke Rudolph requesting that not less than four first and four second violins should be used for a performance of his Seventh Symphony! Mozart's piano solos and duets pose a greater problem than his concertos. His piano gave no strong Beethovenian *sforzando*, nor the strong contrasts of tone we are accustomed to. We must therefore play delicately – especially in duets and works for two pianos. Yet if we scale down contrasts and play too lightly we shall deny the music its own passion and vitality. If we are using a different instrument from Mozart's then we are translating, and a feeble translation does him a disservice. He must sound as if he wrote for the instrument we are playing. That does not mean that we emulate conductors who Beethovenise and Schumannise Mozart, if not Bach and Handel. We do not translate the music to a later style because we use the later instrument; for instance we do not often use the sustaining pedal, and we never use the other one unless Mozart so directs us; yet Mozart had a sustaining pedal and it was probably much used in his singing slow movements.

The Concertos

Whether we like admitting the fact or not, most music of the nineteenth century would have seemed vulgar to the Mozart who died in the eighteenth and was music's greatest natural aristocrat, the most urbane and civilised of musicians, whose art never acknowledges its inspiration from wild nature but only from human nature. It is a condition of civilisation that nature is restrained; to belch, shout, fart, micturate, or rut in public is to rebel against civilisation. In Mozart's art we have to distinguish between passion and emotion (of which we are aware beneath civilised forms and designs) and violence, by which passion and emotion are not put under the restraint of form. The less musical we are, the less we recognise the simple fact that power, in mechanism or in art, exerts most strength when under restraint. Freedom takes away its energy after the first outburst. Listeners untrained in music theory request records and broadcasts of fugues and other works that are under heavy restraint from devices or artifice, because they enjoy the expression

48. *Announcement of Mozart's concert on March 10, 1785 in Vienna, at which the Piano Concerto, K.467 had its première.*

that is spread to give the impression of subdued power that may at any time explode. Thus "artifice" is not simply a term of reproach, and we may understand Eric Blom's inspired comment upon Mozart's piano concertos – "Here we enter a world of enchanted artificiality." It is, of course, true of any lengthy movements that artifice has enabled the prolongation of emotion or mood. Under the leash of restraint they "play out" such diverse emotions as anger and tenderness, humour and anguish. Yet the artifice of Mozart's best concertos is more complex than that of any other Classical designs – more complex than fugues and canons, and more varied.

The high point of complexity was reached in the first movements and rondos of the piano concertos from the E flat, K.449, of 1784, and relaxed only for the somewhat shallow "Coronation" Concerto in D. Analysis lies outside the scope of this study, but recognition of the broad designs of these movements is necessary to an understanding of one of Mozart's major effects on the history of music, an effect that would remain even if the concertos were not works of such intrinsic beauty. Mozart, and Mozart alone, brought what must be distinguished as the "Classical" concerto to a richness that was never exceeded. Beethoven knew it and was modest enough to acknowledge it, both in words already quoted and by tacitly accepting Mozart's design – a remarkable fact in

a composer whose genius could not help transforming the sonata and symphony. The whole difference between the Classical concerto and the splendid concertos by Liszt, Schumann, and most composers after them is this: that the Romantic concertos are shaped like their composers' sonatas and symphonies. They have the designs of sonatas with orchestra or of symphonies with piano. Schumann, Grieg, and the rest rightly dropped the long initial orchestral statement because it was superfluous within their design. It was a mere preliminary canter of main themes. Shaw parodied Milton when a lady asked him why the pianist was immobile for so long at the opening of a Chopin concerto – "He also serves who only sits and waits."

His waiting is essential in the Classical concerto because while he waits the orchestra is not merely playing over what he will later play. Beethoven's piano gambit in his fourth concerto creates no exception to that rule. It was not wholly original for it was anticipated 30 years earlier by Mozart in his E flat "Jeunehomme" Concerto, K.271, but Mozart had the good taste never to repeat a piece of wit. After both Mozart's and Beethoven's surprising early sounding of the piano, the pianist sits and waits for that long piece which, whether it contrasts only three ideas or (as sometimes with Mozart) six, whether it takes incidental modulations or stays in key, comes to a formal close in the tonic, with the "cadentials" or valedictory gestures found at the end of a symphony, overture, or other orchestral piece. Then the piano begins, either with music that has *not* been heard before or with a theme already stated by the orchestra; but it will not continue as the orchestra did. Always it will propose new ideas and move towards the dominant or relative major key, for this first concertante section (soloist with orchestra) is the exposition. There is no "double exposition" as some old textbooks erroneously say. That orchestral opening has an entirely different purpose and function, to understand which we must quickly note the ancestry of the Classical concerto.

It did not develop from the concerti grossi of Corelli, Handel, and others, which have the designs of sonatas or suites of no fixed number of movements; nor was it a special kind of pre-Classical symphony which included the solo instrument. It came from the operatic aria. This is clear enough if we use for examples the best known of arias – those in "Messiah," such as "He was despised" or "The trumpet shall sound." Those two differ completely in expression but are of similar design. Each begins with an orchestral piece containing at least two ideas of contrasted character. It sounds introductory only because we know it to be so. It therefore begets expectation of the solo entry, as it does in a concerto. In fact, however, it comes to a formal finish with the cadentials of an independent piece, and it does so firmly in the tonic key. The modulating and extending of the ideas, along with the possible addition of new ideas, is left to the solo voice, which may or may not begin as did the orchestra. The purpose of the music in that initial orchestral piece is to frame and support the solo, for though the orchestra may sometimes echo a vocal phrase, it punctuates the vocal sentences and paragraphs with *ritornelli* (returns) of music taken from the opening section. At the end of the aria and in the middle, the whole of the initial orchestral piece may make a full *ritornello*. Even when, to suggest urgency, the voice begins without the initial orchestral *ritornello*, the aria proceeds as if the *ritornello* materials (which can easily be synthesised) had been stated at the opening.

A Baroque aria is therefore a concerto movement for voice and orchestra. Substitute a violin, oboe, or cello for the voice and we have the prototype of Classical concerto design; but this substituting had to wait for several decades , after the terms "concerto" and "concerto grosso" had become common. The step was taken early in the eighteenth century by Venetian composers, chiefly Albinoni and Vivaldi, who had already composed hundreds of arias for their operas and oratorios. With this form of solo concerto they also established the three-movement norm, fast–slow–fast. Their influence on the musicians of German court orchestras was enormous, and fortunately one of their admirers who copied, arranged, and imitated their concertos was J. S. Bach, at that time employed at the court of Cöthen. Bach's concertos, including the six for the Margrave of Brandenburg, are probably the best known of Baroque concertos built on *ritornello* principles, but there is another link between Bach and Mozart. We know of no harpsichord concertos before Bach's. In the fifth of his "Brandenburg" Concertos, supposedly a violin and flute concerto, the keyboard instrument is exalted to "cembalo concertato" with brilliant cadenzas. Bach may have used a second harpsichord as "cembalo continuo." Most listeners justifiably take this work to be a proper harpsichord concerto, for the harpsichord is the most prominent solo instrument. The fact that many of Bach's openly titled harpsichord concertos are arrangements suggests the origin of the genre in a practice of the Bach family. The father was in the habit of training his sons to sight-read violin and other concertos with him. Each player sat at a harpsichord, one acting as orchestra to the other's playing of the solo part with improvised harmonies. One happy result was Bach's leaving us two concertos for two harpsichords. He went a step farther in his "Concerto in the Italian Style" by imitating the solo-orchestra relationships on two manuals of one harpsichord. His sons launched the pre-Classical keyboard concerto. Mozart knew several examples from C. P. E. Bach, and we should be ever grateful that fate led him to London in boyhood, to become the close friend of J. C. Bach, the father of the piano concerto.

Before the "Jeunehomme" Concerto Mozart's Salz-

49. Title page of the first edition of the Piano Concerto in F, K.413, published by Artaria, Vienna, 1785.

burg piano concertos were not much richer than J. C. Bach's in the number and organisation of ideas, but much richer in the kind of integration that defies analysis and was called by the Mozarts "the thread" (*il filo*). Some very great composers have felt themselves at times bereft of ideas, of invention that they thought vital. Mozart never complained of that particular sterility, but knew great labour in composing (in the strictest meaning of the word, putting together) so that ideas should follow, as he said, "naturally" – in fact, far from naturally, for their flow and integration depended upon a highly trained mind. The marvel is that the result always seems spontaneous. Sunny concertos like the Salzburg B flat, K. 238, or the first Vienna A major, K. 414, seem to pass in front of us a chain of attractive melodies without making us wonder how they are held together in an impressive whole. Obviously if Mozart could hold his thread so lightly but so securely, minute analysis can discover at least some of the delicate mechanics of construction; but they were probably used unconsciously, as we use healthy limbs and nerves. (Wagner once called composition "the art of transition.") Indeed in his early concertos Mozart is less convincing when he is least overtly melodic, as in the C major, K. 415, which wears counterpoint stiffly. By 1784 the big symphonic paragraph, sustained motivic development, and unlaboured recourse to counterpoint passed the "thread" to and from lyricism with apparent ease, and did not seem out of place in constructions superficially as light as a summer-house.

This is not the place in which to demonstrate the full range of procedures within Mozart's first movements and rondos. Such fertility follows when a first-rate artist rejoices in mastery of a general design. It is paralleled in the fugues of Bach's "Forty-eight" and the first movements of Beethoven's sonatas and quartets. It will suffice here to suggest the broad divisions of first movements, as labelled in a recent study of their designs.* Then we can notice no more than the order of ideas in the first movements of the two great minor-key concertos – the D minor, K. 466, admired by Leopold, and the C minor, K. 491. Nothing need be said of their expressive effect except that the D minor is fiery and passionate while the C minor, under even greater restraint of device, holds its fire with the grandeur of classical tragedy. To speak of a "recapitulation," as in symphonies, would be as erroneous as talking of "double expositions." No such phenomenon occurs even in K. 488 in A, which allows the piano to follow the order of themes in the orchestral prelude. A witty purpose underlies this unique procedure. Mozart's Vienna audiences were accustomed to welcome new ideas either at the entry of the piano or from the piano soon after its entry. In K. 488 they are withheld, only to come surprisingly during the middle section where one expects free fantasy referring to previous ideas.

The contrast in the algebraic representation of procedures which follows might have been greater if we had chosen one of the first movements from a "melodic" type, for both of these examples in minor keys are "symphonic," that is to say full of big paragraphs from the motivic growth of one or two main themes. The small letters represent ideas introduced by the soloist. They show (*a*) that the reprise is never a recapitulation of the "first concerto," (*b*) that the fourth, final section tends to follow the order of the initial orchestral one, which the "first concerto" does not, and (*c*) that Mozart invented ideas that led "naturally" into more than one other idea, so that a sequence of ideas could be telescoped. Thus ABCDx could become ACx in a reprise where condensation was needed to make room for cadenza and cadentials.

Mozart's rondo finales are even more complex and

	K. 466 (D minor)	**K. 491 (C minor)**
1. Orchestral statement	A A B C D	A A B A C
	(*p f p f p*)	(*p f p f p*)
2. First concerto	x a bB y cC	x a y A z
Long *ritornello*	A C D	A C
3. Middle section or Fantasy	x A x A x A etc.	x A cC cC cC etc.
4. Concerto reprise	A y B	A z y B
Long *ritornello*	A cadenza C D	A cadenza C coda with piano

* "Mozart's Concerto Form," by Denis Forman. London, 1971.

varied than his concerto first movements. In its simple form, as Mozart inherited it, the rondo is one of the least complex designs, and is therefore among the first used for student exercise. If one can compose a song with chorus, one can compose a simple rondo. If A be the chorus, or refrain, and B the verse or episode, the shape is ABABA. During the eighteenth century rondos came to include another episode, and by Mozart's boyhood the norm was ABACABA, the C often distinguished by key (e.g. the minor in a rondo in the major) and sometimes by change of tempo. Beyond devising beautiful bridges and passages leading from episodes to refrains Mozart did not experiment with the basic shape in rondos for solo piano. Only the one in A minor, K.511, can be ranked with his best works. Even in his early concertos the finales sometimes seem too light for what has preceded them. Possibly Mozart was cautious with the mass of listeners for whom the first movement was demanding and the second serious; he may have felt it wise to secure applause with ear-tickling pianism and a string of memorable rondo tunes. Sometimes he gave them a minuet instead.

The first notable rondo is in the first surprising concerto, the "Jeunehomme." This finale rattles off *presto* as if for harpsichord in the most *galant* of styles. Just as the piano is leading the first episode back to the refrain it goes to a temperamental cadenza with ominous changes of tempo, throws it off again to rattle the refrain, and then begins (for section C) a slow minuet which passes to the next refrain by another cadenza. Mozart so liked this scheme that he adopted something very like it for his last E flat concerto, K.482, wherein the A flat minuet is more chromatic and soulful, though the rondo in general is even gayer than that of K.271. Far more clever than merely inserting surprises is the witty treatment of main ideas in K.449, the middle one of the three piano concertos in E flat (not counting the one for two pianos). This rondo maintains a comically strict tempo all through – a strut that suggests the march of a wooden puppet. The refrain is varied at each appearance as if it were exemplifying in turn the five species of counterpoint in Fux's "Gradus ad Parnassum." That was in February 1784. By December came the rondo of K.459 in F, more concentrated than the splendid first movement, yet having a gay refrain in alliance with a length of tough counterpoint. By February of the next year Mozart had reached the D minor concerto. This has the most wonderfully organised rondo in all music. It needed a wealth of ideas, some to delight us purely as rondo tunes, some pregnant with motives, others capable of metabolism for "telescoping." Algebraic analysis is baffling, and it does little to reveal the thread.

After 1784 all rondo finales except that to the wilfully complaisant D major "Coronation" Concerto are wonderfully constructed, and each is unique even in its type of humour or ebullience. It is much to be regretted that the seemingly artless tunes and child-like playfulness in most of them prevents recognition of their virtuosity as compositions by a large body of opinion that equates greatness with turgidity or solemnity. It was pointed out to Stravinsky that in "The Poetics of Music" he had put forward the proposition that "art is not entertainment," which is as illogical as "food is not apples"; Stravinsky greatly regretted this and said he had not intended, being himself an entertainer, to disparage the entertainment offered by great artists from Aristophanes to Mozart. Even so, if we made a list of Mozart's supreme achievements, those expressing painful or dark moods would preponderate. He can at any point take the smile from one's face during his magnificent comedies, mixing poignance with beauty and raising even basic yearnings to sublimity. Sometimes, as in the last G minor symphony or the variations at the end of the C minor concerto, the rhythms are those of *opera buffa* but the witty music is far from merry. It is not true of Mozart, as of Haydn, that he is more extrovert than the average great composer. Haydn's symphony finales (not usually rondos) are his most highly organised designs as well as his most humorous pieces. They may introduce "clouds" for deliberate contrast but, unlike Mozart's "clouds," they do not sound more personal than the sunshine. Most of the Vienna piano concertos, however, have finales which equal those of Haydn's symphonies both in high spirits and organisation of materials. Schubert declared that he had not mastered rondo. His early symphonies show how well he knew Mozart, and we must therefore believe that when a composer of his enormous natural ability found difficulty with a type of movement mass-produced by far poorer musicians, he meant that he could not bring it to the level of Mozart's and Beethoven's rondos.

Few of the rondos will commend themselves to people who expect the merriment to be offset by the smouldering and scowling of the one in D minor. Most of them are what that superb example becomes after Mozart's brilliant change to the major key. The two last concertos in C major, K.467 and K.503, offer tests of perception, for neither does more than hint at introspective Mozart. The wind-writing in the rondo of K.467 (one of the best) recalls Liszt's quip about Mozart's "concertos for piano and wind instruments," and in many places sounds as if Mozart were imitating a fairground organ; the rondo of K.503, after two unusually spacious movements, begins in gavotte style but itself becomes spacious with toccata-like sequences of figuration such as Bach was fond of using, especially in that first long cadenza of the fifth "Brandenburg" Concerto.

A particularly ingenious rondo is that to Mozart's very last piano concerto, K.595 in B flat. An algebraic diagram is worthwhile:

ABA C D (in F major) cadenza
A extended with *bravura* and wide modulations
A, refrain, in E flat
C and D in B flat cadenza
ABA

All sections are joined by treatments of A, the full refrain

50. Title page of the first edition of the Piano Concerto in B flat, K.595, of 1791, published by Artaria, Vienna.

ABA coming only at the beginning and the end. The themes are like nursery tunes; the integration by development is unusually impressive, and the cadenzas are perhaps the finest in any concerto.

It was in the slow middle movements of piano concertos that Mozart's own playing most enthralled his listeners. To comment upon the construction of such beautiful outpourings of lyrical pathos as the *Andante* of K.453 in G or K.488 in A seems to align one with those who "murder to dissect." Readers may, however, wonder why some theorists write about their "aria form" and others about their "binary sonata form." The stereotype with which they are compared is not of the slightest importance. To make interesting dialogue between piano and orchestra most composers (the Schumann and Grieg concertos illustrate their practice) give the simplest order of a sonata movement some of the characteristics of an aria. They introduce echoes, variations, and *ritornelli*. In the Classical concerto, and normally in a Mozart *Andante*, the *ritornello* is stated at the opening, coming to a close in the tonic key as in an aria; but Mozart is fond of the telling effect of letting the solo piano make the opening statement. It is notably beautiful when, in a major-key concerto like K.488, the pathetic minor mode is used for the *Andante*, and when the phrases and leaps of the melody are like those of a fine singer in an opera. Once or

twice Mozart adopted Haydn's favourite slow-movement procedure, familiar to us in the "Clock," "Surprise," and other symphonies of the great 12 for London. This can be described as a kind of rondo or as interrupted variations; for the initial and attractive strophe returns with light changes of texture and instrumentation between two or three episodes, often vigorous or even stormy, the more to enhance the returns.

The nearest slow movement to the Haydn type is in the E flat, K.482, with its C minor *Andante*; but towards the end of Mozart's career as a concertist and public performer he favoured a special type of strophic slow movement which still seems the most popular with audiences. Some theorists find its design repetitive and almost too simple for juxtaposition with edifices of such intricacy as the average first movements and rondos. This is the type called "romanza" – Mozart writes the German word *Romanze* when he uses it, for with him it is a definite design, not just an indication of mood or expression. (Songs of tender sentiment were known as romanzas or romances in several countries. Mendelssohn's "Songs Without Words" are known in France as "Romances sans paroles.") The best-known example is the slow movement of the D minor concerto. Here the main theme or romanza tune incurs repetition within itself, the first two sentences beginning alike. This happens nearly always when Mozart uses the design and so emphasises its simplicity. As in the C minor concerto, the echoes between solo and orchestra give us seven presentations of the tune, which means in all 14 recurrences of that first phrase – a very languorous phrase. Plainly Mozart loved the romanza shape, and so impressed Beethoven as to inspire the younger composer's *Romanzen* for violin and orchestra. In performance Mozart's romanzas probably maintained vitality, however languorous the theme, but they are a trap to modern sentimental players and conductors.

Three of the slow movements are of a special type called "reverie" by C. M. Girdlestone in his study of the concertos. The first is in the very first concerto, K. 175, but the most notable and beautiful is in K. 467 in C – alas it has already been stolen for film music! This exquisite movement is opened by the orchestra, not the piano, the muted strings having the effect of a gauze curtain over a luminous stage more suggesting the "fields of sleep" than Gluck's Elysian fields. The soft plashing of the piano notes in triplets (slow ones indeed!) against the duplets of the orchestral melody maintains the evocation of a dream world yet suggests figures moving in it. There is no parallel to the dream-*Andante* in any of Mozart's operas and no other Classical composer provides one in concerto or symphony.

Among the chief treasures of the piano concertos are Mozart's three best sets of variations. Without them we should only have those in G for piano duet to show his

51. Maria Theresa Paradis. Etching by Faustine Parmantié, 1784.

advance in an art that was largely ornamental and decorative before Beethoven. Orchestral colour enabled Mozart to diversify variations without bewildering audiences by wider and wider departures from the theme; it also enabled him to let the orchestra enrich the harmony or even sound the melody while the piano indulged in more brilliant or more delicate figurations than were possible in his variations for solo piano. He usually repeated the sentences of the theme between solo and orchestra at the outset in order to impress it on the listener's memory. If his imagination led him to very free variations he followed them by treatments which strongly recalled the theme. The themes for the G minor *Andante* of K. 456 in B flat and of the finale to the C minor concerto are so sublime in themselves that one imagines oneself willing to hear them repeated with little variation. The suggestion that the G minor movement elicited pathos at the blindness of Mlle. Paradis may be fanciful. The C minor theme is hardly pathetic except in one or two treatments; it smoulders with the fire of high tragedy, an effect heightened by trumpets and drums played *piano* in a style rarely used by other composers.

Solo and Duet

Mozart lovers who recall days when radio was only beginning, gramophone recording crude, and opportunities to hear opera (for most people) rare, may also recall a wish that Mozart's sonatas had been withheld from young players, and certainly not used as teaching pieces. Most of us knew Mozart only by them, and therefore thought him inferior to the composer we met in Beethoven's sonatas. We were uneasy about this opinion only when we played movements that seemed to us very fine and without parallel in Beethoven – for instance the middle movement of the Sonata in F, K. 332, which most of our teachers made us learn until we never broke a run. There was an almost Chopinesque beauty in its singing phrases with their turns and appoggiaturas, and in the spaced broken chords of the accompanying left hand; and at least three of the last sonatas showed a mind different from Beethoven's but almost as interesting. (Today with the operas available on record, and the chamber works and symphonies broadcast daily, the danger is that Beethoven will not be given his due!) On the whole, knowing Mozart only from the sonatas, we were ready to accept Parry's false view of him as "The Great Precursor," nowhere more glibly credible to the inexperienced than in the C minor fantasia and sonata.

Today Mozart's sonatas are treasured and played by many of us who once disparaged them. Their distinction is apparent especially to those who, without being unduly mindful of Beethoven's "the piano was still in its cradle," have heard or played keyboard sonatas by J. C. Bach, Vanhall, Wagenseil, and others among Mozart's immediate predecessors. With the right sort of teacher we should no longer deplore their use in training the young, for their main challenge is musical, not technical. Some of the most innocent-looking do have their technical snags, which are not always in the rapid passages. When already a famous performer, Alfred Cortot confessed to "spending hours" over a mere four bars, in two parts and in C major, beginning at the return of the second group (bar 129) in the first movement of the Mannheim C major sonata, K. 309. Most of the difficulties are of a similar nature – demanding both independence and co-operation between the two hands. If one wished to test a player's musicianship one would discover more by hearing his playing of the *Adagio* in F minor of an even earlier sonata (the Salzburg one in F, K. 280) than by asking him to play far more difficult pieces.

It cannot be said of either Mozart's or Haydn's keyboard sonatas, as Wordsworth said of Shakespeare's sonnets – "With this key he unlocked his heart." They include almost the first fine music for the piano, but they do not – nor were they intended to – chart their composers' artistic advances through a whole life, as Beethoven's do. To follow Mozart's sonatas chronologically is to make unfair comparison with Beethoven. A more powerful and suggestive piano than Mozart's was the companion and confidant of Beethoven's solitude, and his music is none the worse for showing that he worked at a piano. Mozart wanted the piano only for its own music.

It is mistaken, however, to regard his sonatas as chiefly for pupils. He carried them around with him to impress patrons in their homes, and he sometimes played them as solos at public concerts. The "Sonata facile" in C, K. 545, called by Mozart "The little sonata for beginners" is the only one overtly intended for teaching. It is followed by one in B flat, K. 570, that is quite as little in length but decidedly not for beginners; and then comes the D major "Trumpet" Sonata, K. 576, that reflects the athletic workmanship of certain quartets and quintets. The more likely teaching pieces were among the 15 sets of variations, mostly on popular airs, to be found in Vol. XXVI of the collected works. Young ladies and their parents liked them because they were easy to follow, sounded more difficult than they were, and took their themes from tunes that were "all the rage." Yet some of them are known to have been played at concerts. Mozart used those on a minuet by J. C. Fischer, K. 179 for a long time, though he was only 18 when he wrote them. Many copies of these rather shallow variations were sold, especially just after Mozart's death. The only set of solo piano variations which seem any more valuable than the pretty little ones opening the A major sonata, K. 331, are those on the song from Gluck's "The Pilgrims of Mecca," K. 455. They were certainly played in public to honour Gluck, and were supposedly "extemporised" for the purpose at Mozart's concert of March 23, 1783.

Far finer than any variations for solo piano are those in G for piano duet, K. 501. The theme sounds like a popular tune but is, as far as we know, original. It is also excellent for its purpose. To participate in this work is to find difficulty in naming any other so sensitively laid out for the two players. In most of Mozart's variations we can expect an interesting one in the minor key; in this set that minor-key variation is in four lovely contrapuntal and chromatic strands. It is music as nearly perfect as can be imagined. Not even Mozart wrote a more admirable 16 bars. The Mozart family portrait by Della Croce shows the children duetting as they did on public exhibition, for duets were novelties with audiences. Mozart's early duet sonatas, K. 381 in D, of 1772, and K. 358 in B flat, of 1774, were composed for use on tour and are known to have been played in Paris and Vienna. A long time afterwards came the duet sonata in F, K. 497, the finest work of its kind before Schubert's Grand Duo. During its first movement the Mozart work actually reminds us of Schubert's Fifth Symphony, the one in B flat. Yet it is on a grander scale, having a fine slow introduction and a spreading slow movement in which we seem to hear pairs of bassoons and horns, and the interplay of wind and strings. On a modern instrument the rattling bass of the last movement needs careful treatment not to sound heavy, yet the whole work admirably suits its medium, despite the curious feeling that it is the piano-duet arrangement of a symphony. Admirable but not quite as fine is the duet sonata in C, K. 521, composed in May 1787 for Gottfried von Jacquin and his sister and later dedicated to the daughters of a rich merchant called Natorp. The attractive piano figuration in this work shows much that had evolved while Mozart was engaged on his concertos. We have already mentioned the two fantasias for Count Deym's clock mechanism and their arrangements as effective piano duets. The better known one was issued while Mozart was alive, the other after his death by one Johann Mederitsch.

Another work which can sound crude on modern pianos unless it is more sensitively played than usual is the popular Sonata in D for two pianos, K. 448, written in 1781 for the composer to play with Josephine Aurnhammer. Einstein speaks of "the art with which the two parts are made completely equal, the play of the dialogue, the delicacy and refinement of the figuration, the feeling for sonority in the combination . . . of the two instruments" which make this "apparently superficial and entertaining work one of the most profound and mature of all Mozart's compositions." Most of us agree with the technical qualities specified by Einstein but are perhaps surprised at the word "profound," which would have been applicable to another sonata for two pianos in B flat of which we possess only impressive fragments, K. App. 42.

The fugue in C minor for two pianos, K. 426, was composed in 1783. At the time Mozart did not finish the prelude to it, although the beginning – an *Allegro* in C minor, K. App. 44 – seems a fine piece. When he scored the fugue for strings in 1788 (K. 546) he added the beautiful *Adagio* which is always given with it when it is played by strings and often when played as a piano duet. The noble but strenuous fugue is far finer than any of

Mozart's fugues for single piano, the best of which is the one in C major that goes with the preceding fantasia, K. 394. The fantasia is the better work, for the fugue is crabbed and too long for its limited subject matter and treatment. It is on the kind of subject that needs episodes of attractive phrases, not devices affecting the subject entries. Simon Sechter finished the fugues in E flat, K. 153, and G minor, K. 154, which fail to make even the entries eventful. These are an able student's essays in what was still to Mozart parody, for nobody – certainly not Albrechtsberger – could have taught him to make fugues beyond archaism. It is easy enough for us to see what he had to learn, because at about the same time in 1782, he arranged five Bach fugues for string quartet. The exercises were as valuable to Mozart as to Beethoven, and at least the C minor fugue for two pianos is vitally his own music, transcending parody. Did he know that, towards the end, where the left hand openly gives arpeggiated harmony instead of contrapuntal strands, he was doing nothing shameful, but introducing relaxation just where Bach would have done so?

Fascinating as showing how Mozart and his contemporaries heard Handel's music is the Suite or Overture, K. 399, "in the style of G. F. Handel," for it reveals perception of the French elements in German Baroque music. There are first a fine, pompous slow opening, more like Rameau than Handel, then a good fugue, because it is not too long for its slight materials, and then two attractive Baroque-gone-Rococo binary pieces modelled on allemande and courante (in C minor and in E flat respectively).

Two rondos for solo piano are in F. One of them is the Andante for clockwork translated. Its passages in thirds, *staccato* notes with melody above or below, and its ornaments all betray the original purpose. The chromatic passages and splendid finish show it to be late Mozart. The other rondo in F, K. 494, is used as the finale to the sonata K. 533, and contains the F minor section of a quality we find arresting when we play the sonata. The rondo in D, K. 485, is dedicated to a pupil, thought to be Charlotte von Würben, and is merely charming in the manner of J. C. Bach. All the rondos are eclipsed by the one in A minor, K. 511, which it is difficult not to find subjective. It may have nothing to do with Mozart's personal moods of morbid introspection and despair, but if it has, then he was a great enough artist to express himself with such beauty that the home pianist always wants to repeat the work after coming to the end, then repeat it again until it is decided to leave it alone for a long time lest its mood infect the player!

Two very short pieces for solo piano are among Mozart's most virtuosic compositions. One shows the wealth of his harmonic and the other of his contrapuntal resources. The first is a minuet in D, K. 355, dating from 1790 and boldly chromatic, here bitter, there sweet. The other is a witty binary gigue in G ("Eine kleine Gigue," K. 574), its *fugato* inverted after the double bar. It is very difficult for the average player. Lastly we mention Mozart's finest work for the piano, the profoundly tragic Adagio in B minor, K. 540, of 1788. Here is diversity of texture, in some places chromatic harmony and counterpoint with yearning discords, and a Classical control of pathos which does not exclude delight in pianistic technique – the embroidery, the hand-crossing, the sudden full chord which is especially effective when it makes a momentous modulation. There are fine movements in the sonatas, but this piece is finer than any. The form does not seem imposed even in the splendid middle section developing the main theme. The conception within the restraints of form is what imparts the power and pathos.

Pictorial Essay: Art in Mozart's Time

Stylistic advance in any art has never been an isolated phenomenon, and the establishment of Viennese classicism in the music of Haydn, Mozart, and early Beethoven had its parallels in the paintings of Mozart's time. But while music moved from the Rococo towards Romanticism by natural evolution, the pictorial arts, in France particularly, progressed more by revolution, and it is no coincidence that the first two artists represented in this very brief survey died in obscurity – Fragonard (*No. 46*) as a result of the French Revolution and David (*No. 47*) as a result of the Restoration.

Styles changed more by influence than reaction in the German states and Austria, where many Italian artists were employed, including the Venetian Bernardo Bellotto (*Nos. 1 and 48*). The traditional warmth and vibrance of Venetian colouring influenced the Austrian artists more than the German, whose more restrained formalism is represented here by Tischbein (*No. 49*). Indeed, in the frescoes of the Austrian Maulbertsch (*No. 50*) there is a hint of Romanticism in both the colouring and the freedom of execution.

Britain in the meantime pursued its insular development. The assurance of the Protestant succession made artists who valued fame and prosperity heavily dependent on society portraits instead of religious subjects. Gainsborough (*Nos. 27 and 51*) disdained the work almost as much as the Italian influence then prevalent in the recently founded Royal Academy and his work preserved Rococo characteristics in the capital while neo-Classicism took root in the provinces and Romanticism was born unnoticed in the work of the visionary William Blake.

46

In Spain another great individualist, Goya (*No. 52*) had begun to paint from inner compulsion rather than external influence, and by a curious coincidence he was forced into the emotional introversion – a prerequisite of true Romantic expression – by deafness, the very affliction that altered Beethoven's life and the course of music with it.

46. "The Swing" (detail). Oil painting by Jean-Honoré Fragonard, c. 1766.

The frankly hedonistic Rococo art of Fragonard, more than any other, was bred in the shallowness and indolence of life at Versailles in Mozart's time, and his characteristic sensuousness is fully apparent in "The Swing," his most famous work, commissioned by the Baron de St. Julien, who wished to be portrayed with his mistress. Fragonard, a pupil of Chardin and Boucher (see *No. 54*) later studied in Italy together with his friend Hubert

Robert (see *No. 8*), but he continued to paint in the French Rococo style as long as he was patronised by the king and court. He did turn eventually to neo-Classicism just before the Revolution and for a time obtained work under the Revolutionaries through the kindness of David (*No. 47*) but he soon fell out of favour and died forgotten in 1806.

47. "The Oath of the Horatii." Oil painting by Jacques-Louis David, 1784.

Nothing could be further from the fragility of Fragonard than this picture by David, completed in Rome in 1784. The contrast was intended, and the work became not only a symbol of artistic reaction against the Rococo and the firm establishment of neo-Classicism but also one of political rejection of all that Fragonard's patrons stood for. Although it is unlikely that David had any political motive in choosing his subject (the oath of

the Horatii triplets to their father to fight to the death in a symbolic battle against the Curiatii triplets to decide the war between Rome and Alba Longa), he soon became a purveyor of political idealism and later, under Napoleon, of personal propaganda. Having miraculously maintained his popularity through all the political upheavals from Jacobinism to Bonapartism, he did not survive the downfall of the Emperor and was exiled to Brussels, where he died in 1825.

48. "Christ driving the money-changers from the temple." Oil painting by Bernardo Bellotto, 1765.

It was as a topographical artist that Bellotto won his fame and fortune in Mozart's time in Munich, Vienna, Dresden (as court painter to Frederick Augustus II), and later St. Petersburg and Warsaw. We have already seen an example of his draughtsmanship (*No. 1*)

47

49

(28)

and can compare his work in that field with that of his uncle Antonio Canal (see *No. 4*) under whom he studied and whose name, Canaletto, he used after he left Venice in 1742. Bellotto's heavier contrasts of light and shade and his cooler colour are apparent in this canvas of 1765, painted during his Dresden period and exhibiting a classicism almost as uncompromising as David's. Bellotto, however, lacks David's moral conviction and the ornate head of the Corinthian column is as important (if not moreso) as the central figure of Christ himself.

49. "Goethe in the Campagna." Oil painting by Johann Heinrich Wilhelm Tischbein, 1787.

Neo-Classicism in the German states was an intellectual study rather than a practical art style and is well typified in this soberly coloured work by Tischbein, who, after beginning his career as a portraitist at the Prussian court in Berlin, travelled in Italy like most of the leading artists of his time. It was his friend Goethe, with whom he journeyed and whose portrait is here set against symbols of Rome's glorious past, who persuaded Tischbein to turn to classical subjects; two years later, in 1789, he settled in Naples as director of the academy there.

50. "The Assumption of the Virgin." Oil sketch on paper by Franz Anton Maulbertsch, 1764.

The frescoes of Maulbertsch represent the peak of Austrian painting in the eighteenth century, which was markedly more colourful and lively than German art. In this respect Maulbertsch drew inspiration, like his compatriots, from Venice; it came, however, not from the static art of Bellotto (*Nos. 1 and 48*) and Canal (*No. 4*) but rather from the swifter brushwork and sense of movement of Guardi (*No. 57*), Tiepolo, and the Genoese Magnasco. Indeed, in the intensity of his feeling and his freedom of execution there is a foretaste of Romanticism which confirms the fact that the bridge between the Rococo and Romanticism in central Europe was shorter than elsewhere. The illustration here was a preparatory painting for a fresco in the Pfarrkirche (parish church) of Schwechat, near Vienna, which was destroyed during the Second World War.

51. "The Morning Walk." Oil painting by Thomas Gainsborough, 1785.

There were many rebels in eighteenth-century English art and Gainsborough was one of them in a peculiarly conservative way. Although he was a founder-member of the Royal Academy in 1768 he scorned academism in general and the Italian influence in particular. Till his death in 1788 he continued to paint in the French Rococo style with a lightness of

touch that occasionally recalls Fragonard (*No. 46*). Although Gainsborough had to paint portraits for economic reasons, his heart really lay in landscape painting and he combined the two when he could. This may be the case with "The Morning Walk," but if so the subjects' names are unknown; Gainsborough's disdain of portraiture was reflected in his carelessly kept records of sitters. Music was one of Gainsborough's greatest passions and although he had not yet moved to London when Mozart was there as a boy, he must have heard later much about the young composer from the Linleys, who were his close friends.

52. "The Picnic." Oil painting, 1788, by Francisco de Goya y Lucientes.

Although certainly the greatest individualist of all the painters represented here, Goya like most of the others, travelled to Italy in his younger years and his religious art particularly reveals Venetian influences. He was, however, the master of many styles and subjects. "The Picnic" was part of the collection of the Duke of Osuna with whom Goya became friendly in 1785 and who commissioned a series of decorative genre scenes similar to the cartoons Goya painted for the Royal Tapestry Factory between 1775 and 1792, representing his nearest approach to the Rococo art of Fragonard, to which he was indifferent. In 1792 an illness which brought temporary paralysis and permanent deafness wrought a radical change. As with Beethoven aural isolation brought to the surface an emotional intensity which exploded conventions of subject, form, and technique. When Goya finally settled in France, where he remained till his death in 1828, the impact of his genius shaped the French art of a new age in the Romanticism of Delacroix and was felt far beyond in the work of Manet and even in schools of the twentieth century.

51

VII

Withdrawal to opera

"The Impresario"
Preparation of "Figaro"
Lorenzo da Ponte
"Figaro" Produced
"Don Giovanni"

52. *"The Count discovers the Page." Detail of an illustration from the first Paris edition of Beaumarchais's comedy "Le Mariage de Figaro," engraved by Jean-Baptiste Liénard after Jacques Philippe Joseph de Saint-Quentin, 1785.*

Until the end of 1786 Mozart remained the cynosure of Vienna's concert-goers in spite of the counter-attraction of concerts at the Augarten which marked the summit of popularity enjoyed by Dittersdorf. If there was any rivalry it did Mozart no serious harm, for Dittersdorf always sincerely sang Mozart's praises. We have already quoted from his autobiography his answers to the emperor's questions during the contest with Clementi. From the same source we also hear that the emperor thought Mozart's operas inclined to "overwhelm the singers by their full accompaniments" – no doubt a valid criticism with weak singers, for conductors know to be careful even with fine singers when Mozart is enjoying his delicious little decorations with wind instruments. More significant, however, was the emperor's comparison between Mozart and Haydn; the former was likened to Klopstock, "whose poems must be read more than once," and the latter to Gellert, who "revealed all his beauties at a first glance." No doubt love of epigram made too summary a generalisation, but there was some sense in the observation. Dittersdorf added his own explanation to his report of the emperor's remarks:

> He [Mozart] is undoubtedly one of the greatest of original geniuses, and I have never known any other composer to possess such an amazing wealth of ideas.

53. Karl Ditters von Dittersdorf. Engraving by Hieronymus Löschenkohl.

I wish he were not so spendthrift with them. He does not give the listener time to catch his breath, for no sooner is one inclined to reflect upon a beautiful inspiration than another appears, even more splendid, which drives away the first, and this continues on and on, so that in the end one is unable to retain any of these beauties in the memory. – *A. D. Coleridge's translation.*

One fact that suggests Dittersdorf's accuracy of statement, even if we disagree with his judgments, is his reporting the production of some of his own works as failures when contemporaries called them successes. He is most famous for the symphonies illustrating scenes in Ovid's "Metamorphoses" which Vienna sampled during that season of 1786.

Elsewhere, in dealing with Mozart the man, we took some pains to emphasise that after 1786 Vienna did not suddenly turn against him as is commonly supposed: it was he who withdrew. And after his first brief withdrawal it was as a dramatic composer that he was to win public acclaim. He had always loved opera more than any other engagement of his art and not even Mozart could have composed four great operas, two minor ones, the last four symphonies, the chamber works, as well as arrangements for Baron van Swieten, and at the same time have kept himself before the concert public.

The first withdrawal was for the composition of "The Marriage of Figaro," but before the first performance of that opera and while still working on it, Mozart received a commission from the emperor for another work for the stage, to be performed in February 1786 at Schönbrunn. After a banquet there the guests were to sample the rival types of opera in miniature, a German *Singspiel* and an Italian *opera buffa*. Mozart was to provide the music for the former, Stephanie's "Der Schauspieldirektor," usually called in English "The Impresario." The *opera buffa* was Salieri's "Prima la musica e poi le parole" (First the Music and Then the Words) to a text by Casti.

The title character of Mozart's work deals with rival termagants, Mademoiselle Silberklang and Madame Herz, each regarding herself as *prima donna*. Non-singing characters add to a long-winded and heavy-handed satire on theatrical conditions. One of the ladies declares herself the mistress of a rich banker who will see that she gets her way or the impresario will be ruined. After Mozart's brilliant overture, still a concert favourite, the arias and concerted numbers are spaced out between far too much talking, right up to the musically delicious trio in which the principals hymn the moral that all will go well if we give and take and co-operate.

It is a pity we do not often hear this little work to Eric Blom's text or to any other neat compression of Stephanie's story. Unfortunately theatres do not favour operas which do not last an evening (except the paired "Cav. and Pag.") and "The Impresario" needs good players and singers, although it is not exceptionally difficult. It seems an excellent choice for production by university or conservatory students.

Preparation of "Figaro"

Although the scales were heavily tipped in Salieri's favour at Schönbrunn, "The Impresario" did Mozart no harm. The knowledge that the emperor had commissioned it impressed Vienna and provided advance publicity for "Figaro" which, however, had the best of all publicity – the knowledge that the play by Beaumarchais from which the story was taken had caused a scandal in France and Austria.

We know that Mozart read "hundreds of plays" in his long search for a libretto, including one – "Lo sposo deluso" (The Deceived Husband) – by Lorenzo da Ponte, the very man with whom he later collaborated so wonderfully. He began a setting of it but finished only the overture and the arias collected under K.430. He also began

setting "L'Oca del Cairo" (The Goose of Cairo), a text by Varesco, his old collaborator, whom he had approached during his visit to Salzburg in 1783, and in K.422 we have most of the music for the first act. But in February 1784 he laid that aside. What did he want and find so much difficulty in getting? We cannot tell entirely from his letters, from which we hear only such remarks as "An *opera buffa* must of all things be funny." To which we could say: "Plenty of people would have found 'The Goose of Cairo,' inhabited by an actor, quite comic."

We have to bear in mind the subtle changes in verbal expression and atmosphere that make a play sound contemporary, for Mozart was sensitive to them. Previously Italian comedies derived much of their fun and satire from caricature, by presenting comically rigid, stock types of personality such as were familiar in the street productions called the *commedia dell'arte*. We meet only a few of them in "Figaro," for instance the peppery Dr.

54. Pierre Augustin Caron de Beaumarchais. Engraving by Augustin de Saint-Aubin after a painting by Charles Nicolas Cochin, 1773.

Bartolo with his long words and professional jargon. The not-so-young woman he has to marry, Marcellina, is another type – the middle-aged widow or spinster desperate for a husband. (She, too, evidently has pretensions, for Susanna calls her "Sibylla decrepita" and "Dottoressa arrogante.") But most of the persons both in "Figaro" and "Don Giovanni," even if their parts can be traced to the *commedia dell'arte*, are warm, passionate, human, "real" characters, not just caricatures. Only the tone-deaf or utterly unmusical can fail to see that music serving humour and verbal wit, however ebullient and efficient, cannot equal music that can serve the comedy yet at any moment glow with human emotions. It then fulfils the very nature and purpose of music.

Einstein makes us suppose that Mozart unconsciously knew what he was after some time before he found "Figaro." He compares two early comic operas, "La finta semplice" of 1768 and "La finta giardiniera" of 1775. The list of characters in the later one is divided into "serious parts" and "comic parts," and Einstein connects this with the fact that the work was popular for many years in a German translation. A similar comparison can be made between English Restoration comedy and the popular plays of Sheridan, whom some critics disparage for such features as Lady Teazle's "serious" declaration of married love at the end of "The School for Scandal." Let us notice that no musician in his senses would set the coldly brilliant wit of Snake and Lady Sneerwell to any music that aspired to do more than let the words be heard while it crackled in the background; but at such points as the one just mentioned, music could "take the stage" so to speak. When Mozart told his father he wanted a really comic libretto there was no need to tell him that he wanted one which gave music the opportunity to express human feelings in its own right, not just let most of the words pass in recitative. We do not know when he first read Beaumarchais nor when it first occurred to him that one of the "Figaro" comedies might be the basis of an ideal libretto. (There are three "Figaro" plays, but the third, "La mère coupable," was not written until 1792, after Mozart's death.) The thought must have been spurred, if it had not crossed his mind before, when he saw Paisiello's "Il barbiere di Siviglia," which came to Vienna in 1783. It was originally composed for St. Petersburg where the empress Catherine kept the composer on a huge salary. Although the wit of Beaumarchais was ruined by Paisiello's feeble Italian librettist, the opera proved enormously popular in most European capitals within a few years.

Though "Le barbier de Séville" shows Almaviva courting his Rosina, and "Le mariage de Figaro" shows him on his estate some years after marriage, the second play is not at all an artistic sequel to the first. "Le barbier" was first seen in Paris in 1775; "Figaro" came nine years later when France was only five years from the Revolution. It is far less a comedy of manners or a comedy of stock characters using the devices of farce. Most of the characters in "Figaro" are so real that the

55. Giovanni Paisiello. Engraving by Vincent Alloja after a painting by Elisabeth Vigée-Lebrun.

censorship is thoroughly understandable. Despite modern insistence *ad nauseam* upon the social and political overtones of the Mozart–Da Ponte opera, they affected its advertisement, not its musical vitality. Sociological, political, or religious beliefs may lead a composer to words and a state of inspiration, but they are incapable of making their own distinctiveness explicit in music. If, as high priest of the Supreme Being, robed amid braziers on his stage mountain, Robespierre could have commanded really great music for his own apotheosis, that music could have served as well for a Te Deum at the reconsecration of Notre Dame or the coronation of another Bourbon. Elgar's five splendid ceremonial marches could have been elicited for fine effect in Red Square as well as in The Mall.

Although Mozart seems to have enjoyed seeing Almaviva outwitted by servants, Mozart the musician was greater than Mozart the thinker, and we actually find ourselves sympathising with the cruel and naughty Almaviva's longings for Susanna as we are moved by the yearning chromatics of his duet with her, "Crudel! perchè finora." Why? Because the Count is warm-blooded as we are, not just a *type* of haughty seigneur, landlord-bully, ineffective rival lover, or tailor's dummy for fine clothes. How lucky for Mozart that Paisiello had already used "Le barbier de Séville," and forced him, even if his musico-dramatic instinct did not, to choose the more human story. Mozart was also sensible to resist any temptation to invite direct competition with Paisiello, with whom he was on friendly terms, for Paisiello would not have remained friendly after a challenge. When he was an old man of more than 70 he organised a claque to "kill" the first performance of Rossini's "Almaviva," which we now know as "The Barber of Seville." (Rossini and his librettist, Sterbini, were too terrified to use the original title until the work became a triumph that ousted Paisiello's.) It was Rossini's humour and sparkle, not Sterbini's, which secured that triumph and the deserved permanence of the work in repertory, for Sterbini did little more justice to Beaumarchais than did that nonentity Petrosellini, who arranged the story for Paisiello. It was also Mozart's musical humour and sparkle which secured the triumph of "Figaro," yet it would be grossly unfair not to insist that Mozart's brilliance responded to a superb text by a man who, though seven years older, was also anxious to achieve a long-desired success in the theatre.

Lorenzo da Ponte

The life story of the flamboyant Da Ponte, who was born in the ghetto of the place now called Vittorio Veneto near the hills north of Venice, can be traced in his refreshingly shameless memoirs (available in German and English translations) and his published letters to his friend Casanova. After an affair with a prominent citizen's wife he had been banished from Venice and the Veneto for 15 years on pain of a long prison sentence, and had naturally shifted to Austrian territory. He knew better than to set up in Vienna while Maria Theresa was alive, but he visited the capital and made himself known to the poet laureate Metastasio. Not even Da Ponte's conceit ran to the hope of securing the old laureate's office after his death in 1782; what drew him to Joseph II's Vienna was the revived cult of Italian opera. By ingratiating himself with Salieri he became engaged by the imperial theatre at a regular salary, and immediately showed his talent in translation and adaptation by supplying a good Italian version of Gluck's "Iphigénie en Tauride." Mozart first mentions him in a letter of May 7, 1783:

> Our poet here is now a certain Abbate da Ponte. He is laden with work adapting plays and is bound to supply an original libretto for Salieri which will take him two months. After that he has promised one for me . . . but as you know these Italians are all very pleasant to your face . . . If he is thick with Salieri I shall get nothing out of him.

But he got "Lo sposo deluso." We have no documentary evidence of Mozart's telling Da Ponte why he would not finish that libretto if he could find something more up-to-date, but subsequent events make us certain about the trend of their discussions. They closely followed all new productions and must have been specially impressed by two of them, human comedies set to music rather than neatly turned old-fashioned *opere buffe* with "type" characters. Paisiello's "Il rè Teodoro" (King Theodore), about a German who was temporarily chosen to reign over Corsica, but ended in a Venetian prison, was to a libretto by Casti full of subversive social criticism; it was produced in August 1784. In November 1785 Vienna saw "La villanella rapita" (The Raped Peasant) set by Bianchi to a libretto by Bertati. This presents the story of a count, more like Don Giovanni than Almaviva, who drugs a village wedding party and carries off the bride; the peasants enter the castle in disguise and rescue her. If the story had been presented as a spoken play (supposing that it had got past the censors) its dialogue would have landed Bertati in prison.

Dent assures us that there were several German translations of "Le Mariage de Figaro" available by 1785, and that those who heard the opera included many who could supply what Da Ponte omitted from Beaumarchais. But he omitted nothing that matters at all for an opera. With the music, the Mozart–Da Ponte work is actually more amusing than the play in the comic parts and, of course, more moving in the emotional parts, some of which are hardly touched upon in the play. Mozart himself first suggested using the play as the basis of an opera, and we shall see when we look more closely at the Italian comedies that Mozart suggested the alterations in the arrangement of acts and scenes that made his brilliant finales effective. But Da Ponte takes the credit for missing nothing, not even a word or phrase of Beaumarchais that could serve the opera well. To him goes the credit for knowing how to omit certain characters and give others credible names, to avoid scenes of mere repartee or discussion, to simplify yet to expand into verse where rapturous lyricism was wanted. He had good reason to desire a notable success, for his "original" work for Salieri had come to a notable failure, and the angry Salieri turned to Casti.

56. Playbill for the première of "Figaro" on May 1, 1786.

Allowing for Da Ponte's entertaining boastfulness (e.g. the frequent "I told Mozart"), we have to bear in mind that there are only three great Mozart operas to Italian texts, apart from "Idomeneo," and that all three are to libretti by Da Ponte. The old rogue is not to be pitied for not becoming poet laureate. He made Europe too hot for himself and passed through Holland and London to New York, where he finished his days as a teacher of Italian – of course with his fingers in a few shady commercial pies!

"Figaro" Produced

There were many obstacles of malicious origin in the production of "Figaro." Da Ponte, for instance, relates that the Intendant of Theatres, Count Rosenberg, said that the emperor had forbidden use of the ballet, asked to see the libretto that Da Ponte was holding, tore out two of the sheets and put them on the fire, saying: "You see, Signor Poeta, that I can do anything!" Mozart was desperate but "I begged him to allow me just two days' time, and to leave everything to me." Fortunately the emperor himself attended the dress rehearsal. In the adapted dance scene he saw only the Count and Susanna gesticulating. "There being no music, it looked like a puppet show," and the emperor said to Casti, who was sitting behind him, "What's all this?" Da Ponte handed the emperor the manuscript in which he had cunningly restored the scene. When asked why the dancers had not appeared, Da Ponte's silence "gave him to understand there was intrigue," and the emperor turned to Rosenberg and told him to let Da Ponte have as many dancers as he needed. They were collected in "less than half an hour," and "this new manifestation of royal kindness redoubled the hatred of my powerful persecutor."

Michael Kelly's "Reminiscences," printed in 1826, are worth quoting at length:

> There were three operas now on the tapis, one by Regini [Righini], another by Salieri ["The Grotto of Trophonius"], and one by Mozart by special command of the emperor . . . These three pieces were ready for representation at the same time, and each composer claimed the right of producing his opera first. The contest raised much discord, and parties were formed . . . Mozart was as touchy as gunpowder, and swore he would put the score of his opera into the fire if it was not produced first; his claim was backed by a strong party; on the contrary, Regini was working like a mole in the dark to get precedence.
>
> The third candidate, *maestro di cappella* to the court, a clever, shrewd man, possessed what Bacon called crooked wisdom, and his claims were backed by three of the principal performers, who formed a cabal not easily put down . . . I alone was a stickler for Mozart, and naturally enough, for he had a claim on my warmest wishes, from my admiration

57. *Michael Kelly. Mezzotint by Charles Turner after a painting by James Lonsdale.*

of his powerful genius, and the debt of gratitude I owed him for many personal favours.

> The mighty contest was put an end to by His Majesty issuing a mandate for Mozart's "Nozze di Figaro" to be instantly put into rehearsal; and none more than Michael O'Kelly enjoyed the little great man's triumph over his rivals . . .
>
> All the original performers had the advantage of the instruction of the composer, who transfused into their minds his inspired meaning. I shall never forget his little animated countenance when lighted up with the glowing rays of genius; it is as impossible to describe as it would be to paint sunbeams.
>
> I called on him one evening. He said to me: "I have just finished a little duet for my opera; you shall hear it." He sat down to the piano. I was delighted with it, and the musical world will give me credit for being so when I mention the duet, sung by Count Almaviva and Susan, "Crudel! perchè finora farmi languir così?" A more delicious *morceau* was never penned by man, and it has often been a source of pleasure to me to have been the first who heard it . . . At the first rehearsal of the full band Mozart was on the stage with his crimson pelisse and gold-laced cocked hat, giving the time to the orchestra. Figaro's song, "Non più andrai, farfallone amoroso,"

Benucci gave with the greatest animation and power of voice.

I was standing close to Mozart who, *sotto voce*, was repeating "Bravo, Bravo Benucci!"; and when Benucci came to the fine passage "Cherubino, alla vittoria, alla gloria militar," which he gave out with stentorian lungs, the effect was electricity itself, for the whole of the performers on the stage and in the orchestra, as if actuated by one feeling of delight, vociferated "Bravo, Bravo Maestro! Viva, viva grande Mozart!" Those in the orchestra I thought would never have ceased applauding by beating the bows of their violins against the music desks.

The work proved just as popular with the public and when it was performed for the first time on May 1, 1786 it took nearly twice the expected time because of repeats. Immediately after the nine Vienna performances which ran into December, rehearsals began for a production in Prague. The triumphant first night was on January 17, 1787, and when Mozart returned home in February it was with a commission for another opera for production there in the autumn.

"*Don Giovanni*"

Mozart went immediately to Da Ponte, who was himself under pressure to produce two libretti for other composers. In his memoirs he makes the assertion that the idea of using the Don Juan story was originally his and it seems safe to accept it. We need not review here the many dramatic versions of the story preceding his. Mozart certainly knew Gluck's "Don Juan" ballet – for, as we have already pointed out, the eerie, rising wood-wind scales associated with the statue and first heard in the overture are derived from it. Goldoni's "Don Giovanni Tenorio" of 1736 must also have been amongst the plays perused, but Da Ponte needed more modern writing to engage his talent for adaptation and/or translation. Audaciously he used a libretto by his rival Bertati, "Il convitato di pietra" (The Stone Guest), written for that year's Venice carnival and set by Giuseppe Gazzaniga. His adaptation was brilliant, but he needed a source even for his improvements and that source was almost certainly Goldoni's play.

"Don Giovanni" is full of producer's problems because Mozart added and altered for later performances; but few people are willing to cut fine music just to make the work unfold consistently as a drama. Whatever its defects Da Ponte responded to the two outstanding achievements of "Figaro," namely the delineation and contrast of characters by music, not merely the suiting of music to "given" types, and the cumulation of interest in huge act-finales, which might have many movements, last longer than symphonies, begin with few voices but at the end employ all or most of the cast in an imbroglio or denouement. Thus whereas other dramatists made no

use of Donna Anna after she had bewailed her father's murder, Da Ponte gave her a leading part so that Mozart could present musically the contrast between three female personalities – Anna, Elvira, and Zerlina. He knew he had nothing to fear by offering Mozart so much stage business in each of the two great act-finales. Mozart had done wonders, would do wonders, and did. He would be stimulated by any challenge that made for "good stage" unless it impeded or held at "neutral" the forward thrust of music. If he met what thwarted musical expression he was capable of cutting it out or of telling Da Ponte to supply something else, giving clear indications of his own ideas.

An ability to excel in beauty while surmounting complexity is one of the distinctions between Mozart and his contemporaries, indeed between Mozart and Beethoven or later composers. Even in a post-Wagner style, with more fluid forms than those of the eighteenth century, could any composer – even Verdi, even Ravel (to mention two who could be dramatically ingenious) – have better advanced the action from the opening of "Don Giovanni," the overture leading into Leporello's "Nott'e giorno faticar," thence to the seduction, alarm, murder, and complex of emotions, including Anna's horror and fainting, her turning to vengeance, Ottavio's attempt to comfort, and the passionate outburst of the lovers? To look at the score is to see only the conventions, sections of recitative, *arioso*, aria, duet, and the complex called *scena*. To hear it is to be aware of an unbroken unifying excitement to which the orchestra, even with quiet solo instruments, contributes considerably; yet the secret is not revealed by analysis, not explained by talk of motive development, for perhaps the most remarkable feature of this wonderful section of drama-in-music is the amount of sheer beautiful melody.

It must be insisted that Mozart could not have produced even that section, any more than he could have produced his treatment of the infamous supper and the arrival of the statue to pronounce the Don's destruction, unless Da Ponte had known what to supply. Though it is amusing to quote, little credence need be given to the old rogue's account of his work. His memoirs frequently boast about his (no doubt uneasy) favour with the emperor, and it is certainly true that Joseph liked the ridiculous comparisons between poets and musicians (for Dittersdorf also mentioned them).

Martín, Mozart, and Salieri came all three at once, to request a play ... Having found three subjects I went to the emperor, explained what was on my mind, and informed him of my intention to work on these three operas at the same time. "You will not be successful!" he responded. "Perhaps not," I replied. "But I shall try. I shall write at night for Mozart and count that as reading Dante's 'Inferno'. I shall write in the morning for Martín, the equivalent of studying Petrarch. The evening will be for Salieri and that will be my Tasso." He found my simile very good. As soon as I returned

58. *Caterina Bondini (Zerlina) and Caterina Micelli (Donna Elvira), two of the singers in the first performance of "Don Giovanni." Anonymous silhouettes.*

home, I settled down to write. I went to the desk and stayed there continuously for 12 hours – a little bottle of Tokay to the right, the inkpot in the middle, and a box of tobacco from Seville to the left. A pretty 16-year-old girl (whom I had wished to love only as a daughter, but . . .) stayed in my house with her mother, who took care of the home, and came into my room at the sound of a hand-bell which, to be truthful, I rang a great deal, and especially when it seemed to me that the inspiration was beginning to cool down: she fetched me now a biscuit, now a cup of coffee, now nothing but her own pretty face, always gay, always smiling, and perfectly fashioned to arouse poetic inspiration and the witty idea.

The rehearsals for "Don Giovanni" were difficult for the work needs patient stage management. Despite ingenious situations, most of "Figaro" can be sung standing upright and upstage, straight at the audience, whereas "Don Giovanni" calls for good acting as well as fine singing in difficult ensembles that allow little improvisation of movement. Positions, gestures, inflexions of voice must all be learnt thoroughly yet seem to be swift and spontaneous. Moreover the music itself was then full of surprises. Mozart worked hard, commending and thanking whenever he could. We can well believe the story that Caterina Bondini, playing Zerlina, was not easily persuaded to emit a loud enough shriek behind the scenes. Mozart is said to have crept behind her and suddenly gripped her, so that involuntarily she produced what was wanted. Evidently the last music added was that of the favourite airs from contemporary operas, played by the wind waits during the Don's supper, for the original text does not contain the words used by Leporello and his master during the "bel concerto."

According to Mozart, the first performance on October 29, 1787 "was received with immense applause." But when the work was performed in Vienna on May 7, 1788 – with a cast so brilliant that they demanded extra arias and alterations of the work (listed by Einstein as K. 540a–c) – the reception was tepid. The work did, however, have 15 performances, one of which was attended by the emperor.

VIII
Mozart as dramatist

Action and Pace
Musical Wit
Delineation of Characters
Solo Items

59. Illustration from the title page of the first edition of "Don Giovanni," published by Breitkopf and Härtel, Leipzig, 1801. Engraving by P. Bolt after a drawing by Vincenz Georg Kinninger.

Action and Pace

In the strict sense of the word neither Mozart nor Da Ponte was a dramatist, and we should merely waste time by arguing the likelihood of either having the successful playwright's full ability if he had been forced to earn his livelihood in producing plays. We know only that they loved the theatre and were astute judges of plays. Mozart was a rarer creature than a great dramatist for he could maintain the pace, progress, and expression of drama in fine music. When he did not do so, either he failed to do so, or he decided to let fine music "get past" dramatically weak spots. Why? Either because he had to meet a date of production or the demands of singers, or because he wanted a particular mood and type of music. A notable instance is just after the opening of the second act of

"Don Giovanni." We have had the brilliant finale during which forces are combined to seek out and bring the wicked man to justice. A series of items so beautiful that nobody in his senses will forgo them (including the Don's serenade and Elvira's "In quali eccessi" and "Mi tradì") merely delay the dreadful denouement of the story. If Mozart and Da Ponte had been given time to spend on a perfect drama-in-music, they might well have decided to open the second act with the cemetery scene, and invented (or taken from Goldoni) scenes which at least kept the tension of the drama.

What *could* be done by these unrivalled technicians of drama-in-music is shown in other parts of "Don Giovanni" and in most of "Figaro." The latter serves best to illustrate their ability to let the events move at a swift pace, not just by recitative with stage action, but by and in music which gives the aural impression of fulfilling its own processes as attractively as in a symphony. Someone

60. Title page from the piano score (by August Eberhard Müller) of Mozart's "Don Giovanni," published by S. A. Steiner of Vienna, 1810.

may say: "Not half their ability was needed to make a good evening's entertainment from Beaumarchais's rollicking comedy! Just think of the brilliant second act, which piles situation upon situation at increasing tension – begins with one actor, adds another and another until the whole cast is engaged in a noisy imbroglio, and needs only Mozart's horns to 'Tally ho!' as the curtain falls." But that is *not* Beaumarchais's second act at all. His play does not provide that unbroken *crescendo* but lets the second act finish with a scene in which only the Countess and Suzanne are on stage. Even more to be admired than this Mozart–Da Ponte second act is the tragic stretch near the opening of "Don Giovanni," together with the act-finales in that opera, because these impressive sections have to carry extremely complex stage action and unify music in which extremely differing emotions must be heard as nearly simultaneously as possible.

The difference between the dramatist and the master of drama-in-music is illustrated by the most popular item in Mozart's operas – Figaro's "Non più andrai." Cherubino has been ordered to join his regiment. "No longer you amorous little butterfly, no longer you young Narcissus can you go running around after the ladies. No longer the fandango but the march, with a concert of trumpets, drums, and guns." If he doesn't get killed first, perhaps Master Cherubino will come home after a victory covered in military glory. To the mock magnificence of a pantomime march, a *pompa* round the servants' quarters, down comes the curtain on the first act; but in the play the only suggestion of an *aria militare* comes from a few words muttered to Chérubin when the Count sends him packing. They occur neither at the end of the act nor in its last scene, which is a battle of wits between Figaro and Basile from which neither Mozart nor anyone else could have drawn great music.

Could Mozart's genius have shone without Da Ponte's? Dramatic imagination, by which one can see and hear the effect of a passage before it is staged, has never been utterly reliable in great composers. It can be stronger in a Puccini or a Menotti than in a Beethoven. It quite eluded poor Schubert, who tried time after time to succeed in opera. Mozart possessed it as strongly as any great composer, and therefore knew where the words of a libretto halted the action. When he could have wished there were no halt but had to meet a production date, his greatness as a musician hid the weakness, for he simply cast the spell of great music, as we have noticed in the delayed ending of "Don Giovanni." Such passages are not always undramatic entirely, for in the "static" arias and *ariosi* Mozart could show facets of characters. It is not accidental that Mozart's finest score and most ravishing melody is in a Da Ponte opera which we have not yet discussed, and which requires little discussion, for its appeal is almost entirely musical. As a play "Così fan tutte" would be the lightest of entertainment, a most contrived and artificial comedy with few characters all neatly opposed and paired. Mozart's warm and tender music prevents their being puppets, though the range of

their emotions merely circulates around the weathercock of flirtation and true love. It would be ridiculous to disparage the opera which many musicians love more than any by Mozart by comparing it with such a different conception as "Don Giovanni." Of course Da Ponte provided Mozart with material for brilliant act-finales and for the witty suiting of music to comic business on the stage, but they are not solutions to the problem of pace. They are Mozartian luxuries.

Here, almost with apologies, it seems necessary to intone platitude. We can talk ourselves silly about "drama," but no "dramatic" faults have yet kept from the musical public a work wherein human experience and feeling is touched by the music itself. Otherwise "Fidelio" would be a museum piece and Giordano's "Andrea Chénier" a repertory favourite. Attempts to blame a libretto, or the inability to find the right libretto, for a composer's failure are persistent but unconvincing. The platitude is that opera is a musical genre and that people, whether they acknowledge the fact or not, keep an opera, an operetta, or a mere film "musical" among the evergreens only if the music casts its spell. The finest "drama" will not save it from ultimate oblivion. (This is not to deny the constant discovery of works which did not deserve past neglect.) On the other hand not even a tissue of inconsequential and naïve dialogues, allied to a plot in which villain turns hero and heroine into malevolent schemer (for so has "The Magic Flute" been described) can prevent generation after generation from hailing as great the opera in which its absurdities are not even recognised, for they are but pegs on which to hang music that ranges from the deliciously ebullient to the passionate and tender and even the solemn and profound. How futile, from Goethe's time to ours, is the desire to replace Schikaneder's naïve pantomime by something more dignified and literary! Equally futile are attempts to find profound meanings in the descriptions of Mozart's operas on their title pages. We have already seen the historical significance of a change from *opera buffa* to *commedia in musica*, but it was used for hundreds of other operas than "Figaro," as was *dramma giocoso* for other operas than "Don Giovanni," however grimly satirical it sounds as applied to that work.

Like Wagner, Mozart knew that fine music needs *time* to fulfil the form which is also its expression. How could he combine dramatic pace with an apparently unshorn musical growth of the highest order known in his day? Is the speed illusory? Yes, very often. Is the growth of the music illusory? Again, yes, very often. Consider what immediately follows the overture in "Figaro." That overture has suggested unprecedented comic speed for the events of "La folle journée" (Beaumarchais's sub-title) and Mozart will not negate its effect with an opening aria. The orchestra continues with a conspiratorial tune and a witty bass, which Figaro, groping on the floor with a measuring stick to see how the furniture will fit into the bedroom, punctuates at intervals with "Five," "Ten," "Twenty," etc. Susanna, sitting at a mirror and trying on

61. *Francesco Benucci, the first Figaro. Silhouette by Hieronymus Löschenkohl.*

her wedding hat, has longer phrases joining the second group of the orchestral sonata form – "Don't you like it, Figaro?" etc. The first illusion is that the singers carry the piece forward, but in fact their contributions are largely exclamatory; it is the orchestra which holds the thread. The second illusion is that the music grows into a perfect little "first movement."

Schoenberg exposes the means of illusion in "Brahms the Progressive," a chapter in his collected lectures, "Style and Idea." He thinks Brahms learnt from Mozart how to use asymmetrical phrases, but still more how to juggle with small ideas. He points out that Mozart's little ideas spring straight from the action, but what happens when the action changes? A mass of little ideas can go in varying order during developments and recapitulations that occur after a change of stage situation, whereas a long, arresting idea is sensible only if the drama recalls what it first signified. Now the point to which that scene in "Figaro" takes us is not connected with the measuring or the hat, but with Susanna's suspicion of the Count's designs upon her. She grows forceful in recitative when she says Figaro is wasting his time, for she does not intend to accept the offer of a room so near the Count's. Then, as she begins to dominate the movement our ears are fully deceived. The modulations and rhythms make us imagine that the symphonic movement is being com-

pleted to the usual design; but if we follow Schoenberg and examine the music we see that it has no conventional reprise. Figaro's little motives do not recur in the second half, whereas Susanna's are extended and developed. If Mozart had used more imposing ideas they would have become incongruous as the dramatic situation advanced. His "small change" does not produce a contemptible movement because it is full of wit, which, as we shall now try to prove, is a quality not to be confused with humour.

Musical Wit

Wit comes from the materials of an art, not only from the response to humour outside it. In words wit comes from a knowledge of double meanings, homophones, metaphors, etc. Because it so often makes some allusion or association it is understandable that in music wit needs the same resources as variation, and may indeed inhere in nothing more than a variation or distortion. Normally it depends upon more than one of the facets of music – rhythm, harmony, instrumental colour, modulation, counterpoint, dynamics, etc., whereas simple humour can be served by a sudden loud or soft, an unexpected change of pitch or key, a discord, or merely the gurgling of a bassoon or the high squeak of a violin or piccolo. Fortunately Mozart did not scorn simple humour, which we can compare with wit in the same piece.

Amusing indeed is Susanna's suddenly entering the room at Aguas Frescas and finding herself alone with Marcellina, who eyes her as if to say: "So that's the baggage he thinks he's going to marry!" In return Susanna boldly stares back at the not-so-young madame who claims that Figaro promised marriage to her. Beaumarchais makes this meeting an openly hostile confrontation. Surely it was Mozart who let Da Ponte know that his music could add to the wit and humour of the situation by almost overplaying the courtesies and compliments each woman sarcastically pays the other. Nobody can mistake the opening orchestral music for this duet as suggesting several mutual curtseys; we almost see the spread of the arms, the swoop of the skirt, the inclination and proud upward toss of the head to its highest point of recovery. Why the music has this effect, even before either of the ladies has curtseyed to the other, one can hardly say. Rhythm, harmony, melodic shape, the very bow marks of the violins – all contribute to a piece of rare musical wit. But when Susanna's mock flattery pretends to defer to Marcellina's superior "gravity and experience" (meaning age!) Marcellina's dignity is ruffled for a moment. For just that moment she cannot contain her anger, though she quickly collects herself; for just that moment, and for just one chord (thrice rapidly sounded in an unexpected triplet) the strings suddenly play *forte*. Wit or humour? One is inclined to say "Humour" while being thankful for it, for the musical means are quite simple – a sudden loud in a soft context, a naïve form of humour used by plenty of other composers, including Haydn and Beethoven.

Difficult though it is to isolate wit from humour entirely, we can specify the combination in several places where wit is predominant. The best known is probably Leporello's infamous catalogue aria. To Elvira, who is outraged at being loved and left, Leporello says words to this effect: "Oh milady, you are not the first by any means. Have a look at this list of my master's conquests to date!" – and he proceeds to read from a notebook. "In Italy 640; in Germany 231; 100 in France, 91 in Turkey, but here in Spain already 1003!!!" Sullivan and others learnt from Mozart how to keep accompaniments extremely simple and quiet by repeated chords when comic words were to be clearly heard. Between sentences, however, delicious little phrases cover the joins. One of these clearly suggests the flicking over of the pages to the next entry; more witty, however, and unthinkable from any

other composer, is a point of instrumentation. Not until Leporello repeats the list, and with it makes the musical reprise, do we hear the double-basses. Instead of the "flicks" whizzing upwards we now hear, after each number of victims, a zooming upward of the double-basses from their lowest note, E, as if they say "Ooogh! How monstrous!" (Wit, along with musical variation at a repeat.) By radio or in the concert room the second part of this aria, a slow minuet, rather hangs fire. Here Leporello tells how the Don woos different types of lady – the grand and tall, the petite and saucy, the big-built dame, etc. The humour here is evidently meant to parallel the gestures of the actor, and needs them.

One who explains wit may seem like another of those who "murder to dissect," yet the excuse must be that we are examining the musical means and not explaining jokes. Moreover musical wit need not go with something amusing. It is at work in pathetic and even terrifying

62. Title page from the piano score (by Christian Gottlob Neefe) of "The Marriage of Figaro," published by Simrock, Bonn, 1796.

63. *Autograph manuscript of the opening of the serenade in Act II of "Don Giovanni."*

situations, but more easily observed when allied with humour. Mozart's own favourite number in "Figaro" illustrates the extreme subtlety of his wit. There is nothing spritely or quirky about it, and it is allied to no buffoonery on the stage. If sung "dead pan" the piece as a whole grows more and more what it is intended to be – malicious under external sweetness. It is the sextet in the third act. Having admitted that they are Figaro's parents, Bartolo and Marcellina are now friends of the young people in the plot to outwit the Count. The music creams along in an almost smug hymn of reconciliation and parental affection, the musical equivalent of an enfolding to a capacious bosom. As the Count smothers more and more anger it goes over the offensive truth with an old gossip's persistence, as if it will not end – "And this is his mother, as I said before"; "His mother! Ah, fancy that, his mother." "Did you say his Mother?" "Yes, actually his Mother" (more embracing). "And this is his father..." etc., etc. Let us be snobbish for a moment. Here is such high wit that one almost resents the intrusion of an incident of plain, popular humour. Before Susanna hears of this discovery of Figaro's parents, she enters during the reconciliation and, seeing Figaro embracing Marcellina, promptly gives him a slap on the face in the middle of the sweet croonings.

There is a parallel in "Don Giovanni" to this whole piece of wit (instead of a piece with only incidental wit). Mozart has the good taste to make it short, for it reaches the point of cruelty. The passionate Elvira, entering just as the Don has been exercising his blandishments upon the little country girl, Zerlina, declares that she will "save this innocent from the barbarous snare." She sings the swift aria "Ah, fuggi il traditor" – "Escape from the traitor." For this moral lecture Mozart deliberately uses what his audience recognised as the old-fashioned musical style of Lent cantatas and oratorios – a style which he mastered while arranging Bach and Handel for Van Swieten's concerts. Parody it is, but not to be classed with weak imitations served to the musically naïve as "in the style of Handel," most of which disgust musicians of competence by their lack of Handelian idiom under the feeble aping of a few mannerisms.

Possibly the most accomplished displays of wit allied to humour are two in "Figaro." One is a sly piece of invertible counterpoint during that series of ensembles that builds up the tremendous finale to Act II. The Count is questioning Figaro about the anonymous letter, and this little piece of counterpoint comes as a "cadential" while Figaro is trying to gain time. In Dent's nimble translation the words are: "In your face I read the truth, sir; I can see you've told a lie." "Then my face, sir, is the liar." Once more a smouldering situation is covered by a hymn-like part-song:

> Per finirla lietamente,
> E all'usanza teatrale,
> Un'azion matrimoniale
> Le faremo ora seguir.

"To conclude the dispute according to dramatic custom, a wedding scene should now follow." While the characters chant their ecclesiastical strains the Count mutters: "Marcellina, Marcellina! Where is that woman with the documents and lawyer?" The other brilliant instance of wit-from-musical-form is in "Cosa sento," an ensemble that could be played as a symphonic or serenade first movement, with woodwinds taking the parts of the voices. The Count is questioning Susanna while Cherubino is hiding behind the chair. Hearing Basilio coming, the Count himself hides behind the chair, so as not to be caught alone with Susanna, while Cherubino creeps into the chair and has a cloth thrown over him. Basilio's "You know what they are all saying" is too much for the Count's curiosity. He reveals himself, demands to hear what Basilio has in mind, and is fobbed off with "Only an innocent little scandal about the page Cherubino, who is still only young, poor boy." "Young? Poor? I'll stand no more of him . . . Why, only the other day in Barbarina's room, I had my suspicions and lifted up the cloth from the table . . ." – and to illustrate his story the Count lifts the cloth from the chair, revealing Cherubino again.

At this point the ensemble has developed a "sonata form" to its middle section. Its "principal subject," with which it opened, is a terse one in the rhythm of the words "Go . . . and find him!" ($\textit{♩. ♪|♩♩}$) – three descending notes, the last one repeated. As the Count tells his story, repetitions of this musical idea go farther and farther down in pitch, easing the tension as all join the Count in amusement. Very quietly the theme is then inverted and begins *ascending* as the Count lifts the cloth, thus gathering tension to the climax, at which it goes on rising to each of three exclamations:

> Count: Ah, cosa veggio?
> Susanna: Ah, crude stelle!
> Basilio: Ah, meglio ancora!

(Very freely translated: "Ah, what's this?" "Oh, dreadful fate!" "Oh, better than ever!") Dent's version brings the climax with malicious Basilio's high tenor squeaking "Ah, how delightful!" The dramatic tableau is like that in "The School for Scandal" when the screen is drawn aside in Joseph Surface's room:

> Charles Surface: "Lady Teazle, by all that's wonderful."
> Sir Peter Teazle: "Lady Teazle, by all that's damnable!"

Yet sheer musical wit makes the scene in "Figaro" even more effective.

Wit is found often in the incidental painting of single words, which poses problems for translators of the libretti; but it must be emphasised that musical wit need not be allied with humorous words, and possibly Mozart's wit is at its highest in lovely pieces like the farewell ensemble in "Così fan tutte" which evokes the idea of a soft breeze blowing the sails that will take away the soldier lovers and then turn to bring them back safely.

Delineation of Characters

The technique of ensemble to gain pace played right into Mozart's hands as a means of delineating character. In a spoken play character can be made evident in dialogue rather than in soliloquy, because the latter is unnatural even amongst sleepwalkers and people who talk to themselves, whereas the former shows contrast between the reactions of different people to one another and to the same situation.

The French playwright whose list of actors is labelled "Personnages" is more accurate than the English one with his "Characters in the play," because many a fine play may have no characters in the sense we are now considering. Wilde, in his most famous comedy, did not trouble even to use likely names, but named his puppets after railway stations – Mr. Worthing, Mr. Hastings, Lady Bracknell. The comedy is of ideas and manners rather than of real people. Many a great opera takes us out of the world of real men and women into a world where the clash is of ideas or ideals. Siegfried, Wotan, Alberich, and the rest represent ideas in a latter-day morality drama that is not inferior to "The Mastersingers" with its real characters. Consequently in "The Ring" dramas Wagner does not need ensembles of argument and conversation; his supernatural beings may declaim in turn and at length in a vast vocal-orchestral symphony. Why are these characters not "real"? Why is Sarastro or Papageno or the Queen of Night not "real"? Because real characters are complex, have more than one facet to their (i.e. our) nature. Consequently the dramatist who wishes to make a character seem real must bring about the effect of a stereoscope on a photograph – we must view him or her from at least two sides. There is more than just a bullying master in the Count. He shares amusement with others in two ensembles, and in the duet with Susanna we actually feel for him in his longing for her. (We can discount his final pleading for forgiveness from his wife as being the conventional ending of such a comedy.)

We could say that the Count is shown from not much more than two angles, just enough to make him a real man and not simply the personification of feudal arrogance. No more than this is needed, for he is not the central figure of the story, as is Susanna. She is therefore on stage when the work opens, a participant in six duets and in every larger ensemble; we thus get her reaction to every situation in the story. At the opening we know she has a will of her own and will be the dominant character in the happy marriage; we then see her as the spirited schemer who can bring her mistress into the cabal against the Count; she can be pert and humorous, but is much more than the saucy maid in the old kind of *opera buffa*; she is also courageous, even when terrified for herself, Figaro, Cherubino, or the Countess, and can keep her head in a moment of danger; she can also play the coquette, but coolly and without compromising herself. Until the last act Mozart does not allow her the aria which proves her the heroine, the finest woman of the play. This simple "Deh vieni, non tardar" is utterly serious and meltingly tender. It also happens to be harder to sing well than the more florid and symphonic arias for the Countess. It is not usual for the *prima donna* to have the part of a soubrette and it is natural to make the mistake of supposing that the Countess is the main role. The withholding of the most important aria until the last act is unique, and it is characteristic of both Mozart and his Susanna that she should sing this outpouring of strong, radiant love at Figaro, whom she knows to be hiding in the garden, and to torment him because he thinks she is singing it at the Count.

So character may be revealed in solo items, though with Mozart it is not very fully revealed by them. Sometimes, however, the solo item plays the stereoscope by showing two moods, or a conflict of two emotions. The most wonderful example, justifying its place among items which impede the advance of the story in "Don Giovanni" is the recitative-cum-*arioso* "In quali eccessi." Opening with a theme expressing violent rage, the orchestra introduces Elvira's "Ye gods! what monstrous crimes! Why does not Heaven strike him?" She pauses for breath and the orchestra repeats its rage theme. She

64. *Teresa Saporiti, the first Donna Anna. Engraving by Ferdinando Fambrini, after an anonymous portrait, 1791.*

TERESA SAPORITI
Hic effigies: ubique fama

continues, still determined upon vengeance, until the orchestra again takes up the theme, but with different harmony and with a subtle cadence which shows anger melting to pathos; not surprisingly the next words are of self-pity – "Misera Elvira! Che contrasto d'affetti!" What a change of mood indeed, for the poor creature is still in love with the seducer! While she asks why her heart still flutters, why she still sighs, Mozart's music is of an order which would not be out of place in "Tristan and Isolde." Not even Wagner's chromatics ever produced such a rich evocation of heartbreak.

Mozart has been compared with Shakespeare for various reasons, one of which is his uncanny portrayal of female as well as male emotions and motives. His chief claim for comparison with Shakespeare is his creating of characters when his sources gave him only the name, sex, age, profession, and general features. In Plutarch, as in any other source Shakespeare could have used, Brutus and Cassius were two Romans amongst others who would have Caesar die rather than turn the republic into a monarchy. It was Shakespeare who made Brutus "the noblest Roman of them all," showing him, under a dramatic stereoscope, consenting to the killing with deep regret and behaving stoically on the night before Philippi. If Shakespeare had so chosen, Cassius would have been the nobler of the two protagonists. The Brutus we know

65. Luigi Bassi, the first Don Giovanni, depicted singing the Act II serenade (see No. 63). Engraving by Medardus Thoenert.

was made by Shakespeare. Thanks to Da Ponte this full creation of a character purely by imagination was not often forced upon Mozart. Yet it must be emphasised that another great composer, for instance Beethoven, provided with the same text by Da Ponte, could not have presented us with those highly individual and real personalities. It is customary to pay tribute to Mozart's special gift by pointing out that there are three women in "Don Giovanni" – the aristocratic Anna, the passionate Elvira, and the peasant Zerlina – that all are sopranos, yet that we cannot mistake the music of one for the music of another; nor, if we hear "Figaro" by radio and do not understand Italian, can we be uncertain whether the Countess, Susanna, Cherubino, or Barbarina is singing. The character is established by music.

Characters were clearly established in Mozart's mind before he made their music but had determined their voices. Most composers make their heroes tenors. Mozart never made a "real" man either tenor or bass. Why? Because the usual "real" man does not sing very high or very low notes, but is some kind of baritone. So Figaro, the Count, and Don Giovanni are baritones. When we hear the pretty ornamental tenor arias of Don Ottavio, Anna's virtuous suitor, and then Don Giovanni's manly baritone in "Là ci darem" or the famous serenade, we quite understand why the ladies fell for the wicked man. Tamino in "The Magic Flute" can be a tenor, because he is not a "real" contemporary man but a fairy-tale Japanese prince. Sarastro is a bass, because he is something above ordinary men, the personification of wisdom and probity. His voice is always used with slow dignity, like that of an oracle. The chief tenor and bass in "Figaro" are comic characters. The tenor voice, heard in malicious chuckles through the texture of an ensemble, suits the scheming Basilio. The bass voice is right for an elaborate vengeance aria by the testy old Dr. Bartolo; but later on we hear another vengeance aria by the Count. Even when his baritone voice smoulders in its lower compass we cannot find it comic or amusing; it is nasty and cruel, too real to amuse. The "real" sopranos are not given great display or extreme high notes, as is the Queen of Night.

No other composer before or after Mozart has equalled his skill in the chain of ensemble movements which (going by page numberings in a score) often occupy more of an act than does the total of solo singing. The word "chain" is used because dramatically the most important ensembles are those which follow one another without break like short movements in long symphonies, and they cumulate after Mozart has written "Finale," usually far earlier in the course of an act than we recognise until we look at a score. Da Ponte calls the long and elaborate act-finale "a little comedy in itself." The previous recitatives and arias, maybe with interspersed duets or trios, have loaded the dramatic gun afresh; from the word "Finale" ensembles draw together both actors and action with increasing urgency towards a climax.

Other composers know that a good finale with plenty of ensemble satisfies audiences and shows commendable planning – it is simply "good theatre." Only Mozart brings the cumulative effect of ensemble and at the same time maintains in each participant's contribution the musical distinction of character that has been established in the previous solo items. This we can see by thinking of a scene leading up to a splendid finale by another composer – the last one in "The Mastersingers," showing the song contest with the crowds and pageantry of the guilds. Just before the trumpet summons to the event comes perhaps the most sensuously beautiful ensemble in any opera, the quintet. The duty of the singers is to blend as perfectly as they can, to stand still and contribute their loveliest tone and expression to music that makes no attempt to treat them as distinct characters, and would be spoilt if any one took precedence. We saw, however, that Mozart's favourite item in "Figaro" was a hymn-like sextet, also deliberately calling for perfect blending, for the smoothest, if not the most unctuous expression of the new alliance between old opponents; yet in this ensemble, even without gestures or movements to the words "And this is his mother," and so on, each musical line maintains the distinct character of its singer.

Solo Items

Despite what has just been written, we probably treasure most the outpourings of lyrical melody or the passages of dramatic eloquence that Mozart writes for his principals. They sound so spontaneous that we suppose them to have been composed quickly, i.e. not carried around for long in his mind. In fact some of the finest gave him much trouble. The most beautiful in "Figaro," probably the most beautiful in any of his operas, Susanna's "Deh vieni, non tardar," was actually written out several times, and the version that finally satisfied Mozart was the most song-like, the least externally elaborate.

Operas of a quality nowhere near Mozart's can be effective when their composers and librettists have the common sense (alas, uncommon among several composers of high literary pretensions) to recognise what music does better than words and what it never has done well. Music cannot easily be admirable itself, showing some quality when deprived of its theatrical circumstances, if it remains continuously changeful and restless in mood and rhythm, forgoing thematic interest, because it hugs a mass of conflicting elements. It needs moments of repose because it has no equivalent of "while," "during," etc. And, having no powers of reasoning, it goes dead or neutral with words implying "because" or "therefore." On the other hand, it is envied by poets and playwrights because it can prolong a situation or an emotion for our relish where verbal prolongation would be absurd or tedious. If it is musically good enough it can

even seem not to hold up a story. Consider a simple case. Dido is deserted by Aeneas. As long as Purcell's music on a ground bass holds our attention and moves our feelings, she may continue her lament with repeated "Remember me." Without the musical processes what words could prolong the pathos? Not many, or they would become comic: a few rhetorical questions – "Why should he so treat me?" "What have I done to deserve this?" "How can I bear it?" "What shall I do?" might bring satirical replies from the gallery. At best she could remain silent and make a slow tragic exit. Granted a poet as fine as Shakespeare or Racine she might declaim a soliloquy which, though less powerful in effect than music, usurped the functions of music. Walter Pater's belief that "poetry constantly aspires to the state of music" was a gross exaggeration. The poet whose work *always* aspires to the state of music cannot be a master of his materials – at least not a full or great master. Such a poet fails to use words for their distinctive quality, the conveying of thought, the appeal to the reason and the rich development of mental associations. Mindless poetry is to be classed with heartless music.

These words are metaphors, for nobody knows fully what the mind or the heart is. We do know today, however, that the processes of conation and feeling are not totally separate, so that the mind is engaged in the judgment of music. Even when a solo aria comes at a moment of repose in the unfolding of a drama, and Mozart is merely drawing lyricism from a passing situation, the mind is engaged, often in no more than the recognition of the composer's own mental powers. There is space here to consider only one aspect of them – the multifarious shades and types of sexual love that are found in his arias. One of the most difficult for most composers to catch (Strauss hardly attempts it in "Der Rosenkavalier") is the first bloom of the emotion in adolescence. Can there ever be another Cherubino in music? We should not blame Strauss, whose Octavian becomes "real." Only Mozart's own musical language, which cannot be faked, has so far caught the subtle differences between the expression of love by one character and another, amongst men and women, boys and girls, the noble and the ignoble. Shaw called Mozart a psychologist. He was not. Stendhal called him a philosopher, but the description is inept today. When the impudent Alfred Jingle said to Mr. Pickwick "Philosopher, sir?" he was answered: "An observer of human nature, sir." So was Mozart, but he also happened to be the greatest of dramatic musicians.

Pictorial Essay:
Music and Society

53. "The Garden Concert." Oil painting by Peter Jakob Horemans, 1736.

54. "The Music Lesson." Oil painting by François Boucher, 1759.

55. "The Concert." Oil painting on panel, attributed to Jean-Honoré Fragonard.

Twentieth-century musicologists have long been dependent on the visual arts, particularly for their studies of instruments and techniques of the ancient civilisations. Obviously eighteenth-century painting offers less to be learned as so many actual instruments have survived (see *Nos. 29, 32, 33, 35, and 41*), and many pictures are unreliable in the study of techniques (e.g. *Nos. 53 and 62*). Their true worth is in placing music in its social setting – letting us see the who, when, and where of the matter rather than the what and how. On the other hand, many of the paintings shown here are of intrinsic artistic value (notably *Nos. 54, 55, 57, and 61*) and as such they represent a useful supplement to the section already devoted to the art of Mozart's time.

53.
In this genre painting by Horemans (see also *No. 60*) the instruments are probably painted from memory and that none too accurately, but it seems to have been the artist's intention to portray a lower middle-class group of amateur musicians made up of two violins (or violin and viola), two oboes, a bassoon, a theorbo (the bass lute), and a viola da gamba (or perhaps a double-bass viol as it rests on the ground, though its proportions are too small). The gamba and theorbo were often associated in the Baroque and pre-Classical periods in providing the continuo in the absence of a keyboard instrument. The fact that Horemans has confused features of the cello and the gamba is an unwitting reminder that the last of the viols persisted almost till the end of the century as the traditional alternative to the cello in this role (see *Nos. 62 and 63*). The hybrid instrument depicted here has the sloping shoulders, fretted fingerboard, C-shaped sound holes, and bow associated with the viols, but it has the cello's four strings instead of six and is being bowed as a cello would be.

54 and 56.
The guitar was the most fashionable instrument, superseding the lute, among the musical dilettantes of the French aristocracy in the Rococo period and it is to be found everywhere in the *fêtes galantes* and scenes of garden dalliance which provided the favourite subjects of Watteau, Lancret, Boucher, Fragonard, and Hilaire. One of the most admired professional performers in French high society was the singer/guitarist Jélyotte whom the child Mozart accompanied at Prince Conti's in 1766 during the second visit to Paris.

55.
Another very fashionable instrument among the aristocratic ladies of the eighteenth century was the harp. The daughter of the Duc de Guines attained more than ordinary competence on it and

56. "The Music Lesson." Oil painting on panel by Jean-Baptiste Hilaire, 1781.

Mozart, who described her playing as "magnifique," wrote the flute and harp concerto, K. 299, for her to play with her father. The harpist is depicted in this painting, thought to be by Boucher's pupil Fragonard (see also *No. 46*), in concert with violin, flute, and horn.

57.

Dr. Charles Burney in his diary tells us of the conservatoria of Venice, originally attached to hospitals, where foundlings were given musical training at state expense. The most famous was that for girls called the Ospedale della Pietà, of which Vivaldi was director, and it is most probable that the uniformed female singers and instrumentalists depicted by Guardi in the galleries to the left are from the same institution.

58.

The dance depicted here by the fashion-able Saint-Aubin is probably the eight-eenth-century form of the allemande, a heavily stylised dance for four couples which in French court circles ousted the minuet as the most popular dance after 1750. Soon, however, the French were to be infected by Vienna's enthusiasm for the Deutsch (Teutsch) or Ländler, a fore-runner of the waltz, a number of which Mozart wrote for court balls in his capacity as court composer after 1787.

59.

This is one of the popular engravings from the lighter works of the Swedish artist Lafrensen, who studied under Nico-las de Largillière and became known in Paris as "Lavreince." The afternoon salon concert was an important social function in France when this softly satirical scene was painted, but more for the gossip than for the music. Vain efforts to still the conversation in this case are being made by the conductor, who holds the roll of paper with which it was then customary to beat time (see also *No. 62*). Mozart was much put out to find himself providing not much more than back-ground music to a sketching session when he played on such an occasion in 1778 for the Duchesse de Chabot.

60.

In this painting by Horemans (see also *No. 53*) it is high Bavarian society that is portrayed. Ismaning was the summer re-sidence of the Prince-Bishop of Freising, brother of the Elector Karl Albrecht. The figure at the harpsichord, accompanied by flute, violin, and gamba, is the distin-guished castrato Fillippo Ballatri, who was 55 at the time and who died in the year of Mozart's birth. Private, informal concerts such as this (note the card-playing and table-laying in the portico) were common at the Bavarian courts and Dr. Burney

57. "Gala Concert by Conservatorium Students in Venice." Oil painting by Francesco Guardi, 1782.

58. "Le Bal Paré." Engraving by Antoine Jean Duclos after a painting by Augustin de Saint-Aubin, 1773.

59. "L'Assemblé au Concert." Engraving by François Dequevauviller after a painting by Nicolas Lafrensen, the Younger, 1785.

60. "Concert at the Schloss Ismaning." Detail from an oil painting by Peter Jakob Horemans, 1731.

describes one by the Elector Maximilian Joseph III which he attended in 1772, when cards and the meal were again part of the proceedings. Adding to the relaxed atmosphere on this occasion are the seated child (see also *No. 61*) and the artist himself enjoying a glass of wine on the balcony.

61.
In society portraiture of Mozart's time intimacy and informality became the aim. This led to a new vogue for the group portrait, particularly family groups in which the specialists were Longhi, Zick (*No. 63*), and Zoffany, the German-born artist active in England. Children (instead of Baroque cherubs) often lent the right informal air and Zoffany also found room for pets. As a social activity music was an ideal binding element pictorially, but often the sitters were not as musical as the "props" suggested. Instruments here depicted are (left to right): cello, violin, serpent (the bass member of the now extinct cornett family), oboes, horns, clarinet, harpsichord, and lute.

61. "The Sharp Family Making Music on the Thames." Detail from an oil painting by Johann Zoffany, 1781.

62.
In this extravaganza by Platzer, Vienna's leading Rococo painter and stage designer, the main point of interest is the long-necked chitaronne (largest of the lutes). The white keys of the harpsichord (whose curvature should be on the right) should not lead us to mistake it for a forte-piano. Although black keys persisted in Austria, Germany, and France till the 1790's (see *No. 29*), bone or boxwood keys with black accidentals were common on Flemish and English instruments. Note too that the cellist bows his instrument like a viol.

63.
Coffee and billiards provide the social accompaniments in this bourgeois family portrait (see *No. 61*), by the Bavarian genre painter Zick. The music is provided by a quartet of strings and a clavichord. The cellist, however, is playing continuo and reading in the traditional manner from the keyboard music. His instrument has not yet acquired the modern spiked rest and is supported by the legs like a viola da gamba.

62. "The Concert." Oil painting by Johann Georg Platzer, c. 1740.

63. "The Remy Family." Oil painting by Januarius Zick, 1776.

IX
Under the cloud

Van Swieten and Bach
String Quartets
"Così fan tutte"
String Quintets
"La clemenza di Tito"

66. *Frontispiece of the piano score (by Siegfried Schmiedt) of Mozart's "La clemenza di Tito," published by Breitkopf and Härtel, Leipzig, 1795. The engraving is by Johann August Rosmässler.*

Van Swieten and Bach

After Vienna's limited response to "Don Giovanni" a cloud descended on Mozart's life – widely attributed to financial embarrassment, but more probably caused by the onset of the kidney disease which is now believed to have been the cause of his death and which sapped his strength for years before the end. In spite of his borrowings he had at this time two dependable sources of income. One was the stipend of 800 gulden a year which went with his appointment as "Imperial and Court Composer" – a title bestowed on him by the emperor after Gluck's death in November 1787. The other was the money he received for services at Baron van Swieten's concerts, the direction of which Mozart officially took over in 1788.

Van Swieten's idea was to let a wider musical public hear some of the choral-orchestral masterpieces of "old" composers. The concerts, inaugurated in 1787 were held in various places, though the favourite one for works requiring large forces was the splendid hall of the National Library. In February and March 1788, Mozart directed two concerts at the Esterházy Palace, each of them including C. P. E. Bach's "Resurrection of Christ." For subsequent concerts in the series he made his famous (to purists notorious) "arrangements" of Handel's "Acis and Galatea," "Messiah," "Alexander's Feast," and "Ode for St. Cecilia's Day." His task was to supply orchestral parts more in the taste of his time than were the stolid, string-polarised accompaniments of the high Baroque.

To sample an extreme case of the kind of work which Mozart's friends thought necessary, we may compare Handel's accompaniment of "The people that walked in darkness" with Mozart's additions to it. Handel suggests the groping in darkness by gloomy unison with the voice, including the heavy lower octave of the double-basses, and he does not greatly alter the texture at "have seen a great light" – there are still no chords, though no doubt the continuo keyboard strayed from a strict *tasto solo* at these words. Mozart supplied delicious woodwind decorations, including parts for clarinets. Those who are not offended at the late eighteenth-century belief that good taste and civilisation had at last arrived can gain from such exquisite "additional accompaniments" the same kind of delight and amusement that can be enjoyed when we see a Rococo architect's "improvements" of a Palladian palace.

Mozart had the further opportunity to delve into music of the past when in 1789 he undertook a trip with his former piano pupil Prince Lichnowsky to Berlin. Passing through Leipzig in April he met Johann Friedrich Doles, who had taken lessons from J. S. Bach while studying at Leipzig University. According to a report by Johann Friedrich Reichardt, "Mozart played unannounced and without payment on the organ in the St. Thomas Church. He played beautifully and skilfully for about an hour to a large congregation . . . Doles was completely delighted and thought that his teacher, old Sebastian Bach, had been reincarnated . . . With great skill and facility Mozart improvised on 'Jesu meine Zuversicht'." Doles was 74 when Mozart met him. Several reference books do him great injustice because, when he followed Harrer (Bach's immediate successor) as cantor at Leipzig, he did not perform much of Bach's music and because his own compositions were *galant* and Italianate. The same accusation might be made against the two most distinguished of Bach's sons, both of whom venerated their father. The whole pattern of Lutheran worship changed during the eighteenth century from the ceremonious eucharistic *Hauptgottesdienst* which Bach loved to the Pietist prayers–hymns–sermon type more close to the Swiss or Scots Protestant pattern. Bach fought the change, which was delayed at Leipzig, a centre of high orthodox Lutheranism and of clergy training; in fact it did not come there until 1776, after which Bach's long and elaborate liturgical works would have brought objections. Doles had something of Van Swieten's admiration for the skill displayed in the older style, though his taste was that of his time. Under Hiller, his successor, Leipzig seems to have relegated all Bach's music to limbo. But to continue, this time from an account by Friedrich Rochlitz:

> At Doles's suggestion the choir surprised Mozart by performing the motet for double choir "Singet dem Herrn ein neues Lied," by the patriarch of German music, Sebastian Bach . . . When it was over he cried with delight: "Now there is something one can learn from!" He was told that this school possessed a complete collection of Bach's motets which were preserved like a saint's relics. "That is fine . . . let me see them." As there was no full score of these pieces he examined the separate parts, and it gave the silent onlooker great pleasure to see how eagerly Mozart distributed the parts round him in both hands, on his knees, on nearby chairs. Oblivious of all else, he did not rise until he had scrutinised all Bach's available music. He asked for copies.

String Quartets

In Potsdam Mozart was welcomed at the court of Frederick William II who played the cello and whose musical tastes were less rigidly conservative than those of his stern uncle, the flute-playing Frederick the Great – he brought the latest French and Italian operas to Berlin and encouraged *Singspiele*. "The Seraglio" delighted him and he also knew Mozart's music through the quartets. It is not surprising then that he should have commissioned six new string quartets as well as six easy piano sonatas for his daughter. Mozart completed only three of these quartets, with prominent and not very difficult

67. The St. Thomas Gateway to the St. Thomas Church and School, Leipzig. Engraving by Benjamin Schwarz, 1793.

cello parts designed for the royal performer, and they proved to be his last works in the genre – though by no means his best, an honour which belongs to the six quartets dedicated to Haydn, composed between 1782 and 1785.

If we exclude Mozart's quartet arrangements of Bach fugues, K.405, and his Adagio and Fugue in C minor, K.546, there remain to us no less than 23 of his string quartets, of which only the last 10 – comprising the six "Haydn" quartets, the three for the King of Prussia, and the Quartet in D, K.499, of 1786 – are highly valued on more than documentary grounds. These 10 show the full range of his genius as well as his superb response to the medium.

Listeners still unacquainted with all of the six "Haydn" quartets have yet to be thrilled by a musical experience comparable only with their personal discovery of the riches hidden in Mozart's string quintets. The word "hidden" is used deliberately. Bülow spoke of Bach's "Forty-eight" and Beethoven's piano sonatas as the keyboard player's Old and New Testaments; by the same metaphor those six Mozart quartets are the chamber musician's Gospel. The mere listener may respond to them with near-religious devotion, yet much may remain hidden to him unless he is enabled to use his eyes as well as his ears – an opinion that needs explaining.

Today the scanning of printed music before the ear has been fully exercised upon a work is to be deplored. The map is not the journey. Eyes which continually scan the map may miss the beauty and interest of the scenes, and the mind which is intent upon the map loses time for contemplation and imagination. For similar reasons eyes should not normally be used to study a score until movements have been given good attention by the ears, after which more may be revealed for the ears and mind to relish at future hearings; yet a few forms of music are best appreciated with an earlier recourse to scores. They are such forms of music as only the performers can fully enjoy.

An example is the sixteenth-century madrigal. A concert of madrigals may become tedious even to a sympathetic listener who cannot simultaneously follow the contribution of each voice to the ensemble; but he may be helped by printed copies. The connoisseurs of such a concert are those who have themselves at some time sung in the pieces. Madrigals were written for the five or six voices prescribed. If others join them they turn "vocal chamber music" into public choral music. This difference between addressing participants intimately and composing for a public audience with enough players to suit the auditorium determined the emergence of the string quartet as a great genre long after plenty of music had been composed with four staves as if for the four instruments of a Classical quartet. The emergence was brought about by Haydn and Mozart – not before them, nor before their own advance to awareness of the difference, despite the fact that plenty of composers are said to have written "string quartets" before theirs.

We can understand the difference from a justly popular work we have already discussed, Mozart's by no means immature "Eine kleine Nachtmusik." Although entitled "Quintet" on the cover it is attractive enough if given with only four instruments, but much more attractive if given by a small string orchestra, as we usually hear it. We do not disparage its very great merits by declaring that as a string quartet it cannot rank amongst those which Mozart dedicated to Haydn, nor amongst any of the great quartets. Its exclusion has nothing to do with its light, sunny nature, for some of Haydn's choicest quartets are consistently happy. For the same reason, two profoundly eloquent quartets in G which happen to be their composers' last essays in the genre are not amongst their best quartets. For all their riches, Schubert's Op.161 and Dvořák's Op.106 strain towards orchestral colour. Not so Beethoven's last quartet, nor any quartet or quintet composed by Mozart from 1782 onwards. It is interesting to notice that a large stretch of the opening of Beethoven's Third Symphony would make an admirable string quartet, whereas the corresponding part of his First Symphony would not; this comment is made simply to illustrate the truth that the deciding factor is a textural one, an ideal of performance and performers, rather than of emotional content and range.

The earliest of Haydn's quartets were conceived as successors to Baroque *sonate, concerti,* or *sinfonie a quattro;* they were Rococo serenades, divertimenti, or symphonies (whether they had one minuet or two), scored in their smallest format. Parts might be doubled or trebled and the ensembles might include harpsichord or fortepiano continuo (except those which show the texture of "open-air" music: players in streets or the gardens of great houses did not transport harpsichords). The manuscripts of Mozart's first quartets actually bear the title "Serenade," and Eric Blom declared that nobody "would ever determine whether the string quartet reached perfection through Haydn or through Mozart, so inseparably are their reciprocal influences entangled." By "reached perfection" he meant "took the step of making the string quartet *sui generis* with a great future, a form defying any kind of transcription or arrangement; a form addressed to four players and only those four players."

When Mozart embarked on those first six quartets of his "perfection" he had composed no quartets during the previous nine years, 1773–1782, and when he resumed quartet-writing he was aged 26; in that year, 1782, Haydn was 50. Is not Blom's statement therefore questionable? Was not Mozart's dedication an acknowledgment of the older master's priority in "perfecting" the genre? Mozart may have thought so, but posterity's verdict depends upon the relative value of Haydn's Op. 20 set of six quartets, issued in 1772, and his Op.33 set, issued nine years later. By one of the strangest parallels in musical history the nine-year interval in Haydn's production of quartets corresponded almost exactly with Mozart's, and even if we regard merely as good advertising Haydn's declaration (in a letter to subscribers)

68. Title page of Mozart's six string quartets dedicated to Joseph Haydn, published by Artaria in Vienna in 1785.

that his six quartets of Op. 33 were composed "in a new and special way," they are still regarded as the first of Haydn's quartets to show his full mastery of the form.

We know that Mozart began playing some of Haydn's Op. 20 set when he was 17. It is possible to suppose that the finale to the first of his own quartets dedicated to Haydn pays tribute to the fugal finales in four of Haydn's six, and that the pathos of the D minor quartet owes something to the example of Haydn's few movements in minor keys; but however Mozart at the age of 26 may have been affected by the mood or manner of another artist, he had long ceased to seek ideas or expression that did not well up spontaneously in his own imagination. The "great time and labour" he acknowledged in composing these works was not given to the invention of ideas but their control. Those who wish to note the younger Mozart still influenced by Haydn's ideas may find much evidence in the six quartets composed before the "interval" in the summer of 1773, K. 168–173. Unlike previous quartets by Mozart they are recognised as Viennese rather than Italian in style, pointing to Haydn rather than Sammartini, and readers are referred to Einstein's "Mozart" for parallel quotations between them and Haydn's Op. 17 which show direct debts. The parallel between Mozart's K. 421 in D minor and Haydn's Op. 33 No. 5, with a finale in the form of variations upon a six-eight tune of similar shape, establishes no such debt. Haydn's tune is in G major, Mozart's in G minor, and the latter is more reminiscent of an item in Gluck's "Don Juan" ballet than of any idea conceived by Haydn. Nowhere in the six quartets does Mozart emulate the rustic joviality which leads Haydn to call a movement "scherzo" or to recall items in serenades. Even when gay, Mozart's movements in this set are fashioned with dignity and seriousness. One of them even troubled Beethoven for this reason.

Beethoven's favourite in the set was the Quartet in A, K. 464, today the one least often played – probably for reasons implicit in the comments just made, for it immediately becomes a prime favourite with anyone who follows the score. Beethoven seems to have been perplexed because this quartet finishes *pianissimo*, and with cadences that incur descending chromatics which impart a certain sadness to one of Mozart's "sunny" keys. It is to be regretted that we do not know Beethoven's reactions to the last quartet in the set, known as the "Dissonance," the only one with a slow introduction. From it the nickname is derived. The rest of this K. 465 in C scarcely allows any shadow to pass over its limpid moods, even in the C minor trio to its C major minuet. Its play of textures is brilliant, but its emotional range never suggests any intense personal experience, despite the use of chromatics. It has become customary to belittle the objections made to the dissonant introduction when the quartet was first published. Buyers suspected mistakes – incorrect accidentals which had not been corrected at proof stage. It is true that every note is logical to a modern musician who has studied true counterpoint from Bach or from those English sixteenth-century polyphonists who were often even more dissonant than Mozart; yet if Mozart's opening were "frozen" at the first note played by the first violin we could be deluded into supposing we were listening to music of our own century. It is not easy to imagine that Mozart was playing a joke by leading listeners to expect highly poignant movements to follow this introduction; nor is it easy to suppose that, in a work dedicated to Haydn, he deliberately abandoned the intention to compose a highly unconventional and disturbing quartet. If he had merely wished to please his patrons in Vienna he could have produced another set with little trouble, all in the styles of movements in his Italian operas.

Jahn suggests that in the single D major quartet of 1786, K. 499, Mozart actually did "attempt to meet the taste of the public without sacrificing the dignity of his quartet style," and Jahn's opinion may have led people to think less of the work than it deserves. The spirit of its movements is almost *galant*, though Viennese rather than Salzburg *galant*, the minuet being almost courtly for all its wit. The first movement is Schubertian. As a quartet (in its play of textures and demands on the players) it is by no means second-rate Mozart. In fact the ideas are on the whole better than those in the later quartets requisitioned by the king of Prussia, which we should esteem more highly if we had not been surfeited with wonder and admiration at the six quartets dedicated to Haydn. The "Prussian" quartets reach the former ebullience and inventiveness only in certain movements, such as the finales of the second (in B flat, K. 589) and the last (in F, K. 590). One cannot agree, however, that the conspicuous cello parts for the royal performer, who in some movements initiates all the main themes, cramped Mozart's style or technique. On the contrary we learn much from them of the difficult art of making fine texture with high cello parts and of accommodating showy ornamentation without apparent discrepancy. Contemplation of Mozart's great quartets reminds one of Pope's couplet

> The spider's touch, how exquisitely fine –
> Feels at each thread and lives along the line!

But the spider's instinctive design goes to type, and the marvel of Mozart's is its variety and unpredictability – not just in the "outside" movements with their brilliant developments, but in slow movements and minuets. The couplet speaks only for the vitality of the threads while being felt by the fine performers they deserve. It also applies to the duets for violin and viola, K. 423 and K. 424, which were written at the same time as the "Haydn" quartets and share their superb rank. They have never been rivalled by later composers.

We do not disparage Mozart's chamber works with piano by saying that we should not seek in them the particular qualities we admire in the string quartets; some compensation is found in reflections of that instrumental interplay most admired in the piano concertos.

It is especially evident in the quintet for piano and four wind instruments, K.452, the trio for clarinet, viola, and piano, K.498, and the two piano quartets, K.478 and K.493. Each is original and personal enough to be more than just charming, but the string quartets, especially those written in the 1780's, constitute a unique legacy none the less wonderful after our acquaintance with Beethoven. The key to Mozart's heart is found among the great operas. If these no longer existed, many musicians might think that the chief key to Mozart's musical intelligence – not just his heart but his mind and imagination as well – lay in the six works dedicated to Haydn.

"Così fan tutte"

Only a month after his return from the court of the king of Prussia in June 1789, Mozart was again in financial distress and deeply depressed by illness. This made all the more welcome a commission by the emperor for a new opera from his *Hofkomponist* and the Abbate da Ponte and the news of a revival of "Figaro" planned for August. Mozart's notebook catalogue, in which the only significant entry for the rest of 1789 is the marvellous quintet for clarinet and strings, K.581, for Anton Stadler, indicates his preoccupation with the new work, "Così fan tutte, ossia La scuola degli amanti" (This Do They All, or The School for Lovers), which was eventually produced in January 1790 with great success. Because of the feminine *tutte*, signifying "all females," this is the single one of Mozart's great operas known in English-speaking and other countries by its Italian title. The

suggestion that it should be known by its translated sub-title and called "The School for Lovers" is not wholly acceptable to musicians, for an amusing *Leitmotif*, heard solemnly in the fast-moving overture, and then again just before the Act II finale, distinctly pronounces (if instruments alone can do so) the words "Così fan tutte."

Little was said about this opera in the chapter on Mozart the dramatist, partly because it engaged Mozart in no dramatic problems, only in musical challenges of the kind he enjoyed. In some quarters it is held that critics value works according to the amount they say or write about them, but when one approaches the task of "saying something" about "Così fan tutte" one's emotions are difficult to express. For reasons I cannot explain and do not think worth discovering, despite the glories of other Mozart operas, I personally derive the greatest pleasure from "Così fan tutte" and therefore suffer intense attacks of spleen when either players or singers fail to rise to its beauty.

Da Ponte's memoirs tell us nothing about the origins of the opera, so that we could suppose it the one libretto he wrote for Mozart without the need of inspiration from other dramatists. Not quite. His "crib" was his great rival, Casti, who wrote "La grotta di Trofonio" (Trofonio's Grotto) for Mozart's great rival, Salieri, in 1785. In that story two pairs of lovers change partners after going into the magician Trofonio's grotto, and change back only by returning to it. Substituting Don Alfonso and his wager for Trofonio and his magic, and adding the maid Despina as the soubrette, Da Ponte had three couples to "live happily ever after" at the end of the neatest *opera buffa* to hold the stage, for to complete its neatness the plot observes the classical unities of time and

69. *Title page of the piano score (by Schmiedt) of Mozart's "Così fan tutte," published by Breitkopf and Härtel, Leipzig, 1790.*

70. *Giovanni Battista Casti. Anonymous engraving.*

place. Nobody cares that the plot of "Figaro" does so, nor that "Don Giovanni" was intended to do so, for the many characters put us off the scent (the stonemasons must have had an express order and been paid overtime to honour the Commendatore by an equestrian statue on the day of his murder!). But the compact setting and small cast of "Così fan tutte" is tailored for the unities, and we are unlikely to ask how the girls can believe their soldier boys to be ordered overseas in the morning and sent back to reproach them in the evening.

The characters express a wide range of feelings – playful, tender, arch, conspiratorial, passionate, languid, etc., yet how profitless it is to ask ourselves which of them are "real" as if this were another "Figaro"! Back in 1913 Dent commented upon the "shocked" disapproval which the would-be chivalrous nineteenth century expressed towards the cynical infidelity of the girls within hours of their tender farewells and protests of undying love.

> If the realists maintain that the story is an insult to human nature let them read reports of the Divorce Court during a period of war. Such embarrassment as modern listeners feel is due to the sheer beauty of the music; they cannot bear to think that it is the deliberate expression of sham feeling or comically exaggerated passion ... Don Alfonso, the only person consistently honest with himself, has no emotions; the four lovers, who are all emotions, are never quite sure how far their emotion is genuine.

No more bothered than we are about cynicism in comedy, or the "frivolity" which made Beethoven dislike the work, or what Victorians called its immorality (though nothing about it could displease a cast in a convent), Einstein wrote:

> This opera is iridescent, like a glorious soap-bubble, with the colours of buffoonery, parody, and both genuine and simulated emotion. To this is added the colour of pure beauty. In the Farewell Quintet ... the two young ladies were weeping real tears while the officers knew that there was no occasion to do so. Mozart raises the banner of pure beauty without forgetting the old cynic in the background who is "laughing himself to death." There is an evening glow over the whole score.

The secret of this libretto's excellence is its utter simplicity – a quality Gluck and Wagner wanted in stories of very different operas, and always a necessity if fine music is to make its own appeal, expanding its beauty by its own processes.

String Quintets

With "Così fan tutte" the Mozart–Da Ponte collaboration finished, for just after its production Joseph II died. For the rest of 1790 Mozart was in bad health and composed little, although there was a brief revival of spirit when he decided to try giving a concert in October in Frankfurt during the festivities there for the coronation of the new emperor, Leopold II. The programme included the D major piano concerto, thereafter called the "Coronation" Concerto, but he also played another – it may have been his last, K.595 in B flat, one of the most beautiful and enigmatic. If so then the performance was a "try-out" for he continued to work on the concerto after he returned home in November and settled (if that is the word) to solitude and composition again. Apart from "finishing" K.595 early in 1791, he completed Count Deym's mechanical organ pieces, some minuets and dances for the court and, most important, the two wonderful string quintets in D and E flat, K.593 and K.614 (the latter described in Artaria's edition as "composed for a Hungarian amateur").

For many listeners the quintets are even more enjoyable than the great quartets because their texture and variety is of a different order – indeed unique, for neither Boccherini before him nor Mendelssohn and Brahms after him wrote quintets to equal his in quality. Haydn's quartets inspired him, but Haydn's quintets could show him nothing. Beethoven's quintets are hardly of importance; the great Schubert quintet uses two cellos, not two violas, and belongs very much to its own century. As we should expect, the splendid quintets of Mendelssohn, Brahms, and other nineteenth-century composers who notably developed the orchestra show much concern for texture and colour; they tend to keep all five instruments constantly in play. Mozart, too, exulted in the resource made available by the extra viola and achieved rich textures but also an athletic movement of the parts which others seem to forgo when colour is ascendant. Only Mozart makes the warp and woof of a string quintet even more interesting than that of a quartet; only he notably seeks the "vocal scoring" that characterised five-part writing in sixteenth-century polyphony, brilliantly producing antiphony and overlap of upper and lower instruments.

Thus, though the map again is not the journey, readers who enjoy following their favourite works with scores can hardly find any more profitable for their pleasure and instruction than those of Mozart's quintets; and amongst those one thinks first of the D major, K.593, structurally the most original. Indeed only inspection of the score reveals that the slow movement of this work (at bars 51–56, the "lead-in" to the reprise) contains the most astounding piece of polyphony of the whole Classical epoch, the kind of counterpoint which Beethoven could never have achieved. It all sounds euphonious and facile, yet it incurs ingenious "vocal scoring" and a movement of parts through the boldest discords. (The much-mentioned discord just before "O Freunde, nicht diese Töne!" in Beethoven's "Choral" Symphony was not the first to use all notes of the scale at once!) Perhaps one's partiality for the D major quintet comes from the fact that every movement achieves first Mozartian level – even the finale, which proposes light, almost trivial ideas at the opening, yet proves them to be highly fertile germs which produce some of the most enjoyable, and therefore the best counterpoint in the chamber works.

To compare the quartets with the quintets to the disparagement of either is stupid, but the quintets are the work of Mozart's fuller experience and are greater luxuries now that some of the quartets can be heard broadcast almost every week. There is no "best" among them. The opening of the C major, K.515 poses an enigma which for musicians is more fascinating than any which psychologists or sociologists discuss. The materials are the common chord of C as the background to a dialogue between cello and first violin, the one using the same common chord melodically, the other answering with a cadential figure almost as common; yet even before we reach the glorious modulations through which this dialogue is extended we know that this is very late and very great Mozart, that nobody else could have brought such gold from such apparently common clay. Gay and strong the movement is indeed, but what a sense of power is here! And so through the whole work to the finale, which achieves the rare hilarity and organisation of the best Haydn finales without making us for a moment think of any composer but Mozart.

It is curious that many professional musicians seem to think the last of the quintets, the E flat, K.614, to be the finest, whereas the peculiar poignancy of Mozart's works in G minor makes the quintet in that key, K.516, the popular favourite. It is not merely one of the most moving on account of its sentiments. It is no less marvel-lous than the others technically, and possibly the best of them all to show how Mozart became more and more highly thematic in his last years without sacrificing the initial melodic and harmonic appeal of his ideas. An obvious illustration of this is the invertible "first subject," but let us consider a more subtle one, the "cadential" to the minuet. This is hauntingly beautiful and original in itself, yet Mozart heads off the trio by making it a theme, and not even Schubert more bewitchingly used his favourite trick of immediately turning a minor melody into a major. We should not too easily believe those who write of the pathos of this quintet as if it were the direct expression of Mozart's mood at the time. Two of the four great string quintets were written before Mozart went with Lichnowsky to Berlin in 1789, the second being this G minor, and two after, when he had yet more reason to be depressed. It is not denied that experience "comes out" in an artist's work but it is usually worthless unless it passes through the subconscious. A work written during an air raid is not likely to convey the emotions it arouses at all well, though who would blame anyone who declared a fine work was written during such an event if thereby he could make money by its popularity?

Is there a note of pathos in the C major quintet, or in the last of Mozart's symphonies, also in C major? Blom carefully speaks of a "hectic" sadness behind the superficial gentleness and sweetness of the clarinet quintet, but its mood cannot be equated with Mozart's desperation during the autumn of 1789; nor can the very similar

71. Frankfurt-am-Main. Engraving by Johann Oswald Berndt after a drawing by Johann Jakob Koller, 1777.

mood of the clarinet concerto dating from a few months before Mozart's death provide evidence of his illness and anxiety. All we can say is that the key of A major and the clarinet-playing of Anton Stadler, which affected Mozart as Mühlfeld's playing did Brahms, induced in him that particular vein of melodic beauty. These two works for solo clarinet are so well known that little need be said about them here except that the remarks previously passed on the texture of the string quintets do not apply. The clarinet quintet is a miniature concerto as regards its prominent solo part, but it is shorn of the superficial display of Classical concertos in general and therefore has some of the concentrated interest of the quartets, especially the one in A major. Indeed the clarinet concerto itself is not in the usual sense a display piece.

"La clemenza di Tito"

Although Mozart had had no official invitation to compose for Leopold II's coronation festivities in Frankfurt and the concert given there in 1790 had been on his own initiative, he did receive in July the following year a commission through the Prague National Theatre for an opera to be performed there in September during the celebration of Leopold's crowning as king of Bohemia.

By then Mozart had already begun work on his last great stage work "The Magic Flute" and the music of the Prague opera, "La clemenza di Tito" (Titus's Magnanimity) does not suggest that he undertook it for more than the good fee it would bring. As Dent shrewdly puts it: "Here is Mozart, definitely in his 'third' period, being

72. *Title page of the piano score (by Schmiedt) of Mozart's "La clemenza di Tito," published by Breitkopf and Härtel, Leipzig, 1795.*

forced to revert to the style of his first." The story, a reworking by Mazzolà of one of Metastasio's frequently set libretti, was intended to show monarchy in its best light, and one might almost think that local Freemasons did some of the adapting, for the Roman emperor Titus is portrayed as a noble and wise creature like Sarastro. Vitellia, the daughter of the previous emperor, piqued that Titus has not married her, plots his destruction and sends her lover Sextus (supposedly Titus's closest friend) to fire the capitol and murder Titus. Having already shown his first incredible magnanimity by allowing his beloved Servilia to marry the man she loves, Titus decides, after all, to make Vitellia his queen; but his messenger arrives after Sextus has already put Rome in flames – a situation that enables Mozart to make a finale to Act I as brilliant as the one in "Idomeneo." The plot is discovered and Sextus condemned by the senate, but Titus tears up the death warrant. At last Vitellia makes a grand public confession of her guilt in the amphitheatre where Sextus was to die, and Titus pardons "everybody" so that all may end happily.

As well as the act-finale just mentioned the opera contains two very fine arias which are often given at concerts and recitals. One of these includes a part for clarinet, the other for basset horn (which resembles a tenor clarinet but has a reedier bite); at Prague they were both played by Anton Stadler, and it was immediately after returning from Prague that Mozart wrote for him what is known as the Clarinet Concerto. In fact it was composed (like the clarinet *obbligato* in "Tito") for the so-called "basset-clarinet" which could be played down to C, a third lower than the modern instrument. When the concerto was published in 1802 the solo part was "adapted." Modern reconstructions of the obsolete "basset-clarinet" would have made performance of the original possible but for the unfortunate fact that the autograph of the work has been lost. Nevertheless a performing edition by the English clarinettist Alan Hacker now gives us the chance to hear how it may have sounded.

"La clemenza di Tito" was written in 18 days, much of it in the carriage on the way to Prague. Franz Xaver Süssmayr, who had been Mozart's pupil for two years and who later played an important role in the completion of the Requiem, probably helped on this occasion with the composition of the recitatives and the copying. We lack much information about the first performance and its reception, which is generally supposed to have been merely polite. Of Mozart's other musical activities in Prague we know only that he was invited to a Masonic lodge where a cantata, K.471, which he had composed to honour Ignaz von Born at "Crowned Hope," the oldest lodge in Vienna, was given in his own honour.

Pictorial Essay:
"The Magic Flute"

65

66

67

Specialisation within the theatre is a fairly recent development. Until the mid-nineteenth century the history of stage design was dominated by great names from the history of art in general – sculptors like Bernini, painters like Boucher, and architects like Inigo Jones and the great Prussian classicist Karl Friedrich Schinkel, whose work forms part of this pictorial section.

For these artists theatre was total entertainment (in words, music, or dance, and often all three) and their aim was to make it spectacular in a sense that survives today only in the cinema. This is what Schikaneder meant by "good theatre" and he found the ideal opportunity for it in "The Magic Flute," which Professor Hutchings describes as "a glorious mixture of comedy, magic fantasy, sheer farce, and religious ritual." Mozart found the artistic scope it provided exhilarating, and so must all those who have presented the work, from the first stage version of 1791 to Ingmar Bergman's film version of 1975.

In the early eighteenth century German states and Austria, simply because of a lack of permanent theatrical companies, lagged behind Italy, France, and England in the art of stage design and remained largely dependent on the services of the famous Bibiena family, but by the early nineteenth century artists such as Anton de Pian and Johann Platzer (see *No. 62*) in Vienna, the Quaglio family in Mannheim and Munich, and Friedrich Christian Beuther and Schinkel in Berlin had established distinctive national styles and paved the way for the great Romantic décors of later decades.

Designs for three important productions of "The Magic Flute" are featured here – comprising three by Joseph Quaglio for the Munich production of July 1793, four of 12 celebrated designs by Schinkel for the 1816 Berlin production; and four by Joseph Quaglio's son, Simon, again for Munich in 1818.

The Quaglio family came from Italy in 1777 to Mannheim, where the first German national theatre was established in 1778, and moved with Karl Theodor's court to Munich in the same year. It was Lorenzo Quaglio who provided the sets for the first production of Mozart's "Idomeneo" in Munich in 1781 – and, as was customary at that time, the stagework was regarded as more important than the music or libretto.

Joseph Quaglio's work perpetuates the Italian Baroque tradition of architectural settings with deep perspective, but the progressive influence of Ferdinando and Giuseppe Bibiena is apparent in the angled perspective in *No. 65*.

Both Schinkel and Simon Quaglio belonged to the neo-Classical school. Schinkel represents, however, a remarkable synthesis of style in his work for the theatre – designs for 32 different productions between 1813 and 1832. Without entirely abandoning Baroque principles of geometrical depth and architectural symmetry he yet managed to be an important forerunner of Romanticism in his ability to evoke mood and atmosphere in his scenery (see *No. 75*). His spatial concepts were probably influenced by the Italians Nicolo Servandoni, mainly active in Paris, and Filippo Juvarra, whose curvilinear sets revolutionised Italian Baroque design.

The impact of Schinkel's designs, which take full advantage of the link with Egypt, is clearly felt in Simon Quaglio's sets of 1818. His imaginative architecture, though perhaps more Indian than Egyptian (*No. 69*), succeeds, as Schinkel's did, in capturing the majesty and mystery missing in Joseph Quaglio's early designs, which do not look much farther than Venice for exotic effect. Schinkel's back-cloth (*No. 71*), with its stylised stars in dome formation, clearly inspired Quaglio's curvilinear set (*No. 68*) and the tentative path towards Romanticism is opened up more positively by Quaglio's landscape setting (*No. 70*) in which the view is very much towards the future.

64. "The Queen of Night." Design by Simon Quaglio for Munich, 1818. Like *No. 68* this owes much to Schinkel's dome concept of 1816 (see *No. 71*).

65, 66, and 67. Three sets by Joseph Quaglio for Munich, 1793. All are in the old Italian Baroque style and *No. 66*, for the trials by fire and water in the Act II finale, may have been derived from Ludovico Burnacini's designs for the Venetian-style opera "La monarchia latina trion-

68

69

70

fante" by Draghi, produced in Vienna in 1678.

68, 69, and 70. Three sets by Simon Quaglio for Munich, 1818. Like *No. 64,* the Sun Temple (*No. 68*), with its zodiacal signs on a starred blue band representing the arching of the heavens, is influenced by Schinkel (*No. 71*). The palm grove (*No. 70*), however, is even more daringly Romantic in its use of landscape than Schinkel's evocative garden design (*No. 75*).

71. "The Queen of Night." Wash-coloured engraving after a design by Karl Friedrich Schinkel for Berlin, 1816. Comparison of this with *Nos. 64 and 68* shows how Simon Quaglio developed this concept for Munich two years later. The backcloth can be seen behind the set in *No. 74.*

72

73

74

75

72 and 73. Sarastro (*No. 72*) and the Queen of Night (*No. 73*). Coloured engravings by Carl Friedrich Thiele after costume designs by Stürmer for Schinkel's Berlin production, 1816. (See also *Nos. 76–78.*)

74 and 75. Wash-coloured engravings of designs by Schinkel for Berlin, 1816. The first (*No. 74*) depicts the entrance to the Queen of Night's palace. In the production this was withdrawn in a swift scene-change to leave *No. 71* for her first appearance. *No. 75* is Schinkel's imaginative and almost Romantic response to the libretto's request for "part of Sarastro's garden." One might mistake it for a set in Verdi's "Aida," yet Simon Quaglio's palm-grove design (*No. 70*), also with water, is more truly Romantic in its use of landscape.

76, 77, and 78. Papageno (*No. 76*), Pamina (*No. 77*), and Monostatos (*No. 78*). Coloured engravings by Thiele after costume designs by Stürmer for Schinkel's Berlin production, 1816. (See also *Nos. 72 and 73.*)

76

77

78.

79. "Before the sun temple." Wash-coloured engraving of a design by Schinkel for the closing scene at Berlin, 1816. The seated figure is Osiris.

79

X

Masonry and magic

Masonic Music
Emanuel Schikaneder
"The Magic Flute"
The Requiem

73. *Sketch by Joseph and Peter Schaffer of the Act I stage-setting possibly for the first performance of "The Magic Flute," 1791. The characters are (left to right) Tamino, three Ladies-in-waiting of the Queen of Night, and Papageno.*

In these last years of financial and physical distress there is little doubt that Mozart found solace in his associations with Freemasonry. It was to his fellow-Mason Puchberg that his begging letters were addressed and many of his patrons and special friends were members of the brotherhood. Mozart was first admitted to a lodge in December 1784 and his music for later Masonic ceremonies and occasions must have made him highly valued as a member.

After he had become immersed in Freemasonry a new vein occasionally revealed itself in his musical expression. It is not easy to say if it should be called mystical. The English writers most associated with studies of mystical philosophers and poets, W. R. Inge and E. Underhill, define mystics as those who attempt to convey what cannot be apprehended except by "spiritual" experience – the condition which makes Beethoven's late quartets "difficult" to musicians who find no difficulty in their technique. Mystics, say these authorities, must use symbols. Unfortunately all artists must use symbols, and we are merely left arguing because we call an artist a mystic or non-mystic according to our personal response. There is general agreement that Mozart should not be numbered amongst the mystics, any more than Shakespeare should. His music conveys human moods and feelings. If we sometimes call it unearthly we use licence, meaning that such beauty is fit for the gods. If Mozart is uncanny then he is deliberately seeking an uncanny effect in an opera. Yet his Masonic vein is indescribable and inexplicable, beyond religious solemnity.

It can be savoured by listening to two pieces in succession, first one of Mozart's most moving "human" works, then his most serious Masonic tribute. The Adagio in B minor for piano, K.540, for all its intense pathos, could not replace the "Masonic Funeral Music," K.477, even if it were transposed to C minor and scored to include basset horns – instruments specially associated with Mozart's Masonic music. The funeral piece was played at the "Crowned Hope" Lodge in November 1785 in homage to two departed brothers, the Duke of Mecklenburg-Strelitz and Count Franz Esterházy. According to Einstein "One could find in its 69 bars all the symbols of Masonry – the parallel thirds and sixths, the slurs, the knocking rhythm..." Jahn says: "It is the musical expression of that manly calm which gives sorrow its rightful place in the presence of death, but without exaggeration or artificiality." The final "Picardy" chord (major where minor is expected) was archaic in Mozart's time, but is used to beautiful effect, confirming Jahn's words: "He leaves the narrow limits of corporeal life to take up the spiritual. The brilliance of the Eternal East guides him across the darkness of the grave."

The quotation is made second-hand, along with much information given here, from "Mozart's Masonic Music," contributed by "Bro. Arthur Sharp, P.G.D." to the proceedings of the Quatuor Coronati Lodge for 1957. This lecture was illustrated by professional musicians of the brotherhood at a meeting evidently held either in England or America; but since several non-Mason musicians like myself are grateful to possess a copy there seems no discourtesy in referring to it. Most useful are its unembittered comments on the relations between the Roman Church and Masonry. It may well be asked how the quotation already given differs from general church teaching about death, unless a peculiar meaning is attached to "the Eternal East." Still more noteworthy is the fact that Mozart's "Masonic Funeral Music" treats the two phrases of the first plainchant psalm tone in the manner of a *cantus firmus*, as Bach would a chorale melody. Now in the "Liber Usualis" this Tone i is set to the verse of Psalm 65 ("Te decet hymnus in Sion"), used in the introit of the Mass for the Dead. It would be recognised by Catholic Masons and by others who had attended funerals, and its meaning approved. (This leads one to wonder why, in his Requiem, Mozart set this verse – most beautifully – to Tone ix, known as *Tonus peregrinus*, instead of Tone i. If this was a local departure from general custom no other composers seem to reflect it.)

In 1946 Austria abandoned its old Hapsburg anthem, "Gott erhalte Franz den Kaiser" (better known as set to "Deutschland über Alles") with Haydn's tune from the "Emperor" Quartet. It was replaced by the "Österreichische Bundeshymne" with words set to a melody associated with Mozart's Masonic cantata, K.623. That melody ("Lasst uns mit geschlungnen Händen") represents the average quality of his songs and cantatas for the lodges, which are neither mystical nor magnificent. They are more solid, more German than corresponding choruses and solos in his theatre and church music before those of "The Magic Flute," which contains finer music in the same style. One of the details that contributes to the hymn-like character of some of them can also be found in choral passages by Beethoven and Schubert – the slurring of two or more notes to a syllable to symbolise the holding of hands in German lodges, as in Britain for "Auld lang syne."

Some of the Masonic cantatas are published with soprano and contralto parts, which may be regretted, for all the vocal music for the lodges is for men only, their tone imparting a certain solemnity. The texts often contain references to the emperor. "Die Maurerfreude," K.471, already mentioned as honouring Ignaz von Born, includes the words: "Sing, brothers, for Joseph the Wise has bound the laurel crown upon the Mason's temple."

Mozart's two finest Masonic works are instrumental – the funeral music and a quiet, mysterious Adagio in B flat, K.411, for two clarinets and three basset horns. According to Einstein this piece accompanied an entrance procession. It may have been the first of a suite covering the complete lodge ceremonies. Supporting this theory is the Adagio in Canon in F, K.410, for two basset horns and bassoon, and two unfinished movements for clarinets and basset horns, an Allegro in B flat, K. App. 95, and an Adagio in F, K. App. 93. Several writers describe as Masonic Mozart's last piece of church music (except the Requiem), the justly beloved motet "Ave verum corpus," K. 618, because it is so unlike his earlier church music and has the slurred notes and general style of Masonic hymns. Yet if it were intended even for a church service of the brotherhood it would not be for the usual four voice parts with strings and organ, but for men's voices with wind instruments. In fact it was composed for Mozart's friend the choirmaster at Baden in the June of 1791. He was visiting Baden to see his wife, and since Corpus Christi usually falls in June the motet seems to have been intended for that feast. The basset horns in the Requiem are often evocative of the Masonic works and were surely intended to be so. The wind instruments carry the main thought, the strings merely accompanying; they are a notable feature of Recordare, possibly the most beautiful item in the whole work.

Emanuel Schikaneder

Mozart's last Masonic cantata, "Eine kleine Freimaurer-Kantate," K. 623, a necessarily joyful work, was commissioned from the sick composer for the dedication of a new Masonic temple in November 1791 and the event saw Mozart's last public appearance. The words were written by his friend and fellow-Mason Emanuel Schikaneder, the same colourful and extravagant character who is thought to have written "The Magic Flute" and asked Mozart in 1790 to provide the music for it. He had been born at Straubing near Regensburg in 1751. After his father's death he worked with various theatrical troupes which travelled round the south-German states. Eventually he married the leading lady of one and formed his own company. He is honoured as one of the first Germans to play Hamlet, but his admiration for tragedies by Shakespeare, Lessing, and Schiller was not based entirely upon literary appreciation; he sought "good theatre" and mixed great classics with banal productions that also provided blood and thunder, ghosts, transformations, romantic and exotic scenes, ghouls, witches, and any opportunity to use mechanical contrivances or exotic costumes. Yet at the popular level he did cater for sentiments shared by men of culture – the growing romantic movement and German patriotism. After giving a season of *Singspiele* in Vienna during the winter of 1784–85 he secured Joseph II's patronage and permission to build a theatre in the suburbs. Instead he took over in 1789 the "Theater im Starhembergschen Freihause auf der Wieden."

His rival at the Leopoldstadt Theatre, Karl Marinelli, had drawn popular audiences to musical entertainments in their own language, and to satiric plays and pantomime-like "fairy" and "magic" productions. Schikane-

74. *Emanuel Schikaneder. Title illustration of the Viennese "Theatre-lovers' Almanack," 1791, engraved by Ignaz Albrecht.*

der set out to give the same fare more richly served, and did so well with a "magic" *Singspiel* called "Oberon" that he could outshine it only by a similar piece to better music – not that its composer, Wranitzky, was a poor musician or an amateur, as Schikaneder was. Wranitzky had been a violinist under Haydn in Prince Esterházy's orchestra, and Haydn spoke highly of him. What is more, Mozart himself was glad to emulate one or two items in "Oberon," having said, when he consented to begin on his own work for Schikaneder: "If it turns out a fiasco I cannot help it, for I have never in my life attempted a magic opera."

Schikaneder himself is thought to have supplied the words of "The Magic Flute," giving them to Mozart in instalments, for those who speak German recognise them as naïve, not the work of an educated writer; but even those who speak English and have learnt a little German are aware that some of the passages during the temple scenes (as when Tamino is questioned by the Speaker) are in a dignified, almost liturgical style which would have been crudely parodied by an unskilled hand. Because Mozart may have known him better than we can tell from documentary evidence, something should be said of Schikaneder's collaborator, Johann Georg Metzler, known as Karl Ludwig Giesecke. One writer declares that he appeared in Vienna as "a distinguished old gentleman with silvery white hair" in 1818 and claimed to have been the sole librettist. As he was born in 1761, the son of an Augsburg tailor, the "old gentleman" was only 57 in 1818, and for various reasons it is not generally thought that he did more than help Schikaneder with the libretto.

He had been to the university of Göttingen, became fascinated by geology, and was probably in Vienna chiefly to be a disciple of Born, supporting himself by helping with the theatre. Eventually he became professor of mineralogy in Dublin and a member of the Royal Irish Academy. He was knighted for his expeditions to collect rocks in Greenland. Those who aspired to social rank did not reveal their connections with the theatre, especially humble connections with a humble theatre. That explains the surname Giesecke, whereas he was Metzler on the university books. It is therefore remarkable that he finished as Sir Charles Giesecke. He must have preferred his adopted name and thought it safe so far from Vienna. Possibly as Metzler he had suffered from anti-semitism, although it did not seem to worry Schikaneder.

Giesecke was the librettist of "Oberon." The story is the one Planché used for Weber's Covent Garden extravaganza; it comes from Wieland's oriental tales of 1786. The story called "Lulu" in the same collection provided the basis of "The Magic Flute." It is easy to see Schikaneder's determination to use a plot for the new opera that was similar to the plot of the very popular first one, and to farse it with his own comic antics and patter, along with the added attractions of stage animals, exotic costumes, magic effects, etc.

1. "Oberon." Sir Huon of Bordeaux rescues Rezia from the Turks, overcoming obstacles by using a magic horn given him by the King of the Fairies.

2. "The Magic Flute." The Japanese prince Tamino rescues Pamina from an evil magician by using the enchanted flute given him by her mother, the Queen of the Fairies.

That was the story as Mozart dealt with its opening scenes (though not the present opening with the killing of the serpent) at the end of 1790 and the beginning of

75. *Autograph manuscript of part of Tamino's aria "Dies Bildnis ist bezaubernd schön" from Act I of "The Magic Flute."*

1791. He had the advantage of knowing some of the singers and players and the exact conditions of performance. They included Schikaneder himself, who would delight the audience as Papageno the bird-man, his own sister-in-law, Josepha Hofer, with the applause-bringing high notes (Wranitzky took her up to high D; Mozart went up to F!), Gerl the bass singer, and Schack the tenor who, like Gerl, supplied music for some of Schikaneder's farces.

"The Magic Flute"

We know that some of the items for "The Magic Flute" were finished in the spring of 1791, for Schikaneder and Giesecke were delighted with the duet-finale "Pa-pa-pa-pa-Papagena." At some time during the summer came the decision to change the whole course of the plot, making the Queen into the evil Queen of Night and the magician into the wise and virtuous Sarastro. One event which may have prompted the decision was the success of another *Singspiel* produced by Marinelli. It was called "Das Sommerfest der Brahminen," and may have shown the fine effect of mysterious religious ceremonies in a musical play. Taking them from ancient Egypt instead of India was a matter in which the educated Giesecke was surely more useful than his paymaster, for the source-book was already known to others than Freemasons. It was a romance called "Sethos" published in 1731 by the Abbé Terrasson, a university teacher.

The Egyptian prince Sethos escapes the bad influence of his mother and her court friends by journeying with his tutor to the pyramids and ancient monuments of his country. Mozart's opera absorbed many details of their adventures. Sethos traps a monstrous serpent; at one temple he and his tutor are met by men in armour; he seeks initiation into their mysteries and joins their order; he undergoes the ordeals of fire, water, and confinement to subterranean chambers where thunder echoes. He returns to make his court a brotherhood for the advancement of science and virtue, women being excluded from their secrets and counsels, and becoming gratefully subject to their husbands' superior wisdom! When Mozart supplied incidental music in Salzburg for Gebler's "Thamos, King of Egypt" he had already dealt with Terrasson at second hand, though he may not have been aware of the fact. The sources of the temple scenes were not important to him compared with the thrilling fact of their Masonic nature and opportunities for Masonic symbolism in the music. From composing a comic opera he came to compose his musical testament.

In itself the Masonic symbolism need not interest anyone but a Mason. Either it makes for better music or worse, and we are concerned only with the result, not the special meaning. Let us consider that result no further than the overture. We cannot recapture the surprise of the first audience which had gone to a German comic opera and heard those opening three chords with the weight and solemnity of trombones, associated with the supernatural and with worship. But even today we get a surprise and a kind of thrill when, in the middle of the overture, the gaily fugued texture is halted for three times the same chord separated by awe-inspiring rests. The effect would be ruined if a vandal changed the bass and made the chords a progression like those in the same place within Rossini's "Barber" overture. Indeed it is sometimes ruined by today's vulgar conductors who are unable to give rests their full value. (Rests embarrass them. Unlike Wagner, Mahler, and others who thought the beating of time the first requisite in orchestral direction, charlatan conductors regard themselves only as "interpreters" whose task is to alter and bring up to date the dull legacy of Mozart and other classics. What matters is therefore any grimace or pirouette which "shows what the music means." And what can silence show?)

76. Playbill for the first performance of "The Magic Flute" on September 30, 1791 in the Theater auf der Wieden, Vienna.

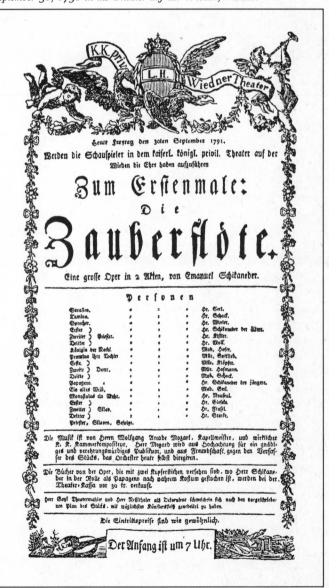

77. *Leopold Hofmann. Anonymous portrait.*

78. *The Act II duet between Papageno and Papagena in "The Magic Flute." Engraving by Schwerdgeburth, 1826, after a design by Ramberg.*

The musical symbolism of "The Magic Flute" has been discussed by several Freemason writers with approval of their lodges. Some perpetuate the list published by M. Zille at Leipzig in 1866, which identifies Tamino with Joseph II, Pamina with Austria, Sarastro with Born, the Queen of Night with the Jesuits, and Monostatos with Hofmann, an apostate Mason who published pamphlets which declared that the brotherhood intended to foment political revolution. Precise identification of characters in the opera is not important. The Queen of Night, for instance, is the personification of a malevolent idea, of "obscurantism" as understood by social reformers, and the first patrons of the opera may have thought her to satirise different people – Maria Theresa, Karl Theodor of Bavaria, the Jesuits. For publicity's sake Schikaneder and Mozart must have welcomed the guessing of possible identities, but they surely conceived no such precise list as Zille's, and today we gain little by trying to establish one as authentic. Their original intention was to provide a comic and fantastic entertainment with Masonic scenes. As the most devoted Mason engaged in the production Mozart was responsible for the uncanny impressiveness of the Masonic symbolism, the elevated glorification of wisdom and virtue, because his most truly religious music was inspired by the apotheosis of Masonic ideals of manhood and womanhood. As Einstein says, this opera "was his bequest to mankind, his appeal to the ideals of humanity. His last work is not 'Tito' or the Requiem; it is 'Die Zauberflöte'."

The music forces us to recall the hackneyed application of "chameleon-like" to Mozart's complete change of style when he deals with the temple scenes and expresses ideas instead of delineating characters. Other composers change their moods, but only Wagner approaches Mozart in completely changing style between "The Ring," "The Mastersingers," and "Tristan." Mozart goes farther and seems to change style with change of key! Confining our observation to his operas we find no precedent for much of the music in "The Magic Flute." We can compare "Idomeneo" with early essays in Italian *opera seria*; we can compare the music for the Italian comedies to Da Ponte's words, our only difficulty being Mozart's unique response to a unique character or situation. Perhaps we exaggerate if we say that we could not imagine Susanna singing *any* of Zerlina's music or Almaviva singing *any* of Don Giovanni's; but where (in the operas at least) is there any precedent for Sarastro's music, or indeed for Papageno's? Even the ensemble items in the act-finales of this last Mozart opera cannot be imagined in any other, and the explanation does not lie only in the contribution of the Three Genii singing together as one personified idea.

Yet if we know a great deal of Mozart's previous music we can find what may be called anticipatory veins. There is a sudden angry shift to C minor near the opening of the Piano Concerto in E flat, K. 449, in the same vein as the opening of "The Magic Flute" with Tamino's "Zu Hilfe!" Choruses of loyal acclaim like "Es lebe Sarastro!"

are foreshadowed in Masonic cantatas and church music. The Queen of Night raves in German with Italianate *bravura*, and music not unlike hers was provided for the raging Electra in "Idomeneo" and for Fiordiligi in "Così fan tutte." One cannot find, even in Mozart's previous German works, such as "The Seraglio" and "The Impresario," any parallel to the short airs or the songs with stanzas. It has even been suggested that the simpler of them, such as the famous "Bird-catcher's Song" with which Papageno introduces himself, were sung to Mozart by Schikaneder or one of the others to show him the sort of thing they liked in Wieden Theatre farces. The rather more elaborate items like Tamino's rapturous contemplation of Pamina's portrait – items hardly to be called arias, yet not simply songs – are not entirely new in Mozart. Even in the Italian operas he sometimes wrote short pieces like Figaro's "Se vuol ballare" or Barbarina's little song about the lost pin; but there was ample precedent for "airs" (rather than arias) in musical plays like those Gluck sent to Vienna from France, and therefore in all German *Singspiele*.

It is only from a sense of duty that one seeks precedents. There were plenty of precedents for marches of priests and ritual scenes in Gluck's tragedies alone; but where in opera is there anything quite like the march of the priests and Sarastro's invocation "O Isis und Osiris" with the answering male voices and trombones at the opening of Act II? Where else is there such an item as the chorale prelude sung by the Two Men in Armour? This "Der, welcher wandert" is in fact set to the Lutheran chorale "Ach Gott vom Himmel sieh' darein" and treated in Bachian *cantus firmus* style – if a precedent, then one utterly forgotten in Mozart's Vienna. (The declamation of the melody in octaves between the tenor and bass is queer in effect from such a lover of euphony as Mozart. One has never heard it sound acoustically satisfactory, and supposes that Mozart imbued this outlay with Masonic significance. If the octaves were played by instruments, as in the funeral music, they would surely sound in tune.)

The greatest musical enigma about "The Magic Flute" is its astounding unity embracing such diversity. Einstein cannot believe that there was any very radical change of plan after Mozart had set Schikaneder's first act, or most of it. "He began and ended the work in E flat major, the Masonic key." Yes, but when was the overture written? Much depends on the meaning of "radical." Why should the Queen of Night still retain the services of three good genii (originally her ladies-in-waiting and afterwards boys, since there could be no Masonic females) when she was no longer the distressed mother but the personification of obscurantist hatred? Surely the truth is that Schikaneder would not waste the excellent music Mozart first showed him, that he was not willing to postpone production just because Mozart approached the work with a new seriousness. So far from disliking the heterogeneous scenes and items, he saw in them what would please a diversity of listeners and beholders. The

79. *An anonymous costume design for Tamino.*

truth seems to be that the Masonic significance of the work, the chance to express his final commentary on life, grew upon Mozart while he worked, for let us remember that he lived for only five weeks after its production and finished it only on September 29, the day before it was first performed.

It was characteristic of Mozart that, as far as music can reveal a man's philosophy, his was revealed in this glorious mixture of comedy, magic fantasy, sheer farce, and religious ritual. The fact was beyond the understanding of Beethoven or most other artists from the north, though Beethoven knew the work well and critics have been at pains to show its influence upon "Fidelio." One can understand those who regard it as Mozart's greatest opera, but they go too far in declaring that the awakening of a German opera tradition to equal the Italian or French would have been impossible but for Mozart's two great German operas. (Though the language of "The Seraglio" is German the music is hardly that of a *Singspiel*, whereas most of the music in "The Magic Flute" is so.) Maybe "Fidelio" and "Der Freischütz" would not have been quite the same if their composers had not known Mozart's music, but Beethoven and Weber, as well as poor Schubert had he lived, would have fulfilled their talents in such works even if Mozart had never existed.

The Requiem

In July 1791 (the exact date is not known) a man called on Mozart and left an anonymous commission for a Requiem. We now know that the caller was Anton

80. *Frontispiece from the first edition of the Requiem, K.626, published by Breitkopf and Härtel, Leipzig, 1802.*

Leitgeb, son of the mayor of Vienna, acting for an amateur musician, Count Walsegg-Stuppach, who wanted a Requiem for his late wife which he could pass off as his own (a not unusual practice in Mozart's time). Since the C minor mass Mozart had composed no important church music. The Requiem, to which his mind continually reverted during his final illness and which at the end remained unfinished, recalled to him the style he thought fitting. Though tinged with Masonic features, that style had the ceremonial decorousness of archaism, for our formal dress is never modern. The choral forms and textures of the Requiem point back to solid Baroque practice, but the exquisite accompaniments (except for certain passages) could have been devised only by Mozart. If his pupil Süssmayr either composed or orchestrated a great deal of the work then where is the rest of the music by such an admirable composer? It would be misleading to say without qualification that Mozart managed to finish only the Introit and Kyrie and sketch the five items of the Sequence (Dies irae) and two of the Offertorium (Domine Jesu Christe and Hostias). In a letter to the publishers written a few years after Mozart's death, Süssmayr gave an account of his part in the work which was neither boastful nor falsely modest.

He declared that he had to compose only the close of Lacrimosa, the whole of Sanctus and Benedictus (though Mozart had indicated the vocal parts of Benedictus without the Osanna), and the opening of Agnus Dei. For the close of Agnus Dei (which in the Requiem turns to "Lux aeterna" and "Cum sanctis tuis") he repeated music from the Introit and Kyrie, which some writers call "unfortunate" without saying why; to many of us the hearing of this fine music at the end as well as the beginning of the work is most satisfying. If we met these portions in a work by Haydn when he was aged between 30 and 40, or in a mass by the younger Reutter or even Michael Haydn, we should not think them poor. The first is Sanctus – efficient and effective, but simply lacking the stamp of Mozart. Much the same could be said of the opening of Agnus Dei and of the accompaniments and orchestral interludes of Benedictus, the Osanna fugues being simply the kind of music that secures a fair "pass" in examinations for music degrees.

Elsewhere, but not in lovely things like Recordare, the indications left by Mozart were inadequate for Süssmayr quite to recapture the master's beautiful use of the wind instruments. They are never misallied but are sometimes given mere chords. At one point, however, comes an obvious mistake. Süssmayr surely thought it a mistake but was unwilling to change what he had taken down from the dying Mozart. After the solemn opening of Tuba mirum for solo trombone, the same instrument continues with grotesque *legato* arpeggio accompaniments to the bass solo. The part is written on the tenor clef, which is used for bassoon or cello in its upper compass. Can it be that, trying it on the piano, Süssmayr satisfied Mozart with the sound, so that he did not mention a change of instrument where only one stave and clef was needed? Surely we have good reason to use our own discretion about the instrumentation when we perform this item.

The Requiem is a glorious work, but it is romantic nonsense to call it Mozart's last testament, his comment on death and life; it is too much a display of his musical culture, his study of older masters, too "specialised" a work for us to take it, like "The Magic Flute," as revealing almost all the veins of his expression. It restricts the free play of his fancy by its very nature as liturgical music for a solemn occasion. It has no place for the kind of art which, had one to name the most original and evocative simplicity that distinguished Mozart from all musicians, would be illustrated from the little flute melody with eerie drum taps that leaves us both charmed and awestruck as Tamino and his bride pass through fire and water.

Acknowledgements

In the following acknowledgements of sources of illustrative material the figures represent illustration numbers, *not* page numbers. Those in parentheses refer to illustrations in the inset colour sections.

Archiv für Kunst und Geschichte, Berlin, *(53, 55, 56, 60, 62, 63)*

Bayerisches Nationalmuseum, Munich, *(57, 60)*

Bibliothèque Nationale, Paris, *63*

Civico Museo Bibliografico Musicale, Bologna, *(27, 28)*

Dr. Josef Dapra, Salzburg, *(19, 24, 26)*

Walter Drayer, Zurich, *(61)*

Foto Blauel, Munich, *(49, 57)*

Foto Gmeiner, Vienna, *43*

Foto-Hofstetter, Ried/Innkreis, *(39)*

Germanisches Nationalmuseum, Nuremberg, *(63)*

Gesellschaft der Musikfreunde, Vienna, *2, 9, 10, 18, 21, 24, 25, 32, 35, 39, 45, 49, 53, 55, 57, 60, 68, (31, 37, 38, 42, 44, 45)*

Graphische Sammlung Albertina, Vienna, *(59)*

Haags Gemeentemuseum, Musical Department, The Hague, *7, 8, 22, 28, (32, 33, 35, 41, 43, 58)*

Herzog-August-Bibliothek, Wolfenbüttel, *52*

Historisches Museum der Stadt Wien, Vienna, *41, 73, 74, 78, 80*

Interfoto, Munich, *(1)*

Mrs. O. Lloyd-Baker, London, *(61)*

Buch- und Kunstantiquariat Hans Marcus, Amsterdam-Düsseldorf, *6, (2, 3, 5, 9)*

Mozart-Gedenkstätte, Augsburg, *44, (12, 25)*

Mozart-Museum der Internationalen Stiftung Mozarteum, Salzburg, *3, 4, 5, 11, 30, 33, 34, 36, 38, 40, 47, 48, 50, 54, 56, 59, 62, 64, 66, 69, 72, 76, 79, (29)*

Municipal Museum of Prague, *58*

Musée Carnavalet, Paris, *(7)*

Musée Cognacq-Jay, Paris, *(54)*

Musée National du Louvre, Paris, *(30, 47, 48)*

Museum für Geschichte der Stadt Leipzig, *67*

National Gallery, London, *(51, 52)*

National Gallery of Prague, *(4, 62)*

National Museum of Hungary, Budapest, *46*

Werner Neumeister, Munich, *(20)*

Niederösterreichisches Landesmuseum, Vienna, *43*

Collection of Prof. Dr. Karl Niessen, Cologne, *65*

Österreichische Galerie im Belvedere – Österreichisches Barockmuseum, Vienna, *(50)*

Österreichische Nationalbibliothek, Vienna, *12, 13, 14, 16, 20, 23, 26, 37, 51, 61, 70, 71, 75, 77*

Abbey of St. Peter, Salzburg, *(39)*

Phonogram International/R. Nooy, Baarn, *6, 22, 28, 42, (32, 33, 35, 41, 43)*

Photo des Musées Nationaux, Paris, *(30)*

Photo Erwin Meyer, Vienna, *(50)*

Photographie Giraudon, Paris, *(4, 7, 8, 47, 48, 54)*

Private Collection, Salzburg, *(36)*

Residenzmuseum, Munich, *(1)*

Residenz Verlag, Salzburg *(19, 24, 26)*

Rijksmuseum, Amsterdam, *(6)*

Royal College of Music, London, *(34)*

Salzburger Museum Carolino Augusteum, *15, 17, 19, (15, 16, 17, 21, 22)*

Jack Skeel, Pluckley, *(46, 51, 52)*

Staatsbibliothek Preussischer Kulturbesitz, Berlin, *1, 27, 29, 42, (10, 11, 13, 14)*

Städelsches Kunstinstitut und Städtische Galerie, Frankfurt-am-Main, *(49)*

Städtische Galerie im Lenbachhaus, Munich, *(53)*

Städtisches Schlossmuseum, Mannheim, *(40)*

Theatermuseum, Munich, *31, (64, 65, 66, 67, 68, 69, 70, 71, 72, 73, 74, 75, 76, 77, 78, 79)*

Wallace Collection, London, *(46)*

Westermann-Foto/H. Buresch, *2, 3, 4, 5, 9, 10, 11, 17, 18, 19, 21, 24, 25, 30, 31, 32, 33, 34, 35, 36, 38, 39, 40, 41, 45, 47, 48, 49, 50, 52, 53, 54, 55, 58, 59, 60, 61, 62, 64, 66, 68, 69, 72, 73, 74, 76, 78, 79, 80, (12, 15, 16, 17, 18, 21, 22, 23, 25, 29, 31, 36, 37, 38, 40, 42, 44, 45, 64, 65, 66, 67, 68, 69, 70, 71, 72, 73, 74, 75, 76, 77, 78, 79)*

General Index

126

Index of artists and engravers

Listed here separately are the original executants of illustrative material. As in the general index figures in italic refer to illustration numbers. Those in parentheses refer to the inset colour sections.

Index of Works

Only works specifically referred to in the text are included in this index, which should not be regarded as a complete catalogue of Mozart's music. Within the type classifications works are listed in order of their original Köchel numbers, which approximate to but do not necessarily indicate the order of composition. Spurious works, noted as such, are included in their respective classifications. Figures in italic are illustration numbers and *not* page numbers. Major references are indicated in bold type.

K.475 Fantasy in C minor (with Sonata, K.457), 71, 74, 80
K.494 Rondo in F (with Sonata, K.533), 82
K.501 Andante in G and five variations for four hands, 74, 80, 81
K.511 Rondo in A minor, 78, 82
K.540 Adagio in B minor, 74, 82, 112
K.574 "Eine kleine Gigue" in G, 82
K.594 Adagio and Allegro (Fantasia) in F minor, 70 (see also Organ Music)
K.608 Fantasia in F minor, 70, 71 (see also Organ Music)
K.App. 44 Allegro in C minor for two pianos (fragment – with Fugue, K.426), 81

See also Sonatas – K.533

X CHAMBER MUSIC

1. Works for Violin and Piano (or Harpsichord)

K.6 Sonata in C, 8, *5*
K.7 Sonata in D, 8, *5*
K.8 Sonata in B flat, 8
K.9 Sonata in G, 8
K.10 Sonata in B flat,* 8
K.11 Sonata in G,* 8
K.12 Sonata in A,* 8
K.13 Sonata in F,* 8
K.14 Sonata in C,* 8
K.15 Sonata in B flat,* 8
K.26 Sonata in E flat, 8
K.27 Sonata in G, 8
K.28 Sonata in C, 8
K.29 Sonata in D, 8
K.30 Sonata in F, 8
K.31 Sonata in B flat, 8
K.301 Sonata in G, 22
K.302 Sonata in E flat, 22
K.303 Sonata in C, 22
K.304 Sonata in E minor, 22
K.305 Sonata in A, 22
K.306 Sonata in D, 22
K.396 Adagio in C minor (fragment), 71 (see also Piano Music: Miscellaneous, K.396)

* For harpsichord and violin or flute, with cello *ad libitum*.

2. Duos for Violin and Viola

K.423 Duo in G, 22, 106, (21)
K.424 Duo in B flat, 22, 106, (21)

3. Trios

K.254 Piano Trio (Divertimento) in B flat, 106
K.442 Piano Trio in D minor (fragments – completed by M. Stadler), 106
K.496 Piano Trio in G, 106

K.498 Trio in E flat for clarinet, viola, and piano, 107
K.502 Piano Trio in B flat, 106
K.542 Piano Trio in E, 106
K.548 Piano Trio in C, 106
K.564 Piano Trio in G, 106

See also Divertimenti – K.App.229; Masonic Music – K.410

4. Works for String Quartet

K.80 Quartet in G, 12
K.168 Quartet in F, 16
K.169 Quartet in A, 16
K.170 Quartet in C, 16
K.171 Quartet in E flat, 16
K.172 Quartet in B flat, 16
K.173 Quartet in D minor, 16
K.387 Quartet in G,* 38, 63, 64, 106
K.405 Five Four-part Fugues, (arranged from J.S. Bach's "Well-tempered Clavier"), 82, 104
K.421 Quartet in D minor,* 38, 106
K.428 Quartet in E flat,* 106
K.458 Quartet in B flat, "The Hunt,"* 106
K.464 Quartet in A,* 106
K.465 Quartet in C, "Dissonance,"* 106
K.499 Quartet in D, 104, 106
K.546 Adagio and Fugue in C minor (arrangement of K.426), 68, 81, 104 (see also Piano Music: Miscellaneous)
K.575 Quartet in D,** 102, 104
K.589 Quartet in B flat,** 102, 104, 106
K.590 Quartet in F,** 102, 104, 106

  * Dedicated to Joseph Haydn.
  ** "King of Prussia" Quartets.

5. Miscellaneous Quartets

K.370 Quartet in F, for oboe, violin, viola, and cello, 56
K.478 Piano Quartet in G minor, 107
K.493 Piano Quartet in E flat, 107

See also Masonic Music – K.App.93

6. Quintets

K.46 String Quintet in B flat (spurious arrangement of Serenade, K.361 "Gran Partita"), 37
K.174 String Quintet in B flat, 16
K.406 String Quintet in C minor (arrangement of Serenade, K.388), 38
K.452 Quintet in E flat for oboe, clarinet, bassoon, horn, and piano, 107
K.515 String Quintet in C, 109
K.516 String Quintet in G minor, 34, 109

K.581 Quintet in A for clarinet and strings, 43, 46, 107, 109, 110
K.593 String Quintet in D, 108
K.614 String Quintet in E flat, 108, 109

See also Masonic Music – K.411 & K.App.95

XI MASONIC MUSIC

K.410 Adagio in Canon in F for two basset horns and bassoon, 39
K.411 Adagio in B flat for two clarinets and three basset horns, 39, 112
K.471 Cantata "Die Maurerfreude," 110, 112
K.477 "Maurerische Trauermusik" (Masonic Funeral Music), 112
K.623 Cantata "Eine kleine Frei-maurer-Kantate" (with final chorus, K.623a), 112, 113
K.623a Masonic chorus "Lasst uns mit geschlungnen Händen" (with Cantata, K.623), 112, 113
K.App. 93 Adagio in F for clarinet and three basset horns (unfinished), 113
K.App. 95 Allegro in B flat for two clarinets and three basset horns (unfinished), 113

See also Divertimenti – K.App.229